DIGITAL MIDDLE EAST

MOHAMED ZAYANI

(*Editor*)

Digital Middle East

State and Society in the Information Age

جـامـعـة جـورجـتـاون قـطـر
GEORGETOWN UNIVERSITY QATAR

Center *for* International *and* Regional Studies

OXFORD
UNIVERSITY PRESS

OXFORD

UNIVERSITY PRESS

Oxford University Press is a department of the
University of Oxford. It furthers the University's objective
of excellence in research, scholarship, and education
by publishing worldwide.

Oxford   New York

Auckland   Cape Town   Dar es Salaam   Hong Kong   Karachi
Kuala Lumpur   Madrid   Melbourne   Mexico City   Nairobi
New Delhi   Shanghai   Taipei   Toronto

With offices in

Argentina   Austria   Brazil   Chile   Czech Republic   France   Greece
Guatemala   Hungary   Italy   Japan   Poland   Portugal   Singapore
South Korea   Switzerland   Thailand   Turkey   Ukraine   Vietnam

Oxford is a registered trade mark of Oxford University Press
in the UK and certain other countries.

Published in the United States of America by
Oxford University Press
198 Madison Avenue, New York, NY 10016

Library of Congress Cataloging-in-Publication Data is available
Mohamed Zayani.
Digital Middle East: State and Society in the Information Age.
ISBN: 9780190859329

Printed in India on acid-free paper

CONTENTS

v

ACKNOWLEDGMENTS

The chapters in this volume grew out of two working group meetings held under the auspices of the Center for International and Regional Studies at the Georgetown University in Qatar. I would like to thank especially Mehran Kamrava, the Director of the Center, and Zahra Babar, the Associate Director for Research, for initiating, supporting, and guiding this project. Special thanks go to Suzi Mirgani, the Managing Editor of CIRS Publications, for her invaluable assistance with all editorial matters. This project also benefited immensely from the assistance of Dionysis Markakis, Haya Al Noaimi, Elizabeth Wanucha, Valbona Zenku, Barb Gillis, Dwaa Osman, Jackie Starbird, and Misba Bhatti. In addition to the authors of the individual chapters, I would also like to acknowledge the contribution of the following scholars to this project: Joe Khalil, John D. H. Downing, Shafiz Affendi Mohd Yusof, Amy R. Nestor, Amal Al Malki, James Onley, and Daniel Varisco. Last but not least I would like to thank the anonymous reviewers for their constructive feedback, and Michael Dwyer, Jon de Peyer, Daisy Leitch, Camilla Wyatt, and Jack McGinn for their editorial input and support. Grateful acknowledgment goes also to the Qatar Foundation for its support of research and other scholarly endeavors.

CONTRIBUTORS

Ilhem Allagui is Associate Professor in Residence at Northwestern University in Qatar. Her academic experience includes more than ten years of teaching at the University of Montreal, the American University of Sharjah, and Northwestern University in Qatar. Her research interests focus on the social integration of new media, Arab cultural industries, and marketing communication practices in the MENA region. She joined the World Internet Project network in 2007, and launched the Emirates Internet Project, which was awarded a UAE National Research Foundation grant in 2009. She serves on the editorial board of the *International Journal of Communication*. She earned her MSc and PhD in communication sciences from the University of Montreal.

Jon Anderson is Professor of Anthropology at the Catholic University of America and has also taught at the Universities of Oslo and Bergen in Norway, the Free University of Berlin, and at Georgetown University's Center for Contemporary Arab Studies, where he was co-director of the Arab Information Project. His interests include civil society, cyberculture, and globalization in the Internet age. He is the author of *Arabizing the Internet* (Emirates Center for Strategic Studies and Research, 1998), and co-editor with Dale F. Eickelman of *New Media in the Muslim World: The Emerging Public Sphere* (Indiana University Press, 1999, 2002), and with Jodi Dean and Geert Lovink of *Reformatting Politics: Information Technology and Global Civil Society* (Routledge, 2006). His current research focuses on comparing technocratic, public roll-out and social media phases of Internet pioneering in the Middle East.

Muzammil M. Hussain is Assistant Professor in the Department of Communication Studies at the University of Michigan, and serves as a faculty affiliate of the Harvard Kennedy School of Government's Science and Democracy Network (SDN) and the Michigan Ford School of Public Policy's Program on Science, Technology, and Public Policy (STPP). He is co-author of *Democracy's Fourth Wave? Digital Media and the Arab Spring* (Oxford University Press, 2013) and co-editor of *State Power 2.0: Authoritarian Entrenchment and Political Engagement Worldwide* (Routledge Press, 2013). His website is mmhussain.net and he tweets from @m_m_hussain.

Gholam Khiabany is Reader in Media and Communications at Goldsmiths, University of London. He is the author of *Iranian Media: The Paradox of Modernity* (Routledge, 2010), co-author of *Blogistan: The Internet and Politics in Iran*, with Annabelle Sreberny (I. B. Tauris, 2010), and co-editor of *Liberalism in Neoliberal Times: Dimensions, Contradictions, Limits* (Goldsmiths Press, 2017) and *After Charlie Hebdo: Terror, Racism and Free Speech* (Zed, 2017).

Suzi Mirgani is Managing Editor of Publications at the Center for International and Regional Studies, Georgetown University in Qatar. She received a PhD in Communication and Media Studies from Eastern Mediterranean University. She writes creatively on the intersection of media, politics, and popular culture, and has worked extensively on issues of piracy and copyright infringement. She is the author of *Target Markets: International Terrorism Meets Global Capitalism in the Mall* (Transcript Verlag, 2016) and co-editor of *Bullets and Bulletins: Media and Politics in the Wake of the Arab Uprisings* (Hurst/Oxford University Press, 2016) with Mohamed Zayani and *Food Security in the Middle East* (Hurst/Oxford University Press, 2014), with Zahra Babar. She is also an independent filmmaker working on highlighting stories from the Gulf region.

Mark Allen Peterson is Professor and Chair of the Department of Anthropology and Professor in the International Studies Program at Miami University in Ohio. He has conducted fieldwork in Egypt, India, and the US. His research interests include ethnography of communication, mass media, information technologies, nationalism, transnationalism and globalization, semiotics, drama, and spectacle. His most recent book is titled *Connected in Cairo: Growing Up Cosmopolitan in the Modern Middle East* (Indiana University Press, 2011). He has published extensively in such journals as *Anthropology Today*, *Childhood*, *Contemporary Islam*, and *New Review of Hypermedia and Multimedia*, and contributed chapters to several edited volumes. He earned his PhD from Brown University and blogs at connectedincairo.com.

CONTRIBUTORS

Damian Radcliffe is the Carolyn S. Chambers Professor in Journalism at the University of Oregon's School of Journalism and Communication; a Fellow of the Tow Center for Digital Journalism at Columbia University; an Honorary Research Fellow at Cardiff University's School of Journalism, Media, and Culture Studies; and a Fellow of the Royal Society for the Encouragement of Arts, Manufactures and Commerce. He is an experienced digital analyst, consultant, journalist, and researcher who has worked in senior and mid-level editorial, research, and policy positions for two decades in the UK and the Middle East. A lifelong digital intrapreneur, Radcliffe has led new creative and research initiatives at the BBC, Ofcom (the UK communications regulator), CSV (a volunteering and social action charity), and Qatar's Ministry of Information and Communications Technology (ictQATAR).

Vít Šisler is Assistant Professor of New Media at the Institute of Information Studies at Charles University in Prague, and formerly a visiting Fulbright scholar at Northwestern University. His research focuses on Information and Communication Technologies in the Middle East and educational and political video games. He has published extensively on issues related to information technologies, identity in the digital age, video games, networked public spheres, and online communities in the Middle East. His work has appeared in the *Communication Yearbook*; *European Journal of Cultural Studies*; *Information, Communication and Society*; *Global Media Journal*; and the *Middle East Journal of Culture and Communication*. He is the editor of *CyberOrient*, a peer-reviewed journal of the virtual Middle East published by the American Anthropological Association.

Annabelle Sreberny is Emeritus Professor of Global Media and Communications at the School of Oriental and African Studies (SOAS), University of London. She is the past-president of the International Association of Media and Communication Research (IAMCR), 2008–12, and was the first chair of the Centre for Iranian Studies at SOAS. Her books include *Small Media Big Revolution: Communication, Culture and the Iranian Revolution* (University of Minnesota Press, 1994) with Ali Mohammadi; *Blogistan: The Internet and Politics in Iran* (I. B. Tauris, 2011) with Gholam Khiabany; *Cultural Revolution in Iran: Contemporary Popular Culture in the Islamic Republic* (I. B. Tauris, 2013) edited with Massoumeh Torfeh; and *Persian Service: The BBC and British Interests in Iran* (I. B. Tauris, 2014), also with M. Torfeh.

Ingmar Weber is the Research Director of the Social Computing Group at the Qatar Computing Research Institute (QCRI). He studied mathematics at

Cambridge University, before pursuing a PhD at the Max Planck Institute for Computer Science. He subsequently held positions at the École Polytechnique Fédérale de Lausanne and Yahoo Research Barcelona. In his interdisciplinary research, Dr Weber applies computational methods to large amounts of online data from social media and other sources to study human behavior at scale. His work incudes studying lifestyle diseases and population health, quantifying international migration using digital methods, and looking at political polarization and extremism. He has published over 100 peer-reviewed articles and is co-editor of *Twitter: A Digital Socioscope* (Cambridge University Press, 2015). Since 2016 he has been selected as an ACM (Association for Computing Machinery) Distinguished Speaker.

Norhayati Zakaria is Associate Professor at the University of Wollongong in Dubai's Faculty of Business and Management. She earned her PhD in Information Science and Technology from Syracuse University. Her research interests include cross-cultural management, international business, and computer-mediated communication technology. For more than a decade she has established international research collaborations with global scholars from the United States, Japan, and Canada, and obtained international research grants from the Asian Office of Aerospace Research and Development. Since 2006 she has served as a Senior Research Faculty Associate at the American University's Center for Research on Collaboratories and Technology Enhanced Learning Communities (COTELCO), where she undertakes projects involving global virtual teams.

Mohamed Zayani is Professor of Critical Theory at the Georgetown University School of Foreign Service in Qatar and Director of the Media and Politics Program. He is also an Affiliate Faculty with the Georgetown Communication, Culture and Technology Graduate Program and co-director of the CCT Institute on Media, Technology and Digital Culture in the Middle East. His works include *Bullets and Bulletins: Media and Politics in the Wake of the Arab Uprisings* (Oxford University Press, 2016), co-edited with Suzi Mirgani, and *Networked Publics and Digital Contention: The Politics of Everyday Life in Tunisia* (Oxford University Press, 2015; winner of the ICA Global Media and Social Change Best Book Award; the NCA Sue DeWine Distinguished Book Award; and the ASA Communication, Information Technologies and Media Sociology Book Award). Currently, he is a Research Fellow with the University of British Columbia's Liu Institute for Global Issues in the School of Public Policy and Global Affairs.

MAPPING THE DIGITAL MIDDLE EAST

TRENDS AND DISJUNCTIONS

Mohamed Zayani

Much of the Middle East has been facing formidable challenges. Undemo-cratic political systems, non-participatory forms of governance, economic stagnation, lagging human development, social inequality, high rates of unem-ployment, demographic pressures, youth radicalization, and escalating politi-cal and sectarian violence are only the pointed manifestation of these challenges. But the Middle East is also in the throes of change, politically, socially, economically, and otherwise. One facet of the region's transformation is its gradual immersion in the digital era. Increasingly, states, groups, and individuals alike are attempting to capitalize on transformation opportunities enabled by information and communication technologies (ICTs). Advances in information technology infrastructures and the fast pace of digitization have impacted the Middle East remarkably, albeit to varying degrees. Enhanced connectivity and high levels of use of ICTs favored a wider adop-tion of the Internet and related technologies by different players and forces in the region. Ease and speed of communication, along with broad diffusion, are engendering a gradual restructuring of the public communication space. Rapidly expanding access to mobile communication has enhanced the potential for increased connectivity, and the exponential growth of connective social platforms has further facilitated interactivity and intensified the public sharing of information, images, and videos. From interactive devices to smartphones to immersive websites and beyond, digital technologies—when affordable and accessible—have never been more enmeshed with everyday life.[1]

While these technological changes are far from turning Middle Eastern societies into "information-intensive societies" or "network societies,"[2] their impact is nonetheless increasingly felt. The growing adoption of a wide range of e-technologies and digital tools in almost all spheres of everyday life is introducing complex dynamics that beg for a better understanding: How have digital transformations and adoption of ICTs affected Middle Eastern societies? What are the social, cultural, and economic implications of these unfolding changes? How are the various participatory technologies that Web 2.0 affords redefining state-society relationships, and how is the Internet reconfiguring power relations? What are the security implications of a wired Middle East for the state and for individuals? How are digital technologies affecting the region's local cultures and, in turn, how do adopted social norms and ingrained cultural practices shape online activities and experiences? How do issues of Internet governance play out in the region and how do competing interests and values, both internally and externally, determine Internet policies? What does it mean for an evolving society—one that increasingly operates in a high-tech environment—to navigate the disjunction between tradition and modernity? Is the adoption of ICTs promoting social inclusion or is it engendering new forms of marginalization? And finally, to what extent can these ongoing digital transformations truly alter the reality and disposition of a region long known for its aversion to change?

By engaging with these questions, this collaborative volume hopes to shed critical light on unfolding changes in the Middle East that are deeply intertwined with the increasing adoption of ICTs. It seeks to unravel the multifaceted digital transformations that the region has been experiencing and to understand the dynamics associated with these technology-related changes. The book offers a grounded reflection into how fast-changing information technologies that have been introduced and widely used over the past decade or so are impacting the region at the level of the state and society. The research pays particular attention to the complex ways in which advances in ICTs have affected individual and community experiences, communication habits, social relations, commercial transactions, cultural practices, and political realities.

MAPPING THE DIGITAL MIDDLE EAST

Conceptual framework

Before delving into the intricacies of the digital Middle East, it is fitting to provide a conceptual framework for understanding and analyzing the multiple dimensions and various articulations of the digital turn. A number of observations, caveats, and propositions are in order here.

First, studying how the advent of the information era has impacted the Middle East is fraught with considerable challenges, not least the risk of homogenizing a complex region. The Middle East, as Annabelle Sreberny reminds us, "reveals remarkable differentiation among almost any indicator one cares to choose."[3] While identifying broad trends and capturing general tendencies that came to characterize a digital Middle East, this project also recognizes the need for differentiation-based analyses.

Second, the dynamics that define the digital Middle East are as much rooted in ongoing social, political, cultural, and economic reconfigurations as they are associated with evolving communication developments and changes in information technologies. To that extent, information technology-induced developments and digital practices are of interest not simply because of their ability to produce change, but because they are in and of themselves manifestations of ongoing changes in the region. The digital Middle East merits renewed attention because the widespread adoption of ICTs is deeply intertwined with ongoing mutations within society. Seen from this perspective, the question of how the contemporary Middle East adopted and adapted new information and communication technologies is as revealing as the question of how those technologies are affecting the region.

Third, increasingly the adoption of digital technologies is consolidating global dispositions, not least the ability to produce content and to consume information that is unbounded by temporal frames and spatial constraints. Many of the digital developments that can be observed in the Middle East are indicative of the advent of a global digital culture that spreads far and wide—being itself tied to the global cultural economy. In fact, there are several striking commonalities between emerging tendencies in the region and trends that can be observed more globally. Yet, these global interactions and intersections, to which Arjun Appadurai draws our attention, often result in disjunctions.[4] The digital Middle East is as much imbricated in processes of globalization as it is shaped by local exigencies, national realities, and regional dynamics; it lies at the intersection of the local and the global. In its twin cultural/symbolic and economic/material dimension, this interpenetration entails complex overlappings, multi-directional flows, and fluid dynamics that define the digital Middle East without delimiting it. Equally important is the need to highlight the ambivalent nature of this digital turn. Capturing the digital Middle East in its complexity requires not only mapping out the nature and scope of the changes that information and communication technologies have brought about, but also highlighting their uneven development and asymmetrical dynamism. The digital Middle East is an intricate development that is equally marked by promises and challenges, and by enchantment and resistance.

Finally, while the digital Middle East is associated with the adoption of new forms of ICTs, such development is not purely technological; nor does it designate circumscribed media forms and narrowly defined communication practices. Defining the boundaries of what may be termed the digital sphere is a challenging endeavor, considering the multidimensional nature of the ongoing transformations and the coexistence of the digital and the non-digital. The digital turn merits attention not so much because emergent forms of communication technologies are supplanting more traditional forms of communication, but because they favor the rise of an even more complex communication sphere that is marked by the coexistence of the two. A rich interpretative account of what the digital Middle East means and how it works calls for particular attention to these fluid dynamics and points of intersection, but also begs the question of what is new and what is old. As Henry Jenkins points out, the process of "convergence" that ensues from ongoing digital transformations does not amount to legacy media being simply absorbed by emerging technologies; rather, the two interact and intersect in complex ways, giving old concepts and practices new meanings.[5] Drawing out the significance of where and why the distinctions between newer and older media have become more visible or have dissolved can yield valuable insights about these ongoing transformations.[6]

Changes and adaptations

In recent years, debates about the effect of ICTs on the Middle East have focused intensively on the political sphere. Considerable attention has been paid to the extent to which the adoption of communication technologies can induce change, reconfigure political action, and redefine the state-society relationship.[7] During the 2011 uprisings that swept through many Arab countries, social media platforms extended activism, facilitated collective action, and mobilized social networks. Online networks played a significant role in stoking protests, mobilizing protesters, coordinating street action, and precipitating turmoil. Whether they were capturing evidence of police brutality, recording protests, diffusing information, rallying support on Facebook, trilling tweets, or posting scrawled anti-establishment graffiti on social media, new forms of digital communication emerged as central to the narrative of the Arab uprisings. The tendency of many commentators and pundits to be eager and enthusiastic in characterizing these uprisings as digitally enabled revolutions reflects a fervent belief in the power of technology to effect socio-political change even in undemocratic contexts. Significantly, this widely celebrated narrative about the empowering role of ICTs did not go unchallenged, and several critics took issue with the overstated effect of mobile technology and social media platforms during these historical events. The deepening of crises in the Middle East and the uneasy transition to democracy in the tumultuous post-uprisings period further lent credence to a growing skepticism about the transformative power of information technologies.

Beyond the celebratory accounts of cyber utopians and the skepticism of cyber dystopians, the potential that information technologies hold for the region remains highly pertinent to any discussion of change in the contemporary Middle East. One of the key arenas affected by the adoption of digital technologies is the social sphere, which is shaped by unique demographics, with youth constituting nearly one-third of the population. Internet access, high smartphone penetration, and the intensive adoption of social media among youth is not without effect on social relations. The exponential growth in the use of such platforms as Facebook, Twitter, and Instagram in the region calls for a better understanding of both usage trends and the nature of interactions on social media. In particular, it calls for a better grasp of how social ties, family networks, and friendships are affected by new and emerging social media platforms, and the extent to which online dynamics are redefining lived experiences and reformulating the nature of social relationships.

Communication practices that are enabled by a wide range of digital tools are restructuring the public sphere and revitalizing citizen engagement. If wider access to the Internet is undermining censorship in a region that has traditionally been averse to the free flow of information, the ubiquity of digital technologies and the low barriers to entry have facilitated the rise of citizen journalism. User-generated content by various actors, activists, bloggers, and social media users has helped give voice to many disenfranchised individuals and groups in the region. With the rise of networked publics, engagement in community life is further extended and its effect enhanced. Whether it is breaking the state's traditional inclination to control what is said in public, providing alternative views, or offering counter-narratives to mainstream media, citizen journalism is one of several forms of "disruptive power" wielded through digital communication technologies.[8] While these trends can be observed globally, in the context of the Middle East they stand out considering the region's enduring authoritarian legacy and ongoing limits on press freedom.[9] More than shattering dominant narratives and reconstructing discourses, the contestatory digital culture that is taking hold is helping to reconfigure power dynamics.

Going hand-in-hand with the rise of citizen journalism is the proliferation of youth-generated media. The appeal of video-sharing platforms like YouTube and micro-blogging sites like Twitter in the region is in many ways dramatic. The Middle East registers one of the highest video-viewing rates in the world. YouTube has become an important part of the lifestyle of young users, with "a strong impact on both the cultural industry and underground movements."[10] In the Kingdom of Saudi Arabia, for instance, where there is a sizable young Internet population, YouTube channels are particularly popular (second only to Google), creating vibrant spaces of entertainment for a highly active online video audience. These platforms offer alternative forms of engagement in a conservative society where entertainment is subject to restrictions and where local media content is state regulated and government controlled.[11] Youth-generated media like YouTube channels are noteworthy not only because they are altering traditional processes of media production and consumption, but also because they are enhancing the exercise of agency.[12]

Significantly, while new and social media are making it easier for users to communicate and to create and share content, preference for certain forms of media usage often obey hybrid logics whereby the local and global intersect in complex ways. When considering how the adoption of social media platforms is altering communication practices and changing socialization habits, it is important to take heed of the ways in which new online forms of engagement are shaped by the cultural contexts where they occur. For example, while the social networking site Facebook is the dominant social media platform in the region, the photo- and video-sharing app Snapchat is particularly popular among the locals in the socially conservative Gulf countries, due to the greater privacy protection it offers.[13] Snapchat's core concept of content mortality—enabling users to send images which are automatically deleted shortly after they have been seen—is especially appealing for many female users who do not feel comfortable sharing images or videos of themselves for fear these may be re-shared beyond one's circle of friends or become permanently public. By and large, a messaging app like Snapchat meshes well with the desire of young women in the region to embrace new forms of information technologies while remaining anchored in cultural values. More broadly, evolving communication habits and preferences for certain messaging platforms point to a fine line between societal expectations to abide by cultural norms and the lure of cyber freedom, between conformity and creativity, and between tradition and modernity. This interplay determines individual communication and socialization choices but also informs state strategies when it comes to the use and appropriation of ICTs. This is the case, for instance, of emerging Gulf states with rapidly growing global cities that are making concerted efforts to preserve their culture and heritage while embarking on a path of modernization and embracing the information age. In such a context, investing in digital library archives and setting up virtual museums, as in the case of Qatar, afford the opportunity to leverage technology in order to revive the national memory, celebrate the local culture, and preserve the region's heritage in the face of increased globalization.

But the adoption of ICTs in the Middle East cannot be reduced to a simple story of adaptation. The use of the microblogging site Twitter in a sizeable country like Saudi Arabia is a case in point. Curiously, Saudis are among the world's most active Twitter users.[14] More than merely a new form of connecting, communicating, and networking, Twitter is proving useful for negotiating the lived reality and creating alternative communities. For the venturesome, it became a means for shedding restrictive lifestyles and further loosening rigid gender barriers, by allowing young Saudi men and women to interact in ways that are typically not tolerated in public spaces. These maneuvers are not specific to Twitter, as Saudi youth have never ceased to devise ways to break such barriers. For the more creative Saudis, these inhibiting conditions have often fueled their artistic and literary sensibility and unleashed their ability to imagine and revel in an alternative world. One noteworthy example is *Girls of Riyadh*, an epistolary novel in the form of emails that vividly describe Saudi women's attempts to expand their freedoms and to negotiate their existence in the face of limitations imposed by society.[15] As an enabling reiteration of such forms of contestation, the widespread use of social media platforms like Twitter exemplifies the ways in which various forms of contention that are henceforth at the intersection of the real and virtual worlds are making it harder for the authorities in the conservative kingdom to continue to exert strict control over public life, dictate norms for social conformity, and in some cases maintain expectations of acquiescence.

Increasingly, wired Saudi women are using Twitter to voice their views on various issues, to challenge limiting gender roles, to promote women's rights, and to call for social change. A case in point is the plethora of Arabic language hashtags and tweets calling for an end to the state-sanctioned male guardianship system to which women in the kingdom are subjected, and which bans them from various activities, including travel and marriage, without the consent of a male relative (or guardian). More tenacious, perhaps, is women's online activism against a longstanding driving ban the kingdom placed on women. While a number of defiant Saudi women activists posted videos of themselves behind the wheel, others took to Twitter to challenge the ban. Evidently, the fight for Saudi women's right to drive predates online activism. With social media, though, such forms of activism gained an added momentum and attracted more attention. Additionally, the various online forms of engagement that ensued have helped women negotiate their realities by envisaging modes of self-representation that contest prevailing cultural constructions of gender identities within Saudi society.[16] It remains to be said that although the ban was eventually lifted, change was not simply the result of social media campaigns or online activism by women rights advocates. The post Arab uprisings context, change in leadership, the desire to project a better image of the kingdom, and economic necessity are all factors that favored a reconsideration of such severe restrictions on women (Saudi Arabia being the only country in the world that had a ban on women driving). Even so, the dynamics that developed around the issue of women driving are noteworthy because they are indicative of more widely shared dispositions and ongoing changes within society that are unfolding at the intersection of the online and offline worlds and that cannot be dissociated from everyday uses of communication technologies.

Noticeably, popular and emerging digital platforms are as enticing for governments in the region as they are empowering to their populations. The wide appeal and high usage of Twitter—along with the challenges of effectively regulating the Twittersphere and managing users' activities and the negative publicity generated by requests from authorities for content removal—have prompted many governments in the region to adapt to the digital age. Thus, while continuing to monitor dissenting voices, state authorities in the region have embraced new forms of communication, with many politicians adopting Twitter as a tool to engage citizens on public matters, and government departments increasingly using Twitter to reach out to engaged citizens and interested publics.[17] Wary about how competing religious authorities have taken to the Internet to promulgate their religious views, even state-sanctioned religious figures and religious establishments in the conservative Gulf monarchies have capitalized on the popularity of Twitter to issue e-*fatwas* (or Islamic rulings) that enable them to reassert their role in preserving morality and enhance their ability to maintain authority.[18]

Efforts such as these to reclaim the public sphere often proved ineffective in the face of popular social media platforms that have been adopted by many actors and players to effect social change. From the Iranian Green Movement of 2009 to the Arab uprisings of 2011, digital media have been tightly connected to protest movements that have shaken a region long known for its authoritarian resilience. In the wake of the Arab uprisings, revolutionary fervor, new-found freedoms, a persistent sense of injustice, renewed disposition for political activism, and loosening of state authority contributed to the rise of contentious voices, the increased appeal of online activism, and the wide adoption of citizen journalism. These evolving dynamics also favored the rise of digital counter-cultures, particularly among digitally enabled youth. More than undermining regime narratives, such counter-cultural tendencies are helping previously disenfranchised segments of society to ascertain their rights as citizens and to claim a voice in what has traditionally been a tightly guarded public sphere that discouraged dissent. For decades, traditional media, from newspapers to radio to television, have served authoritarian regimes. But that control is no longer as seamless as it once was. Today, the abundance of information, the multiplication of platforms, and the emergence of citizen journalism are breaking that monopoly. In the digital age, the vibrancy of the online public sphere is making it harder for authoritarian governments to censor cyberspace or control the message. Increasingly, ICTs are facilitating citizen participation, encouraging civic engagement, and empowering civil society. They are also enhancing grass-roots activism and providing an outlet for disfranchised voices.

In spite of these dynamics, the effect of ICTs on the region's political landscape is not always evident. The enthusiastic discourse about the role of the Internet in political change and the celebratory rhetoric concerning the influence of new and social media during the Arab uprisings notwithstanding, there is deep skepticism toward the potential for these digital transformations to alter the region's political realities, to have a significant effect on democratization efforts, or to live up to aspirations for shared governance. Although access to ICTs has empowered populations to challenge the ability of the state to control the flow of information, overall it has not weakened authoritarian impulses nor altered repressive inclinations.

In this respect, the ability of regimes in the region to adapt and to deal with the challenges that arise with the spread of information and communication technologies cannot be underestimated. It is telling that restrictions on the limits of free speech persist in many countries in the region, with more governments introducing new laws that tighten Internet controls and make existing restrictions on traditional media applicable to new media.[19] While some Middle East governments continue a blunt censorship of cyberspace, others have devised legal and administrative frameworks that enable them to exert various forms of subtle control over the online world. Social media activists and online journalists often face the same restrictions on freedom of speech that traditional journalists have been facing, and more governments are requiring online publications and websites to be registered. By and large, Middle Eastern governments continue to stifle online dissent by filtering and monitoring online content, investing in sophisticated technical tools, devising restrictive legal frameworks, and instituting regulatory bodies, among other forms of control. These restrictive measures are bound to constrict the digital space and circumscribe free speech further.

This is not to say that governments in the region are not challenged by the changes that ICTs are bringing about. In many ways, the Internet proved to be a double-edged sword. Increasingly, Middle East states are faced with daunting and rapidly developing challenges, ranging from cyber security to cyber crime and from cyber attacks to cyber terrorism. If in today's digitally connected world the threat of international terrorism has never been more real, it is more intensely so in the Middle East context. In this respect, the appropriation of the Internet by violent or extremist groups like the Islamic State of Iraq and Syria (known as ISIS, ISIL, or IS) and the use of social media platforms to recruit fighters, disseminate ideology and propaganda, spread spectacles of terror, and foment radicalization is a serious cause for concern.[20]

Beyond these growing security concerns, Middle East governments are constantly confronted with the need to rethink their approach toward information. Traditionally, unhindered access to information has been considered threatening, and warding off such a threat required devising various forms of information control. Paradoxically, while eroding the ability of governments to control information, digital connectivity and information intensity have enhanced state surveillance and given it added impetus.[21] The proliferation of data generators in the digital era means that states now have at their disposal more data on their citizens than ever before. For governments who are seeing their hold on information being seriously challenged by constant shifts in communication technologies, digital-era data collection, data mining, and data surveillance—made all the more effective with the growth in mobile networks and the Internet of things—afford new opportunities to exert control and enhance security. For states that are facing massive waves of refugees from war zones (like Turkey and Lebanon), or whose economies rely predominantly on massive numbers of foreign workers (as is the case with Gulf micro-states that suffer from "unsettling levels of demographic unbalance" created by large expatriate populations that far outnumber the national citizens),[22] data generated through mobile phone use acquires a security value. In the absence of adequate personal data protection regulation, the resulting asymmetrical power risks undermining the empowering potential of the Internet.[23] This is all the more noteworthy considering the authoritarian legacy and aversion to transparency that characterize much of the region. Determining how open-source information gathering is appropriated and how big data systems are managed and used could reveal a great deal about the various states' adaptation to and appropriation of the digital turn.

Beyond these applications, the potential of the ongoing digital transformations is not fully exploited. Massive digital data communication and rapidly growing social networking sites can prove to be valuable "observatories" of evolving everyday societal dynamics in a complex region like the Middle East.[24] Similarly, using data mining to understand current developments and future trends in society can support development and help devise knowledge-based policies.[25] So far, big data remains unwieldy and its applications more urgently felt by information-intensive and network societies than by a region that is defined by its uneven development. It is also unclear whether Middle East governments are disposed to use productively and innovatively an increasingly daunting scale of data to benefit the region, and how they can capitalize on the opportunities afforded by the advent of the era of big data. In a parallel development, the business sector is also tapping into the potential of big data. The advertising industry is perhaps second only to government in terms of monitoring, profiling, and trying to benefit from growing online consumer data. Further complicating this new tendency is the fact that considerable information on user behavior and inclinations is in the public domain and acquiring it does not necessarily call for consent, even though its use and appropriation raise concerns about violation of privacy.[26]

In spite of these challenges and hindrances, the adoption of digital technologies does hold promise for the region, particularly in the areas of social and economic development. In fact, the implications of digital technologies on the region's economies are arguably tremendous, and many countries have either embraced the knowledge economy or are transitioning in that direction. Increasingly, Middle Eastern states are realizing that GDP growth rests on their willingness to participate more fully in digital economies and their adaptability to the demands of such economies. Not only does the adoption of a knowledge economy facilitate the creation of communities of expertise and practice that can add value to the region and enhance development efforts, it also energizes other supporting sectors. To position themselves for such changes and equip the workforce with the necessary skills in ICTs, several countries in the Middle East and North Africa (MENA) region, most notably the oil-rich Gulf states, have been open to private investment in education ventures while also funding state-of-the-art education cities and setting up research parks that draw on world knowledge and international talent. Promising initiatives such as these, which rely heavily on environments supported by ICTs, are expanding opportunities for learning and research, helping to build capacity in knowledge development, and enhancing the prospects for advancement—even though, so far, the potential of digital learning and e-education is not yet fully exploited for reasons that range from the bureaucratic, to the infrastructural, to the cultural; nor can digitization be said to have transformed education and learning in ways that adequately respond to development demands and job market exigencies.[27]

Capitalizing on digital innovations, governments throughout the region have adopted e-government in varying degrees to help provide better integrated and more efficient service delivery to their citizens, as well as to improve the business environment and raise the business standards in ways that stimulate the development of the private sector and attract foreign investment. The launch of government websites, portals, and applications by various ministries and government entities has increased accessibility, enhanced transparency, improved the quality of services, and reduced bureaucracy. Still, the effect of such a transition from entrenched bureaucracies to online technocracies should not be overstated, as these changes are not uniformly implemented or universally adopted by the general public. What can be ascertained is that these changes are accompanied by adjustments considering how social relations in various parts of the region are generally rooted in traditions that tend to favor social hierarchies, nepotism, and face-to-face interaction—markers of traditional forms of sociality that are being affected by evolving communication practices and dispositions. Even if these challenges are overlooked, government automation is not necessarily transformational; it does not fundamentally change the nature of governance. So far, the effect of these dynamics that are induced by ICTs is less evident in modes of governance than it is in everyday practices and dispositions.

But there is more. The efforts of many countries in the region to boost e-government services and their desire to digitize and modernize are also impelled by security, strategic, and economic considerations. For example, in the case of the Gulf countries with sizable populations of migrant laborers, investment in e-government is partly driven by a security dimension. The use of smart ID cards containing digital information for various functions ensures better identification and authentication, while equally enabling governments to improve their management of immigration issues, monitoring of foreign workers, and tracking flows. In this regard, investing in high-tech identity systems and adopting sophisticated biometric technologies is part of a strategy to enhance "soft security" and "preventative surveillance."[28] Interestingly, while digitally enhanced government surveillance and its growing ability to monitor cyber activities are increasing concern over online privacy, users are finding corporate surveillance ever more intrusive.

In much the same way that digital technologies are redefining how governments are dealing with their subjects, so they are altering the relationship between businesses and consumers. Although the development of the business sector is held back by several barriers and challenges, digitization holds great promise for business and commerce. The adoption of new information and communication technologies has fueled the development of e-commerce and encouraged online shopping, especially within the more affluent states. Desire to leverage a growing array of communication tools and media platforms in order to capture the wired consumer market has led more retailers to adopt integrated marketing strategies, while changes in consumer behavior, partly driven by the widespread use of smartphones, is prompting more businesses to establish a stronger digital presence and to adopt direct marketing on social media. Expectedly, pressure for performance indicators has resulted in the increased adaptation of consumer habits and behavior tools. More businesses and brands are also resorting to content generators and "social influencers" with marketing prowess and large followers on social media to promote their products.[29] Although compared to Western countries online shopping in the region is still a fledgling sector, the e-commerce market is gradually developing and the digital economy is steadily growing, even luring established global companies to eye the Middle East market for potential expansion. The acquisition of Maktoob by Yahoo and Souq by Amazon may prove to be the enabling trends whereby local and global processes intersect and interlink more intensely with processes of information flows, economic expansion, and technological innovation.[30]

Noticeably, the economic impact of Internet growth and enhanced connectivity in the region is bound to increase as ICTs sectors and technology-related industries are well positioned to support further development and diversify the structure of the economy in ways that could stimulate job creation for the region's sizable young generation.[31] These technological developments can also push the boundaries of urban growth and development, as evinced in the emergence of innovative and sustainable smart cities with energy-efficient buildings. This is particularly the case in the ambitious, fast-growing Gulf region with the vision and wherewithal to modernize and transform their societies further, the drive to build social capital, and the keenness to ensure sustainable development.[32] While it is hard to envision a large-scale replication of ambitious and futuristic urban projects like Abu Dhabi's Masdar City and Doha's Lusail City, these smart cities are nonetheless noteworthy initiatives that are indicative of the opportunities that ICTs are affording the region.

Hindrances and challenges

Significantly, the digital transformation of the region remains hampered by a number of structural problems. In spite of the technologically enabled changes that the Middle East has witnessed, enormous challenges remain. Foremost among these are issues of technological access and digital divides. As Becky Loo reminds us, "digital divides are not just about e-technology availability but also other dimensions like accessibility, affordability, reliability, and speed of utilization."[33] There are remarkable differences within the region when it comes to technological infrastructure. Similarly, access to the Internet is not universal, and there is a huge disparity in terms of connectivity levels. In much the same way as digital technologies in the information age are increasing the gap between the developed and developing world, so too are they reinforcing disparities between lagging societies and more affluent states within the region.[34] Noticeably, Internet penetration rates vary considerably, ranging from high in Gulf countries like Qatar (94.1 per cent) and the UAE (90.6 per cent); to relatively high in countries like Iran (70 per cent); to medium in countries like Turkey (59.6); to low in countries like Iraq (33 per cent) and Yemen (24.1 per cent).[35]

While the growing adoption of mobile Internet technology could help reduce this gap in the future, notable differences remain within the region's individual countries, as the digital divide is acute between well-off and impoverished populations, as well as between under-served rural areas and more resourceful and developed urban centers. As Emma Murphy points out, equitable and universal access to ICTs in the region is often hampered by both regional imbalances, which favor selective investment in ICTs infrastructure in certain regions over others, and the very commercialization of ICTs, which links access to those who can afford it.[36] What the lack of equitable or universal access does is create hierarchies of knowledge, which in turn translate into hierarchies of power. Many people in the region remain either disconnected from the world of the Internet or disenfranchised, without the knowledge of digital tools and with low technical literacy. For all its promise, the digital transformation of the Middle East is far from being an equalizer. For many, it raises the specter of economic marginalization, exacerbating social divisions and reinforcing inequalities. These inequalities are particularly pronounced when considering the demographics of users. Access to ICTs and technical knowledge is especially a barrier to Internet use among women in many parts of the region, and a hindrance to their inclusion in the knowledge economy. Traditional gender barriers, class differences, and inter- and intra-regional disparities are all the more important to note because they impact on people and determine future social and economic opportunities.

Not only does Internet connectivity vary from country to country, but high-speed broadband connectivity also lags behind in many parts of the MENA region.[37] Where broadband technology is accessible, it is not always affordable as the cost of broadband speed services remains high throughout much of the region. The availability of affordable high-speed Internet is particularly important for supporting sustainable development, driving growth, and creating jobs both within and outside technology-intensive sectors. It is all the more important considering the region's aspiration to pursue economic diversification and to transition toward a knowledge-based economy.[38]

Further hindering the development of the full potential of the Internet for the region are rigid market structures, unchanged regulatory frameworks, and continuing monopolies in the telecommunication sector.[39] Not only have many Middle Eastern countries been slow in introducing legislation covering ICTs to advance Internet freedom and protect the right to access information, but there is also a lack of adequate policy reforms to keep up with the demands of a fast-changing, digitally enabled world. If the mutation of capitalism has increased the reliance on data and information, spawned the information society,[40] and intensified information flows, it has also redefined the nature of the economy by prioritizing such intangibles as creativity and knowledge.[41] Considering the nature of the new economy in the age of the Internet, protecting creativity and intellectual rights in the face of digital piracy becomes a critically important issue. The lack of enforceable intellectual property protection in the region often translates into a lack of innovation incentives to capitalize on the region's digital potential and to modernize local economies.[42] In spite of its phenomenal growth, the Internet has not consistently honed local talent or sufficiently fostered regional capacity building—except in the case of Israel, which has advanced digital industries. Even though there are growing numbers of online companies, technology start-ups, tech-sector venture capital investments, and innovative digital practices, development in this area has been uneven. For example, the development of Arabic online applications and content has not kept up with the notable increase in online Arabic language usage; while the amount of local Arabic language content has increased over the years, overall it remains distinctly low.[43]

These challenges do not undermine the digital potential of the region as much as they draw attention to the intricate nature of the ongoing transformations. The digital Middle East that is taking hold is complex and multidimensional, but is also uneven and nebulous. While weaving these complexities into a coherent narrative is an ambitious task, drawing out the significance of these overlapping dynamics can help shed new light on change in the region. How the digital Middle East is likely to unfold is hard to predict with certainty. Capitalizing on new opportunities that the ongoing digital transformations have opened up for people in the region and coping with the many challenges, hindrances, and limitations these countries continue to face will determine the long-term impact these digital transformations are likely to have on the Middle East.

Overview of the individual chapters

This book unfolds along key areas of digital transformation that have affected Middle Eastern societies in the social, cultural, economic, and political spheres. The individual chapters offer various perspectives on the digital Middle East. They capture a wide range of changes that are intimately connected with the increased adoption of information technologies, but also highlight the asymmetrical nature of these changes. They point out new dynamics and emergent trends associated with the advent of a new digital culture, while also mapping out discordances that have manifested themselves with the intensification of digital connectivity. The following outlines the individual contributions to this volume.

Ilhem Allagui's chapter examines intergroup communication and interaction on social media platforms in light of the increasing number of users connecting with friends on social media.[44] Focusing on the nature and effect of these Internet-mediated forms of socialization in the Arab world, Allagui sheds light on the everyday social experiences of Arab youth who are widely connected and increasingly more active online. Drawing on media narratives and personal stories from informants, she highlights the complexity of social interactions in today's media-intensive environment, paying particular attention to the significance of the Internet for social networking and how closeness and intimate connections are reformulated in the virtual public sphere. Digital technologies do more than enhance connectivity among users; they foster online forms of engagement that redefine how social relationships are constructed, how they are managed, and how they evolve. The use of social media is not only making it easier to enlarge a circle of friends, form new ties, and maintain links with existing friends, but is also altering the very nature of friendship. The informality of the interaction and the instantaneity of the technology often hide complex dynamics. Contrary to what the seeming spontaneity of social media and the casualness of online exchanges suggest, online relationships are often the product of strategic positioning, whereby digitally connected youth carefully craft the image they want to project.

Technologically mediated forms of interaction are particularly noteworthy because today's youth operate in an open online environment. This promotes and facilitates practices that simultaneously feed off and diverge from gauged interactions and guarded forms of sociality. One of the central questions the chapter tackles is how online practices of socialization are themselves affected by culture and how they are affecting cultural dispositions. Ready access to new and social media and the widespread use of telephony have increased connectivity and enhanced the networking capability of individuals and groups. They have also affected the social construction of relationships, such that connecting with people one does not know or communicating with strangers is becoming the norm. In an environment where social conformity and family values are important considerations, the kind of free interaction the Internet affords and the degree of autonomy that users enjoy in making connections are typically perceived as potentially undermining cultural norms and expectations. The case study in this chapter, however, challenges this perception. The adoption of ICTs, Allagui suggests, is not necessarily at odds with traditional values. Youth are embracing a wide range of new technologies and immersing themselves in social media while remaining embedded in their cultural systems. Online forms of socialization do not so much defy traditions or go against cultural expectations as much as they expand the sphere within which identity negotiation takes place.

In some ways, managing social relations on the Internet is a form of play—a ludic activity that is inherent to the participatory culture which digital networks promote.[45] Not surprisingly, perhaps, the pervasiveness of social media usage in the region has enhanced the popularity of video games. These have captured the interest of youth and adults alike, and the gaming industry has grown phenomenally in recent years. It is this thriving market of video games and the complex ways in which these games are produced, adapted, and consumed in the MENA region that Vít Šisler examines in his contribution. Focusing on youth's growing interest in and attraction to video games, he looks at the relationship between the digital and the ludic, drawing attention to the ways in which digital games are woven into subversive modes of representation. Constituting a global passion that has captured the imagination of the digital public, and a fast-growing industry that is facilitated by advances in digital technologies, video games have a particular significance in a region that is marked by a sizable young population and by improved Internet access and mobile device penetration rates. Although the video game industry remains dominated by artifacts, products, and applications that are developed in the United States, Europe, and Japan, the adopted gaming culture is increasingly hybrid in nature, combining elements of transnationalism and translocalism. Further complicating this reality is the fact that the gaming culture in the MENA region has developed over the past decade and a half within regulator frameworks, local cultural contests, and divergent stakeholders, whose intersection often leads to contradictory processes. It is the disjunctive tendencies that characterize the technological processes and the cultural flows influencing game development in the region that Šisler proposes to dissect. He combines insights from interviews with game developers and producers from across the region with rich content analysis. In his account, video games constitute "imaginary spaces" that encompass evolving dynamics, which lie at the intersection between "global cultural flows, media policies of nation states, visions and engagements of private entrepreneurs, and migration and appropriation of Western game genres and rule-systems."

Yet, the fact that video games come to life and become "finished texts" only when placed in the hands of players calls for both an analysis of the particularities of play and an understanding of the cultural, political, and social contexts within which these games are developed and practiced. The specific patterns of interaction and the forms of communication associated with games and gaming are important to note. As spaces of representation, Šisler argues, video games are also necessarily arenas of contestation. The development of local and regional video game production is partly motivated by the need to tell one's story. It reflects a conscious attempt on the part of successful game developers to reflect appropriately the history, culture, and religions of the Middle East. To the extent that they deconstruct misrepresentations of Arabs and Muslims in mainstream Western video games, locally produced games serve as "counter discourses." Šisler further argues that several developers see their primary drive as educational. As an alternative form of edutainment to mainstream Western games, many of these locally developed video games promote virtuous, Islamic, and family values. Interestingly, the culture that these games promote does not insulate users as much as it enables them to value authenticity, originality, and locality, while allowing them to participate in the global gaming culture, to forge networks, and to be a part of vibrant transnational youth communities. These dynamics that surround game development, Šisler concludes, suggest that the evolving digital entertainment culture constitutes an extended "arena where multifaceted political, social, religious, and economic interests compete and coexist."

Shifting the analysis from everyday spaces of communication to media usage and consumption, Mark Peterson examines how the experience of intense historical events is mediated through information and communication technologies. In particular, he probes the lived experience of Egyptians during the 2011 revolution that toppled Hosni Mubarak, one of the iconic figures of Arab authoritarianism. The experiences of lay Egyptians are particularly noteworthy, because they offer a perspective that goes beyond widely adopted narratives that focus on mobile-equipped protesters in Tahrir Square and activist bloggers in cyberspace. For Peterson, this is particularly important to note because the dominant narrative about the revolution is, in fact, a "constructed narrative," and the cohesion that was exhibited in Tahrir Square was a "negotiated unity." Glorifying digital technologies as liberating or downplaying their role during the Egyptian uprising are claims emanating out of "media ideologies" that either justify or rationalize certain forms of media usage, and in doing so obfuscate the mediated experience of change during dramatic upheavals and fast-unfolding social events.

To illustrate these dynamics, Peterson offers different media ethnographic narratives about media usage and media experience. The subjects of his study did not participate in the protests or actively engage in revolutionary activities, but experienced the popular protests in Tahrir Square through various types of media channels, platforms, and technologies. These actors came to experience and participate in the revolutionary process through media practices that are entangled with everyday life and which animate a struggle over the symbolic meaning of revolutionary activities. The attention to this process of mediation, Peterson argues, helps to inform not only how "peripheral actors" consume the various forms of communication they are engaged with in their daily lives, but also how such experience turns them into interactive participants in the flow of communication. What is particularly significant about these mediated experiences, according to Peterson, is their multifaceted nature, being both collective and personal, common and individualized.

The mediated reality that Peterson describes in his ethnographic study opens up the opportunity to understand social and political change as lived and experienced both collectively and individually; it also points to the need to differentiate between various social players, actors, and subjects across social class lines and gender demarcations. When considering the relationship between ongoing political processes and unfolding media practices, gender, in particular, is an important category to note because it rests on a social construction of masculinity and femininity, and along with it the delineation of identity and authority, in ways that profoundly shape the actions of individuals in society.[46]

The issue of gender is discussed more fully in Annabelle Sreberny's contribution. Sreberny examines how digital connectivity is complicating such realities and whether it can unsettle established categories and possibly induce change. More specifically, she examines how, and to what extent, the expansion and wide adoption of ICTs is affecting the lives of women, and how communication technologies are potentially changing women's contributions in the MENA region. Of particular interest is how women are using the Internet in various contexts to get their voices heard and how information and communication technologies have been adopted by women "to make change."

In exploring the implications of increased participation of women in today's online environment, Sreberny is not simply focused on women's empowerment. Attention to the gendered dimension of the digital transformations that the region has been undergoing is less geared toward determining whether women are better or worse off in a fast-changing Middle East than it is aimed at reconceiving the identity of women in the age of the Internet. If anything, the study of women's issues, as articulated in the online environments, affords the opportunity to move the discussion on various women's issues beyond delimited gender terms and categories, and to refocus the discussion within a broader context: whom do ICTs privilege and whom do they leave out? Whom do they empower and whom do they marginalize? In this respect, women's issues cannot be sundered from broader social, cultural, and political issues, nor can they be adequately understood outside the structures of power that define relationships within a particular society. While acknowledging that the kind of "online politics" described "are not ontologically different activities, but rather different modes of being political," Sreberny points out that Internet diffusion in a region that has increasingly shown a disposition to change helped produce "a more conducive environment for women's political activities and thus for a general enlargement of what counts as the 'sphere of the political.'"[47] This means that a gendered analysis of the digital Middle East needs to account not only for whether women can effect change, but also how the sphere of the political itself can be expanded.

In an environment like the Middle East where women's voices are frequently unheard and their experiences overlooked, access to and appropriation of the Internet may change the lived reality and alter existing dynamics—although identifying tangible change is difficult. Sreberny reminds us of the reality of the "digital divide," pointing out how disparities in terms of access and Internet diffusion between and among countries make the endeavor to theorize the role of media in development particularly tricky. In fact, cross-country statistical data on women's Internet usage are hard to come by, and in-depth studies about their online activities are lacking.

Increasingly, though, women are capitalizing on the new online environment. While these trends may not be far-reaching, widespread, or generalizable, they point to "a radical shift of focus toward the Internet by women." Such developments point to women's growing ability to make change, and are indicative of the potential that the new online environment holds for women in the region and beyond. Eschewing the facile argument about "Middle East exceptionalism," Sreberny contends that the struggles of Middle Eastern women should not obscure the fact that the issues they face are also shared with many women throughout the world. If women's online activities in the Middle East are interesting to note, it is not because they are specific to the region, but because they offer a vivid account of the range of struggles that women are facing and, as such, are relevant to wider debates about women globally.

At the same time, Sreberny acknowledges the limits of the new online environments for women in a region that is marked with uneven access to information and technology. Although the MENA region has been shaken by forces of change, positive developments are not all that obvious for women. At least, the markers of the environment within which women are living—whether it is an authoritarian state or a patriarchal culture—do not make it particularly easy to press for change. Sreberny concludes that, even if the proliferation of women's voices online does not necessarily amount to tangible gains and material changes, "the political milieu has certainly been altered."

While the issue of women's empowerment in the region cannot be adequately understood when considered exclusively from a cultural lens, as Sreberny rightly argues, cultural considerations are important for understanding the specificity of the digital Middle East. This cultural dimension figures prominently in Suzi Mirgani's discussion of how some countries in the region sought to modernize their economies in the digital era, and how they adapted to technological transformations. In particular, Mirgani's contribution sheds light on the motivations for Gulf Cooperation Council (GCC) countries to adopt foreign-mandated copyright laws that do not reflect the specificity of their environments, and how they adapt such laws to serve their own needs. The aspiration of GCC rentier states to forego their traditional reliance on hydrocarbons in favor of knowledge-based economies that could lead to their insertion into the global economy necessitated the implementation of international agreements on Trade Related Aspects of Intellectual Property Rights (TRIPS). These agreements are maintained through a set of World Trade Organization (WTO) regulations that favor the economic and commercial interests of developed nations and protect them in the face of rampant intellectual property piracy and copyright infringements. The commodification of ideas as forms of property that can be owned and exchanged, and therefore as assets that need to be well guarded, is further enhanced by the conceptualization of knowledge in the digital era. Mirgani notes that "in the language of this reformulated and reimagined discourse, creativity and innovation are aspects that can—and indeed should—be capitalized upon and exploited to achieve their maximum economic value within the digital age."

Significantly, the Gulf countries have high rates of copyright infringement because of the lax enforcement of laws related to copyright and intellectual property theft. This trend has increased with the wide availability of digital technologies and higher Internet speed. Not surprisingly, Gulf countries have come under pressure to take a firmer stance against piracy and to enforce intellectual property and copyright laws. Although GCC governments have increased their monitoring of online activities over the years and have made efforts to update their press laws and enact cyber crime laws, their efforts have not altered existing practices in the region. In fact, many of the measures that were taken were less designed to protect intellectual property and deter copyright infringement than they were aimed at limiting freedoms and managing political dissent.

In more recent years, as the wealthy Gulf states strove to expand beyond hydrocarbon industries and attract new foreign investment, there has been increasing pressure by powerful international players to implement and enforce anti-piracy laws in order to protect intellectual property. With GCC countries positioning themselves to develop knowledge-based economies that thrive on digital production, the need to take measures to protect intellectual property has become even more urgent. In response, efforts have been made to raise awareness about intellectual property and various measures taken to curb piracy and prohibit the use of unlicensed software. In spite of these efforts, though, the problem persists in part because the stakes for the Gulf states are not high.

Where they have been more proactive and probably more effective is in their effort to protect "traditional knowledge and heritage rights," which have been widely appropriated to fashion the modern national character and define the identity of the Gulf states. GCC governments did so by launching well-funded heritage programs aimed at ingraining a particular national memory among their citizens, resurrecting local knowledge, and preserving historical content through digital archiving. Thus, while being agnostic to the implementation of stringent copyright infringement protection measures that are rather foreign to the Gulf culture and the local environment, Mirgani notes, "GCC governments have attempted to use digital technologies and international intellectual property to their advantage by producing and promoting their own locally produced content." In doing so, they have also and in their own way aligned themselves with the international economic framework sanctioned by the WTO, thus partaking in the global digital revolution while serving their cultural needs. Thus far, it remains unclear what these top-down adaptations mean for the region's native citizens and its large expatriate population, and how they alter the way they think about intellectual property and piracy issues. What is certain, Mirgani concludes, is that "by having a personal or national investment in the production and distribution of local digital content ... GCC states can finally have a stake in the future of creative content."

Complementing Mirgani's discussion of the Gulf countries' cultural approach to intellectual property issues in the digital age is Norhayati Zakaria's examination of the Middle East's acculturation to the digital transformations that the region is experiencing. Specifically, Zakaria looks at whether cultural factors are contributing to or hindering the adoption of e-commerce in a region where trade has traditionally centered around souks. Although the fast-paced processes of modernization and urbanization have engendered an immersion in modern forms of consumerism, most notably malls and shopping centers, it is not evident that the region is prone to adopting e-commerce, which Zakaria dubs "the cyber-souk." Although advances in ICTs and access to the Internet, and the wide adoption of smartphones—along with better services, new consumer habits, desire for a wider range of products, and awareness of global consumerism trends—have contributed to the growth of online trade, e-commerce is far from being widely or uniformly adopted throughout the region. In fact, e-commerce is a fairly nascent market, and a great many local businesses and regional companies are not partaking in the global digital economy or embracing digital transformations. The expansion of e-commerce is hampered by a number of factors that undermine people's confidence in using online services. These range from concerns about the privacy of personal information to the security of online payments, and from the unreliability of delivery services to the lack of a favorable online environment. For Zakaria, the biggest challenges to the development and adoption of e-commerce are neither technological nor systemic, but in essence cultural.

Accordingly, Zakaria outlines a number of cultural factors that determine business practices and affect the adoption of, and acculturation to, e-commerce. These pertain to the nature of the culture and society (whether individualistic or collectivist), the degree of tolerance for risk (whether it is a high-uncertainty avoidance and risk-averse culture or a low-uncertainty avoidance and change-tolerant culture), and the manner in which communication is enacted and negotiations are carried out (whether it is a high-context culture in which individuals are relationship-oriented or a low-context culture in which individuals are task-oriented). For Arab societies that have long internalized the culture of the souk, where social and business ties are rooted in face-to-face communication, strong ties, verbal interaction, price negotiation, personal relationships, in-group dynamics, and trust building, acculturating to online shopping and adopting e-commerce is not self-evident. For global businesses seeking to expand in the Middle East, overcoming cultural barriers that hinder the development of e-commerce in the region necessitates the adoption of strategies that are premised on "cultural localization" and not "cultural universality."

The adoption of ICTs in the region is doing more than introducing and facilitating new business practices; it is also altering traditional dispositions of customers over time. Significantly, Zakaria argues, new and fast-growing business structures such as m-commerce (mobile commerce) and s-commerce (social commerce) are likely to bridge the gap between the cultural expectations of consumers and the business imperatives of the sellers and marketers. Zakaria concludes that "e-commerce industries seeking to claim a market share in the region need to take into account the cultural value systems of potential MENA customers and understand how they acclimate to the new business environment before they can make headways."

The digital transformations that the Middle East is experiencing are not only impacting creative content but also consolidating certain economic dynamics. Jon Anderson's chapter explores the hidden aspect of the social and political economies of the Internet, as it relates to the production and circulation of user-generated content, along with the development of communities of practice tied to developers in the local technology sector. His endeavor calls for a critical distance from two perspectives that have largely defined attempts to understand and theorize change associated with the advent of ICTs and the adoption of the Internet in the Middle East: resilient authoritarianism and relative underdevelopment. The former perspective is political in its thrust and focuses on the ways in which information freedom empowers civil society actors and erodes authoritarian control; the latter is economic in essence and relates to the role that ICTs and informational development are positioned to play in the transition to a knowledge economy. In Anderson's view, the kind of "tool-and-impact thinking" that underpins the twin emphasis on "informational freedom" and "informational development"—as forces that are conducive to change—is rooted in "analytical biases toward the supply side," which, in turn, is premised on assumptions about demand as being pre-existing. Such emphasis privileges "impacts" (whether these are political impediments or civil society gains) over "dynamics." As such, the focus is on macro-practices to the detriment of the micro-level of analysis, which leaves unaddressed complex dynamics about IT development that engages its own "digital habitus."

That culture, along with the habitus that characterizes it, was consolidated with the web 2.0 turn. Social media users and developers feed off each other's activities, such that programs and platforms are dynamically configured by users. Engendered types of behavior and forms of usage are then incorporated by developers who attune the system around which social media is based to capture more of the users' social life. Thus, open and free IT-based services induce more data about user behavior that can be turned into a value. For Anderson, these dynamics point to "the economics of 'working for free,'" which are typically elided in either political or economic macro-perspectives that treat IT in general and the Internet in particular as "exogenous" to the systems that engage them, when in fact they are more endogenous. The focus on IT impacts and user agency (what the technology can deliver in terms of perceptible growth or tangible value) does not account for how value "is harvested up the chain from its primary producer." It captures the goods and services which the system yields, but not the "investment value" associated with them. Focusing on how the process works reveals interesting insights and hidden values related to user repurposing, career patterns and opportunities for developers, and communities of practice development.

Anderson pays particular attention to local developers, including programmers, web designers, and system architects. The advent of social media afforded developers the opportunity to integrate user participation and peer-production into media consumption. When considered external to economic activity, the value of these reverse flows of social media are not obvious, which is tantamount to saying that user-contributed content does not have a tangible or tradable value. In effect, however, value (from content produced by users working for free) is extracted higher up the chain—in the metadata which social media companies then aggregate and sell to advertisers, making value "less in the aggregated than in the aggregation."

Interestingly, Anderson notes, although features and patterns of Internet—and more specifically social media—usage in the Middle East are comparable to those in the West, value extraction does not seem to have taken hold in the region, not only because the Arab world is "on the periphery of the informational capitalist system," but also because it is more attuned to "financing trade" than "investment finance." Even though future pay-offs, such as enhancing one's reputation, may motivate local developers, Anderson explains, they do not fully account for the intricate nature of working for free in the Middle East. What is more revealing, Anderson argues, are the informal networks among tech developers that give rise to a wealth of incubators and accelerators who provide a variety of services on the fringe that could potentially lead to "ownership stakes in turning developers' ideas into IT businesses." What Anderson finds particularly interesting is the ensuing "ecosystem" in which the various aspects of the local tech sector intersect, thus giving form to evolving communities of practice that operate in a dynamic network-based system that is characteristic of the digital habitus. It is these complex dynamics and unstable combinations of local and global dynamics, Anderson concludes, that need to be highlighted when attempting to understand how the Internet entails working not just "for freedom" but also "for free."

It is this notion of "freedom" that Muzammil Hussain contemplates further in his contribution to this volume, which provides insights into the politics of Internet governance. Drawing our attention to the politics of Internet freedom, Hussain critically examines the efforts of Western state and non-state players to influence debates, practices, and policies on Internet freedom in a changing Middle East. Western efforts to advocate Internet freedom in the region have often been met with skepticism, emanating out of what is perceived as a long history of either support of or tolerance for political authoritarianism that is motivated by geopolitical state interests. Critics who subscribe to these views tend to dismiss the Western Internet freedom agenda as a "fallacy." They argue, for instance, that official and corporate involvement of the United States in the Internet freedom movement is more harmful than it is beneficial for freedom, and that "a hyper-politicization of the digital activism movement" undermines more than it serves grass-roots digital activism in local Arab contexts.[48]

The unprecedented youth-led protest movements that broke out in Tunisia and spread throughout much of the Arab world were fodder for the technology enthusiasts, who were quick to celebrate what they considered to be digitally enabled change, extolling the role that the Internet played in bringing about political change in authoritarian contexts. The uprisings also constituted a rare opportunity for West-supported alliances to emerge with the purpose of debating, defining, and enforcing Internet freedom. It is these "proto-regimes in formation" that Hussain critically analyzes. What he finds particularly noteworthy is "the infusion of activist, state, and corporate interests in the ambiguous domain of Internet freedom promotion work involving several types of stakeholders as unlikely bedfellows." This is particularly the case with the Freedom Online Coalition (FOC), a partnership of predominantly Western governments that was launched in the aftermath of the 2011 Arab uprisings. Such an initiative represents a departure from standard UN regulatory bodies in the field of ICTs like the International Telecommunications Union and the Internet Governance Forum.

Grasping the significance of these new proto-regimes necessitates moving the discussion beyond the duality of technology-based political activism (users) and state reactions (rulers) to these new forms of challenges and taking account of digital infrastructural politics. In non-democratic contexts, the political uses and affordances of digital infrastructures are premised on a double bind, whereby opportunities for political participation are often met with repressive counter-efforts to repurpose such infrastructures. Digital media enabled networks of activists to express their grievances, contest their realities, and mobilize against authoritarian regimes, while at the same time helping state powers to exert more control over their people and increase their monitoring capabilities. Significantly, attention to the uses of digital technologies by authoritarian states and networked publics often obscures the dynamics underpinning these technologies, namely how these tools came about in the first place. Particularly important in understanding this equation are "multinational technology companies that own and maintain key pieces of the transnational digital infrastructure." Accordingly, Hussain broadens the range of stakeholders to include not only civil society (activists) and state powers (governments), but also the private sector associated with digital infrastructures (corporations).

In the aftermath of the initial Arab uprisings, the different motivations and competing policy interests of various stakeholders further complicated attempts to regulate digital infrastructures, to advance global democratization endeavors, or to ensure that these West-produced and globally exported technologies were used in practices upholding international human rights norms and values. Concerted efforts to "protect digital infrastructures in the name of human rights and democratic responsibilities," Hussain notes, are often politically motived insofar as they constitute a transnational "arena for exercising state power and for shaping international politics." These dynamics call for carrying out complex negotiations and extensive debates among multi-stakeholders that go beyond traditional state actors and establish policy institutions to encompass various communities of practice. According to Hussain, the new spaces of social practices that support and advance Internet freedom are particularly important to study, because they complicate our understanding of how policies relating to Internet freedom promotion are developed, how they unfold, and how they evolve.

The tension between state and non-state actors is also at work within individual states. The intricate nature of cyber politics in post-revolutionary Iran, which constitutes the focus of Gholam Khiabany's chapter, is a case in point. Typically, studies on Iran emphasize what is often perceived as an inherent divide between the traditional and religious nature of the Iranian state, on the one hand, and the modern and secular nature of technology, on the other. For Khiabany, this dichotomy obscures complex dynamics that permeate and define the relationship between the Internet and politics in Iran. In fact, the theocratic nature of the Iranian political system did not preclude the adoption of modern information and communication technologies and the development of a communication infrastructure. The state pursued a dual strategy; while keen on adopting new information and communication technologies and developing the country's ICTs capacities, it attempted from the outset to control public communication. Wary of the implications of the growing popular appeal of new ICTs on its ability to control public expression and to rein in dissenting discourses and independent voices, the state asserted its control over the communication sphere and sought to limit its destabilizing effects. As the state-supported communication industry grew into a vibrant economic sector, so did the public appeal of the Internet and new media as "vibrant politico-cultural spaces," as evinced in the rich Iranian blogosphere. This double bind is particularly important in understanding the country's "contentious politics," which have become increasingly hard to dissociate from media dynamics and digital activism. At the same time, Khiabany notes, contentious politics and cyber activism in the Islamic republic are not mere technological effects. Fueling and sustaining the ongoing struggle in Iran between a repressive central state and an aspiring public over the use and control of communications are internal rifts, struggles, and tensions within the political establishment itself, which are reproduced and amplified in cyberspace. In other words, cyber politics in Iran need to be understood in relation to the kind of factionalism that characterizes the Iranian political scene in general, and "the power of real networks of reformists' circle in Iran" in particular. The interests and agendas of various state agencies necessarily carry over into cyberspace, making it "an intriguing and contradictory political and digital environment."

The last chapter in this volume looks at the potential for information technologies to redefine the relationship between governments and citizens in the region. Focusing on the advent of e-government in the GCC countries (Bahrain, Kuwait, Oman, Qatar, Saudi Arabia, and the UAE), Damian Radcliffe highlights the ways in which ICTs are impacting government services, facilitating communication, and enhancing the ability of state actors to improve public service delivery, support business, serve public needs, engage citizens, and more broadly add civil value. The chapter offers insights into how these Gulf countries have capitalized on the potential for e-government, but also considers the challenges these countries need to overcome in order for e-government to become more fully embedded in their policies and practices.

Over the past decade or so, there has been notable advancement in e-government in the GCC states, leading to a steady rise in their regional and global e-government rankings, which stand above the world average—albeit with varying degrees of progress and different stages of maturity. In many ways, e-government is an economic investment of sorts. Compared to the rest of the Arab states, the GCC countries have managed, even if variably, to project a modern pro-technology environment, harness a pro-business image, and alter the ways in which government agencies deal with publics. Rolling out e-government initiatives allowed for citizens and the large expatriate populations in these countries to have increased access to government departments online. They also benefited from better government services and more effective transactions, whether for paying a utility bill, settling a speeding ticket, renewing a driver's license, requesting a birth certificate, or applying for a visa on e-government portals.

These advances notwithstanding, Radcliffe notes, change has been slow, which is tantamount to saying that the GCC countries' adoption of ICTs is far from turning them into e-societies. In spite of these countries' commendable investment in telecommunications infrastructure, their steady efforts to achieve digital readiness, and their advanced global standing in this sector, the potential of e-government is not fully developed. While there have been improvements in services and more effective transaction capabilities, and while citizens have better access to e-services, Radcliffe points out that e-government is still not deeply rooted in the Gulf region. Even though the GCC countries have attempted to adopt widespread e-government practices, they have not attained "an integrated e-government." The adoption of e-government is hindered by a number of barriers, including the varying levels of users' digital literacy skills, the general public's predisposition to be wary of government services online, varying degrees of consumer satisfaction, as well as the lack of awareness of available government programs, the potential benefits of such services, and the practicality of non-face-to-face transactions.

Equally noteworthy are users' concerns about matters of security and privacy when it comes to personal information. In fact, a key factor undermining the adoption of e-government is citizens' degree of comfort with online security. Although, increasingly, the use of high encryption standards and secured microchips is making the online environment safer and more reliable for transferring sensitive personal and financial data, there is still resistance to these online transactions by consumers and users in the region, stemming largely from concerns over information security. On the government side, e-government initiatives are hampered by the persistence of bureaucratic practices and mindsets among civil servants (and consumers alike), the lack of adequate training for government workers, and a genuine desire on the part of government agencies to change and "to do things differently." So far, not all involved parties are disposed to believe in the value of e-services.

Technical, administrative, and cultural issues aside, e-government neither has broad reach across the various segments of the population in these countries, nor does it extend to all elements of society. For example, the large low-skilled migrant laborer populations constitute an important component of the economic structure of GCC countries, but they fall largely outside the scope of e-government services because of issues of marginality, digital exclusion, poor literacy, and language barriers, as e-services are typically offered in Arabic and English. Rapid advances in information technology pose yet additional challenges. In particular, the widespread use of smartphones, social media, and apps by the general public and businesses alike is impelling GCC governments to adapt to a new information and communication environment that shapes as much as it is shaped by digitally connected publics. So far, Radcliffe notes, "e-government services and communication are in a perpetual state of evolution." In the future, e-government is likely to evolve in order to keep up with the exigencies of changing communication dynamics and the needs, preferences, and habits of e-citizens.

In the final analysis, the implantation of e-government in the region has been remarkable but not transformative. While government portals offer a wide range of e-services, many websites are mere repositories of information and data, functioning as one-way information venues rather than truly interactive websites. Additionally, only a limited range of online applications is available. Engaging citizens calls for "an active two-way relationship between government bodies and the public aimed at shaping decisions, policies, and practices." Although e-government offers citizens the opportunity to participate in certain forms of public consultation, and allows for them to register complaints against the inefficiencies of government departments, overall the proclivity of e-government to foster better governance in the region remains intangible. When it comes to instituting open government, reducing corruption, promoting transparency, favoring inclusion, and enhancing food governance, the promise of e-government is yet to be fulfilled.

Both individually and collectively, the chapters that constitute this volume offer vivid accounts of how digital technologies are affecting the region. These grounded reflections paint a complex picture of a digital Middle East we are only just beginning to apprehend.

2

THE CHANGING NATURE
OF SOCIALIZATION AMONG ARAB YOUTH

INSIGHTS FROM ONLINE PRACTICES

Ilhem Allagui

Digital media have affected the lives of youth in the Middle East and North Africa (MENA) region on many levels, particularly in the social realm. Research indicates that youth are spending increasing amounts of time online. A 2015 social media report shows that 89 per cent of Facebook users in the Arab world access the Internet daily. Among the surveyed social media users, 25 per cent said they spend 16–30 minutes per day on social networking sites (SNSs), 23 per cent spend 5–15 minutes, 20 per cent spend 31–60 minutes, and 15 per cent spend 1–2 hours.[1] More affordable data packages and better access to the Internet, particularly with more places offering free Wi-Fi, are enabling more users to spend extended time online. These changes are not without implications. Not only are social networks evolving with the development of the technical landscape, but the users' own online practices are expanding, their social experiences are changing, and their relationships to the "real world" are being reconfigured. Capturing these changes in their full complexity is a challenge. Existing research on new and emergent media trends in the MENA region tends to focus on shifting media habits. It is largely informed by macro-analyses aimed at understanding who accesses what platform, the amount of time spent online, and where, when, and how users are accessing the Net. Not much attention has been paid to the more profound and subtle social transformations accompanying these technological adoptions; and their potential effects and likely implications on youth have not yet been duly analyzed. A micro-perspective can help yield insights into the nature of these changing practices and shed light on evolving forms of engagement online.

This chapter focuses on online communication practices that are developing among Arab youth. It explores how youth who form online relationships adapt to and interact with evolving digital technologies. It provides a needed understanding of Arab youth friendship practices, in particular how digitally connected youth negotiate social relationships in an environment that is defined by well delineated social norms. Although socializing counts as one of the top online activities, we know little about how the youth experience and negotiate this digitized socialization. What is not clear is how social relationships evolve on the Internet, and what it means for young men and women to move back and forth between the real and virtual worlds—how they move from their screens to experience "real-life" and back again to cyberspace. We do not have a full understanding of how youth appropriate the technological tools at their disposal when they form social ties on the Internet—how they construct new relationships, maintain existing relationships, or abandon old ones. Similarly, we do not know the implications these dynamics have on self and group identities, much less on traditions and values.

My aim in this chapter is to shed light on these technologically mediated forms of interaction. Driving this inquiry is a grounded attempt to understand the impact of social networking on the ways in which Arab youth manage their social interactions and relationships. More specifically, I explore how young adults use the Internet and other digital technologies to form relationships and maintain social relations. Of particular interest are the shifts in the socio-cultural practices of users that are triggered by their immersion in new forms of social connectedness. Using narrative analysis to recount the negotiation of online/offline relationships through stories told in person or in a mediated form, I highlight various strategies that young Internet and social media users tend to adopt to manage their online/offline relationships. A key contention of this paper is that the negotiation of these relationships may not be as spontaneous as the instantaneity of social media leads one to believe. If anything, online relationships tend to be constructed both intentionally and strategically in ways that take into consideration socio-cultural factors and variables.

A second claim that motivates this chapter relates to the underlying dynamics of and shifting boundaries between online and offline relationships. One of the aims of this analysis is to reveal patterns of movement between online and offline relationships as they pertain to the adoption of Internet and social media, and to shed light on micro-practices that develop in a highly connected environment. Contrary to what may appear, online interactions and virtual relationships are not making real-world interactions obsolete. If anything, the various forms of socialization that youth in the MENA region engage in on social networks suggest that the online/offline dichotomy can only be superficially maintained. Not only are the two worlds intertwined in complex ways, but the hybridity that underpins them is key to understanding sociality in a social media-intensive environment.

This chapter unfolds through five sections. I start with a brief socio-cultural contextualization of the research, followed by a review of the literature regarding the development of online relationships among youth. I then lay out my research design and provide a narration of mediated relationships of youth living in the Gulf Cooperation Council (GCC) countries. Drawing on personal stories, user accounts, and media narratives, I then discuss personalized micro-practices associated with social media usage among Arab youth and explain their significance. I conclude with reflections on how digital technologies have impacted social relations without necessarily unsettling traditions.

Arab youth: reaching cliques

In the MENA region, youth constitute a significantly large demographic group.[2] This segment of the population is the most connected generation yet. According to the 2016 Middle East Media Use Survey, 94 per cent of MENA youth use the Internet, compared to 77 per cent of the rest of the population.[3] Watching TV and surfing the Internet are their top media activities (94 per cent), followed by listening to the radio (68 per cent), and reading newspapers (50 per cent). Typically, young people in the MENA region spend an average of 17 hours per week socializing face-to-face with their friends outside work or school. Social networking, online chatting, and texting extend the connected time of these social relationships. In 2015, 65 per cent of MENA youth said that their use of the Internet has increased contact with their friends. Research on Internet practices in the UAE suggests that young people have been spending more time with their friends, and further, that "the younger one is, the more likely that Internet use is to have a deleterious effect upon time that one spends with one's family."[4] Among the online youth population in the MENA region, nearly eight out of ten (79 per cent) use social media or direct messaging at least once a day, almost nine out of ten (87 per cent) belong to family and friends direct messaging groups, and more than half (65 per cent) make or receive phone calls online.[5]

Mobile messaging services, such as WhatsApp or BBM, have also increased. According to a Mohammed Bin Rashid School of Government survey, 36 per cent of Arabs online use mobile messaging apps at least once a day; 52 per cent use instant messaging; 74 per cent connect with friends on social networks; and 33 per cent use VOIP (Voice Over Internet Protocol) with friends and family. The report also points out that nine out of ten respondents said that the Internet enabled better social activity that could not be possible otherwise.[6]

Not only are the youth who belong to the so-called Arab digital generation very active online, but a significant part of their online activities centers around socialization. Internet usage pushes them beyond their comfort zones to undertake socialization they might not opt for without the Internet, because of cultural considerations, social pressures, personality traits, or simply because they might not be ready for the experience. It goes without saying that not all Arab youth experience this high level of connectivity or engage in intensive online socialization, due to lack of technological access, among other reasons.

Any study of Internet culture in the Middle East needs to take into consideration differences within and among users when it comes to Internet usage and online practices. Based on interviews and informed by content analysis, this case study looks at select localized forms of online socialization in the Arab Middle East, with the aim of identifying noteworthy micro-practices and drawing out their significance. It examines social forms of interaction that are mediated through digital technologies in order to understand how and to what extent social relationships are affected by the use of new media. Particular attention is paid to how youth in Arab societies negotiate their online/offline relationships and, more broadly, how such practices are redefining the relationship between their online and offline environments.

In order to identify traits of ongoing shifts in socio-cultural practices triggered by the adoption of new social habits, I discuss two kinds of narratives: the former is interview-based stories of mediated relationships as perceived by informants; the latter is narratives of Saudi youth who reflect on their own stories and media practices when it comes to online relationships through a popular web series. These rich and evocative narratives provide a unique perspective on current practices of using technology for socialization.

Online interpersonal communication

The question of how the Internet intersects with social practices has generated considerable interest. Research conducted in the 1990s and early 2000s portrays interpersonal communication, such as in email or online chat, as one of the main functions of Internet usage.[7] While some studies considered the online and offline environments as separate social spheres,[8] others treated social life as being "multimodal," emphasizing how it is made more complex by the integration of new media technologies.[9]

Both academic and market research have explored the shifting boundaries between online and offline interactions. There is a widely held perception that face-to-face relationships tend to be the predominant form of interaction. Relationships may start or develop online, but they are often taken offline and developed with face-to-face interactions, which suggests that online and offline lives are more intertwined than antithetical.[10] In many ways, online interactions and relationships are not unique or new; rather, they are an extension of heretofore-known interpersonal relationships. For Agosto and Abbas, "the kinds of activities taking place in SNS are the same kinds of activities that took place offline among previous generations of young people. The difference is not so much the kinds of activities that are occurring online, but the amount, frequency, and semi-public nature of these activities."[11]

Mesch suggests that the Internet creates new forms of relationships. In his view, virtual relationships are considered "more intimate, richer, more liberating than offline relationships because they're genuine, built on mutual interest rather than coincidence of physical proximity."[12] From a youth perspective, affiliations with a social networking group strengthen both existing friendships and relationships with family members.[13] While the Internet provides ways of maintaining (or severing) relationships, widely used communication tools like email and messaging enable people to stay in touch. In fact, existing research suggests that "keeping in touch" is the primary reason for texting among teens.[14] Connecting with peers anywhere, any time, staying in touch, expressing oneself, and sharing experiences are key drivers of young people's online and mobile communications.[15]

According to Paul Adams, staying in touch is what youth care most about today; it is their way of being part of the crowd. Like adults, their socialization is structured on the principle of "homophily," which impels individuals to connect to and bond with others who are like them. Young people use the Internet to connect to their immediate circle of friends, develop relationships with peers, and connect with parents, siblings, and others. Generally, people connect with those who have the same interests, attend the same school, do similar activities, or live in the same geographical area. Adams shows that people connect with their strongest ties (the same five to ten people) 80 per cent of the time.[16] They turn to this inner circle for advice and emotional support, particularly during hard times. Typically, people have up to fifteen persons with whom they are very close (a sympathy group) and about fifty they communicate with semi-regularly and know in general what is going on in their lives. The size and structure of people's social networks remain very stable over time.[17] Adams further notes that people use social networks primarily to strengthen the bond with their strong ties and, to a lesser extent, build relationships with their weak ties. In the same spirit, Agosto, Abbas, Boyd, and Clarke point out that youth are more concerned with communicating first with pre-existing friends than developing new ones.[18] What these findings suggest is that online relationships are extensions of young people's circle of contacts.[19] Significantly, the more they see each other face-to-face, the more likely they are to communicate online.

Young people have different motivations when social networking. They want to be associated with groups in social networking sites, manage their relationships, and keep abreast of social activities in their networks. They use Facebook, for instance, for nurturing and maintaining existing relationships, as well as seeking new ones.[20] New connectivity is based on "fitness"; that is, people who fit best with each other are deemed more desirable for connecting with, since they have higher credibility and trust. Compared to texting, teens view SNS as "less intimate communication media, preferring them for less frequent contact with a much wider range of friends and sometimes parents and siblings, and other relatives."[21]

Adams adds that sharing information on SNS makes life easier. The act of talking helps users strengthen social bonds, while the substance of the conversation allows them to manage how others perceive them. People talk about other people and what is around them, and conversations sometimes generate strong feelings. Women focus more on developing social bonds, while men "more often talk about themselves or things they claim to be knowledgeable about, often because they're trying to impress the people around them."[22] While offline conversations are often just to fill in awkward silence, online conversations tend to be more purposeful, even tactical, as users often take their time and choose carefully what might be interesting or appealing to others. In this respect, Adams notes that the "desire to appear a certain way to others is a bigger factor in what we talk about online than offline."[23]

This is not to suggest that there is a disconnect between who one is in the real world and the image one likes to project in the virtual world. People are still commanded by their personalities. For instance, a psychology research study argues that SNS users extend their offline personalities online. If they are extroverts offline, they usually show a higher level of activity than introverts on social networks.[24] Extroverts tend to update their status on SNS more often than introverts. The motivations for doing so are varied, ranging from the desire to feel connected to the need to link up with others. In many ways, the conversation that follows a profile update is more important than the update itself. Similarly, when people like or comment on a post, it is a social sign that they want to build relationships, not necessarily that they like the original post, in which case talking to someone signals in some ways that the initiator of the conversation is worthy of attention.

Youth and social media usage

When studying connected socialization in the MENA region, it is important to consider the cultural and social contexts within which these forms of communication unfold. Such conceptualization is insistent not only because the experience of new and social media among the youth has its own singularities in the Arab world, but also because the Arab nation itself is far from being singular or homogenous. For Al Omoush, Yaseen, and Alma'aithah, understanding the national culture is critical for understanding the usage of SNS and other online practices of socialization. In their view, the online behavior of Arab youth is influenced "by the cultural values that characterize the Arab nation."[25] Whether and to what extent the adoption of new information and communication technologies is affecting cultural dispositions among the youth remains an open question.

The adoption of new communication technologies calls for a reconsideration of how youth think about culture and values. The 2014 ASDA'A Burston-

Marsteller Arab Youth Survey attempts to shed light on how the cultural values of youth have changed over time.[26] The research shows that youth are increasingly reconsidering their traditional opinions and beliefs. Specifically, to the statement "Traditional values are outdated and belong to the past; I am keen to embrace modern values and beliefs," 46 per cent agreed, a dramatic increase from the 17 per cent reported in 2011. While such attitudes may reflect new dispositions among the youth, particularly in the way they think and perceive the world, they are arguably indissociable from the adoption of new and social media. In fact, the 2015 Social Media Report highlights a direct relation to social media. In particular, the report notes that two out of five users in the Arab region believe that "social media help in preserving [their] traditions and habits."[27] Predominantly, users perceive social media as influencing the way they appreciate their world and relate to their beliefs and values. This is amplified by the extent to which the youth are exposed to social media. Increasingly, new communication technologies are shaping youth's conception of time, culture, and beliefs.[28] While earlier studies are of the view that Arab cultural beliefs may be an inhibiting factor when it comes to technological adoption because of such considerations as traditions, customs, and values,[29] more recent research suggests that Arab users who have embraced technology do not necessarily perceive it as intrusive or threatening to their traditions and customs.

The reactions to technology need to be understood within the broader context of social transformation that the region has been undergoing, and the effect of such changes on the nature of patriarchal Arab societies. More independence means that youth are creating more options for themselves—they can choose, for instance, to follow their own career pathways and be what they want to be, or for that matter forgo an arranged marriage to marry a partner with whom they feel a connection. At the same time, the effect of new media on cultural values and beliefs should not be overstated. For instance, a study on Facebook usage among Arab college students found that Facebook does not have any impact on their physical social life.[30] Furthermore, their subjects do not believe that using Facebook may be against their culture; on the contrary, they are embracing new technologies while being ingrained in their cultural ecosystem.

In the Arab region, community-centered ethnographic research about youth and new forms of media and communication technologies has been sporadic, and much of what is available is anecdotal. No large-scale research has focused on the youth's online socializing habits,[31] although a few country-specific studies have attempted to delve into the micro-practices that are becoming prevalent among users with the adoption of the Internet. Deborah Wheeler has looked at Kuwaitis' usage of new media in relation to their culture and traditions.[32] Samia Mihoub-Dramé examined micro-practices of Internet usage among Tunisians in community centers for accessing the Internet known as publinets.[33] More recently, Miriyam Aouragh studied the micro-practices of Palestinians online while also focusing on Internet cafés as a "milieu" of Internet adoption and online communities' development.[34]

Studies such as these, which analyze practices on the ground from the micro-perspective of the "quotidian" usage of the Internet, are few and far between, and studies that examine how Arab youth are using new technology for social networking are even harder to come by. There is a dearth of research that discusses the dynamics of online socialization or the dynamic relationship between online and offline environments with regard to developing or maintaining friendships and building romantic relationships. It is these often-neglected everyday aspects and dynamics that constitute the focus of the second part of this chapter. The key questions are: what are the various strategies that Arab youth use when they are socially connected? And what are the implications of new—online—forms of socialization on identity negotiation and cultural expectations?

Research design and case studies

This research uses narrative analysis as a key approach to discuss the personal stories of my informants. Such narrative methodology draws on a variety of sources. For Reis and Judd, "Narrative material may be elicited from participants; recorded from naturally occurring behavior; or obtained from preexisting sources... Elicited material may be obtained by means of interviews, recall of a story or a film, or writing samples."[35] The qualitative approach is particularly suited to this study as it enables us to capture diverse social interactions and to understand the life stories of informants as they unfold in specific socio-cultural contexts. By putting people's actions and life situations into context, narratives help determine how participants make sense of particular communication events. As Punch notes, "narratives and stories are valuable in studying lives and lived experience,"[36] insofar as they offer a unique perspective for understanding people's behaviors, attitudes, values, and actions.[37] As a process, narrative analysis offers a flexible and evolving structure in the sense that it could follow a theme, event, or plot.

Typically, narrative analysis focuses on a carefully selected single individual and relies on a wide range of materials, including open-ended interviews, participant observation, casual chatting, documents and archival material, and movies.[38] This research uses two types of narratives: stories that are told in person and stories that are narrated in mediated form. In addition to collecting users' accounts of their mediated experiences of friendships and interpersonal relationships, the research draws on representations of media usage and depictions of media habits in the actual media. Since movies or series can be portrayals of the real world and can give a vivid perception of lived reality, another way to look at how youth negotiate these relationships is through the lenses of film-makers. Accordingly, this chapter attempts to explore how technology is embedded in portrayals of real life and to decode the messages conveyed. It does so by using a descriptive film analysis to illustrate specific details in the movie and point out connections,[39] while offering a non-conventional narrative structure to highlight the technology theme in the oeuvre under consideration, and its usage in the social context of the story.

These stories about the practice of everyday life, to borrow de Certeau's terminology,[40] are used to understand the construction of digitized cultural identities. The narratives portray everyday practices that tell us a great deal about the reconfiguration of the culture of connectivity in social media times. Both personal and media narratives are also useful insofar as they tend to "reflect and communicate continuities and change."[41] They provide insights into how media frame the binary dichotomy of online/offline interaction among friends in the era of the Internet and new technology.

Two case studies are analyzed below. My first set of material consists of four life stories collected on audio recordings from three teenage boys living in Qatar, and a young woman in her twenties living in the United Arab Emirates. The range of material offers the advantage of having perspectives from both genders and from different age ranges. My second artifact is a humorous Saudi web series produced by young Saudi artists targeting young Arabs in Saudi Arabia and the larger Gulf region. This popular program offers a self-reflection of the youth using the language and channel of new media. I select these stories purposefully from within the Arabian Gulf for several reasons. The Gulf is interesting to study because of its sizable youth and its large Arab expatriate population. More importantly, the oil-rich Gulf countries have arguably the most advanced technological infrastructures in the Arab region and enjoy one of the highest rates of ownership and use of technology. Finally, it is a sub-region that is increasingly defined by a disjunction between opposing or contradictory forces, being simultaneously modern and fast-evolving societies within traditional and conservative cultures. The region's oscillation between tradition and modernity, between the old and the new, between the local and the global, makes it a particularly relevant "milieu" for studying the shifts in socio-cultural patterns and identity markers in light of technological adoption.

Interviews: life stories of sociability

My first informant is Suha, a young Arab girl living in the United Arab Emirates.[42] Like many second-generation expats, Suha has Levantine origins and her parents moved to the Gulf when she was very young. She grew up in Dubai, and at the time of the interview she was working for a private company. Still at the beginning of her career, Suha is single and living with her parents, but cares a lot about her social life. Enthusiastic, extroverted, and joyful, Suha invests time and effort in maintaining her circle of friends. I asked her about how she uses the Internet and social media to maintain her social life and interact with her friends. I instructed her to make audio recordings while narrating her experience. Over the span of a month, I received ten short audio recordings and five emails and instant messages from Suha.

The other interviews were conducted with three middle-school teenage boys living in Doha, Qatar. Ahmed is a young boy who describes himself as strong and funny, and loves being around his friends. Hamza is of Arab origin; having recently moved to Doha, he still has friends abroad, but started to develop new friends at school. Ali is sixteen years old, loves sports, and spends a lot of time playing outside with friends; he describes himself as shy and introverted.

All my informants have smartphones; Suha, Ahmed, and Hamza have access to the Internet on the go. Suha finds her life "miserable when [the] data package is out," she says. She wakes up to Facebook and other app notifications and frequently checks all her social media platforms, even while at work. At home, she tends to keep her mobile in her hand to make sure she's connected all the time. The boys cannot use their mobiles at school, but have access to the Internet on the school computer for school-related content. They all connect and socialize with friends, either before or after school.

Media narratives: the *Takki* web series

In 2013, Saudi Arabia was rated the biggest user of YouTube per capita in the world. Driven primarily by the intensive use by youth, the time spent on

YouTube by Saudis increased fivefold the same year. YouTube—along with Twitter, which also has more than 40 per cent penetration rate in the country—is an important channel in Saudi Arabia to engage with young people, and to know more about them. The appeal of YouTube has to be understood within the context of the broader, and more restrictive, media culture in the kingdom. Saudi Arabia has banned cinema since the 1980s. With the advent of the 1990s, television became a true mass medium. In subsequent years, satellite television consumption exploded in the country as it did in much of the Arab world.[43] With the introduction of the Internet, young Saudis have turned to YouTube for both content consumption and content creation. For those who love film and drama, YouTube has become a popular platform for challenging the kingdom's ban on cinema. Although TV is still the first choice among Saudi youth, with 98 per cent watching TV, the Internet is a close second that attracts 82 per cent of youth, compared to 62 per cent of the rest of population.[44]

Takki—literally "sit down" or "lay down" in Arabic—is a Saudi web series that began with an idea and a story by Mohammed Makki, a young Saudi who later became a scriptwriter, director, and showrunner. The story is based on his own personal life.[45] The show is very popular in Saudi Arabia and the Gulf region, attracting audiences and advertisers alike. Global companies like Toyota and government entities like Abu Dhabi Tourism and Culture Authority have invested mainly in branded content on the web series. Saudi people like this show, Makki explains, because they relate to its content.

Takki is a humorous drama that reflects facets of Saudi society and the social challenges that its youth are facing. The series provides insights into the lives of a generation caught between conservatism and modernism and is heavily influenced by new digital technologies. *Takki* embodies facets of the complex Saudi reality, but it does so in a simple and effective way. Commenting on the appeal of the web series, script co-writer Nidaa Al-Andanosi says that what makes it unique is the fact that it highlights issues that are hardly ever discussed publicly in Saudi society, such as cross-gender friendship.[46] The five main characters comprise two female and three male Saudi students who chose to be part of this adventure and challenge gender taboos. For instance, while males and females are not expected to mingle in public places, the webisodes show them sitting side by side in places like public cafés and restaurants. The drama mirrors their daily challenges, problems, and, misjudgments, as well as their aspirations. The web series was criticized for mixing men and women and provoking social discussions. Breaking cultural taboos has made the *Takki* web series particularly popular in Saudi Arabia and the Gulf region, garnering as much as 1.5 million viewers per episode (fourteen episodes in total, of about 10–15 minutes each).[47]

A central theme of this web series is relationship formation and development amongst youth. Girls are often caught between their aspirations for fulfilling relationships and their concerns about conduct and reputation; they care about social values, while also challenging them. For instance, girls aspire to meet someone they would love to marry, but they are also keen on succeeding professionally. Bayan, the web series' main female character, prioritized her career over her relationship with her fiancé Majed. She is a video blogger who reflects on society and relationships; she is also active on Twitter, which negatively affects her reputation in the conservative society where she lives.

The following representative frames evince the use of digital technologies for friendship formation and management in the web series: (1) In episode 3, Majed and Bayan argue over the mobile phone. Majed tweets about it. It gets retweeted and provokes a scandal on social media. (2) In episode 8, young boys whistle, flirt, and catcall at Bayan, who is standing alone in the street waiting for a cab. One leans into the window of her taxi and asks her, "Twitter? Facebook? Anything!!—OK, WhatsApp?" suggesting a new way of asking for a girl's phone number. (3) In episode 12, when attempting to reconcile with her fiancé, Bayan uses the mobile to call him and ask him to start over. (4) In episode 13, Abdullah, one of the main characters, talks privately and seriously with Lama over the mobile phone; he tells her he is proposing and will ask her dad for her hand. Finally, (5) in episode 14, Abdullah is opening a new restaurant and invites Lama, the girl he likes, through a Facebook message. He feels he has broken social norms by inviting her and finds himself in need of justifying himself to his friend Majed, who happens to be Lama's cousin, "I sent her a Facebook message, but it was public, everyone saw it!" The fact that the invitation is public implies legitimacy and conformity. In all these instances, there are points of contention between old and new practices, between traditional and modern habits acquired with the adoption of new technologies. Actors negotiate the relationship formation in light of socio-cultural customs and the aptitude to break through traditions thanks to new and social media.

Discussion and analysis

These case studies provide multiple perspectives on how youth manage their mediated friendship and social relationships. They also give insights into the meaning of friendships in the age of new and social media, the ways in which technology enables an easier and more instantaneous access to friends, and the extent to which seemingly spontaneous relationships are subject to management strategies of sorts. I start with a short discussion about the evolution of the meaning of friendships. I then examine the types of connectedness and the youth's involvement in shaping their friendships. While they may be spontaneous at times, they are strategic at others, displaying consciousness with regard to the image they would like to project to others. I conclude with a discussion of relationship development and the case of online/offline connection in the context of relationship formation and development.

Friendship in the age of the Internet

The Internet may have changed the ways we spend our time; it may also have affected the amount of time we spend face-to-face or through mediated platforms with our family members, colleagues, or friends. What is not clear though is whether and to what extent it is also affecting the way in which we construct relationships, the nature and meaning of friendship, and how we appreciate our friends.

In social media, the term "friend" refers to the link between people rather than the deep and true emotional connection between them. In today's media-intensive environment, friending:

> is a "socio-technical practice" that involves creating a profile on a social networking platform and then extending an invitation to another profile to become [one's] friend. The patient work of taming and the uniqueness of the figure of the friend as per Saint-Exupery have been swept aside and replaced by a brief sequence of clicks and a multiplicity of post-stamp images staring and smiling at us from the computer screen.[48]

In Western societies, friendship is associated with enjoyment; people are friends because they enjoy the company of each other.[49] In fact, most of the literature and the sociology on friendship refers to Aristotle, who defines three types of friendship relationships. The first is based on utility, because each in this relationship senses that he or she could get some kind of benefit from the relationship. The second is associated with pleasure that brings some kind of enjoyment because of a shared love for a hobby or passion for something, be it jokes, places, or music; in this type of friendship, people simply rejoice in each other's company. The third kind is friendship for the good, which is the purest relationship as it is based on pure admiration and appreciation of each other's virtues.

In an Arab Middle Eastern context, friendship is also about enjoyment and appreciation. It is about enjoying the company of someone and being there for him or her when the need arises.[50] In his 1923 poem "Friendship," the renowned Lebanese writer and poet Kahlil Gibran offers a laconic reflection on what befriending means. "Your friend is your needs answered," he writes. The Arab language is rich in words that either connote or denote friendship. In his classical epistle on friendship and friends (al-Sadaqa wa al-Sadiq), the tenth-century philosopher Abu Hayyan Al Tawhidi appraises friendship based on virtue. In classical Arabic, "*sahib*," "*sahibi*," and "*sahabi*" refer to friend, though the latter term is usually attributed to the prophet's companions who proselytized with him. The other commonly used Arabic terms for friend and friendship are "*sadiq*" and "*sadaqah*," respectively. Another variations of the word are "*al-sedq*," which means truth, honesty, and loyalty, and "*al-sadeq*," which designates someone who is true and loyal to the relationship—someone who is not looking for any particular interest to gain from the friendship relationship, except a true, pure relationship.

Mindful of the development of communication artifacts and the evolving concept of friendship and informed by the respondents' testimonials and insights, the following section sheds light on the new dynamics of friendship formation among Arab youth. With social media, friendship may be altered in light of the management strategies that are adopted, the communication tools used, and the type of connectivity that is favored.

When asked about what Facebook friends represent to him, Ahmed responded: "people I can talk to." What Ahmed values in Facebook is a sense of social connectedness, but one that is different from what is traditionally conceived as friendship in the real world. Suha considers friendship to have different degrees. A true friend is someone she could talk to, pick up the phone and enquire after; someone she shares the same values with and the same lifestyle as much as possible. Acquaintances do not have the same values or lifestyles, they are just individuals one happens to know. Facebook and social networks made these connections more accessible and closer than ever before. For Suha, having a wider circle of friends and being connected to friends of friends on social networks is good, provided such relationships are kept under control.

This new conception of friendship recalls Tarik Sabry's depiction of the cultural encounters that animate daily spaces in the Arab world, including street corners, cafés, souks, bridges, haras, or houmas.[51] Houma designates a neighborhood, typically a working-class residential area or community, where people know one another and know what is happening in the lives of one another; however, they are not necessarily close friends. Those living in a houma would stop in the street to cheer or chat with familiar members of the community, but, except the very close ones, they are generally not invited to the privacy of the home. In this framework, Facebook could be the virtual version of houma, bringing people together to chat, hang out, or simply touch base with one another. What Sabry finds most interesting is the unsuspected significance of the quotidian of the youth living in these neighborhoods:

> Dailiness and daily spaces of human interaction are often associated with the banal and the ordinary... Whatever happens on the street, in the souk, the queue, the bridge, the work place and the café is common and has a daily structure that makes it appear, at first glance, to be nothing special, not worthy of our curiosity, yet these human settings are the very spaces where much of our existence and everyday politics are played out. The young unemployed in Algiers, Cairo, Casablanca, Beirut and other Arab urban cities spend considerable amounts of time on street corners (*derbs*) and in cafés. This is where their dailiness is acted out; this is where they chat, joke, fight, smoke, watch and discuss the news.[52]

A parallel could be drawn between social interactions in these neighborhoods and other traditional settings and virtual spaces like Facebook. Increasingly, people are getting their news from Facebook and developing new social habits on social media. The youth play games on Facebook, tag pictures, and watch videos, then comment and react to each other's posts. They display solidarity with the hardships and festivities of their "friends." They congratulate one another on achievements, greet one another on birthdays, or simply follow one another's activities. Friends discuss politics, argue, break up, and make up. In all these activities, their dailiness is acted out virtually. Facebook is the new milieu for these "friends," and a place for their interactions.

Social media and modes of connectedness

The interviews with my respondents suggest that there are two types of communication: private connectedness for stable relationships, which flows over mobile-related technology; and semi-private connectedness for friends, regardless of the degree of friendship or level of activity or inactivity.

With private connectedness, interactions take place mainly through mobiles when not face-to-face. Just as one does not publicly post his or her home address, mobile numbers are also perceived as private, and only solid connections—family members and close friends—may exchange them. For

Suha, "exchanging phone numbers makes the relationship more personal." Significantly, speaking over the mobile remains the predominant private form of communicating. I use the term "speak" purposefully, as talk between youth could include WhatsApp or other mobile messaging applications. "Let's talk" often initiates actions such as messaging rather than communicating over the phone. Generally, youth speak over the mobile for mundane purposes like checking on one another and planning outings, but they also use mobiles for more purposes, like sharing feelings and resolving arguments.

The web series *Takki* captures the latter trend, with Saudi Bayan initially arguing and subsequently conciliating with her fiancé, or Lama and Abdallah discussing engagement plans in a private way of connectedness. As Adams notes, privacy is reserved to close bonds that can also form online. "To form social bonds, most of our conversations are a form of reputation management."[53] In her narratives, Suha considers discussing feelings on Facebook private messages a red line—a "big no, no, no," as she puts it—despite the tendency of such communicative acts to bring people together. There is "private" and "public private," says Suha: messaging on Facebook is public private, thus still public; only when there is a private call does communication become truly private.

The interviews with the young boys suggest that public connectedness is the norm. Ahmed is both a frequent Facebook user and an occasional Instagram user. He does not use WhatsApp much beyond making plans and arrangements with friends, enquiring about school assignments, or interacting with a group of friends, because he does not find it particularly suitable for conversation when communicating with others, nor does he readily associate it with entertainment. Instead, he avidly uses Facebook chat, mainly on his mobile. Ahmed considers himself an active and frequent commentator on posts; he often tags friends or makes silly comments on their pictures just for fun. Unlike Ahmed, Hamza does not use Facebook due to parental restriction; instead, he uses Instagram, WhatsApp, and Snapchat. He uses these social networks when he cannot communicate with people otherwise, or when he wants to maintain relationships with his friends abroad. Ali says that most of his communications on social networks are for planning purposes and "simple stuff." He finds it convenient to plan his activities and arrange his outings with his friends on Facebook.

The forming of friendships is perhaps the most interesting social media activity to observe—particularly the way in which negotiations of relationships tend to occur in the zone between public and private communications, irrespective of whether the concerned individuals initially met online or offline. Where people first met is not an important consideration; in fact, connecting with people one barely knows is no longer as threatening as it once was. As the findings of the ictQatar cyber safety survey suggests, people are now relatively at ease when it comes to meeting and connecting with people they do not know.[54] If anything, social media users have developed ways of mitigating the potential threats that come with such forms of connectivity. In the words of Suha, "as long as one manages to keep these relations under control so that they do not evolve or become intrusive, one does not run the risk of being harmed." As the above discussion suggests, this mindset marks a change in the social construction of relationships in the Arab world. The virtual space affords youth the opportunity to be more independent and autonomous in choosing connections, which is tantamount to saying that the forming of social network friendships is evolving in ways that make considerations of social conformity in a patriarchal society less pressing.

This is not to suggest that social media use is necessarily undermining cultural norms or making traditional values irrelevant. The research findings suggest that the values and perceptions of Arab youth are being shaped by their use of social media. For example, in the *Takki* web series, Bayan challenges these traditions. She stands up against the mindset of her conservative Saudi society and refuses to give up work, even if that entails the risk of losing her fiancé. Adams argues that traditions and beliefs have not disappeared in social media times, noting that "our culture is a set of habits and rituals, attitudes and beliefs, that guide how we behave. They are unwritten rules we learn from observing people around us as well as from people's reactions to our behavior... We work hard to conform to the social norms in our culture."[55] Our informants recognize that they negotiate their connectedness on social media in light of traditions and social norms. Although their society is evolving and becoming more tolerant toward experimenting in new ways of relationships, youth care about reputation and still think that social acceptance is an important consideration. Even in the era of social media, traditional values continue to be an important factor in social image formation and cultural perceptions. For instance, a girl's reputation has been a heavy social responsibility to carry.[56] Girls should behave well out of respect for their families and their "social capital"; most often in traditional societies and conservative families, a woman's impeccable reputation would earn her respect in the community.

To understand how young users manage their images, it is useful to refer to positioning theory, which concerns itself with the analysis of perceptions and

identity during interactions. Within social sciences, the concept of positioning was introduced by Hollway in order to analyze how subjectivity is constructed in the context of heterosexual relationships.[57] In this perspective,
positions are presented as "relation processes that constitute interaction with
other individuals. Positioning can be understood as the discursive construction of personal narrations. These are used to construct the actions of an
individual in a way which is intelligible to herself and others."[58] The wide
adoption of the Internet and new media technologies is breeding new forms
of relationships and transforming old practices, often leading to the coexistence of old and new habits. In this new communicative space, users often find
themselves torn between the "self" in its singularity and the mirror of the self
that actors want to project when using digitized technologies.

In the cases under consideration, the subjects position themselves on social
media in ways that reflect their aspirations while taking into consideration
their environments. Suha's narratives prove that she uses discourse strategies
to appear that she is conforming to traditions and upholding values; she is
keen not to offend her family and relatives by posting specific kinds of pictures. She says it is important for her to keep up appearances so as not to
offend anyone with her posts or pictures: "I have uncles in my contacts on
Facebook and my family is conservative, so I wouldn't post a picture of me and
a guy even though he's simply a friend; it's important that I don't disrupt our
values and customs. I would, though, put such a picture on Instagram or
Twitter because I know that they would not follow me there." Suha also commented on how she set her privacy settings in such a way that she would need
to approve being tagged in a photo before it can be posted. On Facebook,
Suha wants to project the ideal "real-life" image her uncles and extended family have of her. But she uses other platforms to project who she "really is" to
her circle of friends. Suha tailors her image based on her target public on
Facebook that has come to include "all kinds" of friends, conservative members in her extended family circle, and fretting mother figures. Throughout
these social interactions, Suha measures her conformity to the conventional
group. Cultural expectations of social conformity lead her to adopt the image
her traditional family has of her and to play the gender role that is expected of
her when she is on widely used and viewed platforms. At the same time, she
uses different platforms to project a particular image of herself. The intentional double discourse that Suha adopts in the context of social interactions
highlights the complexity of online interactions and the role that agency plays
in identity construction and relationships management, as much as it points

to the weight of cultural conformity and social constraints under which social media users operate.

In the interview with Hamza, still a teenager, he says he feels more comfortable speaking face-to-face with people. "It's more honest," he says. "If they lie, you can tell; and if you lie, they can tell." But for Ahmed, the Internet enables him to show a different facet of himself. He feels that the Internet improves his relationships with friends. Attempting to be funny online, as he sees it, helps him to be more popular among his friends: "Being funny helps my friends to see another side of me. I can be funny online because I can think about what to say and not find myself acting on the spot. Online, I'm less stressed and less nervous. I can think what others might think regarding what I post." Just like Suha, Ahmed thinks ahead of time what to say online so as to improve his image. However, Hamza is keen on being the same online and offline: "I don't want to showcase online what I don't want to talk about in person," he says.

In both cases, social media users have different views on what to share online, how much to share, and if it would be better to remain faithful to real life or project a slightly different self. These interrogations raise interesting questions about the image and perception of the self when projected to others. Positioning theory helps capture the construction of these interactions and the creation of social identity.[59] First introduced in marketing and then adopted within the social sciences, positioning theory suggests that brands select attributes which they communicate to their audiences in order to be perceived in a specific way, and build an image of the brand in the minds of this audience. Ideally, brands reach for a convergence between perceptual positioning (the way the target audience perceives the brand) and desired positioning (the image that the brand wants to carry), so that audiences perceive the brand as desired by the brand.

In the aforementioned case, the positioning games that Ahmed and Suha play out are intentional; they aim to please their social groups by reflecting an image of someone who is funny, traditional, or modern. Not only do online interactions enable these roles and the positioning to occur, but also the online environment itself documents and archives these interactions in a way that builds up the social image of these informants, which are available on their social media "walls." One can see the same strategy played out in the web series *Takki*, when Abdullah thinks he is socially "correct," respectful of traditions and values, and causing no harm to Lama's reputation when he invites her to his restaurant opening event on Facebook. "Everyone can see [the invitation]; it's a public message," he says innocently and convincingly. On Twitter, Bayan's reputation plummets when people criticize her vlogging. This act is met with disapproval from Lama's would-be mother-in-law, causes arguments with her dad, and eventually leads to a break-up with her fiancé. In her pursuit of professional freedom and self-actualization,[60] Bayan cares more about her career than her fiancé and in-laws; she seems to resist bad reputation, wanting to be a model to young girls in her conservative Saudi society and speaking for her generation about standing up to these traditions. The image that Bayan constructs and projects is intentional and goes beyond her circle of interactions. She aims to reach out to her society and tackle taboos that the society ignores or avoids discussing. Her interactions with her fiancé acquire a broader significance when considered within the context of her society. Bayan's actions and social interactions are consistent when interacting with close or extended ties; they are also consistent in her social media posts, conversations, and actions. They all converge toward the image she wants to reflect: a modern, professional woman who stands against traditions and outdated beliefs.

The following narrative, which is another example of social identity creation, describes attempts to construct and manage social relations. In this example, Suha points out the complex dynamics associated with developing social bonds. While at a birthday party, Suha met someone she liked, but did not have the chance to interact much with him. Unexpectedly, a few weeks later he sent her a friend invite on Facebook. They occasionally talked to each other by posting on each other's Facebook pages. A Nutella image posted on her wall provoked some conversational jokes between them, and a few days later she drove to his office and dropped off a jar of Nutella. Shortly thereafter, the two engaged in a WhatsApp conversation and ended up meeting for coffee. Trivial as it may be, the incident speaks to evolving forms of social interaction that tread both the real and the virtual worlds. While some researchers emphasize the prevalence of "real-life" as opposed to "digital-life" relationships, others take issue with the dichotomy between real and virtual, arguing that online spaces are becoming integrated into the offline. The case of Suha suggests that online and offline spheres are becoming inextricably intertwined. A picture posted online then, an object as simple as a Nutella jar, becomes an artifact of connectedness as the online relationship between the two develops, giving a "real" sense to an online relationship formation. Facebook friendships usually do not develop beyond virtual relationships, Suha said. She is strategic about how she develops friendships on Facebook. If she likes someone, she checks his interests and posts. She might comment a couple of days after he posts a comment, offering a different perspective in order to intrigue him and to draw attention to herself. In the words of Suha, online communication in this case is designed to induce a calculated effect: "I would 'trap' him so that he initiates the conversation. Sometimes I would make a not so obvious joke or make an ambiguous comment that arouses his curiosity and that helps start the conversation."

The second stage of such a relationship would go from what Suha calls "public social media" to "private social media"—for her it is WhatsApp—and then ultimately the phone. Private messages on Facebook are still public social media and Suha uses such forms of communication when friends are intrusive, but she remains hesitant to engage in such a relationship. The pace and volume of social media conversations that follow the in-person encounter give an indication as to whether the relationship is deepening or lightening, and help determine whether there is sufficient mutual interest to warrant a second meeting.

The development of social bonds portrayed in Suha's private communications and Bayan's conciliating communications with her fiancé reflects how social connectedness becomes rather "intimate" in the private social realm. The fact that these dynamics are associated with the use of mobiles or smartphones indicates that they take place in the private domain, and not on Facebook. It is safe to assume that refusing to get in a private chat on WhatsApp (since it is associated with a phone number) is like refusing to give someone one's mobile number.

Strategies for communication vary with the different modes of social networks that are available and used. The privacy or public connectedness as discussed above is tightly linked to the multimodality of social networks. On Facebook, for instance, the practices of the young users interviewed in this study are consonant with those described in the literature, particularly when it comes to micro-practices on social media. In this respect, Ahmed's practices of perceptual positioning when crafting an image of a funny boy, for example, fit under what Boyd describes as "enacting celebrity practices."[61] Teens in particular like to draw attention to themselves and enjoy the visibility that public platforms such as Facebook enables. WhatsApp is subject to multiple modes of usage and practices. It enables a group to manage everyday life pursuits, including school-related work, outing plans, jokes, and casual discussions, but WhatsApp also enables semi-private discussions involving emotions and ethos, as will become clear further down.

Developing networks and relationships

Nowadays, relationships easily kick off with Facebook and "friending." When Suha meets someone she likes at a birthday party, the two do not engage right away in a conversation; instead, they opt to become friends on Facebook, thus allowing the relation to develop online.

In the *Takki* web series, when Abdullah wants to meet Lama, he invites her, publicly, through Facebook. Even young catcalling practices in Saudi Arabia refer to Facebook. Facebook has become the strategic public place to socialize and manage social objectives and expectations, depending on who the interlocutor is (whether that person is a close friend, a family member, or just an acquaintance). The development of SNS helped many young Arab users tailor their identities and messages to specific audiences based on the degree of social proximity, social norms, and values, and guided by objectives and expectations or intentional positioning.

Relationship formations on SNS are negotiated depending on the degree of friendship, the objectives of the connectedness, and the expectations of both interlocutors. Social media bring together connections, be it friends or referral acquaintances, from online and offline, but texting and private chatting are what seems to deepen the relationship. Ultimately, these connections through mobile communications aspire to "the next step," which is to meet face-to-face. The artifact used by Suha to "provoke" a face-to-face encounter concluded the five months of online exchanges with a male user and opened the door to an offline relationship.

After the initial meeting, friends continue maintaining and deepening their relations on social media while keeping alive the prospect for meeting again. A face-to-face encounter largely determines if the relation is bound to grow. In the case of Suha, the real-life encounter is not likely to enhance the relationship. "Usually it goes down from there," she notes. This assessment of the fate of the relationship raises the question of whether, with the social world of SNS, it is easier to dream up someone. Suha is often disappointed after face-to-face interactions because she may have "imagined" the person, rather than seen the reality. Suha wants to be interesting and uses strategies to project a certain profile. She also wants to look smart and attractive, or perhaps mysterious, when she posts provocative comments—which she describes as "traps"—to make others comment on her posts, comments, or pictures. In the same manner, Ahmed uses strategy to reflect an imaginary image of a funny, cool boy. Significantly, all of these strategies may make a person's real identity diverge from what he or she shows on SNS.

These examples provide insights into how youth who feel the pressing need for connectedness transpose personal lives with public exposure. The young generation has a need to externalize opinions and feelings as "SNSs have been able to neutralize the effect of some traditional cultural values, especially those governed by self-disclosure, power distance, and feelings of shame restricting the free social interaction, freedom of speech and expression, and satisfying the curiosity."[62] In a study exploring self-presentation to relationship formations on social networks, self-presentation is found to be affected by the potential to form romantic relationships.[63] The findings of this research suggest that there is no significant differentiation between typical Western case studies and non-Western case studies. Young users seem to have similar motivations for social construction and forming of relationships. The cases at hand also speak for the multimodality of today's social lives and suggest that we move beyond the online/offline dichotomy. Both online and offline spaces are so well integrated and continuous today that it becomes meaningless to try to weigh which drives which. At some point, online and offline interactions are becoming so intertwined that, like the chicken and egg causality, one is unable to say which came first. Relationships offline drive online interactions, and vice versa.

Concluding remarks

In 2007, I presented a paper at the Arab German Media Dialogue in Jordan on blogging practices among Arab youth and the emergence of romantic online relationships. Testimonials collected from Arab youth then suggested that young people were strongly against dating online.[64] At 18 years of age, Ashraf said he was against dating online, but he used email and went on chatting websites for entertainment and discovering new things. Rafaf, 17 years old from Lebanon, said she used the computer for typing and found that the Internet and chatting sites contributed to the development of one's identity, although she also recognized that chat rooms group people together while also setting them apart. Rayya, 18, used emails and the Internet, and found chatting meaningless, a poor way to meet people. Samia, 15 from Bahrain, found herself addicted to the Internet; she contributed heavily in chat rooms, but with a fake name. Tunisian Farida, 17, tried chatting in Internet cafés, but she did not like the experience, preferring to interact with people face-to-face.

A lot has changed over the past decade. Chat rooms were attractive for the many users who preferred to hide their true identities.[65] It was common for people to create fake names for chat rooms in order to speak freely. That was the fun part of it, says Boyd, invoking her own experience.[66] Chat rooms have lost popularity with the adoption of SNS, which are built on a different mindset—one that is premised on being authentic. The basic assumption is that the more people reveal who they truly are, the more likely they are to connect and bond with others. As for using the Internet to form romantic relationships, it is already accepted among adults and increasingly normalized and accepted among adolescents.[67] In less than a decade the situation has flipped. But many of the practices that have been introduced with this transformation are not all that new. It is worth noting that non-face-to-face contacts for romantic and relationship formation were a common practice. Not long ago, as history tells, marriages between European dynasties were arranged through letters. The technology is surely changing, but the practices are in some ways similar; they serve a basic need to communicate, connect, and get together.

Mobiles are enabling more socialization and faster communications. They are giving more freedom and power to women, who have shifted their behavior from hiding their identities online to a full acceptance of who they are, confidently vlogging in a country such as Saudi Arabia despite social constraints. Sreberny's chapter on women's digital activism, in this volume, is evidence of their partaking in a whole range of activities, challenging state power and male hegemony. Let us not forget that in this region the mobile has not been widely adopted as a "multifunctional everyday tool" that supports banking, health, education, e-government, and a host of other services; it remains largely a communication tool, though in the near future we may see more functions and services integrated through the mobile.

3

VIRTUAL WORLDS, DIGITAL DREAMS

IMAGINARY SPACES OF MIDDLE EASTERN VIDEO GAMES

Vít Šisler

In his famous manifesto, game theorist Eric Zimmerman declared the twenty-first century a "ludic century" that is largely defined by games.[1] If linear media and non-interactive information were defining elements of dominant cultural forms like film and video in the twentieth century, today "information has taken a playful turn."[2] With the advent of game-induced experiences, media and culture are becoming "systemic, modular, customizable, and participatory."[3] As a result, the ways in which people spend their leisure time and consume art, design, and entertainment are increasingly game-oriented; at the very least, they are amenable to experiences that are connected to games in one way or another.

Video games are a global phenomenon; they pervade much of society irrespective of age, gender, or social status. Half a billion people worldwide play games online for at least an hour a day, and an estimated one billion people play regularly on consoles, personal computers, and mobile devices.[4] Correspondingly, video games are a strong engine for economic growth. In

2013, the industry sold 160 million games and generated more than $21 billion in revenue in the United States alone,[5] with the global industry revenue estimated at $93 billion.[6] In 2014, these figures rose to $22 billion in revenue in the US,[7] and $101 billion estimated globally.[8]

The new global cultural economy constitutes a complex, overlapping, disjunctive order that cannot adequately be understood in terms of prevailing center-periphery models.[9] Arjun Appadurai has coined the term "mediascapes" as a part of his analytical framework for exploring global cultural flows.[10] By mediascapes he means both the distribution of the electronic capabilities to produce and disseminate information (newspapers, television, and films), which are now available to a growing number of private and public actors throughout the world, as well as the images of the world created by these media.[11]

Video games are inherently transnational by virtue of their industrial, textual, and player practices. As such, video game cultures transect mediascapes in ways similar and dissimilar to television and film, transcending national boundaries and migrating between cultures. Video games emerge as spaces of exploration; their reliance on player activity to become "finished" texts calls for an analysis of the particularities of play, including local cultural, political, and social context.[12]

Until recently, research on the social and cultural aspects of video games tended to focus on the "traditional" centers of the video game industry and consumption (North America, Western Europe, Australia, Japan, and South Korea), while the international flows of gaming and digital media cultures remained largely underexplored.[13] Yet, video game cultures and game development flourished in many other regions, including South Asia, South America, Eastern Europe, and the Middle East. New scholarly research that focuses on digital gaming in regions not usually examined by game studies is slowly emerging, offering a more nuanced picture of gaming across diverse global contexts.[14]

According to a recent survey on entertainment media use in the Middle East, four out of ten people in the region play video games.[15] These figures suggest that compared to film, television, or music, in terms of consumption, video games attract fewer people, but those who do play video games do so frequently (an average of five hours per week, with a quarter of gamers playing more than ten hours a week).[16] Importantly, video games are played almost exclusively in Arabic and English, though more frequently in English than in Arabic across the region (67 per cent English vs 56 per cent Arabic).[17]

Because of the limited number of games produced in the Middle East,[18] gamers in the region remain largely dependent on games of European, American, or Japanese origin. What emerges as a result are hybrid gaming cultures that are marked by transnationalism and translocalism. What this means is that a "mainstream" Egyptian, Jordanian, or Iranian gaming culture does not exist as such; it consists primarily of the consumption of "Western" games, albeit in new contexts and different social settings.[19]

However, these consumption patterns are likely to change in the future. According to an LAI Global Game Services report, the video game market in the Middle East and North Africa (MENA) region is one of the fastest growing markets in the world, earning over $100 million in revenue from online gaming alone.[20] As in other emerging markets, the MENA region has one of the largest populations of young people in the world. In addition, Internet and mobile penetration rates, which are higher than the global average, make the region particularly attractive for business.[21] Several global video game companies have expressed their interest in translating and localizing their production into Arabic,[22] and others have invested in local video game production.[23] At the same time, a number of local video game companies have entered the market in the last decade.[24]

Arguably, the first video games to be developed in the Middle East were educational games created by the Sakhr Software division of the Kuwait-based Al-Alamiah company in the 1980s.[25] These games were designed for the MSX Sakhr personal computer and built on the Microsoft-Japan MSX computer platform. While most of these games had general educational aims, some of them focused on Muslim culture, such as *Trip to Mecca*, which is an educational trivia game about Islam. The Iraqi invasion of Kuwait in 1990 put an end to this early video game development attempt, although the company continued to produce other software.[26] Another iconic game from the region appeared a decade later: *The Stone Throwers* was created by Syrian medical student Muhammad Hamza in 2000.[27] It was a technically simple game dealing with the Al-Aqsa *Intifada* and putting players into the role of a Palestinian defending the Al-Aqsa Mosque from Israeli soldiers.

Since *Trip to Mecca* and *The Stone Throwers*, Middle Eastern game production has come a long way and has evolved in interesting ways, bringing various concepts and interpretations of Islam and Islamic culture, as well as local history, mythology, literature, and popular culture into the realm of digital entertainment.[28] Simultaneously, a variety of actors with different interests and motivations have entered the field, ranging from individual visionaries struggling to realize their dreams to private entrepreneurs seeking economic interests, and from business companies operating within the framework of an Islamic piety movement to state agencies following national interests and political agendas.[29] Significantly, the local video game development and emerging gaming cultures in individual Middle East states are subject to different regulatory frameworks, cultural values, societal norms, and religious traditions. As a result, we are witnessing a highly complex, overlapping, and contested environment, encompassing state and private actors, local and global cultural flows, and supportive and contradictory processes.

My aim in this chapter is to explore these disjunctures and tie them into a coherent theoretical framework. In doing so, I hope to shed light on the cultural and technological processes and flows influencing both video game development and gaming cultures in the Middle East. I conceptualize Middle Eastern video games as imaginary spaces that entangle diverse and contradictory processes: global cultural flows, media policies of nation states, visions and engagements of private entrepreneurs, and migration and appropriation of Western game genres and rule-systems. On a more general level, this chapter explores the structures and mechanisms underlying video game production, and how these evolved within the broader historical, cultural, and political context of the Middle East.

There is a limited, yet growing body of research on video game development and gaming cultures in the Middle East. Pioneering research in the field focused on analysis of the symbolic and ideological dimensions of in-game representational politics related to the Middle East, particularly the Arab-Israeli conflict, US action games related to the "war on terror" discourse, and the representation of Islam and Muslims in mainstream video games.[30] More recently, research focus has shifted to video games produced in the Middle East and how they deal with issues of representation and identity.[31] In my own previous research, I have analyzed how mainstream European and American games construct the representation of Arabs or Muslims,[32] how identity is constructed and communicated to players in Arab and Iranian games,[33] how video games are used as an educational tool within the emerging Muslim consumer culture,[34] and how video game development operates in Iran and the Arab world.[35]

The material I present in this chapter is theoretically grounded in the existing research, including my own, which I systematize within a newly introduced framework of ten imaginary spaces. Empirically, this chapter stems from content analyses of more than one hundred games developed in the Arab world and Iran between 2005 and 2014; it is also informed by a wealth of in-depth interviews with the Arab Middle Eastern and Iranian game producers. A substantial portion of the materials and interviews I draw on were gathered during fieldwork trips I conducted in Damascus in 2005, Beirut in 2006, Cairo in 2007, Tehran in 2008, Abu Dhabi in 2014, and Doha in 2014.

Conceptually, I utilize "gamevironments" when analyzing the imaginary spaces of Middle Eastern video games. Gamevironments is an analytical concept based on the actor-centered approach, which integrates the analysis of video games as digital artifacts with the broader cultural and social context in which these games are consumed and produced.[36] Gamevironments consists of two levels: first, the technical environment of video games and gamers (including the game in relation to textual and audiovisual narratives, interactivity options and in-game performance, production, and design of the game, and gamer-generated content); and second, the cultural environments of video games and gaming (including the social, political, and religious contexts and national regulations and policies).[37] The analytical concept of gamevironments helps investigate the diverse and heterogeneous digital spaces of Middle Eastern video games and link them to the places of their production.

I am aware of the problematic use of the term "the Middle East" as an umbrella term, as well as the analytical risk of subsuming the diverse national video game industries and markets into one chapter. The region usually labeled as the Middle East is geographically, historically, culturally, socio-politically, and economically diverse and multifaceted. The countries of Western Asia and North Africa that are put together on the map as the Middle East neither constitute a continental landmass nor are sufficiently bound together by any unifying characteristics.[38] Yet, as much as the term Middle East denotes a "virtual space," I find it a useful analytical construct for video game studies, particularly as it corresponds with the representational politics of US and European video games and has been adopted by many Arab and Iranian video game designers.

Finally, it is worth noting that the research sample presented in this chapter is selective insofar as it leaves out significant sub-regions (such as North Africa) or entire countries (such as Turkey). Rather than surveying the region as a whole, I point out trends. The following conceptualizations of Middle Eastern video games as imaginary spaces does not present a complete or fixed catalogue, but rather a starting point for us to think about the processes and flows influencing the video game industry in the Middle East during the first fifteen years of its existence.

Video games as cultural spaces

Video games are a pervasive medium that is woven into our everyday lives. On the surface level, they have become part of our daily media spaces. Yet, video games present a new challenge to the traditional dichotomist view of culture and technology.[39] Unlike other new media and virtual environments, they open up cultural spaces which are framed as "playful" from the outset.[40] Video games stimulate the emergence of practices and networks characterized by specific patterns of interaction, communication, and shared meanings.[41] The emergence of cultural spaces that are tightly connected by games has profound implications for the ways we play, relax, work, socialize, and learn.

Video games have become a common aspect of contemporary life in even its sacred and profane expressions.[42] Heidi Campbell and Gregory Grieve argue that video games are an important site of exploration into the intersection of religion and contemporary culture, helping us understand what religion is, does, and means in a changing contemporary society. Echoing Zimmerman's proclamation that we live in a "ludic century," they contend that in the same way as films helped to illuminate and expose the religiosity of the twentieth century, so digital games now depict the religious within the twenty-first century.[43]

In spite of the multifaceted relationship between our socio-cultural world and games, the latter have been largely neglected by academia, leading Phillip Reichmuth and Stefan Werning to coin the term "neglected media" to describe their strong popular appeal and economic relevance, contrasted by their lack of cultural prestige and scientific coverage. Neglected media include audio clips, video clips, video games, comic strips, and a host of new forms of digital media that are emerging almost overnight and quickly gaining a broad audience (like *Let's Play* videos on YouTube, in which players document a playthrough of a video game while simultaneously commenting on it). These forms of neglected media often have a profound impact on the collective imaginary that has not been fully recognized or accepted as culturally relevant.[44]

Understanding the properties of a medium gives us insights into its nature and its implications.[45] Video games have properties that precede their content: games are models of experience rather than textual descriptions or visual depictions of them. When we play games, we operate those models, but our actions are also constrained by their rules.[46] As Gonzalo Frasca puts it, video games open a form of representation based on rules that mimic the behavior of the simulated systems. Games typically do not represent a particular event, but a set of potential events. Because of this, we need to think about them as systems and consider what laws govern their behaviors.[47]

At the same time, video games allow us to play a role within the constraints of a model world. Unlike playground games or board games, video games are computational, which means that the model worlds and sets of rules they produce can be far more complex.[48] The rule-system of a video game is particularly important as it shapes and limits the choices and decisions players can make during the game and determines their possible outcomes. In this regard, Ian Bogost argues that games open a new domain of persuasion.[49] He calls this new form "procedural rhetoric"—the art of persuasion through rule-based representations and interactions rather than spoken words, images, or moving pictures. Bogost predicts that, through their procedural rhetoric, video games can disrupt and change fundamental attitudes and beliefs about the world, leading to potentially significant long-term social change, as well as the support of existing social and cultural positions, including organized religions.[50]

As cultural spaces, video games are being studied within the field of game studies, which places games in their broader social context. In this context, a number of formal video game definitions have emerged, commonly aiming to explain how games work, how they differ from other types of entertainment, and the appropriate methods for analyzing them. For the sake of this chapter, I have adopted Jesper Juul's definition of a game as "a rule-based formal system with a variable and quantifiable outcome, where different outcomes are assigned different values, the player exerts effort in order to influence the outcome, the player feels attached to the outcome, and the consequences of the activity are optional and negotiable."[51] Importantly, this definition is unconcerned with matters of audiovisual representation and digital computation, making it more a definition of a "game" than a "video game." Throughout this chapter, I use the term "video game" as an umbrella term for a broad variety of digital artifacts, regardless of the platform or system on which they operate.

Video games as spaces of encounter

I grew up in the 1980s in Europe, in communist Czechoslovakia. Video games were an important part of my childhood, so in this sense I belong to the first video game generation. I used to play games with my friends; socialization revolved around these games. Over time, we started to modify existing games and design our own. My first encounter with the Middle East was through a video game I came across back in 1990: a US-produced quasi-historical game called *Prince of Persia*.[52] Although this game is seemingly about the historical land of Persia, it uses topoi, concepts, and imagery that have nothing to do with Persia at all. While in the first screen of the game the Sultan's palace bears traces of Mughal India, in the second it resembles the Andalusian-style of the Alhambra palace in Granada. Similar ahistorical assemblage applies to clothing, decoration, and characters. In a manner that recalls Edward Said's work, the "digital Orientalism" of *Prince of Persia* recreates Iran as a timeless and exotic entity. Naively and ahistorically, it conflates Arab and Indian imagery, thus constructing Iran as a place without history, excluding it from the discourses of modernity, and obscuring its contemporary reality.[53]

Tarik Sabry argues that the "overabundance" of media technologies and floating signifiers of the other has undermined the role of place as a necessary element of cultural encountering.[54] Increasingly, witnessing or encountering other cultures has little to do with actual physical space; it has become a symbolic phenomenon. Video games are one such type of non-physical space where cultural encounters take place.[55] As games become globally pervasive media, it is crucial to study critically the symbolic and ideological dimensions of in-game representational politics, particularly in relation to contested spaces of conflict and political hegemony.

As previously shown, video games are increasingly becoming part of the media landscape in the Middle East. They constitute a popular leisure-time activity, especially among youth. Until recently, games of US, European, and Japanese origins dominated the market almost exclusively. Due to loose copyright enforcement, the young generation in most Middle Eastern countries has easy access to global video game production.[56] Foreign video games have become an inseparable part of Middle Eastern mediascapes and consumer culture. These mediascapes are already awash with technologically mediated interconnections.[57] Internet, satellite television, music, movies, and video games are all appropriated elements of transnational flows, integrated by Middle Eastern publics into their social relationships. In this process, translocal goods and ideas are transformed by their contextualization, while at the same time the contexts themselves are transformed. As Mark Peterson notes, certain forms of consumption in the Middle East are indexical of "the West" or "the global" and serve as valuable means for displaying cosmopolitan identity.[58] This applies in particular to specific urban settings, such as North Tehran or Central Cairo, where buying Western games and consuming Western gaming media could be part of displaying both cosmopolitan identity and class distinction.

Such encounters with global entertainment media production are not without contestations. Religious and political authorities in the Middle East have repeatedly criticized foreign video games for explicit display of sexuality, corrupting morals, and misrepresentations of Islam.[59] Several US games have been banned in countries like Iran, Saudi Arabia, and the United Arab Emirates.[60] Before analyzing these contestations, it is fitting to discuss another dimension of video games—as a space of representation—and explore how the Middle East is represented in video games.

Video games as spaces of representation

Particularly after 9/11, there has been an increase in US-produced video games dealing with the representation of the Middle East, Islam, and Muslims. A substantial number of these games tend to portray Arabs, Muslims, and Iranians as enemies (as in the case of *War in the Gulf, Delta Force, Conflict: Desert Storm, Full Spectrum Warrior, Conflict: Global Terror*, and *Assault on Iran*).[61] Typically, games such as these, which feature first-person shooters, allow the player to control American or coalition forces only, whereas the enemy is represented by visual signifiers such as head covering, loose clothes, or dark skin color, flattening the diverse religious and ethnic identities of the region into a few simplistic images. Usually the enemy is collectivized and linguistically functionalized as "various terrorist groups," "militants," or "insurgents."[62] Most of these games exhibit strong cultural bias when schematizing Arabs and Muslims as enemies in the narrative framework of fundamentalism and international terrorism.[63]

As Johan Höglund argues, the first-person shooter war games render the Middle East a perpetual military frontier, where the conflict between American democracy and Islamic fundamentalist terrorism is acted out indefinitely.[64] With the reduction of the Middle East to a perpetual frontier within this game space, war is effectively transformed from an extreme and unusual measure to a state of normality. In Höglund's words, in the above-mentioned first-person shooters, warfare as performed by American soldiers in the Middle East "ceases to be a politically problematic and expensive confusion of resources and instead appears to be a part of the natural order."[65]

Other US and European games, especially adventure and role-playing games, exploit Orientalist imagery, topics, and narratives (as in *Prince of Persia, The Magic of Scheherazade*, and *Arabian Nights*).[66] These games typically feature stock characters (Bedouins, caliphs, jinns, and belly dancers);

they also navigate players through bazaars, harems, and the desert, and contain plots like saving a kidnapped woman or assassinating an evil vizier. The "Orient" is construed as an exotic and ahistorical entity, meeting in particular Edward Said's concept of Orientalism.[67] In his classic work, Said discusses Western culture's long tradition of false and romanticized images of Asia, particularly the Middle East. He analyzes the social and political implications of Orientalism as the source of the inaccurate cultural representations that are the foundation of Western thought toward the East and which have served as implicit justifications for the colonial and imperialist ambitions of the European powers and the US.

The in-game representations of Arabs, Iranians, and Muslims have to be contextualized in a broader narrative structure that covers the Middle East and Islam as it appears in news and popular media. The dominant mode of representation of Middle Eastern cultures in European and American media generally exploits stereotypical generalizations and clichés.[68] Philipp Reichmuth and Stefan Werning argue that the study of Orientalist topoi and rationales in video games requires understanding of the specificity of interactive media and the logic of their production.[69] They point out that game producers draw from a rich repertoire of Oriental topoi and representations that is well established in Western culture. In other words, the imagined Orient is a complex cultural metasign that "is" everything that can be associated with it and could be applied successfully in a video game design with a "Middle Eastern" theme.[70]

These two modes of representation of the Middle East in US and European video games are by no means the only ones. There exist a number of mainstream games (*Age of Empires 2, Civilization* series, and *Assassin's Creed*) as well as independent games (*Peacemaker, 1000 Days of Syria*, and *Global Conflicts: Palestine*) that provide more diverse and accurate representations of various Middle Eastern cultures. Yet, the above-mentioned two modes of (mis)representation constitute a dominant framework of reference to the Middle East in the US and European video game industry. As a result, many video game producers in the Middle East do not perceive video games as neutral artifacts but as a medium that communicates and appropriates particular cultural, political, and religious messages to youth.[71]

Video games as spaces of resistance

In the initial phase of video game development in the Middle East, there has been an urge to present Arab and Iranian youth with alternative games, which would reflect their culture, history, and religion more appropriately.[72] These games can be considered as "counter-discourses."[73] Anchored in "authentic" memories and places, they constitute responses to hegemonic spaces of representation created by the US and European video game industries.

It is important to emphasize that such a resistance framework by no means applies to all the early video game production in the Middle East. There have been other significant motivations behind local video game production, including a realization of the medium's strength, a deep personal interest in video games and gaming, and the desire to produce games that are technologically and conceptually advanced and which do not pale in comparison with global production. Nevertheless, the designers' statements and the paratextual materials accompanying the games suggest that countering Western (mis) representations was a driver and a motivation for developing a more indigenous and more authentic video game industry.[74]

The first group of games developed within the resistance framework was action games based on real conflicts with Israel in Palestine and Lebanon (*Special Force, Under Ash, Under Siege,* and *Jenin: Road of Heroes*).[75] These games provide Arab and Muslim youth with heroes of their own and retell the story of the conflicts from the Muslim and Arab perspectives.

One of the first games of this kind, *Jenin: Road of Heroes* (created by Tamir Majed Malas and Ali Fayez Ismail in Jordan), has a plot based on the Battle of Jenin, which took place in April 2002 in a Palestinian refugee camp. The game starts with a long introductory video about the history of Palestine, the Jenin refugee camp, and the Battle of Jenin itself. The video combines real historical footage with digitally produced material in a way that resembles pro-Palestinian activist videos and video clips of the Lebanese Hezbollah movement. The narrative of Jenin is loosely based on real events, in the sense that the player witnesses the initial attack of Israeli helicopters and takes part in installing landmines in order to prevent Israeli soldiers from entering the camp. At the same time, and as is the case with the aforementioned US-developed war games, reality is depicted in a selective way, reshaping the comprehension of the conflict, its reason, and its outcome.

The trend of resistance games is most clearly pronounced in the games of the Lebanese Hezbollah movement. The series of first-person shooter games *Special Force* and *Special Force 2* retell stories from the 2000 and 2006 wars between Israeli defense forces and Hezbollah.[76] For the most part, the series' gameplay does not differ from a typical scheme for the genre, like destroying army trucks, eliminating snipers, and retrieving confidential documents from the enemy's military camp. Nevertheless, some mission objectives exhibit an ideological bent that serves to glorify the struggle of the Lebanese movement Hezbollah against Israel (for example, preventing Israeli soldiers from raising a flag in a Lebanese village or shooting katyusha rockets at the Israeli settlement).

Obviously, the use of video games as spaces of resistance is limited to the Arab world. A number of "counter-discourse" games have been developed in Iran, both by private producers and governmental agencies, such as *Resistance, Mir Mahna, Special Operation*, and *Black Years*. The first-person shooter game Resistance, developed in 2008, is set in the year 2015 and directly engages in an ideological struggle with the United States and Israel. Players in the game control Hezbollah commandos who are sent to Israel to seek and destroy a secret military program. This game is a clear response to the US game *Assault on Iran*, in which players are sent to Iran to terminate its nuclear program; while appropriating *Assault on Iran's* framework and game mechanics, Resistance reverses its narrative.[77] Recent examples of Iranian counter-discourse games include a first-person shooter *Mir Mahna*, which takes place in a seventeenth-century Persian Gulf occupied by the British and Dutch navies.[78] The game puts the player into the role of a "gallant warrior," who leads his soldiers in a quest to save a rural girl imprisoned by Dutch soldiers and "drives out the occupants."[79] Another example is *Special Operation*, in which the player takes the role of a special forces commander who is appointed to rescue an Iranian nuclear scientist who was kidnapped by American security forces in Iraq while visiting the tomb of Iman Hussein.

All of these games—from Iranian *Special Operation*, to Hezbollah's *Special Force* series, to Jordanian *Jenin*—generally reverse the polarities of the narrative and graphical stereotypes observed in the aforementioned US action games. They substitute the Arab or Iranian Muslim hero for the American soldier. The games of Hezbollah, in particular, borrow considerably from their US counterparts, including game design and structure. But unlike the US games, where the hero is usually individualized, Middle Eastern resistance games generally promote a higher obligation to a collective spiritual whole.[80] We can observe two different, yet not mutually exclusive trends in these games: promoting both the global Muslim and the national identity of the main hero. By situating the players in an immersive simulation of real conflicts in Palestine, Lebanon, and Iraq, these games aim to strengthen the player's identification with the struggles of Muslim communities worldwide. The focal point is the idea of defending the Muslim community against outside aggression, the emphasis on the just and moral cause of the fight, and the glorification of the Muslim fighters. By schematizing complex and diverse conflicts into a single bipolar scheme of good and evil, these games echo their Western blueprints more than the authors are willing to admit, including the collectivization and functionalization of enemies, the exclusion of civilians from the virtual battleground, and the selective references to real events. At the same time, some of these games aim to emphasize the national aspect of the resistance, particularly when related to defending the nation against the outside aggression of the "imperial and neocolonial forces."[81]

Resistance games are not limited to the early stages of the Middle Eastern video game industry. Although not fully pronounced, this trend has been taking shape over nearly a decade and a half, albeit with different forms and manifestations. The most recent example in the Arab world is *The Liberation of Palestine*, a game developed by an amateur team in Gaza in 2014.[82] It is an online strategy game, in which the players "establish refugee camps, build homes, prepare the camp residents for confrontation, build alliances, buy weapons, swap prisoners, and score attacks."[83] The players also get familiar with "historical, archeological, and religious sites in Palestine."[84] According to the authors of the game, the overarching idea is to develop "the spirit of resistance among Palestinian boys and girls."[85] Similarly, a new game called *Black Years*, which is in development in Iran, takes the players back to the years 1951–3 and retells the story of Mohammad Mosaddeq, the Iranian Prime Minister, who nationalized the oil industry and was subsequently removed from power in a CIA-orchestrated coup.[86] The game is supposed to be "based on historical documents" that expose Western schemes for controlling the region, and serves as an informal educational tool for the youth.[87] And it is to this educational dimension that I now turn.

Video games as spaces of education

The focus on the young generation and the perception of video games as a persuasive and educational medium are consistent features of the Middle Eastern video game production. Emblematically, the first video games produced in the 1980s in the region were educational. In the words of Riyadh Al Sharekh, a former marketing manager at Sakhr, "To think that Alamiah's goal was to solely support video games eclipses the efforts and intentions of the company. We saw ourselves primarily as an educational company."[88]

Educational games are an important category of Middle Eastern games. Typically, these games aim at teaching the basic tenets of Islam, narrate the history of Islamic civilization, or promote "positive and family values."[89] Many such games have been developed in the early 2000s in the Arab world: these include *Young Muslim, Prophets' Tales, Adventures of Ahmad, Children of Jerusalem,* and *The Adventurers.*[90] In most of these games, children learn about Islam through simple puzzles and quests, like putting together al-fātiha from Arabic letters or memorizing verses from the Qur'an. The educational approach of these early educational games is based on the pedagogical approach that characterized edutainment in the 1980s. Practically, progress in these games depends on correct answers to unfolding questions and puzzles; and contrary to recent immersive game-based learning environments, the games themselves are the only reward for the learner.

While it is generally agreed that edutainment games can support the learning of facts, it has been argued that these tools have achieved only limited success in helping players develop advanced knowledge and skills.[91] Nevertheless, there are currently many similar games available on the Arab Middle Eastern markets, suggesting the appeal they have to parents. The primary reason why parents buy these games could stem from their desire to provide their children with Islamic, halal entertainment that has some educational function. At the same time, "Islamic edutainment" offers a safe alternative to mainstream Western games, even to non-religious parents who face a lack of other choices.

In recent years, more sophisticated educational games entered the Arab market, like the strategy game *The Prophet's Wars,* aimed at teaching early Islamic history.[92] Although the game's graphics pale in comparison with its Western counterparts, for the first time Arab players were offered Muslim heroes and real historical scenarios reconstructed primarily according to Islamic historiography, such as Ibn Ishaq's Al-Sira al-Nabawiyya (The Life of the Prophet). In contrast to the aforementioned early Islamic edutainment, this game utilizes the full potential of the video game medium by situating the player inside a virtual and interactive reconstruction of real historical events.[93]

A similar pattern can be found in Iran, where the Computer and Video Games Foundation was established in 2006 under the supervision of the Iranian Ministry of Culture and Islamic Guidance. One of the aims of the Foundation is "the indication, improvement and promotion of cultural bases and Iranian-Islamic identity through the video game industry with a special attention to the children and adolescent."[94]

Several games have been developed within this framework, aimed at diverse age groups, dealing with different topics and utilizing various game genres. For example, the adventure game *Nouruz* teaches children about various aspects of Iranian culture and folklore; *My Homeland* deals with ancient Iranian history and archaeology; and *The Honor* retells the story of an Iranian national sports hero with an emphasis on moral values and fair play.[95]

Recent examples of fully-fledged Iranian video games with an educational twist include the strategy game *Black Gold*, in which "the player takes the role of an Iranian oil industry manager who explores oil in different areas of Iran, builds pipelines, refineries and petrochemical plants, and helps with the development of cities."[96] Another is a science fiction game called *Earth 2124*, set in the distant future, where the Iranian Space Agency leads international research on interstellar travels.[97]

Most of these games are technologically and conceptually more developed than the earlier Islamic edutainment mentioned above, and stem from a concept of immersive learning.[98] As Farshad Samimi, one of the authors of *Nouruz*, pointed out to me, the game is intended to "change the way children in Iran play games and let them contemplate why they are playing" in order to "foster a yearning for knowledge among them."[99]

Video games as spaces of cultural dialogue

The third significant category of games that are developed and produced in the Middle East consists of games that are intended as tools for cultural dialogue with the West. One of the early games in this category is *Quraish*. Designed by the Syrian company Afkar Media in 2005, this strategy game, which bears the name of a prominent tribe in Mecca, deals with the pre-Islamic Bedouin wars, the inception of Islam, and its subsequent spread. Through the unfolding game narrative, players are educated about early Islamic history. During the particular missions, the player takes part in many real historical events and visits places like Mecca or Medina, whose topographies are based on available historical descriptions. The game can be played from different perspectives (pagan Bedouins, Muslim Arabs, or Zoroastrian Persians), and is available in Arabic and English. The aim of the game designers was to educate people both in the Arab world and in the West about the "real history of Islam" and to challenge stereotypes. Radwan Kasmiya, the main author of *Quraish*, told me when I interviewed him in Damascus in 2005 that he perceived the game as the ultimate tool for learning and cultural dialogue: "We are trying to build a bridge that serves both sides. We are trying to break the stereotypical models of thinking on both sides, whereby for

Muslims the West is represented by Britney Spears and for the West our culture is represented by Osama bin Laden."[100] Although the extent to which *Quraish* functions as a tool for a cultural dialogue is not clear, the game constitutes one of the first serious attempts to design an Arab game that addresses cultural barriers and enhances intercultural communication.

As is the case with the previous trends, we can find video games deliberately constructed as spaces of cultural dialogue in Iran. In fact, the first Iranian 3D video game was the 2005 *Quest of Persia*, an action adventure dealing with the history and culture of Iran.[101] As Puya Dadgar, the author of the game, explained to me, he was disturbed by the way his fellow university students in the US perceived Iran. So he decided to create a video game with an Iranian hero based on Iranian history and culture "that would help people understand Iran better."[102] Similarly, Farshad Samimi, author of *Nouruz*, told me that his company produces games also for a foreign audience so that "people can understand the Iranian culture and see that Iran has two thousand years of history."[103]

A recent example of a game deliberately conceived as a tool for cultural dialogue comes from Qatar, where a young team of Qatari entrepreneurs designed a game called *Giddam* in 2014. *Giddam*—which means "in front" in Gulf Arabic—is a free-to-play mobile racing game that includes various elements of Middle Eastern culture. Each player's avatar represents a different character from the Arab world and the game is rich in Qatari symbols. For example, the in-game objects include karak, a strong, sweet tea originating from the Indian subcontinent that is popular in Qatar, or the *agaal*, a cord worn by Arab men to secure their headdress.[104] To add to the game's cultural elements, the first two stages the team designed were set in iconic Doha locations: the modern West Bay business district and Souq Waqif, a historic open-air market that was reconstructed as a heritage site during the early phases of the city's rapid modernization.[105] As one of the designers of the game, Fatima Al-Kuwari, told me, she was disappointed with the way foreign video games misrepresented Qatar and the Arab world and wanted to change the perception of her country.[106] As she and the team behind *Giddam* put it: "We wanted to use video gaming as a platform to help us export our rich culture and heritage to the whole world."[107]

Importantly, all the games I have labeled as tools for "cultural dialogue" are available in foreign languages, typically English, and could be obtained outside the countries of their origin. For example, the English version of *Quraish* could be bought in many Arab or Islamic shops in London. Similarly, the Iranian games, *Garshasp* and *Quest of Persia: Lotfali Khan Zand*, were available for download in Farsi, English, and German versions for US$9.99 and $15 respectively, payable via PayPal. *Giddam* is freely available in Arabic and English, and is specifically marketed to the large Qatari expat community.[108]

The different language versions not only frame the respective games' target audiences but also shape their developers' design choices. The socio-cultural environment in which any information technology is deployed has substantial influence over the technology's success. Beyond the issue of translation, the deployment of a video game cross-culturally needs to include localizations that enhance the "fit" of the game to the culture. Given that many Arab and Iranian video games manifest careful appreciation of prevailing local norms and values, their adaptation for a global audience could pose a challenge to their authors.

The notion of Middle Eastern video games functioning as spaces of cultural dialogue is entangled with non-physical spaces of symbolical encounters with other cultures as well as with imaginary spaces of representation.[109] Yet, this time it is not simply the mainstream US video game industry that is constructing the representation of the virtual Middle East; Middle Eastern designers are themselves carefully crafting their own "authentic" self-representations.

Video games as spaces of authenticity

Game development entails a sense of achievement and is a source of technological pride, but it also articulates a cultural stance. With a striking similarity, I have heard the statement "this game is one hundred per cent Arabic" or "one hundred per cent Persian" from game developers in Cairo, Damascus, Doha, and Tehran. The emphasis on "authenticity" permeates the Middle Eastern game production as a whole. Though game production in the Middle East is considerably multifaceted and diverse, many Middle Eastern game producers share the concern that "their" culture is misrepresented in global video game production and strive to create authentic virtual representations of their countries.[110] The kind of "authenticity" that is constructed by locally developed Middle Eastern video games takes different forms and stems from a wide variety of sources, ranging from religion and politics to local histories, mythologies, and popular culture.

Interviews with game designers provide valuable first-hand accounts of how the notion of cultural authenticity affects game design. Puya Dadgar, the lead designer of *Quest of Persia*, told me when I interviewed him in Tehran, "With *Quest of Persia*, we wanted to show what the land of Persia is truly all about.

Quest of Persia is one hundred per cent Persian, from music to environments, up to characters."[111] By the same token, Mustafa Ashur, one of the designers of the Egyptian game *Abu Hadid*, noted, "We are proud that *Abu Hadid* is one hundred per cent Egyptian, from technology to the content."[112] Finally, Munera Al Dosari, Faraj Abdualla and Fatima Al-Kuwari, the team behind *Giddam*, stated that they "chose to make [their] first game one hundred per cent Qatari."[113]

In the Middle East, modernity and authenticity are continually contested. New practices of speech, dress, consumption, education, and uses of technology emerge as significant indices of both cosmopolitanism and authenticity.[114] The search for authenticity involves reflexive, interpretive assessments of one's own and others' behaviors, evaluated against leisure experiences, consumption practices, travels, family expectations, peer values, and other social relations.[115] Authenticity is thus not a given but is negotiated; it is a field of contestation rather than an essence.[116]

Most of the designers in the Middle East are private, enthusiastic game developers, who have a vision and invest money and energy into it.[117] As the interviews I conducted with game designers indicate, there exists a relatively coherent set of concerns that many producers in Iran and the Arab world share and which fundamentally shape their design outcomes and production strategies. These concerns include primarily emphases on self-representation, personal motivation, and respect for one's traditions, religion, and culture.[118] Some of these producers seek authenticity in nationalism or in Islamic piety. Yet, as Mark Peterson notes, even these often prove elusive as authoritative voices differ on which practices constitute an "authentic" form of nationalism or can be considered "true" Muslim piety.[119]

Middle Eastern game producers face many challenges, most notably lax or non-existent copyright protection and—as is the case in Syria and Iran—an embargo on technology transfers and economic sanctions. At the same time, they often find themselves compelled to take into account different cultural communication patterns and religious and cultural values of their audiences. Ultimately, all the authenticities they construct are subject to public interpretations. Moreover, in some countries, the producers have to cope with governmental regulation of cultural production and media control, which further problematizes the question of authenticity, particularly as a new set of actors—governmental agencies and religious establishments—enter the arena of video game development.

Video games as spaces of contestation

The media landscape in the Middle East is often subject to control and censorship by the state, alongside the regulation of cultural production. Governmental control is most notable in Iran, where video games cannot be released without the approval of the Ministry of Culture and Islamic Guidance. Since 2006, such a function has been carried out primarily through the Iran Computer and Video Games Foundation. The aim of the latter was twofold: to boost economic growth in the video game industry segment and to subsidize the development of games promoting Iranian and Islamic values. The support for domestic games is part of a larger process aimed at the "de-Westernization" of Iranian cultural production since 1979. Paradoxically, the establishment of the Foundation and the support it provides resulted in both the production of games asserting the official conception of an Iranian Muslim identity, and games that directly challenge this identity, as is the case with games on ancient Iranian mythology that include tacit links to the Zoroastrian heritage. The Ministry of Culture and Islamic Guidance often removes controversial elements from games during the pre-approval process. As a result, video game production in Iran is subject to friction and competition between factions within the regime, the institutional interests of various agencies, and the tensions between the state and the visions and engagement of private entrepreneurs.[120]

In the Arab world the situation varies significantly from one country to another. Although national Arab regulatory frameworks exhibit similarities and overlaps, they also reflect the fact that each Arab country has developed media regulations and policies to meet challenges specific to that country, whether they are social, political, or economic. As Marwan Kraidy and Joe Khalil note, national media policies in the Arab world have traditionally reflected a handful of concerns, most notably regime survival and protection of moral and socio-cultural values.[121] Yet, in the 1990s, the rise of satellite television channels and the introduction of the Internet entailed a shift from a "monolithic" state-controlled media model pattern to a more "pluralistic" and diverse media scene where a variety of competing voices representing different political positions and orientations could be heard.[122] As a result, most game developers in the Arab world operate in a highly hybridized and pluralistic media environment where "state ownership" and "private ownership," as well as "government control" and "individual or party control," coexist and shape the media landscape. Unlike Iran, most Arab states do not have a specific national policy regarding the production of video games.[123]

Recently, several Arab countries started to finance local video game production through a system of grants, subsidies, and indirect support. An emblematic example of this new approach is the Qatari company Girnaas, which created the aforementioned game *Giddam*. Girnaas has received government start-up funding and was made part of the ictQatar's Digital Incubation Center, which gave its Qatari founders enough funding to hire team members with more technical knowhow.[124] As Fatima Al-Kuwari from Girnaas explains, ictQatar "provide[d] us with seed funds, and it is where we started our business and kicked off product development and then game development."[125] Similarly, in Jordan, Gaming Lab has been established with funding from the King Abdullah II Fund for Development, "to act as an initial incubator where young Jordanian creative minds can experiment with technology and can work on developing their own game ideas."[126] State support indicates both the economic and cultural relevance that Middle Eastern governments place in the emerging digital creative industry.

Finally, Middle Eastern video games and their content are shaped by an official video game ratings authority for the Islamic world, which was established in 2010. The Entertainment Software Rating Association (ESRA) was founded by the UAE-based Index Conferences and Exhibitions Organization (ICEO) in close cooperation with the Iran Computer and Video Games Foundation (ICVGF).[127] According to Behrouz Minaei, the managing director at ICVGF, the rating system was designed with three considerations in mind: "culture, society and special values of Islam."[128] Given that the rating system is voluntary and producers are only encouraged to adhere to it, it is hard to estimate what its impact will be outside those Muslim countries where similar control mechanisms based on Islamic values are already applied.[129] Nevertheless, as is the case in many Western countries, the rating system provides guidelines that help parents determine which games to buy for their children, thus shaping family consumption patterns.

Video games as spaces of networking

In 2011, a new Arab online game named *Happy Oasis* made its debut on Facebook.[130] This social network game, which was created by the Jordanian company Aranim Games, appropriates the successful pattern of *FarmVille*, a farming simulation social network game developed by the US company Zynga in 2009, and refashions it along Arabic and Islamic principles.[131] As Suleiman Bakhit, Aranim's CEO, explains, the game "tak[es] some of the Arab habits and traditions and turn[s] them into social gaming mechanics."[132] The game-play in *Happy Oasis* involves various aspects of farm management such as plowing land, planting, growing, harvesting crops, and raising livestock. The game incorporates the social networking aspect of Facebook into its game mechanics. Players are encouraged to contact other players in order to improve their oases more quickly, by using their help as farmhands or by gaining rewards from helping others in turn.

Even though *Happy Oasis* was not particularly successful, it is suggestive of how Middle Eastern video games function as spaces of networking. Contemporary Middle Eastern youth are increasingly used to networked forms of communication.[133] According to a study by Northwestern University in Qatar, most residents of Gulf states are online (96 per cent in UAE, 87 per cent in Saudi Arabia, and 85 per cent in Qatar). While access drops considerably among the other countries in the region (62 per cent in Lebanon, 47 per cent in Tunisia, and 36 per cent in Egypt), the region still remains above the global average. Overall, younger users are twice as likely to use the Internet as their older counterparts (86 per cent of those under 25 and 40 per cent of 45 and older).[134] Facebook is by far the most popular social network in the MENA region, used by nearly twice as many Internet users as its nearest rival, Twitter. More than 90 per cent of Internet users are on Facebook in five of the six countries covered in the study.[135]

Constance Steinkuehler and Dmitri Williams argue that for a generation raised with the Internet, instantaneous access to both information and the social networks for which that information is relevant has become the norm.[136] While earlier generations see instant messaging (or even cell phones) as a distraction, for the current generation the opposite seems to be true: it is hard to imagine getting work done without those tools. The so-called "digital natives" increasingly participate in the creation and sharing of their own content. This allows media consumers to become producers, creating "knowledge communities" that form around mutual interests. Their members also work together to forge new knowledge often in realms where no traditional expertise exists.[137] Networked game cultures participate in a collective intelligence, blur the distinction between the production and consumption of information, and emphasize expertise rather than status.[138]

Social networking is an indivisible part of the contemporary gaming culture. Peer groups of gamers exchange games, discuss their qualities, and circulate information to help others win while they are playing a particular game. With the spread of the Internet, these social networks are manifested by fan sites, blogs, and peer-to-peer servers, effectively creating transnational youth communities. The experience of sharing creates a collective bond that is often exploited by game designers. Most of the games mentioned in this chapter have their own websites or social network sites and players are encouraged to take part in online discussion forums. Such peer groups and collaborative networks play an important role in the construction of youth identities; adolescents use media and the cultural insights provided by them to see both who they might be and how others have constructed or reconstructed themselves.[139]

Networking is not only an inseparable aspect of gaming cultures; it is also a fundamental part of game development. Video game programmers, artists, and game designers usually operate as "digital nomads." They join new game development projects based on public calls, personal contacts, and social capital, only to leave them once their job is finished to start new ones. Game development in the West is typically project- and task-based and includes local and transnational networks of experts who re-structuralize and reshape themselves according to concrete project needs. A cornerstone of every project is a lead game designer who coordinates the work of other designers and is the main visionary of the game. In the Middle East, similarly, we can find lead designers who stand behind several successful games. This is the case with Radwan Kasmiya from Damascus, the lead designer of *Under Ash, Under Siege, Quraish*, and *Knights of Glory*, and *Puya Dadgar* from Tehran, the lead designer of the *Quest of Persia* series.

Until recently, the game development networks in the Middle East tended to be local (or translocal) and constituted loosely interconnected "small worlds" organized primarily along the lines of nationality and citizenship. Today, these networks are becoming formalized and international as there are several social networking events and platforms that foster transregional cooperation, such as the MENA Games Conference in Beirut, which aims "to promote and help expand the regional gaming industry,"[140] or the Dubai World Game Expo, which serves as "the leading platform for meeting with interactive entertainment developers, publishers, distributors, investors, and government officials in the MENA region."[141] Among the prominent cross-border game developer networks in the Arab world are the Arabic Game Developer Network and particularly GameTako,[142/143] which is currently arguably the largest and most active pan-regional game developer community. Since 2014, GameTako organizes one of the largest annual game development events in the Arab world, the GameZanga,[144] in which participants from throughout the region create game concepts on community-selected topics.

The processes of formalization and internalization are often connected with financial and political support from the state, as in the cases of the previously mentioned Gaming Lab in Jordan, ictQatar, or the Iran Computer and Video Games Foundation. Finally, several universities in the region recently started to offer formal degrees in game development and programming, such as the Iran Game Development Institute in Tehran or the SAE Institute in Dubai.[145]

Video games as spaces of hybridity

Another imaginary space of Middle Eastern video games, the space of hybridity, is again closely connected to the issues of authenticity, originality, and locality. Despite the emphasis on self-representation, regional traditions, and one's own history and religion, most video games produced in the Middle East almost invariably appropriate genres and game mechanics of global video game production, particularly of successful US games.[146] While these games create new "authentic" content on the layer of audiovisuals and narratives, they replicate the hidden layers of rule-systems, quest structures, goals, and ergonomic principles.[147]

A video game is essentially an imaginary universe.[148] The defining aspects of this universe include the global scenario (topology, main characters, nature, and hierarchy of the levels), images and sounds, the principles of the gameplay (modalities, goals, rules, and game mechanics), and the ergonomic principles (interface and game learning).[149] From this analytical perspective, Middle Eastern games "authentically" create new content in the first two categories of the defining aspects (global scenario, images, and sounds), being the visible and audible layers of a game, yet appropriate the remaining hidden layers (gameplay, rules, and ergonomic principles).

In particular, the rule-system governing the player's interaction with a particular game is one level around which cultural bias may be communicated. While the content of the game may consist of Arab and Iranian topoi, the rule-system that gives it a form reflects American or Western cultural values. In the case of first-person shooters, it is the topos of the lone invincible warrior outnumbered by enemies yet winning against the odds. In the case of role-playing games, it is the topos of life as an individual development project carried out by acquiring new skills and advantages. In the case of strategy games, it is the model of the world as consisting of quantifiable variables offering everyone an equal possibility to "win" if properly managed.[150]

As such, what emerges from the Middle Eastern game production is a story of "hybridization" and cross-cultural exchange rather than "authenticity" and "originality." Certain aspects of Middle Eastern gamevironments (such as textual and audiovisual narratives, production and design, and gamer-generated content) are indexical of the "Arab," "Muslim," or "Iranian" referent, whereas other aspects of these gamevironments (such as interactivity options, rule-systems, and gameplay) are indexical of "the West" or "global." In this respect, Middle Eastern video games are becoming new imaginary spaces where cultural encountering takes place and where cultural authenticities and hybridities are simultaneously represented, contested, and inverted.[151] Class, ethnicity, patriotism, cosmopolitanism, and religious affiliation are all increasingly tied, sometimes in contradictory ways, to these transnational flows.[152]

Concluding remarks: from neglected media to ludic century

This chapter examined video game development and gaming cultures in the contemporary Middle East. My aim was to analyze the cultural and technological processes and flows influencing the Middle Eastern gamevironments and tie them into a coherent theoretical framework. This framework consists of imaginary spaces, which include diverse and contradictory processes: global cultural flows, national regulatory frameworks, visions and engagement of private entrepreneurs, and migration and appropriation of Western game genres and rule-systems. These seemingly heterogeneous processes are interdependent; they overlap, support, and disrupt each other. Seen from a broader perspective, they point out the trends influencing the development of the video game industry in the Middle East since 2000.

Three concluding remarks can be ventured when it comes to the imaginary spaces of Middle Eastern gamevironments. First, these spaces are shaped by a number of heterogeneous actors pursuing different, sometimes contradictory agendas. There are visionary lead designers who strive to realize their dreams: programmers, artists, and testers who create ever-changing networks of "digital nomads" on whom lead designers rely; national governments who aim to boost digital creative industry and/or promote their national cultures; religious authorities who want to translate their messages into the new language of youth; foreign investors who aim to participate in the emergent markets; and local players who want to play high-quality games with heroes and stories to which they can relate. The motivations of these diverse actors are connected to complex processes that are affecting the region, including globalization and localization, cultural appropriation and search for authenticity, cosmopolitanism and nationalism, and traditionalism and modernization.

Second, in spite of their diverse backgrounds, actors share a relatively coherent perception of games as a serious medium communicating important messages and having significant economic relevance. The contemporary regional production includes complex educational, political, and religious games, as well as games promoting different national cultures or aiming to be tools of a cultural dialogue. The emerging Middle Eastern video game markets are similarly perceived as spaces of investments and economic growth, both by local governments who subsidize national video game start-ups and digital creative industries, and foreign investors who seek strategic partnerships in order to secure access to local markets.

Third, over time we can observe both the formalization and internationalization of the various networks forming the Middle Eastern gamevironments. These networks now stretch from independent game jams organized from below to international conferences and expos promoted on the highest political levels. In many ways, regional video game development and gaming cultures are becoming part of a larger cultural shift from "neglected media," marginalized by governments and academia, to the "ludic century," in which systemic, modular, customizable, and participatory digital entertainment culture is the extended arena where multifaceted political, social, religious, and economic interests compete and coexist at the same time.

4

MEDIATED EXPERIENCE
IN THE EGYPTIAN REVOLUTION

Mark Allen Peterson

While much has been written on the role of digital media in the Egyptian uprisings of 2011, there has been little sustained attention to the lived experience of the revolution and the roles that the media played in this. Reconciling large-scale political and social change with everyday lived experience has always been a fundamental problem for understanding social and political change. Social movement theories, rational actor theories, and other macropolitical theories that ascribe causality to contextual variables often avoid phenomenal accounts of the experiences of individual people, precisely because these subjective accounts appear either to contradict or to complicate the assumptions on which these theories are founded. Nowhere is this more true than in times of revolution, when everyday routines, practices, and norms, including those involving media, are disrupted, and people struggle to find ways of being in the world when "'normality' is radically in flux."[1] To study revolutions therefore implies not only a focus on political behavior "from below," but also recognition of moments at which "high and low" are relativized, made irrelevant, or subverted, and the micro and macro levels fuse in critical conjunctions.[2]

This chapter offers a first effort at a conceptual framework that recognizes the intricacy of interaction between mediation and dramatic social change by looking at the lived experience of Egyptians during the Egyptian revolution.[3] I begin with a bird's eye account of the Egyptian revolution from the perspective of media use. I follow this with three brief accounts of people who consider themselves participants in the revolution, but whose experiences differ from the stereotyped depictions of people who massed in Tahrir Square or revolutionary bloggers hunched over keyboards in Internet cafés. I then review the concept of "mediation" that has increasingly been used in media studies to describe the integration of media into everyday social worlds. Finally, I will attempt to link these three sections through an analysis of the revolution as process, drawing on the processual theories of social change developed in anthropology in the 1960s and 1970s and currently going through a critical revival.[4]

The mediated revolution

Central to any understanding of the roles played by media in the Egyptian uprisings is the recognition that in the years leading up to the revolution, media technologies had ceased to be understood as the exclusive provenance of the state. Historically, the Egyptian state had always exerted extensive control over newspapers, radio, and television, even those published by private corporations and opposition political parties. Small media technologies (cassette recorders, photocopies, and fax machines) had long been used by anti-state actors to produce and distribute media outside the routes dominated by state and corporate media, but the rise of digital media dramatically increased the availability and ease of use of the tools of media production (computers, software, recording equipment, etc.) and distribution (Web 2.0 applications) to the extent that they provided significant alternative sources of media content. Initially ignored by the state, except as a tool for measuring progress toward development goals, new media came to provide channels of communication outside state control and, perhaps more importantly, to symbolize the possibility of alternative forms of Egyptian citizenship.

The Egyptian uprisings can only be understood within the context of more than a decade of protests against Egypt's "human security regime" that peaked in 2005 and again in 2010.[5] For decades, the Egyptian state posited itself to its Western sponsors as the only vanguard against an anti-Western Islamic regime, while positioning itself at home as the guarantor of a moral order that supported secular modernity while enforcing racial, gender, and religious boundaries against public transgression. This role as double-guarantor justified the establishment of a strong security apparatus that operated with relatively few constraints. State media played a central role in this project. While everyday experiences with the state were often mediated by fraught interactions with police and other state actors,[6] state media provided an alternative narrative featuring a paternalistic state protecting and supporting its subjects from internal dissension and the invisible hands of external enemies.[7] Aside from voting in parliamentary and presidential elections, Egyptian citizens were confronted with a paucity of available civic practices. Instead they were in practice largely positioned in the role of audience for a political spectacle. Protests occurred, but were largely unrepresented by the media. Although many of these protests were labor strikes at factories or held in small communities disconnected from each other and from larger social movements, many of the urban protests involved closely-knit groups of protesters and organizers who learned from experience, from one another, and in some cases from wider global pro-democratic protest networks.[8] New media technologies played important roles in creating these connections and disseminating lessons. Many of these urban protest leaders also made strong efforts to connect urban and student protests to the labor movements.[9] One of the most important mediated social movements in Egypt, "the April 6 Movement," began as a simple Facebook page calling on protesters in Cairo to support a planned labor protest in the industrial town of El-Mahalla El-Kubra.[10]

While it is true that new digital media "make possible new kinds of civic practices,"[11] they coexist with pre-existing media and civic practices. At the beginning of the uprisings, Egypt's media ecology consisted of widely distributed state-controlled newspapers, radio, and television, and a much smaller number of independent newspapers and television stations, privately owned but subject to ambiguously defined legal restrictions against criticizing government agencies and actions.[12] Blogging emerged as an important alternative system through which writers could explore new literary styles and find alternative voices.[13] For the state, allowing free expression at the margins—in foreign language and online—initially served as "a safety valve and a way of keeping tabs on opponents and alternatives at a safe distance from local arenas."[14] Simultaneously, in response to new initiatives for measuring development by global agencies like the UN and World Bank, the government established initiatives to make the Internet more readily available to larger numbers of people, establishing free dial-up connections and building village Internet facilities.[15]

New media practices enabled many Egyptians to imagine and engage in new forms of action and involvement in the polity. As more and more political bloggers came online writing in Arabic, however, they became increasingly subject to government reprisals.[16] The regime was initially cautious about arresting bloggers out of concern for widespread attention outside Egypt, both because of the capacity of blogging to reach audiences outside the state, and also because of the nature of the cultural values placed on these activities by those external audiences.[17]

In addition to blogging and the creation of protest event pages on Facebook, protesters against the regime found creative ways to employ social media designed in North America and Europe for very different purposes. The Piggipedia, for example, employed the photo-sharing site Flickr to upload pictures of secret police, usually taken with cell phones at protests, which could then be annotated by others in an effort to introduce transparency as a counter to state secrecy.[18] Yet while these types of "tactical innovations" partially liberated activists from a regime-controlled communications grid,[19] the new media tools were also subject to constraints imposed by Western ideologies and practices: Flickr refused to upload images seized from the security apparatus itself on the grounds that the activists did not "own" the images, while Facebook's frequent structural revisions could cause entire networks and conversations to vanish.[20]

The January 25 uprising succeeded in part because it was a continuation of the social and political unrest that had marked the entire preceding year. Events such as the clash of Egyptian security forces with Palestinians during Egypt's unpopular enforcement of the Israeli blockade of Gaza, the murder of blogger Khaled Said by state security forces, and the blatant ballot box stuffing and intimidation used to ensure a National Democratic Party win in 2010, all were exposed and discussed through social media. These became symbolic and mobilizing events for the young, college-educated, underemployed youth, sometimes called "shabab al-Facebook":

> The Internet gave these young Egyptians a view of the Gaza clashes unobtainable through state television. Disaffected government employees posted videos to YouTube taken with cell phones of fellow poll workers stuffing ballot boxes. The Facebook page Kullina Khaled Said (We Are All Khaled Said) became a rallying point for calls to revolution. Blogs became important sites for commenting on

media, both domestic and foreign. Streams of Tweets pointed people to blogs, Facebook pages, and news sites, in an ever-growing web of political resistance.[21]

The uprising itself began not as a call to revolution but as an anti-regime protest to mark National Police Day. Activists wanted to exploit the fact that people did not have to work in celebration of the holiday and mobilized them in protest of the holiday. A famous V-Log by Asmaa Mahfouz challenged young men to come out for the protest; it went viral within Egypt.[22] Protesters used social media sites and cell phone text messaging to organize several of the protest marches, but knowing electronic networks were monitored, they also organized some protests through word of mouth and printed handouts distributed in working-class neighborhoods with histories of labor unrest.[23]

Initially, the protests seemed to follow a familiar script common to protests in Egypt: marchers congregated in one spot (in this case Tahrir Square). State television announced that, although they were breaking the law, the president was graciously allowing them the freedom to express their discontent. Late at night, under cover of darkness, security forces entered the square and broke up the gathering with batons and tear gas. But this attack was far from secret; cameras captured the action from rooftops, and the videos were uploaded to YouTube and broadcast on Al Jazeera.

The next day, disgruntled protesters gathered in small groups throughout Cairo, vowing to resume the protest. This was typical in the aftermath of a protest, and police squads had been assigned throughout Cairo to deal with it. On January 26, however, the numbers of these gatherings were unusually large, in many cases beyond what police could control. As groups began to march toward Tahrir Square, their numbers swelled as they recruited and coordinated, often through text messages, tweets, and phone calls.

On January 27, and in an effort to stem the tide of this "Internet revolution," the regime cut off nearly all Internet service for the entire country.[24] This effort failed spectacularly, damaging the Egyptian economy far more than it did the incipient revolution. The desperate attempt of the Mubarak regime to quell online activism drew the attention of those positing a "social media revolution" to the significance of links between online and offline activity, the important relationships between social media and the traditional mass media of television and newspapers, and the creativity of protesters who again and again turned obstacles into opportunities.

The eighteen-day occupation in Tahrir Square that ended on February 11, with the resignation of Hosni Mubarak, has been described by participants as exhilarating: a breakdown of social norms replaced by an intimate interpersonal generosity, organized by a strong sense of purpose. The protesters suffered hunger, thirst, and exhaustion, punctuated by moments of fear and violence. Participation in the occupation elicited a deep sense of community, as people spontaneously organized makeshift hospitals, security cordons, food delivery, and rubbish removal services. Many of these activities were organized in part through cell phone call chains, Twitter, and text messaging, and these technologies were crucial in coordinating with citizens outside the square who supported the movement and brought in supplies.[25]

It was a period of extraordinary public drama, marked by Muslims and Christians protecting one another as they prayed on their respective holy days, the defection of public figures to the protest movement, the chanting of creative slogans,[26] and the expression of hope through graffiti and hand-made signs. All of these activities had national and international audiences as local participants uploaded pictures and videos to the web, where they were subsequently re-edited by supporters internationally. Al Jazeera covered the entire occupation live, in spite of continued interference from security forces, frequently incorporating digital media taken by protesters in their coverage. Al Jazeera's footage was in turn aired by broadcast media throughout the world.

Thus while occupations of public space, strikes, marches, and protests were crucial aspects of the revolution, so too were the media through which people both gathered information and shared it, expressed and engaged with ideas, and negotiated social action. Media practices in the revolution were complex, broad, shifting, and multi-layered; they were also often unpredictable and creative.[27] The complexity of mediation becomes clear when one considers how indeterminate the interpretations between social meanings and social actions can be. Many people who supported the initial protests were willing to call for an end to protests through social media by January 29, when Mubarak sacked the cabinet, or February 1, when he pledged not to run for a sixth term, or after newly appointed Vice President Omar Suleiman's speech two days later. For example, in an email correspondence, a professor of literature at Ain Shams University, who protested in Tahrir Square on January 26–27, told me that by January 29 the protests had been hijacked by people "with political agendas" and that the protesters should go home and wait for the reforms their actions would engender. A young Egyptian living in London shared a post from a friend on her Facebook page arguing that he had gone home from Tahrir Square after the first week because the protests were going too far, and that they were becoming an embarrassment. The thirty-eight comments that followed took multiple positions, staking claims about what protesters could reasonably demand, what they should settle for, and when they should go home. Other protesters had high hopes and ambitions but became demoralized at certain points and were willing to stop, only to be regalvanized by such events as news of fresh protests in Alexandria or Ismailia, or by Wael Ghonim's February 7 television interview.

The opinions circulating in blogs, tweets, emails, and text messages were broad and variable about why people were there, what they could seriously hope to accomplish, and what they were risking personally and in terms of the nation. The unity of Tahrir Square was a negotiated unity, one continually being argued, debated, and reassessed in the light of shifting events. It was only after the celebrations of Mubarak's resignation that a simple framing of the eighteen days as a clash between the regime and a rainbow cross-section of Egyptians from all walks of life, unified by their opposition to the president, became a dominant narrative.

As with any form of complex action, people made sense of the revolution by integrating their experiences of it into a wider complex of meaning—in this case, as part of a wider media ideology. In his book *Revolution 2.0*, Wael Ghonim makes extraordinary claims about the liberating capacities of digital technologies.[28] By contrast, Hossam El-Hamalawy has insisted in interviews that digital technologies are just one tool among many in the arsenal of the revolutionary, and that protesters exploited whatever tools they thought might work effectively. Both revolutionaries are making claims about the purpose of digital media, and use those claims to justify approaches to how those media can and should be used. These claims express media ideologies; they articulate sets of beliefs that people have about media in general, which are conveyed by media users as rationalizations and justifications of how they use media, and which discursively link media to group and personal identity (e.g. shabab al-Facebook), to aesthetics, to morality, and to epistemology.[29] But while describing and analyzing the media ideologies that organize social, economic, and political activities, and which are struggled over as symbolic capital, we need to be cautious about allowing these media ideologies to predefine our efforts to understand the roles of media in dramatic social change. Finally, we need to be skeptical about studies in which the role of digital media in particular is portrayed as liberatory, transformative, or even "new." We must also be cautious about imagining that direct use of digital communicative technologies to further the revolution was the only, or even the most significant, way through which experience of the revolution was mediated.

Mediated experience in a time of revolution

From an analytical viewpoint, a revolution involves a dramatic social change in which some aspects of the social order are overturned. But what constitutes a revolution from the experiential perspective of those engaged in it, living with it, and affected by it? Is it the distribution of pamphlets, or the micro-blogging of experiences as one dodges tear gas? Is it the crowds of sweating, tired bodies pressed into Tahrir Square, staring at giant television monitors, or scanning smartphones, or singing revolutionary songs, or waiting restlessly as others report, speculate, and gossip around them? Is it the televised reports, and announcements by state officials, and commentary by pundits in English and Arabic on Al Jazeera and state television? How do we know the revolution when we see it? And how do people know they are living through, and partaking in, a revolution?

Case studies are a well-attested method in social anthropology.[30] The examples used in this chapter are not meant to be representative but illustrative. Looking at particular cases of mediated social experiences during revolution can help us to understand changing social experience in a time of rapid political and technological change. What follows are three very different ethnographic narratives about media use and the ways it framed experiences of the revolution. Each of the narratives is rooted in field experiences and interactions with three Egyptians I met: Tamer, Gehan, and Bishoy. These particular narratives are based on mediated data (including emails and Facebook posts) and interactions that took place in 2011. The cases under consideration were selected in part serendipitously—they were cases on which I had enough information to put into a narrative—but they were also deliberately chosen for their distinctiveness. While all three are middle class and college educated, one is female and two are male, two are Cairene and one from outside Cairo, one supported the regime and two opposed it. In terms of age, they are each roughly a decade apart: Tamer in his late 20s, Gehan in her mid-30s, and Bishoy in his mid-40s. Bishoy is a travel agent and tourist guide whose livelihood is dependent on international visitors; Gehan is a college professor at a national university; and Tamer is a landlord managing a handful of small properties that his family owns in Cairo and Alexandria. Their different mediated experiences—using cell phones, computers, newspapers, television news, and face-to-face interactions in managing their lives and ascribing meaning to the events of the revolution—provide detailed examples to ground subsequent discussion of mediation, experience, and social change.

Gehan's revolution

Throughout late January and early February, when she was not traveling to and from her teaching position at the Women's College at Ain Shams University, Gehan would be at home in her house in Heliopolis, checking emails and flicking through Al Jazeera and state television channels. She believed that the stories Al Jazeera aired were false, yet many of the foreign friends she made in her decade as an English literature professor clearly believed its propaganda over the content on state television. They were unable to see what was obvious to Gehan: that Al Jazeera was a tool through which Qatar sought to destabilize Egypt. "Why should I believe gezeera and not national t.v.????" she wrote to her international friends via email.

Gehan's father was an army officer, and her grandfather had been a judge. She supported the regime in general, but was critical of its failures to address more of the economic woes that beset the poor—and it seemed as if there was more poverty every year. She was sympathetic to the young people who had started the protests, because the issues of food subsidies and the sinking economic conditions of workers were real problems, but she felt that the protests continued for far too long. She was not surprised when young people identified as protest leaders appeared on state television to explain that the faces in this crowd in Tahrir in early February were not the same as those who started it in late January. Gehan believed that what had begun as a student protest in solidarity with the poor had become infiltrated by the Muslim Brotherhood and by foreigners.

The protesters impacted her everyday life and work. Her mobile phone became a crucial tool in negotiating the complexities of daily life, at a time when roads might suddenly be closed, security cordons might stop vehicles, and one could never be sure whether shops would be open. Instead of sitting back and letting the driver take charge while she worked, as had been her practice, Gehan alerted him to changing street conditions utilizing a stream of text messages from friends and colleagues who were themselves in transit. Wherever she went—from neighborhood to university to shops—she encountered people who were vocal in their opinions for and against the protests and the government's reactions. At home there was little support for the revolution. "No good can come of this," said her mother, and this was also the consensus of her neighbors. They were shocked when Omar Suleiman announced the president's resignation on television, and deeply shaken by the sudden about-face on the part of the state newspaper *Al Ahram* when it unexpectedly embraced the revolution on February 12.

In time, though, Gehan adopted the newspaper's position: the eighteen days in Tahrir became the "real" Egyptian revolution, expressing the collective will of the people, against which subsequent protests could be dismissed as mere outbursts of disorder. In emails to friends, Gehan defended the army's use of force to clear Tahrir Square in April. She expressed outrage when she saw on state television that protesters were attacking the army, and viewed the reprisals as something the protesters had brought on themselves. When her international friends insisted on describing the event as a "massacre" of the Copts, she abruptly stopped communicating with them.

Tamer's revolution

Having watched the progression of the protests on television over several days, Tamer and two friends finally went to Tahrir Square on February 2, just in time to be caught in the "Battle of the Camels," when anti-Mubarak protesters were suddenly attacked by mounted *baltagiya*, or hired thugs. Returning home slightly injured—not by authorities attacking protesters, but from the crush of people trying to get away from attackers—he was reprimanded by his mother and sisters for risking his life. Tamer was the only adult male to head the family, so in his mother's eyes his responsibilities to manage the family's properties and arrange his sisters' marriages superseded any responsibilities to vague collectivities like "the people" or "the nation." Therefore, instead of returning to Tahrir Square with his friends, Tamer took on a leadership role in the neighborhood popular committee, which had taken on the job of securing the area in the absence of police. Some evenings, Tamer spoke about the events with his friends, many of whom had returned to Tahrir several times. He also followed events on Al Jazeera and Dream TV, and argued in favor of the uprising with neighbors who were following events on state television, which framed the uprisings as a dangerous disruption of Egyptian stability and security inspired by foreign agents. As he described it to me, watching television in his home was an active practice, with imprecations hurled at the screen, and arguments erupting over what political machinations lurked behind the state's media practices. Tamer also followed the tweets of some former American University in Cairo friends who were in the *midan* (Tahrir Square), and watched the video clips recommended to him. When the announcement of Mubarak's resignation was made, he took his sisters to join his many jubilant friends in their celebration in Tahrir Square.

Bishoy's revolution

Revolutionary action did not only take place online and in Tahrir Square. Hundreds of thousands of Egyptians participated in marches, protests, and demonstrations in Alexandria, Ismailia, Luxur, Aswan, and elsewhere. Bishoy was one of hundreds of Egyptians in Luxur whose livelihood was dependent on the tourist trade. Locals in the trade—Luxur's major industry—had for many years seen their enterprises becoming displaced by tourism developments generated by large corporations in Cairo believed to be linked to the Mubarak regime (and particularly his son Gamal). These corporations demolished people's homes and shops, constructed partition walls around tourist sites, and replaced locally-made souvenirs of carved alabaster with Chinese-made resin imports. Police cordons protected construction crews from the wrath of the locals who believed that all these actions were facilitated by Governor Sami Farag. Efforts to find legal remedies had been of no avail.

When Bishoy first learned of the occupation of Tahrir Square from his Facebook page, which he accessed daily from an Internet café as part of his tour business, he immediately called friends in Cairo using his mobile phone to learn more about what was happening. Over the first few days some of his friends reported being terrified, some exhilarated, and two were in Tahrir for twelve days joining in the protests. In Luxur itself, thousands of people and groups were watching and hearing about events taking place elsewhere, and they were responding to the new developments. Strikes were being called and protests organized. Bishoy joined in a march on the governor's palace in Luxur on January 31, demanding he step down.

The televised resignation of Hosni Mubarak was an event of ecstatic celebration, but within a few days unease set in. The governor of Luxur had not budged and there was no sign of normalcy being restored. Bishoy began to wonder whether the flow of tourists would be restored before his savings ran out. As his cash dwindled, his visits to the Internet café were cut back to once or twice a week, and he spent less time following and posting about politics, and more time trying to persuade his customers abroad that it was safe to return to Egypt.

Reflections

For all three of these Egyptians, the media deeply shaped the experience of the revolution but in different ways. For Gehan, state television was the source for an unfolding social drama that enveloped her life, and was reflected on in her interpersonal encounters, including those extended through digital media. Over time, the contradictions between mediated experiences of the revolution as she understood it, and as it was differently understood by international colleagues with whom she was digitally connected, became too great, so she cut herself off from those networks. For Tamer, the revolution was an exhilarating experience enhanced by digital media moderated primarily through a smartphone. This allowed him to track multiple streams of information and interact with networks of friends and acquaintances who were involved in the revolution in different ways than he was, while shouldering the new responsibilities thrust upon him by the collapse of the security state. For Bishoy, images and texts from Tahrir Square hundreds of miles away helped link local protest activities not only to the protests in Cairo, but to those in Luxor, Ismailia, Suez, Alexandria, and in other sites throughout Egypt. In these constructions, Tahrir becomes a heterotopia, a juxtaposition "of the near and far, of the side-by-side, of the dispersed,"[31] a single place that was somehow simultaneously all places in rebellion against the corruption of the regime. Yet the specifics of the local—the economic and political realities in Luxur—shaped Bishoy's actual protest activities.

Media and experience

State television and Al Jazeera, email and Facebook, and cell phones and smartphones—these are a few of the communication technologies that operate as networks in the very diverse revolutionary experiences of Gehan, Tamer, and Bishoy. It is the continued and public presence of such technologies in people's narratives of the revolution that gives rise to common portrayals of the Egyptian uprisings as a new kind of revolution, a "Facebook revolution,"[32] a "Twitter revolution,"[33] or a "Revolution 2.0."[34] Yet the protests also involved the inhabiting of public space, violence, reprisal, and makeshift sodalities organizing everything from food distribution to medical care, to security and rubbish removal. One way to understand how these many different things collectively form the experience of revolution is that humans relate to themselves, to each other, and to events in the world through a process of mediation. Anything can operate as a medium (gestures, words, activities, bodies, technologies, spaces) by conveying meanings. But media do not convey messages neutrally; the meanings they convey are always partially framed by their physical properties, social uses, and aesthetic characters. Broadcast and digital media are, in this sense, but one significant form of a broader notion of mediation.[35]

Mediation makes it possible for people to experience events in ways that allow them to understand themselves as having a stake in those events. One of the extraordinary things about the Egyptian revolution is the number of people who lay claim to having been part of the revolution during the eighteen days that began with the National Police Day protests and culminated in the resignation of President Hosni Mubarak. It was not only protesters, but also civilians affected by work stoppages, the Morsi regime, the Supreme Council of the Armed Forces, Salafists who rejected the protests and sought to disrupt them, and even police injured while trying to force protesters from Tahrir Square.[36] Gehan now describes herself as having been part of the revolution. Tamer's sisters and mother also lay claim to being part of the revolution. Although none of them ever took part in a public protest, their experiences were similar to those of other women in domestic spaces.[37] Winegar rightly suggests that experiences of the revolution are shaped by class, gender, age, and the kinds of spaces one occupies; experience is also shaped by the kinds of media practices in which one engages. Media practices link the spaces one occupies with other spaces occupied by other people in ways that transform understandings of both sets of spaces. In a manner similar to Bishoy's experience, Abu-Lughod describes the media as playing a role in how young people in an upper-Egyptian village came to feel "themselves to be in a national space despite a history of marginalization" and so organized themselves to solve problems in their community, articulating their actions through a locally-inflected "language of social morality."[38] Indeed, tens of millions of Egyptians never participated in a public protest but experienced the revolution through some mix of exposure to state and independent mediated narratives of events, social media (and especially mobile telephony), face-to-face communication with protesters, and so forth. These mixings of personal experiences in the *midan*, face-to-face communication with protesters, consumption of state and independent mediated narratives of events, and discursive negotiation of the meaning of narratives about the uprisings and occupation are all common features of personal accounts that Cairenes give of their experiences of the eighteen days.

Perhaps it is useful to consider revolutionary participation in terms of a relatively small core of people whose lived experience is dominated by their commitment to these activities, and who are actively engaged in revolutionary activities, including the creation of revolutionary communications, articulation of goals, recruitment, and planning and management of protests. This core is encircled by a larger periphery of people who observe the protests through various types of media, discuss the protests with others, and deal with the disruptions of everyday life caused by the uprising; and a semi-periphery of those whose imaginations are captured by the protests, who may dabble in protest (or counter-protest) activities, but whose lived experience remains dominated by other social networks, responsibilities, and institutions. Such a conceptualization is only useful, however, if understood as heuristic; sharp distinctions cannot be drawn between these categories, and like all continua, they bleed together at the boundaries.

Because I was physically in the United States, my own experience of the revolution was almost entirely mediated through information and communication technologies. My wife and I kept a round-the-clock vigil on Al Jazeera, sleeping in shifts and working around jobs and childcare schedules, not wanting to miss anything. Our viewing was supplemented by a continuous flow of emails, Facebook posts, and tweets, posted by friends and colleagues from Egypt, and also those living elsewhere in the world (from London to Berkeley, and beyond). Our networks were, moreover, quite different. My informants tended to be former colleagues and students of both sexes, graduate and undergraduate, now in many walks of life, most of whom had some kind of participation in the Tahrir protests. My wife corresponded primarily with women, Egyptians as well as expatriates. My daughters, whose mediated social worlds involved more tweets than texts and emails, reported the thoughts and feelings of teens living in affluent suburbs—not quite old enough to defy their parents and head to Tahrir—trying to make sense of the rapid, frightening, and exhilarating changes taking place around them. My own blog, initially created at the behest of the publisher of my book on Egyptian globalization, quickly became devoted to observations and quick analytical takes derived from my situated position in this flow of information, and my knowledge of Egypt prior to the revolution. These posts produced further dialogues as Egyptians (and others) read them and commented on them, both online and off.

Analyzing such mediated experiences relies methodologically on a type of "anthropology at a distance,"[39] in which information derived from my technologically mediated experience of the revolution—television accounts, emails, Facebook posts, tweets, blog posts, and similar data—are mined for patterns or reconstituted into narratives like those recounted above. The term "anthropology at a distance" has been used in the past to refer to the study of cultural systems not through direct participation and observation but through analysis of literature, news media, films, music, and other types of expressive culture. Analysis of these stories is usually contextualized by interviews with travelers, migrants, or refugees from the place in question, or (as in my case) by the experience of extensive prior fieldwork. While always subject to criticism within anthropology (even by its practitioners), this approach served anthropologists working in periods like World War II, when most international field sites were closed off, and in the contemporary global world system where ethnography is difficult or impossible, such as Iraq and Afghanistan, or when events are temporally displaced from direct ethnographic participation.[40]

Contemporary digital information and communication technologies allow transformations of "anthropology at a distance" in several ways. First, the temporal immediacy of electronic communication "has made the pursuit of fieldwork in new contexts of time-space (or here, simply a return of an intimate version of 'anthropology at a distance') possible."[41] Second, data can be derived not only from the polished products of the culture industry, but from individuals communicating in real time about events they are viewing, hearing, and taking part in. Third, digital technologies improve the possibilities for dialogical ethnography, in which observations and analyses are shared with members of the community being studied, and their observations, comments, critiques, and corrections significantly shape the final project. My narratives were shared with the three Egyptians whose stories I told above; one of them (Tamer) offered extensive comments, many of which were incorporated into the final narrative. Finally, digital technologies open the possibility of diachronic study—of observing changing accounts as people not only recount events and experiences, but assign them meanings and weave them into a larger cultural narrative. Thus, while dialogical assistance from the originators of the material I collected was sought whenever possible, it is important to keep current reflections of the revolution separate from archived data about the revolution from earlier points in order to describe changing meanings and analyze the contingency of both events and the meanings assigned to them.

One other point is particularly salient. While I was not present during the Tahrir Square protests and make no claims of being a participant in the revolution, some aspects of my wider, mediated participation in the Egyptian revolution are not so different from that of many Egyptians who also experienced it partly, or even largely, through electronic and social mediation. The vast majority of Egyptians were not present in Tahrir Square, and while they experienced the revolution in the form of disruptions of everyday routines, and in face-to-face discourse about events and their meanings with other Egyptians, they also experienced it through television, radio, newspapers, cell phones, and the Internet.

Mediation/mediatization

For all Egyptians, then, participation in the revolution was at least in part a mediated experience involving a variety of institutions, technologies, messages, and contexts in which the media are a central agent. The concept of mediation is intended to draw attention to the ways in which media contents and technologies shape, and are shaped by, the social relations in which they are embedded. A theory of mediation in media and communication studies is rooted in two claims: "first, the media mediate, entering into and shaping the mundane but ubiquitous relations among individuals and between individuals and society; and second, as a result, the media mediate, for better or for worse, more than ever before."[42]

I will reserve the term mediation for the first of these processes, which looks at how tools of communication are used in every aspect of human life, from the intimacies of family relationships to the collective complexities of political revolution. Understanding mediation requires us to examine the micro-processes through which people are, or believe they are, connected through mediating technologies to events, issues, and social formations that allow them to feel part of a wider, imagined public sphere (a movement, a generation, a nation). These engagements—and disengagements—are shaped partly by media affordances, but even more by the media ideologies that inform people's media practices and are entangled with broadly shared values about communication, identity, and nation, among others.

Mediation in this sense involves social actors evaluating, using, and producing a range of media and communications within their complexly media-saturated lives. People engaged in protest activities (core actors) produce continual streams of communications across myriad platforms about what they are doing and what is happening to them, as do state and non-state media professionals. These systems interpenetrate one another: professional media reframe and remediate activist media, incorporating them into their own productions; and activists remediate and reframe material from television, newspapers, and websites, incorporating them into their own communications. Peripheral actors consume these communications, but they also become interactive participants in the flow of communication by remediating communications, incorporating them into their face-to-face interpersonal interactions and their everyday practices. Peripheral, semi-peripheral, and even core actors come to understand their participation in the revolution through the entanglement of media practices and the practices of everyday life.

One way to think about the uniqueness of individual experience within the revolutionary context is through the concept of assemblages, heterogeneous elements or objects, ranging from physical objects and events to signs and utterances that enter into relations with one another within some context.[43] Lacking organization, an assemblage can include any number of disparate elements. Individuals experience the revolution as assemblages of technologies, bodily sensations, activities, texts, and social interactions within the context of their own unfolding social lives. Bishoy, Gehan, and Tamer experienced the revolution in very different ways as they engaged with different technologies, understood media messages through locally inflected interpretive frames, and interacted with others.

Conceived as an assemblage, each person's individual trajectory through time and the spaces of recent events in Egypt is unique, yet all of them are partially shared. These sharings can be conceived as actor networks, in Latour's sense.[44] There are no groups, Latour argues, only group formations, including formations of networks of people connected by common experiences, utterances, technologies, practices, and interactions. An actor network consists of and links together technical elements, such as Gehan's television, computer, and cell phones, but also her knowledge and experience of these technologies and the social networks through which her knowledge and experience are mediated. Gehan's networks link her with various degrees of intensity to those millions watching state television in simultaneity with her, but also the networks of women of similar background in spatial proximity, kin networks, social networks of students, and fellow college professors in the workspace (possibly supplemented by an overlapping network of colleagues connected by email), the production of state television in Egypt and of Al Jazeera in Qatar, and a much smaller electronic network of international academic colleagues. The term "experience" is not intended to be passive, but active. In laying claim to being part of the revolution, Gehan, Tamar, Bishoy, and other Egyptians used different forms of media to participate as citizens in the ongoing political change by passing moral judgment on activities and creating sites where citizens can exchange views on issues involving the common good, whether in the home, the classroom, a taxi, in the streets, through email, correspondence on micro-blogging platforms like Twitter, and social media spaces like Facebook.

Dramas, fields, and media

It remains necessary to theorize the relationship between mediated experiences and the unfolding historical process of political and social change. Many media scholars increasingly use the term "mediatization" to describe processes whereby social systems and media systems are implicated in mutual processes of change. Here the question is whether, and how, the increasing incorporation of media technologies into systems of kinship, economy, politics, and social organization is transforming those systems and thus society in general.[45]

Many people have connected Egypt's changing media landscape causally to the revolution, asserting that the emergence of new media allowed people to bypass the state monopoly on electronic media, forming mass movements, generating protest networks, and organizing revolutionary activity. There are many problems with positing the Egyptian uprisings as a digital revolution, not the least of which is that digital media were hardly ubiquitous. Only about 30 per cent of Egyptians had Internet access at the time of the revolution, and the rapid rise to nearly 40 per cent by mid-2012 seems to confirm that rising Internet access is as much a product of the revolution as it is a cause.[46]

A related approach shifts attention from technologies to technology users,[47] and to attend to the roles that technologically sophisticated activists play in mobilizing popular uprising. This approach is often linked with the broader social movements approach.[48] While some formations of media practice and social movement clearly make an effort to attend to the specific ways in which technologies mediate experience and shape participation, for the most part the lived experiences of peripheral and semi-peripheral participants get lost in the focus on core revolutionaries and their media practices.

Yet another prominent approach to understanding revolutions posits social networks of individuals who make rational cost-benefit calculations in such a way that they can gain more by joining revolutionary activities than they risk by participating. Mediation is invoked by suggesting that social media networks "can trigger informational cascades through the effects of their interaction with independent media outlets and on-the-ground organizers."[49] In turn, these informational cascades "can make it difficult for regimes to maintain their control of information hegemony" and can stimulate collective action "by lowering the 'revolutionary thresholds' of individuals embedded in social networks."[50] While there is certainly some evidence that this approach can work at a small scale—even partisan revolutionaries know that participation in protests increases as perceptions of the likelihood of reprisals decrease—such an approach does not help us understand the assemblages and networks that comprise the experiences of Egyptians like Gehan, Tamer, and Bishoy, and tens of millions of others in the periphery and semi-periphery of revolutionary action.

An approach that allows us to incorporate mediated experience into a larger revolutionary process involves understanding the revolution as a political conflict unfolding across a series of overlapping political and social fields. Fields refers to organized but heterogeneous zones of action in which unequally positioned social agents compete and cooperate over public stakes. The most significant of the stakes over which groups struggle may be the definition of the field itself—what constitutes "the revolution," for example, and thus who is and who is not a legitimate revolutionary.[51] Such fields have "many dimensions, with parts that may be loosely integrated, or virtually independent from each other."[52]

Although the term "field" has been primarily associated with the work of Pierre Bourdieu, who emphasized the field as a site of social reproduction, the concept originated earlier and has recently been undergoing a renaissance. A field is a place in which social actors compete for various forms of social, cultural, and economic outcomes, often drawing on their lifelong socialization into a particular cultural milieu (itself comprised of overlapping social fields). Central to Bourdieu's approach to social fields is the concept of habitus, the product of long years of "reading" our social milieu with our minds and bodies.[53] In this sense, fields are useful ways to see how everyday life plays out as people compete for various social goals, freely and creatively, but within the constraints of objective social relations and the cultural definitions of goals at play.

Bourdieu argued that most political action involves struggles within the field, between an authorized orthodoxy, ideologies expressed and sustained by various actors, institutions, and agencies usually associated with the state, and one or more heterodoxies, alternative ideological positions expressed and sustained by alternative sets of actors, institutions, and agencies.[54] Political practices consist of actors freely and even creatively struggling with one another over political stakes within the field, but within the structural constraints imposed by their habitus and by boundaries and constraints of the field itself. At times, crises may emerge, but they are rarely sustained because they fail to challenge the doxa, the tacit assumptions shared by all actors and which, in fact, sustain the field. For a true crisis, the doxa itself must be objectified, challenged, and possibly even overthrown, redefining the social and political field itself. Such an extended crisis is a revolution. Revolution "involves a rapid, basic transformation of a society's political structures," which includes "an effort to transform not just the political institutions but also the justifications for political authority in society, thus reforming the ideas/values that underpin political legitimacy."[55]

Revolutions are interesting in part because they constitute a breakdown of normalcy, introducing situations in which quotidian social practices, including mediated social practices, cease to be effective. At such times, the political field can be seen as constituted not by practices but by "purposive, goal-directed group action" in which conflict, coalition, and collaboration all play parts.[56] This happens because the doxa itself becomes challenged, and the field becomes a site of what Turner refers to as antistructure. The protests shifted the normative space of everyday life under the Mubarak regime into this kind of field, an interstitial cultural domain in which alternative paradigms for social interaction, values, and symbolic representations are formulated, shared, and come into conflict with existing social and symbolic structures. When social fields become sites of anti-structure, alternative forms of structure and symbolism emerge that derive from and reconstruct the social structure of the cultural mainstream. For example, in anti-structure the gender and sectarian distinctions present in mainstream society may be dramatically exacerbated, or they may be dramatically minimalized, as participants reported happening in Tahrir Square during the eighteen days. Anti-structure opens up enormous possibilities for creativity and the imagining of alternative possibilities, particularly for those who saw Tahrir as a model for the egalitarian, populist Egypt they hoped to create in the aftermath of Mubarak's ouster. Within the larger field, multiple public areas of contestation may arise. Turner called these "arenas,"[57] bounded sites of struggle between groups promoting different goals and outcomes.

Turner's model of political process assumes that these periods of anti-structure cannot last. While they do, however, such situations have enormous transformative possibilities. Indeed, it is that sense of possibility that clearly drove the unprecedented popular struggles that continued in Egypt long after the resignation of the dictator, elections, trials of regime leaders, and other elements that were ushered in when the uprising took place. In the social dramas Turner studied, anti-structure either gave way to a restoration of the pre-existing social order or led to schism, to permanent separation of peoples. This latter possibility is extremely problematic in contemporary nation states, leading to the question of whether other outcomes are possible.

One possible alternative outcome is transformation of the field itself, indicating fundamental social, political, and cultural changes without necessarily ending contestation. Fields are intended to be seen as diachronic rather than static concepts, and indeed the unfolding Egyptian revolution as it moved through parliamentary elections, constitutional revisions, presidential elections, the military ouster of a president, and more elections, all inflected by continual protests and increasingly violent acts of resistance, can be seen as a series of shifting fields, each marked by shifts in the goals at stake, the strategies at play, and the symbolic configurations through which actors seek publicly to rationalize and justify their actions. Emily Crane, who has taken a number of detailed life histories of people's experiences of the revolution, suggests that Egyptians of many different walks of life tend to divide the revolution into seven periods in their narratives, which might be conceived of as fields: first, the eighteen days in Tahrir Square; second, a period of fragmentation in which groups that were unified in Tahrir became separate players struggling for a place in an authority vacuum; third, the period of parliamentary and presidential elections; fourth, the presidency of Mohammed Morsi; fifth, the period of rebellion against President Morsi, culminating in the military coup; sixth, the massacre at Rabaa and the conversion of the Muslim Brotherhood into a militant opposition; and finally, seventh, the return to military rule, culminating in the presidency of Abdel-Fatah El-Sisi.[58] One of the elements that changes across these seven fields is the media ecology. In the aftermath of the uprisings, media's roles in the new Egypt altered again and again. For example, several efforts were made to recapture the "spirit of Tahrir" through social media websites, most of which foundered from lack of participation. Other experiments sought to link social media to civil society, such as the "Tweetnadwa."[59] Social media have continued to be an effective site for disseminating criticism of the government and communicating with mainstream media. It is also a site where particular forms of critique can be "tried out"—an immensely popular series of web videos launched a successful television career for political humorist Bassem Youssef, while others, like the political humor series by actress Mona Hala, failed to gain traction. Lampooning the media and the state through each change in the revolutionary field, Youssef found his program canceled after the election of President El-Sisi and left Egypt to escape a court verdict which required him to pay millions of pounds in damages.

Also, the distinction between the "old" state-controlled media and the new popular digital media has become difficult to maintain since the Tahrir uprising. Even during the Mubarak regime, security forces used technology provided by international contractors, such as the Boeing subsidiary Narus, to monitor and record Internet traffic, including email, online chats, text messages, and even website visits.[60] This surveillance technology remains in the hands of the military, security forces, and the new government, and continues to be used to monitor, detain, and arrest prominent social media dissidents. Simultaneously, social media also became less dominated by protesters as mainstream institutions and political leaders created Facebook pages, Twitter accounts, and websites as ways to reach out to their own publics and to independent media at home and abroad.[61] The revolutionary power of digital media in Egypt was generated by its liminality; as it becomes institutionalized within the Egyptian media ecology, it increasingly becomes more controllable and controlled by the state.[62] And with the Egyptian information and communications technology sector having increased from 3.4 per cent of GDP in 2008 to 4.2 per cent in 2012 (growing at twice the rate of GDP), the state is increasingly interested not only in its content but also in managing its infrastructure and making it a tool for encouraging international investment.

The role of new media in Egypt's media ecology continued to shift among non-state users as well. New applications emerged that sought to address significant social problems, such as sexual harassment.[63] Moreover, "freedom technologists" trying to protest military rule have sought to find ways to extend their activities to the Egyptian majorities that are not connected to the Internet—many of whom are illiterate—by "taking the digital materials back to the street" through graffiti, street performances, and music.[64] These include such projects as Askar Kadhibun (Lying Generals), La lil-Muhakamat al-Askariyya lil-Madaniyyin (Stop Military Trials for Civilians), and Salafiyya Kosta (Salafists of Costa Coffee), and others, many of which transform themselves flexibly and quickly in response to changing conditions online or on the street.[65]

Conclusion

The experience of collective events is necessarily mediated; it is experienced through media technologies whose form and content both shape and are shaped by the events they represent. Mediated experiences are at once experiences refracted through communication technologies and shaped by interpersonal activities and also interactions through which mediated experiences are affirmed, contested, and interpreted. These mediated experiences are both collective, in that people are connected by media uses and practices, and by common activities and spaces, and yet they are also deeply personal and individualized, in that specific sets of technologies, interpersonal relationships, and embodied practices that comprise one person's unfolding experience will be different from another's. I argue that these two dimensions could be theorized using the concepts of network and assemblage.

When Egyptians look back at the events that began to unfold in January 2011, they usually describe a series of events with a unified character. The eighteen-day movement in Tahrir Square, for example, is conceived as a unified body of protesters challenging the ruling regime. Examined empirically, however, such a perception is revealed as a construction, a story collectively composed through myriad media by excluding the contingent moments that existed during the protest process itself. I have argued that we can understand the relationship between mediated experiences of events and agent-driven uses of media technologies—especially digital media—in constructing collective narrative accounts of these events by turning to processual analyses of the sort called "social drama" or "field theory." Field theory allows us to see the revolution as a series of struggles over the symbolic meaning of revolutionary activities, in which media practices play a crucial part. What is ultimately at stake is the definition of the symbolic configurations that define the structure of the field itself, and the contours of the media ecologies through which these struggles take place.

Finally, I have argued that part of what is at stake in these fields are media ideologies: beliefs that people hold about media, and about what media can do, and how media operate in everyday life. I have suggested that these media ideologies often slip from description of the social fields to shape the presumptions of media analysis, and that we must be on guard against this.

5

WOMEN'S DIGITAL ACTIVISM

MAKING CHANGE IN THE MIDDLE EAST

Annabelle Sreberny

The Arab spring of 2017 is profoundly different from that of the Arab spring of 2011. The latter embodied and diffused a considerable sense of hope. The central tropes were of peoples mobilized in many different locations and the imminent end to the authoritarianism that had plagued the region for decades and produced skewed or limited economic development. Countless questions had been posed and books written about the incompatibility of Islam and democracy and whether the region could ever become democratic. And then, as political mobilization seemed to spread from Tunisia to Egypt and elsewhere in the region, challenging long-extant forms of masculine authoritarianism, the multibillion dollar economy of Middle East experts, academics, pundits, and media mavens was completely taken by surprise.

By 2017, instead of basking in the socio-economic benefits of democratization and development, the region has fallen into chaos. It boasts at least four failed or failing states (Syria, Iraq, Libya, and Yemen). War, violence, and the emergence of the caliphate of ISIL/Daesh have together precipitated the biggest population movement for years, with huge refugee camps in Turkey and Lebanon and a European refugee crisis that mirrors that of the Second World War. Egypt seems to be returning to pre-democratic ways. The Turkish-Kurdish accommodation has broken down. Palestinians still do not have a state. Yemen is one of four countries in the Middle East and Africa on the verge of calamitous famine.

All of this has gendered dimensions, insofar as war, resettlement, and impoverishment are experienced differentially by men and women; and as usual, women's experiences are often overlooked. A focus on women's digital activities is one way of exploring unheard voices, weakly articulated issues, and new political realities. As the region descends into chaos, the more considered and mature voices of women need to be heard. This chapter explores how many are trying to do just that.

The Arab uprisings of 2010–11 changed the political landscape in the Middle East. Finally, change seemed thinkable and possible. That history does not come with guarantees is evident, but that is not the point here. Western media pundits, not known for nuance or even local knowledge, immediately pronounced these dynamics as a "Facebook revolution" (albeit developed in regard to Iran's Green Movement) and "Twitter revolution." Such synecdoche for complex political and social dynamics found a home in global public discourse, even as they have been criticized for both overstating and obfuscating the role of social media in change. Such hyped constructions function as zombie categories, explaining little about either new media or political process. Of course Twitter was used within the so-called "Arab Spring" movements of 2010–11. Its use has risen considerably in Saudi Arabia where, as elsewhere in the region, a sizeable proportion of the population is under age 35 and accesses the Internet via mobile phone, making it one of the world's top markets for time spent on the Internet. Clearly, digital connectivity and social media can be powerful tools for change, but that is not the same thing as triggering or producing that change.

Of course, citizen movements and political struggles for democracy and rights in the region did not begin with the Arab Spring, and neither did women's political activity. Online politics and embodied social movements are not ontologically different activities, but rather different modes of being political. Yet it is reasonable to suggest that access to the Internet, the development of social media platforms in English and Arabic, and the growing popular awareness of change have produced a more conducive environment for women's political activities and thus for a general enlargement of what counts as the "sphere of the political." Until now, the treatment of information and communications technology (ICT) expansion and use in the MENA region has often obscured the gender dimension, and more specifically how the new environment is affecting women.

In this chapter, I explore the intricate and evolving relationship between new media practices, gender roles, and political processes, as well as the possibilities and limits of the new online environment for women in a region that is increasingly embracing the Internet and immersing itself in the digital experience. My concern is not to reflect again on whether women are better or worse off in the much-altered and fast-changing Middle East. Nor do I wish to challenge the manner in which the region vividly manifests the stand-off between Shirky's uber-optimism—"here comes everybody"—and Morozov's uber-pessimism—"be frightened of strong states"—about the possibilities of online activism in producing change.[1] I consider this a false polarity since the region—and other locales—manifest the simultaneous existence of both practices, and much contemporary contestation is enacted in that competition of powers. Dissident online activity by women and others is increasingly monitored and blocked by the regional authoritarian states, which have woken up to these novel forms of disembodied resistance that require new forms of policing. In 2010–11, the states of the region understood and could control physical demonstrations more effectively than the more invisible online organizing. But they are learning these lessons fast, now detaining and imprisoning bloggers and journalists. The 1,000 lashes meted down on the blogger Raif Badawi in Saudi Arabia became an Amnesty International case; while, as of yet, the national and "halal" Internets invoked by Egyptian and Iranian authorities have not emerged. Despite the difficulties, the people of the region are making their presence felt like never before, in physical demonstrations of "somatic solidarity" as well as using the full range of new media techniques available for Internet political activism.[2]

This chapter tries to reconceive the question of Middle Eastern women in the age of the Internet. If anything, the study of women's issues in an altered online environment affords the opportunity to theorize such issues beyond the traditional categories of female empowerment and gender equality. If the question of women's digital activism is of renewed interest, it is because it prompts us to reflect on the ways and the extent to which the new online environment has helped turn social issues that have been relegated to a rather narrow gender register into much broader political issues; and in so doing, it has extended their significance and their potential for serious change in the region.

Gender analysis helps us to think about three big questions: the nature of "gendered identity" and its interconnections with other social identities; societal constructions of the private and the public; and the relationship between women and the nation-state, which hinges on broader issues of equality and power. I address each of these topics briefly.

First, a gendered lens is not just about women, although women are typically omitted from many official accounts, academic analyses, and development plans about the region, both as objects of the process and as possible participants within it. A gendered lens asks broader questions about the nature of social definitions and practices around masculinities and femininities, and the ways in which sexualities are defined, enacted, and socially constrained. It asks about gender norms, ideologies, and discourses about gender roles and relations. If standpoint theory helped the articulation of specific identity-formations in different societies, the theorization around "intersectionality," as proposed by Kimberly Crenshaw and Nira Yuval-Davis—the mutual co-constitution of different categories of social differentiation—suggests that we inhabit a range of subject positions dependent upon the issues at hand and the discursive formation through which events are being defined.[3] Thus "women" as a category intersects with and is internally differentiated by class, race, and ethnicity as well as other minoritarian positions. But we must also resist simply employing and imposing social categories derived from other contexts onto the actors in the region. It is precisely the kinds of identifications that local actors make and how various groups consider that their struggles intersect with those of others that needs to be analyzed, without presumptions as to what we may find. What kinds of "intersectionalities" happen remains to be uncovered.

Secondly, the nature of the boundary, indeed the distinction, between the public and the private is socially constructed and differs from place to place. Cynthia Enloe has argued that feminist-informed gender analysis actually provides the bigger picture, since it includes the analysis not only of macro-power relations, but also the micro-politics of power, hierarchies, and inequalities: the complex situations in which "power operates in ways that sustain unjust and unequal micro and macro regimes."[4] Feminism reminds us that it is not only the state that wields power, especially across the region, but it is also the habitus of patriarchy and the men and women who sustain it, often the relatives and intimates who help to structure women's lives. It is in this sense also that an emergent feminist political economy can open up new veins of analysis that have been occluded or ignored, since "the violation of rights, poverty, and exploitation is not random, but embedded in structural inequalities" that include gender.[5]

All societies make a distinction between public and private matters, but these are made in different ways. The media have always been social boundary-bending, revealing once inaccessible areas of social life to all, while new media provide the possibility of pushing this even further.[6] In addition, access to digital platforms and social media provide new spaces for the "making public" of issues and the articulation of concerns, for the development of voice and capabilities, and for the forging of new solidarities.[7] Some of the debate and the activities might be raw, so that the globalizing digital environment does not mean a rational discursive public sphere but a raucous space of interaction and contestation, an arena of contention. Hence, while this chapter focuses on women's activities in the Middle East, these are not all that different from the struggles being engaged by women in other parts of the world, including in the Americas and Europe.[8]

The third big issue at work in a focus on women's digital activities in the region is the relationship between women and the nation-state or, even more broadly, the relationship between national politics and power. The regimes of the region have been buffeted by unexpected forces for change. Often, their response has been to suppress and curtail emergent demands for greater freedoms, participation, and democratic processes. That has been accomplished through various means. State-sponsored propaganda often paints any opposition as anti-nationalist, in league with foreign governments. There has been considerable surveillance and control of online activities, so that journalists, editors, and bloggers have been arrested in Iran, Egypt, and Saudi Arabia. And pro-government forces, for example in Syria and Bahrain, have sown confusion by using social media—especially Twitter—to baffle publics. Historically, there have been plenty of state-sponsored mobilizations of women; Farah Pahlavi's activities in Iran or Suzanne Mubarak's National Union for Women in Egypt are two examples that come to mind. There has also been strong resistance to women's movements for rights and equality, often by using the argument that such dynamics are originally Western and external to the region in order to suppress nascent activity. In addition to state surveillance and suppression, women's public activities often face a negative response by social institutions and practices supportive of patriarchal cultures and by direct monitoring by family members, especially menfolk. These are not easy environments in which to press for change.

In 2011, it did appear that the political opportunity structures of the region were opening up and that new media might be particularly significant in social mobilization. In this chapter, I look with a degree of empirically-informed realism at the diffusion of a set of new communication technologies in the region and how these are being adopted by women in particular to make change. One of the challenges of studying the Middle East as a region is to avoid false binaries. This implies avoiding accounts based on models of Western development that overemphasize regional deficiencies of one kind or another. But it also means avoiding accounts based on some odd notion of Middle Eastern exceptionalism. This means that it would be a mistake to start by defining a social "object" found in the West, such as "women's social movements," and then to hunt for this in the Middle East. I adopt a more grounded approach to examine how women are using the Internet, what they are discussing, and what they think, building up a detailed analysis out of the different practices in very different contexts.

Digital communication in the MENA

Some of the original theorizing about the role of the media in the process of development was triggered by Western analysts' understandings of the Middle East. Daniel Lerner's now infamous book, *The Passing of Traditional Society: Modernizing the Middle East*, published in 1958, suggested that media were mobilizers of modernity. While not wrong in itself, the argument was so wrapped up in a single teleology of Western modernity that it was roundly and properly criticized. Yet contemporary globalized discourses about the "digital" often manifest a similar teleological outlook and a digital technological determinism. This is not the place to dispute such arguments, but simply to make the point that it is evident that a "digital divide" remains a powerful reality in this region, with considerable disparities regarding access between and within countries, with rural dwellers and women among the worst connected and weakest users. Even the Global Information Technology Report recognizes that "the 2015 results, which cover 143 economies, confirm the dominance of advanced economies and the persistence of the multiple-faceted digital divides not only across but also within economies. They reveal the pervasive digital poverty that deprives the neediest from the opportunities offered by ICTs."[9]

The region manifests considerable uneven development. It includes some of the (oil-)richest and some of the poorest states in the world. In aggregate data, MENA scores the lowest of all regions in economic participation and political empowerment, and the second lowest for educational attainment.

Regarding gender equality, one of the many sad ironies of the so-called "Arab Springs" is that the gender gap in the region was actually higher after 2011 than before. Of the sixteen MENA countries, Kuwait is the highest ranked at a poor 113 out of 142 countries. Women in Iran have enjoyed the vote for decades, while in other countries no one votes. The Egyptian blogger Aliaa al Mahdy posted a naked photograph of herself on Facebook, while in Saudi Arabia women still operate under a strict guardianship system that restricts their freedom.[10]

In regard to the Internet, the 2014 Arab Social Media Report makes the point that Internet use is relatively recent in the eight countries that were surveyed.[11] Over one-third of adults in Qatar had signed up for access only in the previous year, and Internet use is still nascent in Jordan and Egypt. It is evident that the spread of mobile telephony is improving people's access to the net. This is especially marked in Bahrain, Lebanon, Libya, and Oman, where 11 per cent of the population accesses the Internet via mobiles, while the figures are 18 per cent for Saudis and 19 per cent for Kuwaitis. At the other end, less than 3 per cent access the Internet by mobile phone in Algeria, Egypt, Morocco, Palestine, Tunisia, and Yemen.[12] Many people have limited access, or do not understand what to do when they have access, and encounter considerable issues of language, of technological and information literacy, and of security, privacy, and trust.

Unfortunately, recent regional reports on trends in the Arab online environment and social media pay little or no attention to gender, so that it remains extremely difficult to gain any kind of statistical picture of women's online usage and activities.[13] The 2013 Media Use in the Middle East study, conducted in eight Arab countries, did produce a table with age and gender breakdowns which suggested that the highest levels of Internet usage by women were: UAE 88 per cent; Qatar 80 per cent; KSA 79 per cent; Bahrain 78 per cent; while the lowest were in Jordan at 37 per cent and Egypt at 15 per cent.[14] Such statistics, however, tell us little about what kinds of women are online, nor about their usage. The 2014 *Arab World Online* points out that "social media in the Arab world is dominated by young men under age 30, with only 1 in 3 social media users in the region being a woman."[15] The Arab World exceeds our focus on MENA, with the MBRSG/Bayt report covering twenty-two Arab countries, including Somalia and the Comoros. Other international measures such as the World Economic Forum's 2016 analysis of the "gender gap" suggest that the region ranks the lowest in terms of reducing the gaps between men and women across a number of economic and political indicators, with its gender gap at 40 per cent (noting that the highest ranking region, Western Europe, still had a gender gap of 25 per cent).[16] As is evident here, the picture is rather confusing and poorly-researched. As such, I make no claim that the kinds of activities reported in this paper are popular or widespread; we simply don't know that. But they do indicate a radical shift of focus toward the Internet by women, a major change in and of itself and a potential harbinger of more to come.

It is also important to ask why the analysis of women's digital activities is important and of relevance not only to the region, but also to wider debates. Globally, there is widespread physical violence toward women, with media debates making it a significant domestic issue in the US, the UK, India, and elsewhere. In 2014, a global summit was held in London to end rape and other forms of conflict-related sexual violence, and a new research center was established at the London School of Economics to focus on women, peace, and security. There is ongoing misogyny and lack of gender equality everywhere. Thus, the MENA region is most interesting not as an example of any kind of exceptionalism, but rather as a vivid scene of the range of difficulties and struggles with which women are currently involved, and the possibilities and limitations of the online environment.

A plethora of women's digital activity

It is fitting here to offer some clarifications. There is clearly political activity that is not digital, although the development of political parties, the dynamics of elections, the organization of civil society, and other phenomena that might be used as formal indices of political development are only weakly evident across the region. And there is political activity that is not gendered in focus, although women are active participants. Many women were and became active in the broad-based social mobilizations of 2010–11, and they and others have been active since. Some blogged, some took photographs, some graffitied walls, and some tweeted. There was no obvious predominant use of one social media platform or form of digital engagement over another. Web pages and websites, Twitter, Facebook, and YouTube were used singly and collectively, as the local practices and preferences combined. There are Iraqi Kurdish Facebook activists and Saudi bloggers. It is interesting that Saudi men and women are the greatest users of YouTube in the region.[17] What does seem clear is that the mobile phone diffusion in the region is giving many more women access to the Internet and the possibilities of all kinds of communication beyond the control of both parents and male relatives, including husbands.

My focus here is on women's digital activity that has specific gendered, feminist aims. Even at an anecdotal level, it is evident that there is a plethora of digital activity by women across the region. Much of women's online activity still has a national origin and focus, with considerable activity in and particular to Egypt, Iran, and Tunisia. Much is conducted in regional languages such as Persian, Turkish, and the various dialects of Arabic. A great deal of material is publicized in English and French, and many sites provide links to other campaigns and events happening elsewhere, addressing transnational feminist sympathies. And it is evident that some of these activities are conducted and aided by what can be broadly termed Middle East diasporas based in Europe, the US, and elsewhere. Online activity seems to be indigenous and locally-driven, although funding from various international and non-local NGOs does support activities around gender empowerment and equality. The Internet makes boundaries porous, blurring the inside and outside, the indigenous and the exogenous, and favoring the emergence of transnational interconnections among the region's women, which are worthy of further detailed analysis. The possibilities of the Internet have pushed further the spatial turn in media studies and the critique of "methodological nationalism."[18] Rather than appropriating a Habermasian notion of a singular "public sphere," it is perhaps more useful to think of online communication in this context as offering a transnational public space, an arena of contestation, in which people are building diverse communicative networks with multiple nodes of linkage.

During the 2011 uprisings, many men became well-known names around the world. But there were many courageous and outspoken women also. Indeed, the online environment can amplify individual voices and these can make a difference. These are spontaneous political celebrities for particular periods of time, and their voice, their courage, and their leadership can provide role models for others to follow. There were and are many individual women activists involved in the Arab uprisings.

Blogging as a space of individualized writing has been popular across the region, with Iranian and Saudi women bloggers exploring a wide range of issues and finding a written voice where opportunities for oral expression and physical participation have not been so accessible.[19] The online environment can amplify the voices of individual women, and these can make a difference. In Egypt, Arab nationalist modernity often embodies the nation in the figure of the woman. State discourses around violence against women during the uprising suggested that the culprits were simply young misogynist thugs; yet women activists turned this around to point a finger at the security state itself. This provided a fascinating example of how the discourses of national identity are reappropriated by women and turned against the security state. As Amar comments:

> when women professors, medical doctors, lawyers, university students and syndicate leaders began to command the barricades at major political protests, it became difficult for the state to draw upon class and geopolitical phobias to portray them as terrorists; and the thugification tactic or *baltagi*-effect unravelled. Granted, the international media, and even many Egyptian reporters, could easily believe that crazed thugs could emerge 'naturally' from within a group of working-class male leftists and Islamists. However, when middleclass Egyptian women were harassed, terrorized and brutalized by men during protests, this allowed for a disarticulation of the body politic of the protestors from that of the brutalizers, enabling a recognition that the *baltagiya* were cops in plain clothes, not men from within the dissident organizations.[20]

What is "political"?

Through such online activities, women are extending not only the content but also the nature of what is thought of as "political." These issues are not simply a function of the sudden availability of new technologies or the existence of a large youthful population under thirty years old (estimated at 70 per cent of total population), although these are both contextual realities. Rather, these issues speak to a fundamental problem with the definition of the "political." There exists a widespread perception—based on a crude distinction between repressive states and democratic ones—that the region is highly authoritarian, with little or no "politics" allowed, despite the adventures of the Arab uprisings. However, what is meant by the sphere of the "political" is always contentious and contingent. Even within liberal democracies, the demarcation between the "public" and "private" as the cornerstone of the limits of state intervention has been revealed by feminist and critical theory as a powerful and enduring myth. Thus while the "social" might be defined as the realm of sedimented social practices, not all of which are put into question at the same time, the realm of the "political" is both where agonistic debate about social practices takes place and where hegemony functions to frame and limit that debate and redefine the social at any one point in time. Chantal Mouffe expresses this clearly:

> The frontier between the social and the political is essentially unstable and requires constant displacements and negotiations between social agents. Things could

always be otherwise and therefore every order is predicated on the exclusion of other possibilities. It is in this sense that it can be called "political" since it is the expression of a particular structure of power relations. Power is constitutive of the social because the social could not exist without the power relations through which it is given shape.[21]

Mouffe has argued that there is no inherent distinction between the social and the political, but rather that a social issue becomes "political" when it is brought into public contestation. That is partly what women's online activity is doing.

The struggle over women's bodies

Women's bodies are the focus of the greatest social and cultural concern. Whether covered or not on the street, whether visible or not on television and film screens, female embodiment is trouble—and especially for women themselves. While organizations concerned about rape and violence against women have existed for some time, a renewed impetus for these concerns was triggered by the spate of attacks that Egyptian and other women experienced while demonstrating in Cairo's Tahrir Square and elsewhere. What came to be known as "Blue Bra Girl" refers to the savage beating of an abaya-clad female protester by Egyptian military forces, with graphic videos of the beating captured on phones and uploaded to YouTube and Facebook.[22] A cartoon image of the assaulted woman became an international meme and icon of the fight against repression and, using the hashtag #bluebra,[23] women took to the streets in one of the largest demonstrations by Egyptian women in a long time.[24] Egyptian women developed the HarassMap.org website to log acts of sexual harassment and assault in Egypt, and created a manifesto to support safe schools and universities.[25] There are similar activities in Lebanon, and numerous online stories of gender harassment from Saudi Arabia and Libya. Syrian women have been documenting sexualized violence in the various conflicts, noting attacks that use rape as a weapon of war, as well as women being sold into sexual slavery by ISIL.[26]

In Iran, a 2014 spate of acid attacks against women on the streets of Isfahan triggered large demonstrations, often mobilized through text messaging and reported through images carried on Twitter, Instagram, and opposition websites. More significantly, in terms of online activity, in May 2014 the My Stealthy Freedom campaign took off with a Facebook page[27] that has attracted thousands of Iranian women who have dared to take off their veil inside the

Islamic Republic and post photographs of themselves, despite the fact that such action is not allowed and that Facebook is banned. Some women are photographed from behind, but many photograph themselves with faces showing, clearly identifiable; some are individual images, while others are group photos. There are even some videos. Masih Alinejad, an Iranian journalist based in London who spearheaded the campaign, was awarded a UN Summit on Human Rights and Democracy award in 2015. She made a fiery speech defending the focus on veiling by explaining the state security effort required to maintain it:

> But when I hear why make a fuss over this piece of cloth, I say that this piece of cloth is a big issue too. This piece of cloth in the hands of those politicians who do not believe in freedom has become a chain around the necks of Iranian women and over the past 35 years has choked their vitality and energy. According to Ismail Ahmadi Moghaddam, Chief of Iran's national police, just last year the security forces issued warnings to 3.6 million women about their bad hijab. Eighteen thousand women were arrested and sent to the courts. Of course, the police don't keep statistics on how many women were kicked or punched or slapped because of their bad hijab.[28]

By spring 2017, the page had been "liked" by over one million people.

Online space is where Iranian women were able to draw attention to an unfolding domestic issue. While four men were arrested over the acid attacks, it is clear that some hardliners within the parliament consider such monitoring in support of good hijab commendable, and they would welcome a bill to protect vigilantes. Iranian President Hassan Rouhani has spoken out against the rise of militia groups imposing their own version of Islamic morality, arguing that "Iranian women are Muslim women of virtue who are all supporting hijab. So a few people in this country should not consider themselves the custodians of morality."[29]

In Saudi Arabia, one of the most prominent campaigns in recent years has been around allowing women to drive. There was a flurry of activity in 2007–8, to little effect, and the campaign erupted again in May 2011. Various women have posted videos of themselves driving; probably the best known is that by Manal al-Sharif in May 2011, which was part of a broader "Women2Drive" campaign. Her video went viral, picking up coverage around the world. She was named as one of the world's 100 most influential people in 2012 by *Time* magazine, and she also won the Vaclav Havel Prize for Creative Dissent. By the end of 2012, her Facebook page had some 18,000 followers, with almost 3,000 Twitter followers. There have been subsequent mass drive-ins, one in October 2013, but the Saudis refused to budge—though in 2017, the kingdom unexpectedly decided to lift the ban on women driving, a positive conjuncture of interests for women. One might speculate that such actions receive much more positive support from outside the region than from within, and are often better recognized as brave and creative by global feminist actors than by local women. Clearly, the cost at a distance of a "like" on Facebook is negligible in comparison to the difficulties and even dangers of embodied protest on the streets of the region.

Other foci of women's online activity follow more traditional political lines. They include promoting women's awareness of their legal rights, getting national ID cards, and participating in elections. Yet other forms of women's online activity tend to be more economic in orientation, raising funds to support female entrepreneurs, allowing women to market goods directly without costly middlemen, or providing information and support for women's economic empowerment. Women have been involved as newly-empowered citizens within the broader social movements directed at the contemporary state-formations that maintain neo-patriarchal policies and at existing legal and regulatory limitations. More specifically, women are challenging the regional state formations to recognize their—and minority—rights as political citizens, consumers, and emerging interest groups. While it remains to be seen whether the proliferation of new voices in the virtual sphere can be turned into material changes, the political milieu has certainly been altered.

Private matters become public affairs

Women are also asking questions about gender roles and sexual identities that challenge older patriarchal cultures, and the habitus and practices that limit not only women's but also men's sexuality. Women in particular are challenging prevailing social attitudes—often as sanctioned and manifest by state-run broadcasting media—and the existing, often policed, boundaries between the public and private. They are turning once "private" matters of domestic violence and sexuality into public and political ones. Women are breaking social taboos, raising new issues, and showing the enduring power of patriarchal values that lies before and behind state power.

Even in the ravages of the Syrian conflict, an active online feminist movement called Estayqazat, literally "she has awoken," was founded in 2014 and has maintained its momentum. The women of Estayqazat argue that "Patriarchy, apart from keeping women marginalized by default, also keeps women in a permanent state of anxiety and guilt."[30] They have made two short films that are available on YouTube. One involves women sharing names for their vaginas, aiming "through the act of naming to restore female ownership and overcome shame around female sexuality."[31]

Across the region, issues of sexual identity and practice are raging. LGBTQI support networks have sprung up and acquired an active online presence. Ahwaa (Passions) is a regional grassroots digital network that aims to create a safe space to debate LGBTQI-related issues.[32] Ikhtyar (Choice) is a research collective aiming to create "indigenous knowledge around gender and sexuality trends" in Arabic, seeking to be "the knowledge producer, not just the subject of the study."[33] Bint El Nas is an online support network for women who identify as LGBTQI in order to combat what is sometimes termed the "digital closet."[34] Helem is an NGO based in Lebanon that supports LGBTQI communities, while Bedaya is its Nile Valley (Egypt and Sudan) equivalent.[35] Women have also raised the topic of domestic abuse, an often hidden enactment of patriarchal power, and are breaking the silence over other such issues.

Clearly, to find a voice in the online environment is a significant step. But there is no automatic correlation between such activity and a change in social mores, state acknowledgement of the issue, or new legal regulation and enforcement. Online voice does not equate to offline power; indeed, that is the rub.

Harassment, physical and virtual

If women are physically harassed in many countries, the online environment has sadly not been all that much safer for them—a contemporary global problem. Women online have suffered from censorship and state surveillance in Egypt, Saudi Arabia, Tunisia, Iran, and beyond; indeed, surveillance and monitoring may increase as women's voices resonate more widely. But also, as in other parts of the world, including the "liberal" West, trolling and online harassment are on the increase.[36] The security states have often harassed the informal online sector as much, if not more, than the traditional media. Journalists and editors have been arrested and imprisoned around the region, but many bloggers, including women, have been dealt the same fate.

Faced with such intolerance, many users pushed back. Many regional political activists are digitally adept and have learned to use Tor to communicate anonymously and filter-breakers to circumvent state monitoring. Within the LGBTQI rights communities, many create fake online profiles, and anonymity offers some protection. And, of course, often men have acted in solidarity with the struggles of women. In Istanbul in February 2015, a number of men dressed in mini-skirts demonstrated against the rape and killing of a young woman, Ozgecan Aslan; while in a parallel solidarity campaign, Azerbaijani men posted photographs of themselves dressed in skirts.[37] Such campaigns echoed the powerful response by Iranian men to the Islamic Republic's attempt to symbolically castrate the student leader, Mohammad Tavakoli, during the Green Movement of 2009, by arresting and dressing him in a chador. The campaign backfired hugely as men posted images of themselves wearing head coverings of various kinds, declaring how proud they were to wear the imposed hijab of their mothers and wives.

The complexity of religion

The ghost of yet another binary, between secularism and religion, haunts much of women's activity in the region. In Iran, Egypt, and elsewhere, the debates about what might constitute a new Islamic feminism is a growing discourse and one around which further cohorts of women are finding their voice.[38]

Equally, supporters of women's rights can sometimes be found in surprising quarters. As an amusing and indicative sign of changing times, in December 2014 a Saudi cleric ignited a fierce national debate regarding the niqab.[39] Ahmad Al Ghamdi, a prominent Saudi cleric and former head of the religious police in Mecca, officially known as the Committee for Promotion of Virtue and Prevention of Vice, replied positively to a tweet by a Saudi woman asking if it was permissible in Islam for her to post a picture of her face on social media. His affirmative answer went viral and his Twitter feed received more than 10,000 comments, ranging from congratulations to death threats. He was subsequently a guest on Badria, the popular weekly TV talk show broadcast from Dubai, together with his wife, Jawahir Bint Sheikh Ali, who appeared without a face veil and wearing make-up.[40]

It is evident that not all regional online activity is progressive or supportive of women's rights. ISIS's digital activities are appealing to many, including women. Some people have been recruited online, and a number of women have volunteered to marry ISIS fighters through online invitations. Some women even act as baits and trolls themselves.[41] Indeed, in March 2015, Dar al-Ifta, the Egyptian state-sponsored Islamic authority, warned women against marrying ISIS fighters, saying that they would be pulled into a "circle of terrorism."[42] It is necessary to make the point that the terrible violence being wrought across the region has a massive impact on women: as terrified victims of war in Iraq, Syria, and Palestine; as abandoned breadwinners left to fend for their families; and as refugees, often with young children, trying to survive in makeshift conditions in limbo on territorial borders. Some women are actively participating in such conflicts, taking up arms in the Peshmerga in Kurdistan, for example, and some are responding to the blandishments of ISIS.

Conclusion

It is evident that women are active across a range of public activities as well as pressing their own specific needs. Strategic alliances are being made with various cross-cutting social groups, often to join in combatting the incursions and repression of the security state. Many men are active in their support of women's struggles. Whether or not these issue-focused activities can be turned into broader feminist movements is debatable, as is whether they are picked up by emergent political parties. Across the region, it is really only in the Maghreb and Iran that there was evidence of women's social networking before the digital period;[43] everywhere else, the digital activities are developing from scratch and might need to develop embodied actions to grow further.

The region's women are speaking out about many issues and with many voices, with or without clerical support, and they are challenging both state power and masculinist hegemony. That is in its own way a significant "political" change and a major contribution to the democratization of the region. If they were not only heard, but also listened to, that would really produce significant socio-cultural change.

6

DOMESTICATING FOREIGN INTELLECTUAL PROPERTY LAWS IN THE DIGITAL AGE

OF PIRATES AND *QARSANA* IN THE GCC STATES

Suzi Mirgani

Emerging from the shadow of British protectionism among other forms of political dependence, and buoyed by an indigenous and lucrative hydrocarbon industry, the six Gulf Cooperation Council states (GCC)—the United Arab Emirates, Bahrain, Saudi Arabia, Oman, Qatar, and Kuwait—overhauled and modernized their developing economic, political, and social infrastructures over the span of a few decades.[1] In the process of nation-building, the young GCC states took "quantum leaps in their national development, to emerge from being quasi-feudal or disputative tribal regions under actual or effective domination into stable and sophisticated independent sovereign states, in just two generations or less."[2]

The Gulf states' large-scale modernization efforts and exploitation of natural wealth reserves secured their place in the international economy. Acting within their new-found positions of power, key GCC states contributed to the founding of powerful consortia and cartels, including the Organization of the Petroleum Exporting Countries (OPEC),[3] and gradually established strong and beneficial protection for their nascent industries. Banking on foreign dependence on energy resources in an industrializing world, the GCC governments commanded powerful negotiating postures and assumed "a not insignificant regional and global influence in international affairs and trade."[4] From the outset, the Gulf states' existential relationship with the world has been defined by trade.[5]

While GCC states maintained substantial control over the trajectory of hydrocarbon-dependent industries, many developed nations attempted to innovate and move beyond their energy dependencies by investing in, and instituting, industries based on knowledge production. In an era of technological advancement, intellectual property can be considered "the driver of productivity and economic growth, leading to a new focus on the role of information, technology and learning in economic performance."[6] Postindustrial success in this digitally-sustained economic environment is being progressively defined by the prevalence and strength of information systems, technological innovation, and knowledge production. Within this transitioning world economy:

> ideas and knowledge are an increasingly important part of trade. Most of the value of new medicines and other high technology products lies in the amount of invention, innovation, research, design and testing involved. Films, music recordings, books, computer software and on-line services are bought and sold because of the information and creativity they contain, not usually because of the plastic, metal or paper used to make them.[7]

World markets are being dominated by globalized networks of developed, industrialized, and technologically-advanced nations, threatening to leave behind the old giants of industry. In this transitioning international economic environment, GCC states have had to keep up with the many fast-paced changes by diversifying their economies and by strategically using their accumulated oil wealth to invest in a future sustained by knowledge-based industries.[8] However, with a new type of global economy based on knowledge production come new rules of engagement. Like most other emerging economies and industrializing nations, the GCC states must submit to new international standards of intellectual property protection enforced by powerful conglomerates and international organizations—standards that are not always in the favor of modernizing nations.

This chapter examines some of the challenges faced by GCC nations as they attempt once again to "modernize" their economies in the digital era and in the face of substantial technological transformations. The GCC states, like many countries in the world, are entering into a transitional phase and a new world order. In order to fit within a repositioned international market, the GCC must abide by the many new rules and regulations in the area of intellectual property protection that have been developed and dictated by the World Trade Organization (WTO) and the agreement on Trade Related Aspects of Intellectual Property Rights (TRIPS).

Since the implementation of TRIPS measures is a strict requirement for WTO accession, this study examines how GCC governments are attempting to harness information industries as well as the related copyright and intellectual property laws that are largely alien to their local legal and social environments. In most cases, these new intellectual property protections are neither strictly implemented nor enforced by GCC authorities, and yet have been written into individual GCC state legal systems at the behest of the WTO. GCC governments are requested by the WTO, the European Union, and the United States to do more to encourage compliance with intellectual property protection in the digital era, even though the majority of GCC societies—local and expatriate—may be unreceptive to, and often fundamentally unfamiliar with, the concept of intellectual property itself and, by extension, the related concepts of copyright infringement and "piracy". It is important to note, however, that resistance to, and unawareness of, copyright and intellectual property laws are not a GCC exception; governments all over the world, even those most vehement in their anti-piracy stances, are struggling to ensure that their own societies comply with intellectual property laws or, at least, understand them in the way that rights holders would like. From the perspective of international content developers and rights holders, the issue of piracy, as it has become known in the dominant discourse and legal lexicon,[9] is rampant and is a key threat that can potentially decimate entire industries.

After outlining some of the main social and economic challenges resulting from the GCC states' adoption of WTO rules regarding intellectual property protections, this chapter highlights some specific examples regarding the practical application and enforcement of these laws. GCC intellectual property laws vary—although not too significantly—from state to state. Each GCC country's idiosyncrasies relate to, among other things, "moral rights and translations of copyright works, compulsory licensing, protection of pharmaceuticals and even the Arab boycott of Israel."[10] Since "the intellectual property laws of the GCC states reflect a common heritage,"[11] this chapter does not propose to inspect the historical development of specific intellectual property laws that pertain to any individual Gulf country, but rather to examine the shared motivations of Gulf governments to introduce externally imposed legal systems, and the means through which these largely unfamiliar—and, in some cases, incompatible—legal frameworks have been implemented.[12]

The study concludes with reflections on some of the ways in which Gulf states attempt to "domesticate" foreign intellectual property laws.[13] Gulf states are endeavoring to gain a competitive advantage by investing in the production of locally produced—as well as Arabic—content, and especially the promotion of niche areas of intellectual property often overlooked by other interests, such as the protection of traditional knowledge rights. This is an area generally neglected by industrialized nations, which tend to promote the concept of "innovation" rather than promoting and protecting collective knowledge.[14] GCC states are attempting to use intellectual property laws to their own advantage with an emphasis on digital archiving and protection of traditional knowledge, heritage, and folklore.[15] Each GCC country has created a dedicated government department to oversee the digitization and protection of heritage materials. This is the case with Oman's Ministry of National Heritage and Culture and Qatar's Ministry of Culture, Arts and Heritage, which "seeks to build a knowledge-economy that reflects its traditions,"[16] by launching the Media, Culture and Heritage National Digitization Plan in which "digitization is a first step in making Qatar's heritage digital and accessible online."[17] By promoting and protecting locally produced content, or "cultural property chattels,"[18] GCC states can aspire to the globalized international economic framework as envisioned and enforced by the WTO.

TRIPS and "universalizing" the concept of intellectual property

In their desire to diversify their hydrocarbon-dominated industries and to become influential players in a future based on knowledge economies, the GCC states have been obliged to join and to abide by the rules of the WTO in its attempt "to ensure that trade flows as smoothly, predictably and freely as possible."[19] As GCC states attempt to become viable players in a newly repositioned international trade community, they must also accept and implement the non-negotiable agreement on TRIPS, which is a prerequisite for WTO membership.[20] Gulf countries are not unique in this respect; other nations are currently facing similar coercion from the WTO and other economically powerful countries, and have little choice but to accept the enforced stipulations or risk being ostracized by international trade cartels. In such coercive ways, "globalization is pushy and intrusive and demands an active re-examination of one's own laws and regulations."[21] Within this framework, as businesses are experiencing a greater form of deregulation, intellectual property laws and copyright enforcements are experiencing increased regulation.[22]

The TRIPS, and subsequent TRIPS-plus,[23] agreements are comprehensive and restrictive international rules that apply to all WTO member states and specify enforcement procedures, remedies, and dispute resolution procedures that, many critics complain, mostly benefit developed nations and those who have a wealth of intellectual property to protect. This is because TRIPS does little to distinguish between nations' needs and capacities in its demand for "universality" and harmonization of the same regulations across the globe: "To its critics, harmonization is the strategy devised by the leading developed nations to achieve and maintain global domination through control of international trade and to protect their commercial interests in the developing and least developed countries."[24]

In their attempts to "harmonize" or "universalize" one-size-fits-all intellectual property laws, international lawmakers seemingly purge and divest laws of their ideological and cultural specificities in the interest of creating "objective" and "universal" laws that supposedly do not serve to benefit one culture over another. As Carroll explains, a "purposeful consequence of the West's dominance of international law over the past century has been to remove cultural, ideological, and religious content from the substantive discussion of transnational issues throughout the world."[25] This is true to an extent. What has been removed is not ideology and culture per se, but, specifically, ideologies and cultures that conflict with Eurocentric modes of thought.

Since laws necessarily evolve from particular, context-driven understandings of the world, creating a purely "universal" law is an epistemological impossibility. Despite sweeping, and perhaps even earnest, claims to "universality" and "harmonization," international intellectual property laws, as conceived and marshaled by a handful of powerful nations, do in fact emanate from a history of European Enlightenment, with European lawmakers and philosophers being the conceptual originators of these laws.[26] In this respect, international intellectual property laws cannot but be Euro- and Western-centric in their basic assumptions and in their epistemological understandings of intellect conceived as "property." TRIPS is:

> predicated on a particular conception of intellectual property as an idea, and internationalising this can be problematic. This may be in the narrow sense that different societies afford greater priority to the public good on a variety of issues, and in the

129

broader sense that some forms of 'traditional knowledge' (TK) as shared amongst indigenous communities do not conform to the codified Western model of individual and exclusive ownership.[27]

In the guise of progressive globalization efforts and competitive open markets, intellectual property laws have been described by critics as a type of neo-colonial exploitation of developing nations' intellectual resources, or what Peter Drahos calls "information feudalism."[28] Because "the transplant of intellectual property laws to developing countries has been the outcome of empire building and colonization,"[29] in most cases those economies considered on the lower end of this hierarchy are previously colonized nations that are still struggling with the vestiges of colonial exploitation.

As GCC states attempt to develop their digital infrastructures and knowledge-based economies in the long shadow of post-colonial influence, there is an uneasy concern that adopting Western-prescribed intellectual property laws "might lead to a renewed loss of national sovereignty."[30] In an era of "neo-colonial" capitalist exploitation of information industries, one need only ask who is most active in promoting intellectual property laws in the international arena to see who stands to gain most from the introduction and enforcement of these laws. As the world's most prolific content developer in the digital age, the United States is also, unsurprisingly, one of the main champions of international intellectual property protection, and "has been persistent in promoting the adoption and enforcement of intellectual property regimes throughout the Middle East."[31]

What is even more telling is that one of the most outspoken and active organizations advocating international protection and enforcement of intellectual property rights is the International Intellectual Property Alliance (IIPA), which is a private sector coalition of trade associations that represent a variety of US copyright-based industries. By applying pressure to specific trade relationships, such powerful intellectual property lobbies have significant international consequences. Through these lobbies, many Western countries are:

> actively seeking to stem the rampant piracy and bootlegging in the Middle East in order to reduce appropriability and increase benefits to captured, extra-Western complementary assets of paradigmatic industrial systems. The West perceives that the most efficient tool to accomplish this economic restructuring is enactment of world-wide, Western-style intellectual property regimes.[32]

Thus, in a transitioning knowledge-based global economy predicated upon information and communication technologies, private actors lobbying for increased protection of intellectual property play as powerful a role as nations did in the era of post-colonial, post-industrial economies. In fact, the TRIPS agreement itself is the result of the demands of a coalition of private sector corporations lobbying for stringent intellectual property protection in an age of increased knowledge production and innovation.[33]

Intellectual property and private interests

Business interests are not only fully intertwined with government interests, in many instances, but steer government policy toward advocating the protection of intellectual property abroad. Moreover, because most research on intellectual property issues and "piracy" tends to be conducted by interested industry partners, it is necessarily biased toward industry interests. One of the main sources of research conducted on intellectual property piracy is the IIPA, which describes itself as actively working to "improve international protection and enforcement of copyrighted materials and to open foreign markets closed by piracy and other market access barriers."[34]

Members of the IIPA include the Association of American Publishers (AAP), Entertainment Software Association (ESA), Independent Film and Television Alliance (IFTA), Motion Picture Association of America (MPAA), and Recording Industry Association of America (RIAA). These members "represent over 3,200 U.S. companies producing and distributing materials protected by copyright laws throughout the world."[35] Other non-governmental organizations working to stamp out piracy worldwide include the Business Software Alliance (BSA), International Federation of the Phonographic Industry (IFPI), Business Action to Stop Counterfeiting and Piracy (BASCAP), and Pharmaceutical Security Institute (PSI), among many others.

International intellectual property organizations such as the IIPA, and individual countries such as the United States, invest heavily in international intellectual property protection, and closely monitor the pervasiveness of information and communication technologies in the GCC states. International copyright industries capitalize on the many opportunities to penetrate the new markets of the GCC for additional international growth, while at the same time attempting to halt the rampant intellectual property theft and copyright infringements that occur on large-scale institutional platforms, as well as at the level of the individual user.

Since "intellectual property rights go largely unenforced in the Middle East,"[36] the GCC states have been on the receiving end of much criticism from rights holders and industry coalitions in developed countries regarding their lax implementation of intellectual property laws and the concomitant lack of enforcement.[37] These coalitions of:

> U.S.-based non-governmental organizations seek to influence the adoption of Western-style intellectual property protection in the Middle East by threatening to expose lax enforcement in an effort to promote U.S. and international sanctions. [...] The IIPA makes recommendations to the U.S. Trade Representative as to which countries should appear on the U.S.'s "watchlist" of countries with lax IP protection in order to encourage the U.S. to pressure Middle Eastern governments to reduce appropriability. In addition, [it] threatens offending countries with private prosecution before the World Trade Organization.[38]

Complaints against GCC states during WTO meetings are common and vociferous, and many Gulf nations have been placed on the United States Trade Representative's (USTR) Special 301 Report "watch list" of offending countries.[39] Most recently, the UAE was criticized for its failure to enforce stringent intellectual property and copyright laws.

Despite internal power struggles and occasional discord between the member states of the GCC, the organization as a whole tends to agree on the importance of establishing unified intellectual property laws—even though, in practice, such laws are hardly fully implemented. From the standpoint of the IIPA, the Gulf monarchies are exploiting the lack of centralized enforcement mechanisms within the organization in order to delay enforcing intellectual property laws in the individual GCC states. The IIPA does not support joint GCC decision-making regarding unified intellectual property laws, and does not hesitate to use tough language in its public accusations against the Gulf states. The IIPA has announced that the UAE is making "a major policy mistake" by "waiting for the Gulf Cooperation Council to establish region-wide collective management" rather than establishing its own royalty collecting society.[40] The IIPA "urges the U.S. Government to engage the UAE Government, through the EPD [Economic Policy Dialogue] or otherwise, to address this long-festering problem by approving a collecting society as quickly as possible."[41] Thus, a non-governmental coalition of businesses such as the IIPA regards itself as powerful enough to go head-to-head with a sovereign nation, and indeed with the GCC as a collection of nations.

Dichotomies of perception

It is important to point out that there is a complex set of assumptions and histories that underlie this perceived blasé GCC attitude toward piracy and intellectual property rights in the digital age. These cultural and religious governing contexts are important for understanding the GCC states' relationship to concepts of intellectual property since, for many non-Western countries:

> there exists a dichotomy between the formal expression of intellectual property protection though the states' laws and their practical application though the states' respective enforcement strategies and efforts. The dichotomy arises as a consequence of the external pressure upon the states to adopt laws for which they have neither the resources nor the expertise nor the infrastructure to effectively execute to the level of satisfaction sought by the more demanding developed countries.[42]

In this respect, there are at least two largely incompatible views on copyright and intellectual property that stem from the experiences of industrialized nations versus industrializing nations. Advocates of stringent intellectual property laws believe that these legal measures:

> stimulate economic growth which, in turn, contributes to poverty reduction. By stimulating invention and new technologies, they will increase agricultural or industrial production, promote domestic and foreign investment, facilitate technology transfer and improve the availability of medicines necessary to combat disease. They take the view that there is no reason why a system that works for developed countries could not do the same in developing countries.[43]

Alternatively, those in developing countries perceive the stringent intellectual property rules, as currently conceptualized, devised, and enforced by the technologically-advanced and industrialized country lobby, as doing little:

> to stimulate invention in developing countries, because the necessary human and technical capacity may be absent. They are ineffective at stimulating research to benefit poor people because they will not be able to afford the products, even if developed. They limit the option of technological learning through imitation. They allow foreign firms to drive out domestic competition by obtaining patent protection and to service the market through imports, rather than domestic manufacture.[44]

In an interesting conundrum, the IIPA acknowledges that the UAE is a technologically advanced economy that does not need to resort, as some developing economies might, to widespread intellectual property piracy and copyright infringement. The IIPA states that in the UAE "the software piracy rate in enterprises is higher than it should be for this economically developed marketplace."[45] Here, in its conflation of intellectual property and economics, the IIPA disregards the UAE's particular cultural and social contexts and focuses only on the economic ones.

The drivers for infringing copyright material and for intellectual property piracy may be very different for some countries in the Middle East. In some of the richer, more conservative Gulf states, the appeal of infringing digital content is much more nuanced, as users may indeed be trying to overcome an expense barrier; but the fact remains that much of the copyrighted material is also unavailable through the market or even online—platforms such as Netflix cannot be accessed easily. A more practical reason for GCC publics to engage in intellectual property piracy is to access banned, censored, or controversial content, so illegal file-sharing may be considered a means of bypassing state control.

Unlike developing nations that resist application of the TRIPS agreement on economic bases, the GCC states' reticence to enforce international intellectual property laws is not necessarily based on issues of wealth. Their failure to comply with implementation of TRIPS rules, therefore, must necessarily stem from a variety of cultural or social factors.

Cultural conceptualizations and the discourse of intellectual property

Like the rest of the wider Middle East, the GCC is "an area where cultural issues inform policy and enforcement but are often ignored by western scholars and governments."[46] Intellectual property laws are being transplanted into GCC digital, legal, and cultural contexts without the same manner of fervent public debate regarding the language, implementation, and negotiation of these laws that has occurred over many years in the European and US contexts. The GCC states have only relatively recently begun addressing questions of intellectual property and piracy. In comparison, Western nations have long histories and traditions, starting with the first officially recognized copyright law in 1710 in the UK,[47] giving ample time for these laws to percolate through the legal system and through the social fabric to be reincarnated in the digital age.

While GCC institutions have accepted international intellectual property laws without much negotiation, this is a highly contested international discourse, beginning with concern over the term "intellectual property" itself. The term is a fairly new manifestation and a modern development regarding the conceptualization of knowledge, especially in the wake of digital technologies. The term is often perceived by critics as being thoroughly inappropriate in that it serves to commoditize ideas as a form of "property."[48]

The quantification of ideas conceptualizes thought as competitive; that is, something that is finite and therefore in need of protection. However, knowledge is generally considered to be "not rivalrous and can be shared without loss of utility,"[49] meaning that "one person's contemporaneous use of it does not detract from another's ability to do so. The institution of intellectual property therefore involves the 'construction of scarcity' where none necessarily exists."[50] With increased availability of digital reproductive technologies, the concept of property to describe "ideas" becomes even more incongruous.

Through the instrumentalization of ideas as forms of property, modern intellectual property laws necessarily conceptualize intellect, innovation, and creativity as things that can be "owned." More importantly, submitting to the notion that ideas can be owned also means that they can be quantified, monetized, and commoditized. Because modern intellectual property laws define "ideas" according to the language of business and profits, it necessarily means that the concepts of "creativity" and "innovation" become irrevocably integrated into market economics. The concept of "creativity" that has traditionally been associated with free-flowing and ethereal notions of art and culture is now, through the discourse of intellectual property, being forcibly tied down to an exchange economy. In the language of this reformulated and reimagined discourse, creativity and innovation are aspects that can—and indeed should—be capitalized upon and exploited to achieve their maximum economic value within the digital age.[51] This has generated a controversial and heated debate in Western cultural contexts, and one that is fundamentally absent in the GCC states, both at governmental and societal levels.

One way in which the conversation can be started in the GCC states is to debate the linguistic and discursive conceptualization of intellectual production in the Arab context. It is argued that "the oldest reference to formal intellectual property protection in the Middle East is connected with original authorship, i.e. copyright" in the pre-Islamic era, especially as it relates to poetry and questions of attribution,[52] even though the poems themselves would have been widely circulated and recited by many without necessitating permission. Pre-dating the modern ascribed characteristic of intellect as property, Arab intellectual tradition, like Western intellectual tradition, has always been built on the cumulative sharing of knowledge. It is widely acknowledged "that appropriation, mimicry, quotation, allusion, and sublimated collaboration consist of a kind of sine qua non of the creative act, cutting across all forms and genres in the realm of cultural production."[53] Seen from this perspective, emulation and contribution is not only necessary, but is inextricable to all cultural endeavors.

In this sense, it is important to highlight the particular cultural, religious, and political contexts that shape the conceptualization of intellectual property in the GCC. The connection between Islamic law and the concept of intellectual property is tenuous, and there is an ongoing debate in which some scholars argue that the idea of intellectual property should "be rejected on the grounds that the concept of ownership in the *Shariah* is confined to tangible objects only,"[54] while others note that copyright, or attribution, is a prized concept in *shari'a* law. Adding yet another caveat to the open-endedness of this debate, others argue further that, regardless of whether or not the concept of intellectual property can be accurately identified within the fundamentals of *shari'a* law, this law has yet to be codified into a practical and workable set of rules and regulations to be enforced by the state.[55] Thus, the transference and translation of Islamic law into codified legal text is a set of translations that must be performed.

Importantly, various complications arise out of the linguistic translation of GCC intellectual property laws, where "the Arabic text is the authentic and binding version,"[56] and the English text, as published by the GCC legal authorities to satisfy the WTO, is used for reference only. Ultimately, no account of GCC intellectual property laws is complete without a critical study of the terms of the debate in both English and Arabic—which is beyond the scope of this chapter. As an example, the word "piracy" to describe intellectual property theft mimics a very particular pejorative Western discourse regarding the disruption of colonial maritime trade.[57] The term carries "a substantial amount of historical and cultural baggage" that cuts straight to the heart of the Gulf region's colonial history.[58] With their attempts to resist or subvert British imperial dominance in the region at the beginning of the nineteenth century, the Qawasim tribe, along with other regional players on the eastern coast of the Arabian peninsula, were labeled "pirates" (or "*qarasina*") for their disruption of British trade with India, ultimately prompting the British Empire to introduce the "Trucial system" that abolished such maritime disruptions, enabling it to assert a controlling influence over the region. Since then, a number of historians and Gulf scholars have challenged the narrative that depicts the maritime activities of local tribes as "piracy" (or "*qarsana*"), pointing out the role such discourse played in safeguarding colonial interests in the region.[59] Thus, "piracy" has historically been a politically charged and loaded concept, and continues to be used today in relation to copyright infringements..

Just as intellectual property laws have been enforced internationally by powerful nations with a vested interest in copyright protection, so too has the discourse of "piracy," and its associated terminology and pejorative framing, been introduced to the language and cultures of other nations. Even though the complacent use of the term "piracy" to describe intellectual property theft is born of a very specific Western history of maritime piracy, it has nevertheless been adopted, hook, line, and sinker, by the Gulf nations in the Arabic language intellectual property discourse, with its literal translation of "piracy" as "*qarsana*."[60] It is thus important to pay attention to how the different languages of Arabic and English are used, and how certain phraseologies attempt to steer the discourse in particular directions and according to particular sets of basic assumptions. The issue of intellectual property piracy then becomes an issue of translation—not only translating language, but also translating the culture of law itself from one cultural context to another.

Intellectual property and digital piracy

Even though GCC copyright laws are criticized for being relatively new and not fully enforced by any of the official institutions, it is important to point out that most internationally recognized copyright and intellectual property laws also take on a piecemeal character as they have been updated a multitude of times to catch up with technological innovations and the new ways in which people engage with cultural materials in the digital era. As such, current copyright laws bear little resemblance to two decades ago.[61] Intellectual property laws are often behind the curve as they attempt to create, pass, enshrine, and enforce increasingly draconian laws to halt the spread of pervasive infringement in the face of increased availability of digital technologies.

Such rapid changes in the digital environment may be one reason why, for many GCC states, "the disinterest or disinclination to embrace copyright and neighbouring rights protection can be explained in part by the entrenched attitude by officialdom that copyright was still essentially a mechanism for the control of local press and publications" rather than newer forms of digital content.[62] Over the years, international copyright laws have been regularly rewritten in order to expand the scope of protected works with the inclusion of digital rights and computer software programs.

The concern for international content-creators and rights-holders stems from the Gulf states having some of the highest penetration and usage rates of Internet and mobile technologies in the world. The Broadband Commission for Digital Development reports that Qatar's household Internet penetration rate for 2013 was 96.4 per cent, the second highest in the world, after Korea.[63] The digital infrastructure in most GCC states is extremely advanced, reaching most homes, offices, businesses, and public areas:

> According to the International Telecommunications Union (ITU), Internet broadband penetration in the UAE has skyrocketed, to almost 952,000 and nearly 10.3%

of the population. ITU also indicates that 7.8 million people in the UAE (85%) now use the Internet, and this may be accounted for by mobile users (the mobile penetration rate far exceeds 100% at nearly 13.8 million), with well over half of those mobile users having access to the Internet through their phones or mobile devices (e.g., tablets).[64]

With increased Internet speed as well as proliferating digital hardware and software, there are reports of an increasing trend toward digital piracy.[65] If Internet penetration and usage are highest in Saudi Arabia above all other Middle Eastern countries, then it is not surprising that this Gulf monarchy will also have the highest rates of copyright infringement and intellectual property piracy.[66]

In the rentier economies of the Gulf states, the wealth generated through the lucrative hydrocarbon industries is strategically distributed among the national population. Because residents have become accustomed to receiving state subsidies and benefits, this makes it harder to introduce restrictive measures regarding intellectual property, and curtailing already widespread practices of infringement. However, in the wealthy GCC states, the national and regional reach and avid use of technology relates to the wealthy national population and much of the high-earning expatriate population. It does not necessarily apply to the majority of the low-income migrant population that resides in basic, company-appointed accommodation generally located on urban peripheries, where residents have little access to digital networks or even the technology itself. This presents a unique dilemma for Gulf authorities in their push toward creating a modern and technologically advanced national digital infrastructure. In most GCC states, there is an attempt to ensure that major government services and bureaucratic offices, including ministries of labor, become primarily accessible online in a push for increased "e-governance."[67]

The more information and communication technologies are used by local as well as the multi-ethnic, multi-lingual expatriate populations, the more these will need to be monitored by authorities, who are unwilling to relinquish control over the digital public sphere, but who do not necessarily have the capacity or reach to fulfill such an undertaking. Importantly, this monitoring comes in the form of increased prohibitions of online behavior and engaging in discourses that are politically sensitive. The introduction of GCC states' cyber crime laws is one such example of increased public monitoring of online behavior.[68] As such, this monitoring is not necessarily the kind stipulated by TRIPS and the IIPA, which is to increase vigilance against piracy of intellectual property, rather than vigilance against political dissent. For example, the

IIPA argues that UAE's cyber crime law "was recently updated to include, among other things, a specific provision on ISP [Internet service provider] liability. However, the Law does not cover ISP liability in connection with IP [intellectual property] infringement."[69] Thus, in the interest of private business, US rights-holder organizations such as the IIPA argue that GCC cyber crime laws should be strengthened and extended, despite their potential to limit freedom of expression in the countries of the GCC.

The Gulf states are central hubs for foreign investment, and yet there are very few implemented laws to protect foreign intellectual property. Uncertainties regarding the enforceable laws pertaining to copyright and intellectual property rights are the biggest cause for concern.[70] In Kuwait, for example, "unauthorized duplication of software" was not considered illegal prior to 1998 with the early institution of intellectual property measures.[71] Computer software, in particular, has been the target of many infringements in the region, both at the level of the individual user and within institutional settings.[72] In the UAE, the "unlicensed use of software in enterprises makes up nearly 40% of all software use, with a commercial value of over $200 million."[73] Even though these businesses openly operate illegal software, there are very few repercussions.

Addressing these issues on the ground necessitated the creation of appropriate enforcement bodies. The Business Software Alliance (BSA) and the Arabian Anti-Piracy Alliance (AAA) are the most integrated of the anti-piracy groups, working closely with government entities to conduct raids and to release reports on infringement issues. In Qatar "the Ministry of Justice has partnered with Business Software Alliance (BSA) to launch anti-piracy campaigns."[74] Throughout the year, GCC authorities conduct high-profile and media-publicized operations against those dealing in infringing materials—mostly goods related to entertainment and apparel. The Shaheen operation in Qatar "raided places that stored illicit and fake goods and counterfeit products that violated intellectual property rights" and was carried out by the Ministry of Interior Qatar in cooperation with Interpol.[75] Apart from these intermittent raids on local merchants, there are few, if any, active campaigns devised by GCC authorities to raise awareness among the public or to enforce broad intellectual property measures.

Digitizing heritage and the future of creative content

Since the WTO's enforcement of the TRIPS agreement, there have been shifts in the power relationship between the GCC states and the increasingly knowledge-based nations. As digital production increases all over the world, intellectual property laws become ever more encompassing in level and scope, finding new ways to limit access to and uses of digital materials, while simultaneously increasing the control of owners.

Other than the production of oil and gas, and investment of the ensuing resources, the GCC states have few other industries, and thus have little else to protect, at least from the standpoint of intellectual property. In their bid to transition to knowledge-based economies, the GCC states are increasingly investing in industries of cultural creation. One area the GCC governments have been advocating is protecting traditional knowledge and heritage rights by digitizing historical content.[76]

As relatively young independent nations, many if not all GCC countries have been heavily involved in shaping national identity based on history and heritage. Most post-colonial countries attempt to fashion their post-independence national character and override decades or centuries of colonial exploitation by harking back to a heritage that pre-dates the colonial era. This heritage is tinged with romantic and fetishized ideologies of origin, but key nonetheless for Gulf nations striving to define themselves according to their own sovereign histories, while simultaneously appropriating elements of this history to rally their people around a common historical narrative in such a way as to shore up political support within a tightly-knit tribal culture. In order to unearth these histories and heritages, each GCC state has its own strategic government-funded institution dedicated to the resurrection of traditional practices and knowledge and the implementation of heritage programs.[77] The GCC states in general have spared little expense in the implementation of heritage programs and the preservation of content through digital archiving.[78]

Thus, despite the frictions caused by the introduction of intellectual property legal frameworks and the general disadvantage experienced by the GCC states in relation to these laws, GCC governments have attempted to use digital technologies and international intellectual property to their advantage by producing and promoting their own locally-produced content. Designed for such purposes, for instance, Qatar's Media, Culture and Heritage (MCH) National Digitization Plan:

> seeks to contribute to the creation of quality digital Arabic content that taps into Qatar's rich Arabic and Islamic heritage and its unique history in the Arab Gulf region. Such content will ground the country's economic transformation in its values while spurring the development of an Arabic digital ecosystem that promotes the culture and economy of the country.[79]

Since GCC nations have had to adopt and implement new legal systems, including the introduction of intellectual property laws that are largely foreign to their local environments, it is by promoting locally-produced digital content that GCC states can fit into the globalized international economic framework as envisioned and enforced by the WTO. The GCC states still face huge legal challenges as they attempt to grapple with the introduction and implementation of intellectual property laws in an increasingly technologically-driven environment, but now they can do so with the protection of home-grown content in mind.

Currently, within all the GCC states, the conversations regarding intellectual property and piracy are taking place at ministerial, corporate, or highly legalistic levels and have not trickled down into social discourse, even though the individual user is often the ultimate target of anti-piracy campaigns. With the production and promotion of local heritage and digital content, this conversation can be steered toward Gulf societies, who ultimately have a stake in their own copyrights.

In order to remain central to the global economic order and to become relevant to any future intellectual property discourse, the Gulf states have made several attempts to modify their engagements with intellectual property laws—though whether these are seriously enforced remains to be seen. Qatar in particular has left an indelible imprint, at least cosmetically, on the future discourse of intellectual property by hosting high-profile international meetings such as the 38th Session of the UNESCO World Heritage Committee and the WTO's latest round of trade negotiations known as the "Doha Round."[80] Although the Doha Round talks hit an impasse and were ultimately disappointing, the fact that the name "Doha" has become synonymous with a discourse responsible for shaping the future direction of intellectual property demonstrates the Gulf nations' willingness to engage, at least symbolically, with the new knowledge-based world order.

The pervasiveness of the concept of intellectual property piracy has increased exponentially since the advent of digital technologies, and so it is important to rethink the terms of the debate that have entered into the everyday vernacular. Digital technologies have radically changed the way people reproduce, distribute, control, and publish information. Similarly, the cost and time to make, distribute, and consume cultural material have been significantly reduced. In much the same way, everyone can be a publisher and producer in this new digital environment, but everyone can also be a "pirate."

Since intellectual property issues involve all those who engage with cultural material and not just copyright-holder organizations, this is a conversation that should not only occur in a top-down manner, as most policies do in the GCC states. In the GCC context, there have been very few studies conducted on what the average person—citizen or expatriate—thinks of intellectual property and piracy issues. Importantly, the lack of debate at the social level means that issues of copyright and related issues of piracy are not necessarily discussed at the institutional level, whether in schools or the educational system more broadly defined. There is an ongoing passionate debate taking place around the world in which the basic assumptions of copyright and piracy are questioned and critiqued, and it is important that the GCC states enter into this international discussion. The lack of public awareness regarding the philosophy of intellectual property needs to be addressed if piracy is to be dealt with and, more importantly for rights-holders, reduced in any significant way. It is by having a personal or national investment in the production and distribution of local digital content that GCC states can finally have a stake in the future of creative content.

7

FROM SOUK TO CYBER SOUK

ACCULTURATING TO E-COMMERCE
IN THE MENA REGION

Norhayati Zakaria

For centuries, the Middle East and North Africa (MENA) region has drawn both local customers and foreign visitors to a local form of market known as the "souk." As a community-based space that brings together buyers from all walks of life and sellers who trade various goods and products, the souk is at the center of public life. Traditionally, the souk constitutes an open-air marketplace that throbs with activity and teems with customers and visitors strolling down endless walkways, eyeing goods and products, getting to know the merchants and examining their merchandise, bargaining on prices, and building relationships. Whether it is the Grand Bazaar in Istanbul, the serpentine souks in Marrakesh, the old Deira Souk in Dubai, Souk Waqif in Doha, Souk Abdali in Amman, or the Taiba Market in Riyadh, the souk is a unique cultural phenomenon that continues to have a special appeal to locals and foreign visitors alike.

Over the years, new shopping spaces and consumer trends have emerged, and the traditional souk culture has given way to a more modern mall culture throughout the region, particularly in the more affluent Gulf societies. While imitating the face-to-face business environment that prevailed in souks, malls have adapted commercial practices to the needs of changing societies. They also afford new spaces for socialization that appeal to people of all ages. In recent years, advances in information technology, changes in business strategies, and demand for enhanced shopping experiences have all contributed to the adoption of e-commerce. In the new cyber souk, business transactions take place "just a click-away," with the convenience of not having to leave one's home. Based on online transaction rather than the traditional face-to-face interaction, this new shopping experience affects both the nature of the shopping experience and the ways in which people relate to it.

This chapter probes the implications that digital transformations in the Arab Middle East have had on the business sector. A number of questions motivate the analysis. Does the absence of cultural practices in the online business environment, which are so inherent to the souk experience, make e-commerce less appealing than traditional forms of trade? Can Arab societies acculturate to the new ways of conducting business, and are they likely to change their norms, practices, and values accordingly? How and to what extent does culture impact the development of e-commerce? Does the continued popularity of the traditional souk and the appeal of the modern mall hinder the development of e-commerce? What culturally-attuned behaviors lead buyers to adopt or avoid the new cyber souk environment? And, more generally, what barriers hinder consumers from engaging in e-commerce?

Addressing these questions necessitates paying attention to the factors that have contributed to the development of e-commerce in the region, and highlighting barriers that hinder its growth. A key contention of this chapter is that the most complex challenges for the development and adoption of e-commerce in the region are not so much economic, technical, or systemic, but cultural. The persistence of various cultural barriers raises questions about the extent to which e-commerce is likely to take hold in the region.

This chapter unfolds along four lines of analysis. First, I explore the nature of the souk in the MENA region, including its origins, business practices, and historical development from souk to mall to cyber souk, describing the similarities and differences between all three of modes of commerce. Second, I provide a critical review of the literature on e-commerce in the MENA region, with the purpose of understanding the previous studies that examined factors affecting e-commerce acceptance and its usage among Arab consumers. Third, I discuss the effect of culture on the adoption of e-commerce by applying cross-cultural theories along several cultural dimensions, paying particular attention to the challenges and impediments for adopting e-commerce. Finally, I offer some reflections on the theoretical and business implications on the development of the cyber souk, and suggest possible future research directions.

From the souk to the e-souk

In Arabic, the word "souk" designates a marketplace. In former times, goods were carried to the docks near the souk, using small wooden ships known as dhows. The cargo was then sold to the merchants who would flock to the docks to examine the newly arrived merchandise and acquire what they could to supply their stands. This proximity encouraged the practice of haggling between merchants—wholesalers, suppliers, importers—and retailers. Once a price was agreed upon and a deal closed, the shop owners would bring the goods to their tents or stalls in the souk, usually set on narrow streets not very far from the docks. The hustle and bustle that accompanied the trading of goods at the docks created a dynamic, haggling-intensive environment that carried over to the souk itself. Although the souk in the MENA region still offers authentic local goods, such as spices, perfumes, and silk, the types of traded merchandise have changed considerably over the years. Today, one can shop at the souks for handmade carpets and authentic delicacies, but also modern electronics.

By and large, though, souks have been taken over by the more modern shopping malls, which have grown more commonplace and popular. The emergence of shopping malls has allowed people to experience a new type of marketplace. The new culture of malls extends the souk culture, but also alters it to accommodate the changing needs and tastes of customers. The shopping mall reflects an affluent contemporary lifestyle in Arab societies, and is visited by those who desire global brands and a refined locale where they can engage in conspicuous consumption.[1] In Dubai, where modern architecture and high-rises are common, high-end malls and luxurious shopping centers are burgeoning, turning the city into a global shopping hub to satisfy the needs of its citizens and expatriate community, and as a means of attracting tourists.[2]

In the mall, customers experience a modern conception of space and a different type of shopping experience.[3] The mall allows people to shop in air-conditioned spaces and offers its visitors an array of services and activities. Some patrons enjoy the enclosed environment, which allows them to shop in comfort, while others use malls as a platform for leisure activities and entertainment, and not so much for consumption purposes.[4] Malls also create an urban lifestyle for their customers, thereby establishing their status in society and encouraging the consumption of goods to enhance their image and build rapport.

Although the mall extends the culture of the souk, it also differs from it. One distinct feature is that, because prices are fixed, people can no longer haggle, as they were accustomed to doing in the souk. In such an environment, people seem to enjoy the variety of local and global brands on offer, and experience a leisure activity that does not necessarily always entail consumption. Mall-goers take advantage of new ways of socializing while shopping, embodying a lifestyle that was not common back when souk culture was dominant.

With advances in information and communication technologies (ICTs) and the adoption of a range of social media communication tools, traditional ways of conducting business are giving way to digital practices and online business transactions. Compared with the traditional souk, the cyber souk—or what is commonly termed e-commerce—operates on a wider business scale, offering products and services that are not confined to particular locations or restricted by geographical boundaries. Anyone with access to the Internet can browse, select, and buy. Unlike the souk, which is confined to a physical location where sellers and buyers converge and engage in face-to-face transactions for a limited time of the day, the cyber souk is a virtual place that spans a global business landscape, where people can browse at any time of day, anywhere in the world, and goods are delivered to them without the inconvenience of leaving their homes. E-commerce is increasingly appealing because it features a wider variety of products and services, has a greater customer reach, and offers better prices.[5]

It is fitting to highlight the elements that make e-commerce appealing, but also to pinpoint the disjunctions that ensue from these new practices. One of the factors that affects people's receptiveness to doing business in the cyber souk relates to how business is conducted online. To start with, e-commerce is based on an impersonal relationship between the seller and the buyer, and does not offer the kind of tactile sensory experience many customers value in a region long accustomed to the more immediate experience of the souk.[6] In the souk it is common for customers to engage in haggling before they close a deal. Haggling has been practiced for centuries and is the primary means of conducting business in the souk. The price eventually agreed upon depends on the level and strength of the negotiating power of the seller or buyer. The business culture of haggling creates an exciting and interactive environment in which the customer can negotiate the optimum price when buying goods.

In online transactions, the price is usually fixed and customers cannot haggle since negotiation is not entertained. A few online vendors such as eBay offer items at unfixed prices, which mimics in some ways the experience of face-to-face haggling. With this practice, sellers set a minimum price to start the bidding and then buyers have the opportunity to bid against each other, with the price set at the end of the selling period. Online buyers compete in a sort of price war, wherein whoever offers the best price gets the desired merchandise. But this is different from face-to-face haggling because it is one-directional (as bids always go up) and because sellers and buyers do not engage with each other in any real sense. The final selling price depends on what other buyers are willing to offer. In face-to-face transactions, negotiation takes place between an individual seller and an individual buyer—a one-to-one relationship—compared to an online transaction, which is a one-to-many relationship.

Communication between buyer and seller is an important component of the souk experience. The physical souk becomes a meeting place for many people because it creates a strong sense of belonging to the society and the local community. As Feghali and Rice point out,[7] for Arab societies that are strongly anchored in cultural values of collectivism, honor, and hospitality, oral communication and face-to-face communication are crucial for weaving relationships.[8] With their personalized touch, sellers establish a bond and a relationship with buyers in the course of their daily transactions. Hospitality is extended to the buyers, which makes them feel a strong sense of belonging and induces them to become loyal customers.

The aforementioned similarities and differences between the souk, the mall, and the cyber souk are summarized in Table 7.1, which is based on Lauterborn's 4Cs international marketing mix strategy.[9] Highlighting the similarities and differences between these three shopping environments can help determine whether, and to what extent, consumers in the Arab Middle East are likely to adopt e-commerce, and why.

Key drivers of e-commerce

Facilitating the development of e-commerce in the MENA region are such factors as Internet penetration, increased accessibility, and improved IT infrastructure. A robust Internet infrastructure has enhanced consumer habits and improved services, giving the consumers more business venues and choices, allowing sellers to conduct business and process orders more quickly and efficiently.

Table 7.1: Comparison of the souk, mall, and cyber souk, based on the 4Cs international marketing mix strategy

Component	Souk	Mall	Cyber souk
Who? Customers/Clients	Authentic: comprised mainly of local sellers with local customers seeking local products All-inclusive: hybrid market Physical presence: see, feel, and touch merchandise	Universal: mixture of local and foreign customers who visit the malls in their locality seeking global brands Offers hybrid market Physical presence: see, feel, and touch merchandise	Worldwide/global: anyone who can access the Internet Virtual market: online presence Global products: offers anything No physical presence: cannot feel or touch
Where and **When?** Channel	Physical bazaars or shopping quarters Limited by shop hours and need to respect hours for prayer	Within a modern building with large, air-conditioned space Limited by the mall operating hours	Online platform: accessible anywhere and everywhere No time constraints; open around the clock
What? Cost	Unfixed; haggling; negotiated prices	Fixed price, no haggling; what you see is what you pay	Fixed or unfixed (e.g. eBay bidding, competitive pricing)
How? Communication	Face-to-face interactions Informal style of shopping, active interactions due to need for haggling and establishing rapport	Face-to-face transactions Formal style of shopping, less interaction due to fixed prices	Virtual interactions at any time, 24/7 Can be formal or informal depending on context

No less important in understanding emerging e-commerce patterns and practices is the make-up of the population. In fact, more than 40 per cent of the population of the MENA region are aged 16–36 years.[10] Youth often champion or become early adopters of new technologies, and naturally contribute to the high rates of Internet penetration. As the use of smartphones takes hold, particularly among an aspiring generation of digital natives, e-commerce is likely to be more widely adopted. According to a 2012 report from PayPal, with the wide adoption of smartphones, mobile consumption is picking up in a number of GCC countries (namely Saudi Arabia, UAE, and Qatar).[11] In 2013, Google's "Our Mobile Planet" surveyed the users of smartphones and found that 38.3 per cent of smartphone users in the UAE and 34 per cent of users in Saudi Arabia had bought goods using their mobile device.

Another important factor that has contributed to the growth in e-commerce activities is the wealth of the population. Populations with high disposable income have the luxury of purchasing goods and services online. Conspicuous consumption and impulsive shopping behavior are growing among consumers in the MENA region, particularly in the rich, oil-producing Gulf countries. This has resulted in changing consumer behaviors and shopping habits.

The Nielsen Global Survey of Consumer Shopping Behavior provides insights into these changing patterns of consumption and the factors that influence people's decisions about what to buy.[12] Interestingly, the survey found that 39 per cent of MENA customers are impulsive and engage in spontaneous shopping behavior. For example, the findings of the survey suggest that Arab consumers frequently tend to buy what they see without a genuine need for the product. They are also inclined to try new products sooner than others, and tend to be early adopters of fashion. The survey further points out that consumers in the MENA region are brand-conscious and that they often select products based on the high status of a brand. They are also highly engaged and easily persuaded to buy products that are on promotion (51 per cent) in stores. Overall, Arab consumers are mindful of the price of a product, attracted to free gifts, and highly aware of promotions and discounts. At the same time, they consider quality as the primary criterion for purchasing a product, rating it as more important than price. In a place like Dubai, which is leading the MENA region in terms of its burgeoning mega-malls and is ranked as a favorite shopping destination, consumers do not compromise on quality despite going for advertised bargains and seeking out good deals. From a retail industry perspective, this market segment has specific needs and demands that require a delicate balance between quality and special offers or promotions. Although wealth and prosperity have dictated new lifestyles and shopping behaviors, shopping preferences remain distinctive due to local cultural values and attitudes.

By and large, e-commerce has shown a consistent pattern of growth in the MENA region and is likely to continue doing so in the coming years. A 2007 report by the Arab Council for Judicial and Legal Studies indicated a high level of preparedness and acceptance among e-commerce champions in Arab countries such as Kuwait, Saudi Arabia, the UAE, and Lebanon.[13] The Council reported that these four countries had brought changes in shopping behavior to more than 5.1 million consumers. In 2012, e-commerce in the Middle East reached a record US$ 9 billion, rising to US$ 15 billion in 2015. Similarly, mobile commerce was estimated at US$ 4.9 billion in 2015.[14] In addition to the 90 million or so Internet users in the Middle East, 15 per cent of businesses now have an online presence. Leading online buying patterns in the Middle East are dominated by Saudi Arabia with 51 per cent of e-commerce consumption trends, followed by Bahrain (50 per cent), UAE (46 per cent), and Qatar (37 per cent), with much lower patterns of online purchasing in North African and Levant countries such as Tunisia (19 per cent), Lebanon (15 per cent), Jordan (10 per cent), and Egypt (7 per cent).

Barriers to the development of e-commerce

Although e-commerce is drawing an increasing number of consumers in the MENA region, it is safe to say that it remains far from being a widely adopted form of business for organizations and consumers alike. Online shopping remains a relatively new culture for many users and consumers who are used to more traditional forms of business transactions. Understanding the nature of the barriers that hinder the development of e-commerce will go a long way toward gauging its potential for growth in the region.

To start with, it would be misleading to suggest that e-commerce is widely or uniformly adopted in a region that is also marked by high discrepancy in wealth, economic means, and individual income. Significantly, there are notable discrepancies within the region when it comes to Internet access and use, which has direct impact on the potential for e-commerce to grow.[15] The highest proportion of Internet users come from oil-rich Gulf countries, while other sub-regions, such as North Africa and the Levant, have varying usage rates. A 2016 report on media use in the Middle East in six nation countries (UAE,

Qatar, KSA, Lebanon, Tunisia, and Egypt) noted that the three Gulf countries in the survey (UAE, Qatar, and KSA) have soaring levels of Internet penetration, reaching 100 per cent for the UAE and 93 per cent for both Qatar and KSA; while Internet penetration in Lebanon, Egypt, and Tunisia is 59 per cent, 84 per cent, and 49 per cent respectively.[16] Promising as these trends in media use may be for the growth of e-commerce, they are far from being uniform throughout the region. In other MENA countries, slower progress in matters related to national information infrastructure and networks, advanced computer technology, and Internet penetration are impeding the wide adoption of e-commerce.

Beyond issues of infrastructure and accessibility, e-commerce in the region is hampered by a number of technical challenges and systemic problems, ranging from concerns about the privacy of personal information during online payment, to the inefficiency of payment systems, to the unreliability of the delivery.[17] For example, Zaied examined barriers to e-commerce in Egypt by looking at the factors that affect ICT adoption in small and medium enterprises (SMEs).[18] He identified thirty barriers which he grouped into six categories: social/cultural, technical, economic, political, organizational, and legal/regulatory. Among these categories, Egyptians ranked technical barriers as the most powerful in constraining their use of e-commerce, followed by legal/regulatory barriers, while social/cultural factors were ranked as the lowest barrier. Shovlowsky concurs; in his view, the strongest barrier to e-commerce adoption in the MENA countries concerns security doubts about online transactions, which make potential online customers reluctant to use credit cards.[19]

Even if these technical difficulties are overcome and online security is enhanced, other systemic factors continue to hinder the growth of e-commerce. Reddy and Divekar suggest that lack of a "favorable" online environment at the nascent stage of e-commerce can discourage customers from visiting a site.[20] For example, if the website's interface is difficult for customers to navigate and they cannot easily search for products, they may have an unfavorable online shopping experience. A study by Lin points out that user recommendations are more effective in driving product sales than system recommendations.[21] As such, e-commerce firms need to ensure that the online shopping environment is attuned to this, and allows for the posting and viewing of user recommendations. Ultimately, what matters most are the preferences and tastes of customers. Thus, according to Aanen, Vandic, and Frasincar, algorithms are one way to map product taxonomies.[22] Such a taxonomy, they suggest, will allow firms to aggregate product information from their competitors' multiple websites, which in turn will enable them to formulate an effective market strategy and assess market competitiveness based on their customers' personalized requirements.

Important as they maybe, the technical and systemic factors are neither the only nor the most complex barriers to the development and wider adoption of e-commerce in the region. In fact, the nature of relationships that develop between the customers and the sellers in the online environment is an important consideration.

Bridging interpersonal and mediated connections

The impact of interpersonalization is most evident when customers engage in shopping activities either in the souk or in modern malls, where the business transaction emanates from the seller to the buyer and vice versa. When it comes to the e-commerce, the practice and expectation of building personal connections tend to be replaced or supplemented by the mediated connections of technological systems. Considering the lack of personalization and the absence of relationship-oriented business dealings, both of which were inherent in the souk culture, it is fitting to ask whether the use of innovative technologies, in general, and the adoption of digital platforms, in particular, inhibit or facilitate relationships between customers and retailers.

Tyler's article "Is the Internet Changing Social Life?" notes that although the lack of face-to-face communication on the Internet could weaken social ties between people, it also weaves the social fabrics of the users into many different forms.[23] In spite of the challenges that accompany online forms of interaction within business environments, the Internet has the ability to function as a social equalizer, specifically in bridging the interpersonal relationships required for achieving an intimate connection in face-to-face business transactions. In effect, with time, "relationships formed over the Internet become very close, of high quality, and rooted in real world connections."[24] The ability of online customers to access products and information can be enhanced by the added ability to engage in a meaningful relationship with retailers to understand their products.

The prevalence of the Internet of Things (IoT) can lead to an enhanced form of personalization, which makes the shopping experience more suited to personal preferences and tastes. A study by Wu, Chen, and Dou found that, with IoT, online consumers have the ability to experience the sense of touch and feel of the products in the same way as in a store.[25] Increasingly, technology is enhancing the ability of retailers to position their brands in the consumers' minds and emotions. Particularly noteworthy in this respect is the effect that interaction styles have on consumers' brand perceptions. For example, friend-like interaction styles (factors like friendly and caring intention, sincere and honest personality, and a pleasant experience and intimate relationship) lead to positive brand warmth and brand attachment; conversely, mechanical styles (such as professional intention, efficiency, sophisticated and rugged personality, and a less pleasant experience) lead to less warmth and attachment to the brand. With the IoT, friendly styles of interaction can make users feel adequately satisfied with the online shopping experience, as if their interaction were personal and not virtual.

The nature of the relationship with the customer can both ensure an authentic shopping experience and also provide value for customers when engaging in online shopping. Lee and Dubinsky found that e-retailers can increase customer satisfaction by helping customers feel as if they were engaging in a face-to-face interaction with a salesperson.[26] For the authors of the article, the role of a salesperson in establishing a relationship between a customer and a seller in their business transactions is crucial. When customers face poor service from staff on the frontline, they immediately experience feelings of rejection and dissatisfaction. Accordingly, Lee and Dubinsky identify three key elements for effective online shopping: service quality, service recovery, and customer relationships. In order for e-commerce retailers to promote the same quality of customer relationships over the web without jeopardizing the authenticity of the shopping experience, they need to incorporate user interface features such as effective customer-based information (customer reviews) and e-contact option (live-chatting with salesperson), which can increase the satisfaction of online shopping for customers.

Another finding by Inman and Nikolova suggests that customer acceptance of technological innovations within online shopping depends largely on the level of intrusiveness of their privacy, which forms their perceptions of the potential relationship with the e-retailer.[27] Although customers would like to establish relationships with the retailers or sellers, they also want their privacy to be respected and protected to the extent that their disclosure of self-related information is done at their own discretion.

The foregoing analysis suggests that the role of digital technologies in the context of e-commerce is instrumental, and further that it is affective in nature. Considering Tyler's claim that the Internet is changing the social fabric of customers, it is safe to say that customers in the Middle East are cognizant of the role of digital technologies, particularly the tendency of IoT to make their experience of shopping authentic, and thus encompass the kinds and meanings of relationships they long for and aim for in an online shopping context. What this means is that the advent of information technologies does not preclude the possibility of forming virtual relationships that thrive on trust and empowerment. Evidently, mediated forms of connection need to be evaluated based on whether cultural practices are congruent with cultural values, in order to determine the level of desirability of e-commerce. Accordingly, the following section approaches customer acceptance and resistance from the perspective of cultural values.

The culture factor

Important as the technical and systemic factors may be, they are neither the only nor the most complex barriers to the development and wider adoption of e-commerce in the region. The more challenging barriers are cultural in nature and relate to values, attitudes, and behavior. According to cross-cultural psychologists like Triandis, beliefs and values are the strongest force shaping a person's thinking, emotions, and behavior.[28] Changes in behavior usually take a longer time to achieve than system or technical changes, as technical elements are relatively easy to fix or alter.[29]

Thus, despite modernization and the wide adoption of a broad range of technologies in everyday life, Arab societies continue to desire the kind of social and business interactions that underpin the experience of the souk and the mall. For example, the adoption of e-commerce is contingent on the users' willingness to accept that business is done through a technological infrastructure such as the Internet rather than face-to-face. But this is not the case in some business practices in the region. The above-mentioned report from PayPal on business trends in the GCC countries notes that while e-commerce is on the rise, its actual practice shows attachment to old shopping habits. PayPal reported that in spite of the increased use of mobile devices for purchases, customers strongly prefer to pay cash on delivery (COD) (80 per cent of users), rather than pay by credit card (12 per cent). While such data on consumer habits may not be representative, they suggest nonetheless that many consumers in the region who adopt e-commerce still prefer a face-to-face element. These findings also suggest that realizing the potential for e-commerce in the region depends not only on enhancing factors that facilitate its adoption, but also addressing the various barriers that hinder its development. E-commerce industries seeking to claim a market share in the region will need to take into consideration the cultural value systems of potential MENA customers and understand how they acclimate to the new business environment before they can make headway.

Taking heed of the cultural nature of the impediments that hinder development of e-commerce, a number of comparative studies highlighted the need for the online business model to customize products and websites according to the habits and preferences of customers from different cultural backgrounds.[30] For example, using cultural dimensions from Hofstede, some studies pointed out that the notion of "one size fits all" does not hold true in the online business environment and its practices.[31] Business owners must understand their target market segment, which may have different cultural values, such as power distance (the level or degree of inequality in terms of purchase decisions and individualism) and collectivism (the level of independence and self-reliance versus relying on collective or community-based references when purchasing goods and services online). Another study by Pavlou and Chai concluded that for online marketers to entice customers around the globe, they needed to acknowledge their customers' distinctive needs and customize their business and marketing strategies.[32] Similarly, Singh, Kumar, and Baack noted how business websites from particular countries depict the culture of these nations, which suggests a high impact of culture on e-commerce websites.[33]

Culture is an important consideration because it creates a way of life as well as a set of behaviors and norms. Additionally, culture determines the extent to which users are inclined to adopt technology. Ulhelkar underlined the importance of cultural fit between a technology and its users—in this case e-commerce adopters.[34] A study by Hosni showed that the reluctance of consumers to accept e-commerce in the MENA region is related in part to a lack of understanding of the advantages of using the Internet, and the cultural perception of the technology as a Western product with Western values that may not be congruent with their own cultural values.[35]

Cross-cultural perspectives on e-commerce

In the field of international business and marketing, the concept of culture is of immense interest, and many scholars have stressed the need to take heed of the cultural dimension.[36] Failure or success when conducting business often depends in great part on the seller's cultural competencies in the international marketplace.[37] In a globalized world, e-commerce is subject to the same cultural influences as international business.[38] The ways in which people conduct business varies depending on the types of products and services they wish to promote, the different segments of customers they wish to attract, the foreign markets they wish to penetrate, and the price negotiation that takes place, among other considerations.

Each society has its unique value systems and norms. For Charles Hill, "societies differ because their culture is different. Their culture is different because of profound differences in social structure, religion, education, economic philosophy, and political philosophy."[39] Numerous studies have established that culture impacts on the way people do business internationally,[40] including processes and transactions that involve an interaction between seller and buyer, from the moment the seller attracts the customer's attention, to the way they negotiate the deal, to the moment the transaction is completed. During this process many factors come into play, including style and mannerism of communication and persuasion when promoting products, the mechanism offered for payments, the relationship of the parties involved, the efficiency of the system, the structure of the organization, and the brand or name of the product—all of which are subject to cultural variations. Cultural values provide a basis for understanding consumer acceptance or rejection of how business is conducted, based on their culturally-attuned preferences, choices, and tastes.

A number of studies have shown that culture impacts on the adoption of e-commerce in certain MENA region countries. Yet, there is still a lack of understanding about the extent to which both local customers and foreign visitors prefer or adopt the cyber souk over the traditional souk. If a transition from one to the other is to take place in the next decades, how can local and global e-commerce players prepare themselves for how Arab societies prefer to conduct business? And further, how can Arab societies and cultures acculturate to the new practices, values, and attitudes of online business cultures?

Doing business online requires a new order of operations, since it differs from the traditional face-to-face method of conducting transactions with customers. These differences arise in both the nature and structure of business dealings, which need to be congruent with the customers' cultural values. In this respect, a number of questions arise. What changes has technological advancement brought to business cultures? To what extent can culture shape and determine how online business is conducted? If these practices are acceptable to a certain society, what are the cultural values that made it so? Conversely, if such practices are resisted by a particular society, what are the cultural values behind such resistance? These questions matter, since e-commerce operates on an international business platform; customers are not bound by national or geographic borders, but can visit any seller around the world. Culture therefore becomes a crucial factor in how sellers and buyers conduct business transactions and how they carry out their business relationships.

In the following, I develop a culturally-attuned theoretical framework for understanding e-commerce practices and preferences using three cultural dimensions derived from Hofstede, Hall, and Trompenaars: individualism-collectivism, uncertainty avoidance, and high context-low context dicohotomies (Table 7.2).[41] These cultural dimensions are important to note because of their impact on online shopping behavior. Following the discussion of each of these dimensions, a number of culture-based propositions are presented.

Table 7.2: Culturally-rooted challenges to e-commerce adoption in the MENA region

Cultural dimensions	Key questions
Individualistic vs Collectivistic (References when deciding on products to buy)	To whom do customers refer when making purchases (in-group vs out-group)? Under what conditions do people prefer online reviews to word-of-mouth?
Uncertainty avoidance (Attitude toward change in business practices and shopping habits/ preferences)	Why do people need to acculturate to online shopping by engaging in e-commerce? What is the level of risk-tolerance among international customers (risk takers vs risk averse)?
High context vs Low context (Use of confrontational vs indirect style during price negotiation, and levels of personalization in business transactions)	What is the negotiation style when sellers and buyers are trying to settle on a price? How do customers learn to trust sellers? How important is it to build trust and develop a solid relationship before customers make a purchase decision?

Individualistic versus collectivistic inclinations

For Hofstede, how people conceive of relationships and social ties, and with whom they prefer to establish bonds, is largely determined by whether they adopt an individualistic or a collectivistic cultural dimension.[42] Hofstede refers to the concept of in-group and out-group to explain the social ties that affect the nature and structure of business. In-group members are family members, extended families, colleagues, close friends, and other individuals with whom one has a close-knit relationship, while out-group members are people one does not know.[43]

When establishing social and business ties, people who subscribe to a collectivistic culture prefer in-group members who are bound by strong social ties. By contrast, people from an individualistic culture that values self-reliance and favors maintaining loose ties with other people make little or no distinction between in-group and out-group.[44] While in a collectivistic culture, achievement comes from group efforts and is represented by "We, us, and ours;" in an individualistic culture, society emphasizes self-achievement and has an ideology of "I, me, and mine" when describing one's success to others.[45]

Another important distinction between these cultural dimensions pertains to the level of autonomy a person exhibits: whether or not a person makes decisions based on himself or herself as an independent actor or relies on group decisions and collective opinions. While in a collective culture decisions are made by someone who is superior in the family (such as the breadwinner) or in the workplace (whether it is a team leader or boss), in an individualistic society empowerment is a primary leadership element and people are expected to demonstrate independence in the workplace and/or in a family setting. In an individualistic society, though, the consumer's choice of product is self-determined and driven by self-interest.[46] People explore the full range of options by independently seeking information about a potential purchase.

For example, Amazon offers thousands of online reviews provided by customers based on their personal opinions about a wide range of product categories. The reviews include narrative statements as well as a numerical rating (from 1 to 5). Such online testimonies allow customers from an individualistic culture to evaluate their options and then make decisions based on independent choice. Although the reviewers are strangers to the new customers, the role they play is instrumental to an individualistic culture because they provide valuable information based on their purchasing decisions and experience. They have no ties to existing or potential customers and hence they are out-group members. In an individualistic culture, the distinction between in-group and out-group is less important.

Conversely, customers coming from a collectivistic culture normally refer to in-group members and trusted people with strong ties, such as family, colleagues, and close friends, when making purchasing decisions. Word of mouth is a powerful marketing tool in a collectivistic society, more so when it comes from in-group members than from out-group members. Friends who pass on information about certain online products or services are considered more credible sources, and their recommendations are likely to be taken into account by potential customers. Khattab et al. found that individuals from a collectivistic culture tend to purchase goods when they are referred by close members of their family or in-group members.[47] This raises the question of whether or not collectivistic individuals prefer the written testimonies available online (given by strangers) over recommendations made by families or close friends when they browse for a product to be purchased. Equally important is the extent to which information that is provided by an out-group member rather than an in-group member is regarded as credible.

In short, any attempt to change business practices or shopping habits and preferences needs to answer two key questions: 1) To whom do consumers refer when they need to make decisions to purchase online? 2) How do cultural values affect the decision-making process? Two propositions follow from this formulation: 1a) Customers from a collectivistic culture prefer to purchase online goods or services referred to them by people whom they trust (in-group members); 1b) Customers from an individualistic culture prefer to seek information from a trusted source and then self-evaluate it before making a purchasing decision.

Risk perception and attitude toward change

For the cyber souk to become a business reality in the MENA region, significant changes must occur in business norms, practices, and values. The impact of these changes rests on customers' attitudes toward change and their risk perceptions, because what is acceptable to one society may not be acceptable to another. Here, the level of risk-tolerance for changes in business norms needs to be considered. For example, sellers project their profits based on demand. If consumers in a given country are unwilling to buy products and services online, then online sellers will be unable to penetrate the market, no matter how sophisticated their goods are. Thus, it is crucial to understand what levels of risk and change are acceptable within different cultures.

According to Hunter et al., in traditional commerce, risk is a perception carried by consumers when they are faced with uncertainty in their purchasing decisions and fear that such decisions may result in unfavorable outcomes.[48] From a cultural standpoint, Hofstede defines uncertainty avoidance as the degree of risk tolerance and level of acceptance of uncertainty.[49] Those with high uncertainty avoidance are unlikely to encounter a situation where they are unable to assess the degree of risk. The higher the risk, the more likely it is that they will avoid the situation or transaction. For such people, security and certainty matter when conducting a business transaction. Conversely, people with low uncertainty avoidance tolerate more risk, as pursuing high-risk ventures is perceived as being likely to bring a higher profit. However, in the e-commerce environment, perceived risk has a more profound effect on consumers' decisions, because it is tied to such factors as product performance, delivery, and credit card information, all of which are considered risks in online transactions.[50]

Arab societies are considered high uncertainty avoidance cultures, where risk is not all that desirable.[51] According to Zaharna, the more unsure people feel about a situation, the more likely they are to resist carrying out the requested action.[52] In the case of e-commerce, Arab customers find themselves shifting from their customary face-to-face way of engaging in business transactions to a virtual setting. The adoption of e-commerce entails a number of uncertainties, including the security of the transactions, infrastructure efficiency, trustworthiness of sellers, delivery mode, and the ability to assess products.[53] Issues such as these, which arise with the transition from the real to the virtual world, hinder the likelihood of a wide adoption of e-commerce.

In many rentier Middle Eastern countries where the state provides for its citizens, the degree of tolerance for risk constitutes an additional cultural barrier.[54] In such systems, the state controls the natural resource and rents businesses to outside parties who pay a certain amount of money on a monthly or yearly basis. The related practice of *kafala* or sponsorship in oil-rich Gulf countries allows the government and citizens to collect money from a person (or expatriate) wishing to work or do business in the country. Less risk is borne by the government (and the *kafil* or sponsor) since its role is that of a collector of fees; the outside business partners are the ones who conduct the business, run the risk, and bear the consequences. Considering how rentier states protect the interests and financial well-being of their citizens, who increasingly enjoy affluent lifestyles, individuals may be less comfortable facing risky conditions and may therefore avoid unsecured transactions. Engaging in e-commerce as a new way of shopping or purchasing products may be perceived as risky since it requires dealing with online merchants or retailers with whom they are unfamiliar. This is not the case with souks, where retailers may be their own family members or people whose families they have known for generations. These kinds of family and business ties provide a much valued sense of security.

The likelihood of such a society using e-commerce also depends on the people who encourage its use. Uncertainty in Arab societies can be reduced or eliminated by the reassurance of those in in-groups. Those from collectivist cultures normally prefer to rely on a circle of trusted people when they establish business relationships. Businesses also need to provide a secured infrastructure or platform that will allow Arab societies to use e-commerce without fear of fraud. Offering a high degree of security and confidentiality in the adopted Internet system can go a long way toward overcoming uncertainty about e-commerce and developing trust among consumers who use such platforms.

In short, any change in business practices or in shopping habits and preferences needs to address two key questions: What is the level of risk toleration among both risk-taker and risk-averse customers? And how can consumers acculturate to online shopping and adopt e-commerce? Two propositions ensue from this formulation: a) Customers from a high uncertainty avoidance culture prefer to purchase online goods or services when they are assured of the seller's trustworthiness and credibility; b) Customers from a low uncertainty avoidance culture prefer to purchase online goods or services when they are assured of the efficiency and effectiveness of the e-commerce system.

Contextual propensity in negotiation and communication

The styles and mannerisms people employ when communicating during business transactions depend largely on their culture. Such differences may pose challenges if not properly managed. For example, some cultures may favor a confrontational style during price negotiation, while others favor a non-confrontational style; in some cultures, people may require a high level of personalization in business transactions, while in other cultures people are satisfied with a low level of personalization.[55] These differences have implications for such considerations as the negotiation style when sellers and buyers determine the price. They also bear on how customers learn to trust sellers and how important building trust and fostering a good relationship are when making a decision to purchase a particular merchandise.

Hall notes that people of different cultures have differing communication competencies based on what he called "context."[56] Context refers to what people pay attention to when communicating their ideas, feelings, and actions, and how they communicate them. Context is a continuum, which ranges from a low to a high value point. These two extremes are critical points to consider when looking at how people in a certain culture communicate. When it comes to e-commerce transactions, context can help us understand how people of diverse cultures prefer to communicate. For high context cultures, people take into consideration many factors before they verbalize or write their thoughts, including whom to speak to, when to express one's feelings, and the reasons for doing so. All of these considerations are based on the context or situation.

During face-to-face business transactions that are characteristic of the souk environment, customers tend to engage in lively interactions with sellers. They try to establish a relationship such that the more familiar they are with the owner of the business, the more likely they are to negotiate and haggle for the right price.[57] The success of the negotiation rests in large part on their ability to communicate and offer a good price, which reduces the level of anxiety and uncertainty about the outcome. Both parties enjoy this interaction as it allows them to establish trust between them. In the MENA region, developing relationships is a way of gaining trust.[58]

Commenting on the different intercultural communication styles between a high context and low context society, Hall notes that people who are high context (as is the case in the MENA region) depend on "affective" cultural values. Being relationship-orientated, they value interaction.[59] Unlike high context people, low context people adopt instrumental cultural values, which make them more task oriented. Thus while high context customers are keen on developing relationships, low context customers have more individual-based goals. While collectivistic cultures look for relationship building and maintenance, and group cohesiveness, individualistic cultures usually focus on performance and outcomes.[60]

In a low context society, the communication style is very different. Emphasis is much less on the context than it is on the content.[61] Everything is spelled out in either verbal or written statements. Business negotiations take place based on what is said, not what is observed through non-verbal cues, and contractual agreements made between the seller and the buyers are the main business mechanism. The contract informs both parties of all the rules and guidelines for how the business deal is to be carried out. The concerned parties need not read between the lines for what needs to be done, but simply abide by the letter of the contract—a total adherence to the rule. This context is characterized by "universalism" in which all people are treated equally according to clearly documented rules and procedures that ensure a rule of inclusivity.[62] High context societies are anchored in "particularism," whereby the treatment of people is based on their identity, status, and position in the workplace.[63] People are treated on a case-by-case basis. In this context, workplace rules and policies may not be uniformly applicable to everyone. What prevails is a rule of exclusivity by which people are handled, based on a particular set of qualities or considerations.

In a face-to-face setting, negotiation is personalized and, at the end of the day, customers can walk away satisfied with the goods they bought during the negotiated transaction. However, in a virtual setting, the online platform is based on a less (or non-) personalized medium for negotiation, if not communication. As such, it lacks many of the interactive face-to-face business aspects that are crucial for high context societies like the MENA region. For example, a retail website lacks the non-verbal features which are inherent in the high context communication style and which provide clues to one's feelings and reactions. High context society relies on non-verbal communication such as eye movement, facial expression, and tone of voice, which can send signals about the direction of the business interactions, including its degree of success.[64] Without such signals, it is difficult for high context individuals to interact effectively.

In short, any change in business practices or in shopping habits and preferences needs to address two key questions: What are the communication styles shown by Arab consumers when they engage in buying-selling transactions? How do cultural values such as relationship-oriented vs task-oriented impact on consumers when purchasing goods or services online? Two propositions ensue from this formulation: a) Customers from a high context culture tend to be relationship-oriented, and prefer to engage in face-to-face price negotiation when buying goods; b) Customers from a low context culture prefer to engage in information-seeking tasks when attempting to get a good deal or find the lowest and best price.

Conclusions and future research directions

E-commerce is almost a one-way interaction. Customers browse what they are interested in, see what they like, click "add to cart," and then move on to making payment and completing the transaction. If in doubt about any aspect of the transaction or product, the only thing they can do is send a message to the seller and then wait for a response. Such non-simultaneous transactions may be met with resistance from customers in the MENA region, who are used to communicating and expressing their concerns and getting a response immediately. The fact that there is less (perhaps no) opportunity for a two-way interaction may inspire a good deal of resistance.

Despite such resistance, e-commerce adoption is expected to increase in the next decade. Higher use of the Internet in some MENA countries is making the region more prone to adopting e-commerce. From a business perspective, the potential opportunities for e-commerce are huge in this part of the world, as it represents a newly emerging market segment. But to be effective in exploiting this market, e-commerce industries need to focus on the cultural values that affect consumers' behavior.

Scholars in the fields of international business and marketing have established that a customer's cultural values impact on taste, preferences, and attitudes toward a product or service offered for purchase. Such findings are important for marketers, because customer preferences will differ depending on the country and culture from which they come. For many years, studies undertaken by these scholars have proved that when a business attempts to penetrate a new—especially foreign—market, their marketing strategy needs to take heed of their audience and their cultures. Considering that universal taste has no positive appeal for international customers, marketers need to customize their products to suit a multiplicity of preferences and lifestyles. E-commerce businesses need to adopt a "cultural localization" strategy, instead of pursuing "cultural universality" when making international strategic decisions.

On a practical note, in the e-commerce business environment, three key stakeholders (namely, governments, business entities, and individual customers) need to accord with the new business models with their heightened challenges. People in the MENA region may find themselves compelled to change their dispositions when shopping online. Stakeholders need to employ a global strategy that takes into account differences in the nature, system, and structure of business dealings; level of risk perceived; tolerance and readiness for change in online business practices; and contextual needs when negotiating and communicating virtually. The phrase "think glocally" should be kept in mind when implementing an e-commerce business environment. Instead of focusing on an e-commerce strategy that fits one specific culture (or adopting a localized approach), businesses should consider the notion of "wherever, whenever, and whoever" and develop accordingly an approach that is not only localized but also globalized in both thinking and actions.

Ultimately, businesses need to deal with people. Marketers frequently conduct research focus groups to understand their local customers' needs and preferences. To ensure that e-commerce is widely accepted in the MENA region, they need to ascertain the cultural values of Arab societies and understand Arab customers' preferences, tastes, and needs when it comes to choosing products and services. All of these are driven at least in part by their cultural values. Two questions arise from this formulation: In what ways does e-commerce create a novel form of business transaction that transcends the cultural values of Arab society? And can the business culture of e-commerce help re-shape or re-orient the cultural values of Arab society to fit with the nature and culture of e-commerce?

With globalization, the e-commerce market is fast becoming a one-stop shopping platform for customers around the world, due to the ubiquity of the Internet and the vast number of sellers operating online. Specific cultural values still matter, however, because customers make choices based on their preferences and tastes. As a result, universal values become less salient and therefore customers' values need to be accommodated by the e-commerce sellers, at least to a certain extent. In the Arab context, although customers are quickly learning about new business practices such as e-commerce, they also have fears and anxieties about trying new things due to their discomfort with change and uncertainty. A key question in this regard is the extent to which e-commerce companies are capable of establishing an international marketing strategy that is congruent with the cultural values of their foreign customers.

With regard to strategy, system, and structure, e-commerce firms need to consider recent business models such as m-commerce (mobile commerce) and s-commerce (social commerce), which provide new opportunities for customers to engage in e-commerce. In m-commerce, customers can use their mobile device to engage in online shopping. This medium is even more convenient, as it takes the concept of "anyone, anywhere, and anytime" to new levels. Such a concept also supports the lifestyles and trends of young customers, who are the most promising market segment for Arab businesses today. At the same time, employing s-commerce can offer alternative ways for customers and sellers to engage socially, which is important for building a relationship. This would promote trust, loyalty, hospitality, and reliability, since these concepts are attuned to Arab cultural values.

8

WORKING FOR FREE

HIDDEN SOCIAL AND POLITICAL ECONOMIES
OF THE INTERNET IN THE MIDDLE EAST

Jon W. Anderson

"You can see the computer age everywhere but in the productivity statistics."

Robert Solow, 1987

"[IT] networking logic induces a social determination of a higher level than that of specific social interests expressed through the networks."

Manuel Castells, 1996

A curious hiatus has run throughout discussions in the Middle East of new electronic media, of the information and communication technologies (ICTs) that support them, and of the Internet that conveys them. On the one hand, political analyses focus on issues around informational freedom, with new actors and activities opening the public sphere and enabling civil society; on the other hand are plans for leveraging ICTs for development, ranging from ICT training and ICT-trained cadres to "free zone" industrial parks for local entrepreneurs and international corporations to bring the post-industrial revolution centered around "knowledge work" into the region. From the initial establishment of Internet connections in the early 1990s, through extending those to more users and more uses around the turn of the millennium, to today's proliferation of social media among youth, discussion has circled in political terms around informational freedom and eroding authoritarian regimes, and in economic terms around informational development laying the basis for development of "human capital" through information technology (IT). Each projection is cast as bringing larger and longer-term global shifts to the region and engaging the region with them, a knowledgeable polity on the one hand and a knowledge economy on the other. Each is also imagined as constrained by different local factors—authoritarian habits of information control, on the one hand, and relative underdevelopment, on the other—prioritized by their own points of view on catching up to global standards or in global frameworks.

This might seem a merely analytical hiatus of political and economic analysts not talking to, or taking account of, each other's analyses; but even that would be consequential, I will argue, for obscuring or disattending processes closer to the grounds specific to ICT development, particularly as met in the Internet. To begin with, both the informational freedom and informational development theses share a bias to the supply side, or as an early theorist of the political economy of networked communications, Ithiel da Sola Pool, put it, build-it-and-they-will-come.[1] Arguably, this works for infrastructure development, such as roads that attract traffic, but it becomes problematic with IT development, which engages additional values and practices, even its own habitus. "Habitus" is a concept cast by Pierre Bourdieu to capture a denser concept of practice than the value-action formulations in mid-twentieth-century social sciences—not only more specific values, but also what he called "dispositions" tied both to structures and to specifically located values—that unify analytically distinguished ontologies of choices and habits.[2] To elicit this IT or "digital" habitus and how the Internet conveys it, particularly in the digital Middle East, I start with the case of social media,[3] which political and media-minded analyses focusing largely on impacts have left problematic, and then back up to values and practices that social media share with Internet habitus more generally, before proceeding to how that is manifest in the Arab Middle East. This is partly a multidimensional project of restoration: first, restoration of other values and practices elided by supply-side biases in projecting macro-theories down to micro-levels as assumptions of pre-existing "demand;" second, restoration of actual features of what Jodi Dean has called "communicative capitalism" in thinking about compulsions of the Internet;[4] and finally, restoration of dense and evolving relations between users and developers in the IT realm, all of which throw up the conundrum that working on, with, and through the Internet often entails working not just "for freedom" but also "for free." Before comparing some key sites where these dynamics arise, I explore first how it is a problem.

Analytical gaps

Consequences of analytical biases toward the supply side in treatments of political and economic development, which are less apparent in macro-level analyses focusing on system features, or the respective "human capital" of civil society and labor force development, elide certain contradictions that become more apparent at micro-levels. Among those are contradictory pulls between trade and investment on the margins of formal and informal sectors. It is on those margins that informational freedom and developing ICT labor make a difference, but differences that are elusive at the micro-level and so, typically, analytically deferred to the long run. I happen to believe that both informational freedom and ICT development will make a difference in the long run, because they are driven by forces in larger contexts separately considered as technological, political, and economic changes left substantively opaque and analytically incomplete in the short run. This is particularly the case with "social media," which fairly burst upon the analytical scene over the last decade as the latest iteration of the Internet, Internet ideology, and searches for "impacts" that have accompanied each stage of Internet development in the region and what that development might portend.

This Internet is not the same as electronic media, which include extensive discussion of satellite television in the Middle East; and it is not the same as information and communication technologies, of which the Internet is compounded. Media and ICTs come together in it, but the Internet itself is grounded in computing and, specifically, in computing that encompasses, links, and redenominates information as communication—in effect, and often in intent, reframing them. This computer-science Internet is fundamentally based in software, and underlines the idea that what the Internet, ICTs, and digital media bring to political and economic development is somehow fundamentally new "software" in an extended sense. This is not how the Internet has featured in political analyses, which overwhelmingly focus on media, nor in economic analyses, which advance ICTs as development tools and as a development sector. In the most global formulation of this idea at the macro-level, the economic sociologist Manuel Castells cast the Internet and its component technologies and applications as "the material basis" of a "new social morphology,"[5] arising from "a specific form of social organization in which information generation, processing and transmission become the fundamental resources of productivity and power."[6] From this come policy prescriptions for fostering "knowledge" work and workers that were embraced for the Middle East in the first *Arab Human Development Report* (in 2002) and in the plethora of studies and commentary on the Internet as, if not itself the agent of informational freedom and development in the region, at least a key enhancer of that agency for actors there.

The many limitations of this sort of tool-and-impact thinking are well known and not my concern in this chapter;[7] my concern is instead with some of the consequences left over in both treatments of informational freedom, on the one hand, and ICT-based development, on the other, which analytically cast ICTs as systemic externalities—as something new—and so pose an Internet-specific version of Solow's paradox that one "can see the computer age everywhere but in the productivity statistics."[8] Robert Solow is an MIT economist who gave precise mathematical specification to the portion of GDP or income growth that could not be explained by endogenous factors (physical capital accumulation and population growth) until Romer identified the remainder as education and, more specifically, as research and development,[9] which came into economic analysis as "human capital." This underlies the idea of "knowledge work" advocated in the first *Arab Human Development Report*.[10] Romer might settle the matter for economic theory, but not the residual problem that the Internet, too, can be seen everywhere except in the value flows specifically posited by existing theories. Political analyses about informational freedom focus on political impediments, and little on costs apart from access; they dwell largely on returns to civil society, while projections of ICTs for development tend to elide the "discrepancy between measures of investment in information technology and measures of output at the national level."[11]

Liberal political economy would hold that what is externality in more strictly economic terms—or was until incorporated into endogenous growth theory as knowledge work—is actually internal (or endogenous) to the growth of civil society; it would even hold that conversion of economic activity into desirable political capital is an unalloyed good that comes from the Internet's leveraging human capital. In political analyses, this is the "enabler" model. But we would still be left with a value chain taking on faith that both freedom, on the one hand, and development, on the other, will emerge in the long run. This is the thinking that betrays a supply-side bias and treats the Internet as an exogenous lever on, or multiplier of, specific social interests that are prior to it, when in fact primary production in or through the Internet's various iterations has variously, but consistently, been "for free" and its values extracted higher up the chain. This is particularly the case with the Internet's latest iteration as "social media," which are not only rooted in working for free, but foreground that. Internet gurus from Nicholas Negroponte to Chris Anderson,[12] the editor of *Wired* magazine, celebrate this structure of work that is baked into the Internet and Internet growth, but pass over how its origins in and its early spread through the public sector affect what is rewarded, as well as practices that foster feelings that the freedom and development dividends that are elusive in the short term will surely come in ways that are now only imprecisely apprehended. It is far easier and more common to make the macroeconomic case (for system growth) than to trace the microeconomics of how it unfolds. This discrepancy becomes acute with the strange case of social media, which seems to replay earlier stories about the Internet without resolving the hiatus between them.

The social significance of social media

Social media have a far narrower profile in Middle East studies than in the Middle East itself. In those studies, the overwhelming emphasis has been on their play in political upheavals of the "Arab Spring" and with increasing attention to Arab youth,[13] particularly as enabled through social media.[14] Relatively neglected—or, where available, less integrated into discussions of political communication and demography—are more quotidian matters of what else people use social media for, how they get into it, and why (apart from politics). A rather less extensive literature on these matters indicates broad features of social media use among Middle Eastern youth that align them and the Middle Eastern Internet with global counterparts.

First, they take up social media as ways to express themselves and to be with friends, particularly outside the gaze and supervision of parental and other authorities. In this sense, attested in blogger self-narratives and testimonials, they do not differ from American youth: the draw of social media is for self-expression and connection with others like themselves.[15] Some of this is political and social expression and connection, but it also includes exploring the technology, how it works, as well as what one can do with it, in it, and through it. That is, it is not, and not primarily, a matter of imitation or diffusion, nor are first uses commonly political. The curve of uptake starts with personal interests, whatever those are, across the range of youth cultures.

Second, this is a process in which users and developers merge, overlap, and network. Users of social media and its developers learn from each other in loose communities of practice that share tips and tricks, which may extend to other such communities with complementary expertise, from tech adepts to the arts, programmers, and hackers (i.e. those who experiment), some with formal training that they share in outreach to others, and with activists in Internet politics. No one blogs alone, and not every blogger starts with political blogging. Many start with personal interests, to explore online, which often extends to others similarly exploring. So, for example, Radsch found a "blogger elite" to whom activists in the April 6 youth movement turned to take their movement online or who turned to them;[16] behind that Valeriani described a network of computer geeks, open-source software developers, artists, and hactivists who coalesced in overlapping networks of participation, peer-production, and remix practices that they took into political activism.[17] Both trajectories resemble the "sharing" culture of their US counterparts' embrace of social media, which extends from special social interests to the techno-social "culture of the net" itself.[18]

Third, outreach in these efforts was multiple and stratified. In one pattern, bloggers turn political in defense of blogging when police arrest, mistreat, or try to suppress bloggers; and in another pattern, to help their friends, or to assist shared causes exogenous to the Internet itself, from clean streets campaigns to university politics. In some cases, techies try their hands at politics; in other cases, to secure space for their technological interests; and in other cases, for interests they share with activists. Surrounding these, in all cases, are less committed, less adept users generally labeled "social" or "recreational," which eerily echoes complaints in studies of e-education about repurposing digital technologies provided for education for "personal" reasons exogenous to those programs.[19]

Fourth, these sorts of repurposing unite users and developers not just in shared communities, which is problematic, but also in practices that extend the programming in social media with users' own data and uses, and in developers' media trying to program such uses, of which they are the first users. A type site could be Facebook, which began by putting student directories online and quickly morphed into date-finding, developed by programming congeries of other relationships (organized as "status updates" and brief posts that linked "friends" could "like" or "comment" on). All social media proceed and are developed by this reciprocal repurposing by users' and developers' attempts to incorporate more of users' behavior into their programming, of which uses by political activists have dominated attention to social media in the Middle East over all other uses generally left over as "purely social" or "personal."

These dynamics are not unique to youth or to social media. Their micro-sociologies are relatively unproblematic. Social media revolve around reference group behavior, to be with and to express one's self with persons like one's self or, at a remove, whom one would like to be. Social media involve a range of applications from expression-intensive, such as blogging, to connection-extensive, such as social network sites, like Facebook or MySpace or Friendster earlier; but all involve some balance of those activities, from Twitter, described as "mini-blogging" and practiced as a game of attention or following and attracting a following, to recommendation sites at one extreme and online games at the other. All involve transactions in social information by users, the "user-contributed content" that developers seek to capture, model, and incorporate into programs through continuous close study of their users' online behavior, which starts with users' repurposing those programs. In implementing these functions and as their sites, social media constitute a habitus around online interaction that is dynamic but structurally less a new departure than a set of recent iterations with precedents in content-management and programming social connections that go back to the Internet's origins. That is, these are dynamics baked into the Internet, and specifically into its patterns of growth by adding new users and new uses into its predominantly "user-contributed" content.

Background of the Internet

For most users "the Internet" is represented by whatever configuration they first encounter, from the original engineers' and scientists' work tool to the World Wide Web, which took it public as a publication medium, to contemporary social media, which made Web publication interactive. But technically, and importantly from developers' points of view, each successive iteration builds on the immediately previous one as its "platform," as its engineers designate a present layer on which to build the next one, essentially by incorporating or programming more specifically social behavior.[20]

173

This actual Internet was created by engineers for their own work and around the practices of that work that they built into it. Their initial iteration combined existing technologies of time-sharing, multi-user, multi-tasking, and interactive computing into a general purpose machine for accessing files and running programs on distant and otherwise incompatible computers.[21] The engineering concept subordinated communication to computer technology, in order to use then (late 1960s) relatively cheaper telecommunications to access vastly more expensive and scarce computers, so that engineers could work from where they were, instead of where the computers were, access functions on distant machines, and pass information from one to another.[22] Sociologically, they built it around their values and habits of work, in teams and on projects, with tools they could operate, add to, and fix themselves. Low administrative and financial overhead was a key design consideration and was conceptualized as pushing as much "intelligence" as possible in the system to its margins, where the individual operators could build it, fix it, and extend it to additional machines and uses. To the original facility (in 1969) of file- and program-sharing on distant machines, the first addition was email (in 1971) for connection to their operators; these facilities were soon merged in newsgroups and listservs that are forebears of the World Wide Web and of today's social media, which use it as a platform.

Two dynamics extended this model. It soon attracted and spread to other engineers and scientists, then throughout the research world of academics, to the professionals they trained, and through them into the wider publics whom those professionals served; and this spread was actively promoted by the Internet's engineers assiduously cultivating patrons, finding allies, and building alliances for their tool and work model.[23] Those users and uses ranged from early computer hackers, who also created do-it-yourself networking,[24] to other networking schemes that by the late 1980s were mostly absorbed into or displaced by Internet-specific software, TCP/IP, first published in 1974. By the 1980s, the Internet model was established around design principles that its users built into it; as peer-to-peer communication, for all content, and as a stack of programs on which other programs could be added. This model was affirmed and took the Internet public with the World Wide Web from 1991.

The Web, like the original Internet and its first extension among engineers and scientists, originated in a public sector project—in the Web's case for organizing access to otherwise dispersed research files—that took the Internet model into the public beyond academic and corporate research.[25] There, its first native format was the portal, or website with original content and connections to others' sites. This is the underlying platform for social media that began to emerge in the late 1990s from content-management software (for creating, not just placing, content on the Web, such as blogs), social networking sites (initially for dating, such as Friendster), and peer-to-peer media-sharing (such as the original Napster). But first, the portal became the platform for e-commerce and other services, from government to news and entertainment.

Of what came to be called social media, Blogger and Napster were launched in 1999, Wikipedia in 2001, Friendster (from earlier models) in 2002, MySpace and LinkedIn in 2003, Facebook and Flikr in 2004, and YouTube and Twitter in 2005. Multi-player games had been online for decades, including the globally popular Warcraft, online since 1994 and forebear of the World of Warcraft brought to the Web in 2004. So social interaction as well as sharing information online was not new but in fact well developed prior to the Web, whose initial impact was to turn the Internet into a publication medium, from which it returned to a medium for interaction with social media. That turn was dubbed Web 2.0 in a 2004 developers' conference to designate their shifting from building e-commerce portals to focusing on "social" transactions following the 2001 financial bust in e-commerce.[26]

Within a year of their global launches, social media programs were already in use in the Middle East, which is usually credited to two factors. One is the advent of a younger generation online in the Middle East; after the other change, the Internet becoming publicly available nearly everywhere between 1999 and 2002: Jordan by stages from 1996 to 1999, Saudi Arabia at the end of 1999, Egypt in 2002 following limited roll-outs since 1996, and Syria in 2001 after a pilot project since 1997. There is also an earlier stage reaching back to 1993, when Egypt, Jordan, Saudi Arabia, and other Gulf countries got their first connections to the Internet, following Kuwait in 1992 and Tunisia (the first in the region) in 1991, all in universities or government research institutes. Broadly, a decade that began with more connections outside these countries than internally ended with widespread public availability intersecting with a new generation of uses and local users also coming online.

If social media were first adopted and with alacrity by the same sort of individual who adopted them in the US and globally—in this case, youth—and for much the same reasons of self-expression and connecting with others like themselves, they follow the precedent of regional Internet pioneers a decade earlier. Those were, for the most part, technocrats who had gone or been sent overseas for advanced training, often in science and engineering subjects where the Internet was developed or spread and which they sought to bring back to continue their work, often in privileged research institutes, including telemedicine in the Gulf. These institutes were for the most part outside universities, or took over modest early efforts in universities, and were more connected to international counterparts than to their own nations. They were also located near to rulers, outside line ministries, and charged with national development. For that, the Internet became a tool and an underlying model that technocrats promoted for administrative modernization, and beyond that for administrative and other rationalizations. Like their counterparts who initially developed the Internet, these technocrats, trained in engineering and sciences, baked working for free and working for freedom into plans for and implementations of it in their own countries.

The first generation of technocrats soon sought aid from international organizations like the World Bank, USAID, the EuroMed, and UN programs (particularly ESCWA), which shifted focus after the mid-1990s from physical infrastructure to development of "human capital," particularly through ICT training and investment. The World Economic Report for 1998, entitled *Knowledge for Development*, registered this shift, which became a policy recommendation in the first *Arab Human Development Report* in 2002, written in large part by a group of these Arab-country technocrats. Earlier, Egyptian technocrats secured World Bank grants for developing and propagating an Internet model to provincial governorates and to neighboring countries in North Africa; like counterparts in other Arab countries, they used their positions to push the Internet into the public, particularly for e-commerce and e-education, partly to secure allies for Internet deployment. Other venues included the Syrian Computer Society, which hosted a series of international conferences in the 1990s, Jordan's Royal Scientific Society, and Saudi Arabia's King Abdulaziz City for Science and Technology, which both conducts and supports IT (and other) research in the Kingdom, each of which functioned as government R&D think tanks.[27] A common habit and imperative of this generation of technocrats in the public sector, but out of the limelight, was to build their professional values and work habits into these projects, no less than their forebears did with the original Internet, and often with intent to transform, not just to automate, the soft infrastructures of government "going back to the Ottomans," as one put it to me. In these national initiatives, development through ICTs "led to the formation of new and more complex networks of relations where ICTs act as a common point of interest" between diverse actors, national and international, technical and commercial, in both public and private sectors.[28]

During this run-up to full public access, each country rolled out plans promoting ICT in schemes for e-education and e-government—i.e. service delivery—and shifted promotion of ICT investment to training ICT cadre as a development sector—i.e. for business and workforce development. Shifting from ICTs as development tool to ICTs as development sector reflected larger shifts in development theory and international aid policies, from modernization via capital investment to globalization emphasizing markets and comparative advantages, such as an ICT-capable labor force. In one country after another, plans were advanced to "leverage human capital" in high levels of education, thanks to two generations of investment in public education, by extending ICT training and opportunities for investment in ICT businesses. Over the same period, Internet access extended from pilot projects to roll-out for the general public, which was basically in place by 2000–2001, thanks first to persistent lobbying by technocrats who found its benefits in their own experiences of enhanced agency through ICTs to validate supply-side theories, as well as in their specific projects (of automation).

Interest that developed toward the end of this period in creating ICT businesses or luring international ones with an ICT-trained workforce mutated with the Web financing bust of 2000–2001. Prior to that was a heady period of speculation about ICT investment and job creation, including state sponsorship and creation of Internet and media "free zone" industrial parks. Arguably, as one Arab financier put it to me, what was envisioned was in practice less investment than "a trader's mentality, not an industrial wealth-creating one, but capturing the margin between buyer and seller, rather than making something that others come to you for." Cast in the context of de-monopolizing and divesting state telecoms, his judgment might underestimate the value added in software development; but it honed in on hopes, spurred by Silicon Valley comparisons, to sell the company not the product, to which a few notable examples lent credibility. The first Arab email company was courted and finally bought by Yahoo, and an early pan-Arab Internet media portal was sold to the Saudi media conglomerate of Prince Al-Waleed bin Talal. Other business plans settled on providing middleware, such as Arabization components, for software products of international corporations. Taken together, plans to compete for outsourcing with cheaper skilled labor followed functionally the concept of the Internet's creators to use relatively cheaper telecommunications to increase access to high-value computing resources; but they also cast the wares more in terms of tradable than investment values. So, in addition to the working-for-free baked into the Internet's very structure and habitus by its initial development in the public sector and by public sector developers, its morphing into a development sector in practice focused on margins of tradable goods and services.

This supply-side focus, paralleling political analyses of the Internet, which at the time cast it in the role of liberation technology,[29] was set in place during pilot projects and partial Internet roll-outs during the 1990s, before broad public access was established through existing telephone companies and new Internet service providers (ISPs). Egypt had perhaps the most aggressive policy, licensing numerous ISPs to provide dial-up access for the cost of a telephone call, with a portion returned to the ISP as a sort of bounty. In the Gulf, telephone companies sold Internet services directly or through subsidiaries. Others fell in between: numerous stand-alone ISPs supplemented the telephone companies' own in Jordan, while Saudi Arabia licensed only a fraction of applicants, limited to those already in digital service businesses in order for Internet investment to grow those businesses (and prevent Internet service from becoming a new source of rent).[30] In these and other countries, percentages of populations using the Internet that were in low single digits in 2000, except in Bahrain and the UAE where local telcos (Batelco and Etisalat, respectively) enthusiastically embraced Internet service, began sharp climbs.

In the first five years of widespread public access, and in the wake of the global and regional Internet financial bust in 2001, percentages of Internet users in the Arab world grew from single digits or less into the low to high teens.[31] For example, Saudi Arabia's Internet users quadrupled to almost 20 per cent of the population; Jordan's tripled from the same base to 14 per cent; Egypt's rose to 14 per cent from a much lower base than either, thanks to virtually "free" Internet service (for the cost of a telephone call); and Syria's spiked from a miniscule 0.35 per cent to almost 8 per cent, a twenty-fold increase. Between these new users of the Internet that had developed around the original portal-based Web uses and the following five years after 2006, when social media expanded what was available online, the numbers show that percentages of the populations using the Internet took off, and on the eve of the 2010–11 Arab uprisings were higher in all countries than the highest 2001 starting points in the Gulf, with the exception of Syria, which had barely passed 22 per cent.[32] Practically, the Internet was being used by almost half the population in Saudi Arabia, around 35 per cent in Jordan, nearly 40 per cent in Egypt, and an estimated 22 per cent in Syria.

The period 2006–11 brackets the advent of social media in the region up to its exploding into public notice during the Arab uprisings; as the latter period built on the former, the former had built on a similar-length "quiet" expansion of Internet public access. By 2006, social media were available internationally and in use throughout the region. Blogger.com came online in 1999 and was acquired by Google in 2003; YouTube arrived in 2005 and was also acquired by Google in 2006; Facebook was opened to all users in 2004; and Twitter in 2006. It is likely that these social media are not the cause of this increased Internet adoption and percentages of users, which are affected by numbers and costs of ISPs and by active management of access to the international Internet in Syria, Saudi Arabia, and other countries—notably, even notoriously, Tunisia.[33] Instead, social media rise and, by attracting a new generation of users, partly drive steeper increases in the portions of the populations using the Internet. At least, they provide more to do, and more to bring, online. The first question is what comes online, and the initial answers focused on blogging.

Blogging, particularly political blogging,[34] was first done to attract analytical attention from outside the region as "bridges" or "transmission belts" to the international blogosphere and media,[35] notwithstanding Weyman's earlier account of more personal blogging, which highlighted self-expression as the attraction and practice of youth blogging about problems in their lives and imagining "how they would like their social reality to look."[36] Its other regional setting is the amalgam that Valeriani found in "techies" and "tech-savvies" embracing the technical "culture of the net" and its "remix culture."[37] They ranged from enthusiasts and experimenters to professionals, from web design and the arts to programming, and notably new devotees of Free and Open Software (F/OSS) development, an interest which had been invisible in the region prior to 2001, when developers I knew in Jordan and elsewhere were only interested in becoming trained and certified in corporate software.

F/OSS has various roots, from do-it-yourself and hacker practices, to movements espousing radical alternatives to corporate software development (such as top-down engineering and proprietary closure), including academic practices of collaborative development and "free" sharing of both results and access. Its counterpart in the arts is "remix," which Lessig identified and celebrated as sharing, modifying, and further sharing of user-generated content on the Web, thus amplifying other people's creative production.[38] Kelty has characterized F/OSS practitioners as a "recursive public" focused on the means of its own production,[39] by which he means a community of practice in which participants come and go while sharing tips and tricks, as opposed to communities structured more formally and by didactic instruction.[40] In

Kelty's analysis, a community of practice becomes a "recursive" public when its participants objectivize and then valorize its habitus ideologically as an alternative to taken-for-granted structures. The characterization applies to the Internet itself and particularly to its initial developers, all in the public sector and dedicated to working collaboratively, peer-to-peer and effectively "for free" or for reputation over remuneration.

In such terms, blogging particularly and social media generally share and extend an underlying pattern by which the Internet grows through new uses, which extend its architecture as a stack of applications using previous ones as their platforms, and new users, who add their practices and interests to overall Internet culture. Uses and users are dynamically related through repurposing by users and counterpart efforts by developers to capture those uses and automate them. In these practices, users extend the programming of new uses with their own data and practices. An early example of these dynamics was the extension of newsgroups and listservs from technical discussions of Internet technology to other vocational and avocational interests of its operators, which in turn attracted others with those interests. Social media are the latest iteration of that habitus and extension of the Internet culture of freely provided and exchanged goods, designated as "user-contributed content" of Web 2.0. That is, social media are not different from previous iterations of the Internet in how or whom they engage, so much as in engaging ever wider publics in recursivities of the habitus that Castells summarized as the "power of flows"—i.e. making connections—over the "flows of power"—i.e. of previously situated interests.[41]

The social economy of social media

Just as the Internet is more than media, social media are more than blogging. They include Wikis and social network platforms, such as Facebook, MySpace, LinkedIn, and Twitter, originally cast as "micro-blogging," as well as review sites and others that together were recast as Web 2.0 to designate companies that survived the 2000–2001 crash in Web companies, which crowded into e-commerce by concentrating instead on "social" transactions and user-contributed content. Online gaming was an early example. For this category, however, the focal member could be Facebook, whose precursors were dating sites and whose initial competitor was MySpace; its key feature is various balances of content and connectivity, itself a kind of content in the form of connections with others that users also contribute. Marketing debates revolve around whether content or connectivity is "king," but as a category, social media combine both in a range from high user-contributed content but limited connectivity between its developers (such as Wikis, which closely prescribe what contributors can do) to lower user-contributed content with more emphasis on connection (such as Facebook) on to low user-contributed content (but high connectivity) in online role-playing games. Blogging would fall between Wikis and Facebook with long-form contents distributed through links to other blogs and bloggers. Designation as "media" invites comparisons to broadcasting, while their sociology is more firmly rooted as networking, although the extent to which that entails domination by a networking "logic" is an open question. The designation "social" focuses on what marketers and Internet interpreters contrasted as user-contributed over professionally-produced content in the flows of commerce and news of the Web's first, and pre-crash, iterations. In this perspective, the developer's imperative is to attract, capture, model, and thus to automate capture of this content, and thereby, through what is known as the "network effect" (that users attract each other), more users.

This was explicitly cast as a "social" economy, of more broadly social than narrowly economic transactions, and in economic terms a version of supply-side economies over demand-side appeals addressed in Web portals for e-commerce or news. Its most aggressive interpretation as free goods was by Silicon Valley guru and editor of *Wired* magazine, Chris Anderson,[42] as, indeed, social media programs are presented to potential users who program aspects of their social lives on them. It is in this sense that social media users extend the programs they use with their own data and attendant programming of their social lives on these platforms. While the actual micro-sociology of online social networks, blogging, and wiki use have only begun to be researched, that research affirms a primacy of connecting primarily with known others around shared interests, especially in self-expression and self-disclosure, in the company of like others,[43] which is broadly affirmed in a disparate and fragmentary literature from the Middle East, ranging from education studies[44] to blogger testimonies and self-accounts,[45] to a few narrative case studies.[46] While suggestive, this direct evidence from the region is mostly anecdotal, and we need to turn elsewhere for profiles.

Over the past few years, a number of Middle East research institutes and policy center reports have started to focus on social media usage in the Middle East and North Africa region. Among these, the *Arab Social Media Report* (ASMR) offers systematic, multi-year survey-based findings on social media use across the Middle East, focusing specifically on Facebook as a key proxy and on the growth of users from just before to the year after the Arab Spring demonstrations which brought it into prominence as a social phenomenon. Between June 2010 and June 2012, Facebook users started at less than 0.5 million in Sudan and 3.5 million in Egypt; they then increased to 11 million in Egypt, outpacing increases across the Arab region which averaged 1–3 million.

While ASMR data show absolute growth in the number of Facebook users, a better picture that ignores relative sizes of these countries is the 2012 percentages comparing key social networks, which show the overwhelming popularity of Facebook in comparison with the similarly short-form but broadcast Twitter and LinkedIn, which focuses especially on professionals networking with others in their professions.[47] Each engages a different habitus (and recursivity) within the social media field (or choices of social media to use, information to share, persona to present, connections to seek), from narrower and more specialized publics (of LinkedIn professionals), to selected but more generic "friends" on Facebook, to the wider but self-sampling publics of Twitter's "followings" of particular "streams." The particular significance of the comparison is that Facebook and LinkedIn networks are with known others, and established by reciprocal agreement, while Twitter feeds are by comparison broadcast and anonymously consumed.

ASMR reports that the average penetration of Facebook across the whole Arab region was 12 per cent in June 2012, up from 10 per cent at the beginning of 2012 and 8 per cent in June 2011. Female users stayed at 34 per cent of the total, while youth (ages 15–29) make up 70 per cent, a figure that held steady since April 2011. While GCC countries dominate in percentages of the population using Facebook, Egypt had about a quarter of total Facebook users in the Arab region, adding 1.6 million new users between January and June 2012. By June 2012, total Facebook users in the Arab region were over 45 million, up from almost 30 million a year earlier and triple the number in June 2010.[48] A year later, Facebook users increased to 54.5 million, Twitter users to 3.7 million, and LinkedIn users to 4.7 million, with 60 per cent aged between 18 and 35.[49] These data are from surveys conducted online, not counts of network traffic, which do not show reciprocal sharing. A study of such network traffic over the period of the 2011 Tunisian and Egyptian Arab Spring uprisings noted that while Twitter and blogging showed rapid information flow, those platforms did not encourage reciprocal sharing,[50] confirming an earlier observation that Twitter operates more like a general (broadcast) information-sharing network than like a social network,[51] which features person-to-person dissemination of information.

A more recent ASMR survey (2014) reports that 88 per cent of its survey respondents indicate accessing the Internet primarily from home, 56 per cent from work, only 17.5 per cent from Internet cafés, and 15 per cent via public Wi-Fi. Few report shopping online. While 41 per cent overall connect with friends and family over social media, upwards of 50 per cent search for entertainment (video and music); 35 per cent report seeking news online, 28 per cent via social media; but the report does not correlate these activities with places. By far the (self-reported) most used social media platform is Facebook (91 per cent), followed by Google+ (70 per cent), YouTube (60 per cent), with LinkedIn at 37 per cent, and Twitter by 2014 up to 57 per cent (and Instagram photo-sharing, new in Facebook that year, at 22 per cent). Overall, ASMR respondents report using social media equally to get news and information and for keeping in touch with family and friends (both 27 per cent), followed by job-searching (14 per cent), and professional uses (7 per cent), with entertainment (presumably professionally produced video and music) at 9 per cent, but again not correlated with places where these activities occur.[52] They show that social media are integrated into social life and among its conveyers, which is also reflected in use of smartphone apps: 26 per cent for social networking, followed by 18 per cent for phone communications, with all other uses below 5 per cent. It is difficult to tease out specifically political uses from such reported data, but they—like professional uses—are clearly dwarfed by personal and social uses of connecting with family and friends and entertainment/information seeking. What they do not show is how uses correlate with or vary across or may segregate to different places. These numbers indicate first-order features, including using multiple social media, but not second-order information about what those choices are, or higher-order behavior, beginning with segregating different uses and different others with different platforms or in different places and going on to more intensive repurposing. While marketers are interested in the flow of social media into social life, sociologically more interesting is the reverse flow of social life into social media. One reason is that social media are provided free to the user, which reflects a core value and supply-side perspective of Internet developers and advocates to "build it [the Internet] and they [users] will come"; and developers of social media pour effort and resources into building uses that not just attract users but engage them in ways that developers can capture and model in further development. Software developers call this "perpetual beta," referring to users' testing their programs. The ASMR surveys capture some interim results of this testing in measures of user take-up, but not the process or the other, developer, side of such engagements. For that, we have to turn elsewhere.

Developer cultures and habitus

Local developers are perhaps the least reported of Internet users in the region, although developers have been the first users of Internet technologies back to the engineers who put it together or, in the region, who made the first installations. Developers in the IT field range from its hard core of programmers to web designers, and may include system designers or "architects." Developers conceive and implement applications or programs in software, and the role may extend to firms and their owners who hire that work. After the global (and regional) users turned to social media when the dot-com investment bust dashed plans for e-commerce, some local developers who were not working in international corporations turned to remodeling the two most common foci of previous development—e-commerce and online news—into more interactive social media models, which were cast as bringing the public into more interactive social media (as opposed to the other way around). In function if not in form, these newer social media joined already popular online discussion sites known as web forums, which emerged for specific social groups, from towns to tribes, or around interests such as in professions, in the arts, literature, women's issues, on to fan sites for or sponsored by musicians and sports teams,[53] all sites where users interact with each other. Structurally trying to develop similar paths are sites that solicit contributions, from stories to user reviews of shops and restaurants, in effect extending social media to bring everyday life online through interactivity and user-contributed content. These extend, ideologically, to common goals to spread participation, peer-production, and remix practices in social media as conscious alternatives.[54]

That habitus is indiscernible in ASMR and similar counts that do not capture these reverse flows of social media in registering flows into social media and the Internet generally. These reverse value flows remain ambiguous, accounted as gains in civil society and economically invisible when rendered as returns to reputation or to a common good, both of which are accounted as "external" to economic activity. In part, also, their economics remain invisible, or pushed out of sight, as Jason Lanier has argued,[55] by the ideology of "free" goods and constructions of the Internet generally and social medial particularly as fostering a "gift economy." Certainly, that is how its first engineer builders thought of it, how F/OSS ideologues cast it, and what social media tend to foreground. Lanier is more dogged in identifying this reverse flow not just as a social good by focusing on where it accumulates in ways that can be turned into money. Basically, this is not in user-contributed content per se but in what programmers call "meta-data" about it which, in effect, map online behavior or are its features. This meta-data, he argues, is what social media companies like Google and Facebook collect, aggregate, and profile for sale to their real customers, who are not the users (who don't pay them) but advertisers (who do pay them). Superficially, this can look like the revenue regime in commercial broadcasting, which is free to users and paid for by advertisers; but Lanier advances a more provocative comparison, to financial trading in aggregations of securities, where the value is less in the aggregated than in the aggregation.

Lanier draws on experiences as both a software developer and a content developer (music) to advance a provocative analogy to the financial derivatives trade, where value was captured by the traders of bundled mortgages. Even when the values of individual mortgages collapsed, their values had already been sold as bundles that were in turn tranched into tradable values; and this was not a case of supply creating demand, but the other way around. Demand for tradable instruments put prices where none had been before, and drove those prices up. Traces of user behavior are likewise bundled and the bundles sold, with no return in those transactions to the primary producers (the users), only an indirect return whose first characteristic for Lanier is that user-contributed content is unremunerated to the producer, or content contributor. Lanier goes on to make two points that move such practices farther from the model of advertiser-supported broadcasting and print. First is that free goods do not merely crowd out goods that are paid for, as with pirated music; free goods drive the price of competing goods toward zero— as, for instance, professional journalists have found when publications can gather information and scrape stories from amateurs, or is on the horizon for education—while their value is harvested higher up the chain from trading derivatives and fees for aggregation. In Lanier's field, music, the counterargument has been that recordings that circulate for free (or "frictionless" in digital form) can function as advertising for live performances that can be charged for. A similar case would be that the return on creating the Internet was reputational and enhanced employment prospects for its engineers. But Lanier makes a second point, that while this may be sociologically true, vanishingly few harvest such value, and economic value is still derived from aggregation and is extracted further up the chain, with no return to the primary producer. User-contributed content has no tradable value and reduces the values of competing goods.

This reduction of value is dramatic and drastic where the competition is direct, such as Wikipedia's competition with encyclopedias, or between "citizen" journalism and the professional product. But the user contributions that interest social media companies are traces of user behavior and users' networks that can be aggregated as profiles and potential markets. It is this connection that is "king" in marketing speak. Where wikis are driven by the network effect (that users are attracted by other users), Google, Facebook, and consumer review sites drive the network effect. Facebook encourages users to make new connections. Google builds searches from connections that users make,[56] and makes money from creating technology to deliver data about those connections that do have tradable value.

This value extraction may seem as removed from the Middle East as are those companies, but that is partly the point. They are removed, and remove value from its primary production in the region (and, of course, elsewhere). That is not unique to social media or the Internet in the region; it is a feature of characteristic value flows of the region. Murphy has observed that Arab countries lie on the periphery of the informational capitalist system, adapting its technologies and tapping into global networks but not generating the core technologies.[57] A primary characteristic of the Arab world's participation in global informational capitalism, she says, has been on the whole to translate and provide services that take informational capital from core to periphery, rather than constituting a core on their own.[58] This leaves few ways to make money with ICTs apart from trading them. The most reliable is to own a telephone company, which provides international connection to the Internet and most local infrastructure, followed by ISPs, which in telco perspectives are engaged in telecoms reselling or, more positively, delivering customers for connectivity services. After that, it becomes more problematic. Software developers in the region complain, for instance, that they can make no money in local markets, where they sell only few copies and the rest are pirated. So their more compelling business strategy is to seek outsourcing contracts from international corporations for components or modifications for their products to Arabic or to Arab-country specifications, such as for accounting, insurance, business management, and personnel management. The most compelling is to sell the company instead of the product, in the style of Silicon Valley, of which the famous example is Yahoo's purchase of Maktoob, the first Arabic-language email product; but that market is also problematic. A few may attract investment, for which the most compelling reason is often a model already proven in Silicon Valley, which lends an often-noted copycat quality to many developer plans. More complain that investment is just not available in a region more comfortable with financing trade (secured by inventory) than with investment finance.

None of this really explains why developers would work for free, even if users are effectively contributing their data to a free service. Working for free is built into the Internet and built important parts of the Internet, starting from its origins in the public sector and as an engineers' tool for doing something else; but the idea of payment in reputation or in professional pride is limited by clear evidence of profit-seeking and of remodeling the Internet to some other specification. The most local economic explanation, that the very conservative financial culture in the region favors trade over investment finance, also only goes so far. The Internet in the region seems to have a political economy and to engage a social economy, but to be under-determined by the former (on the evidence of what else users do on the Internet) while paradoxically pointed elsewhere by the latter. And yet significant economic hopes are invested in it.

Those hopes might be the better place to look, and further comparison may help here. In a study of migrant Indian IT workers,[59] Biao Xiang described a system, known as "body shopping," that recruited and brokered programmers as temporary workers for outplacement firms hired by international corporations operating in Australia, Singapore, Malaysia, in preference to recruiting permanent staff. Questioning what programmers, the hard core of IT workers, would find compelling in insecure employment with high overheads taken by the brokers, who would often and sometimes immediately upon engaging programmers place them in a sort of reserve labor force, a practice known as "benching," Xiang found two answers in his data. One was that the otherwise clearly exploitative system of "body shopping" was organized as a chain from tech schools through professors and alumni who provided tips on recruits to body-shops, and from there to outplacement firms servicing personnel needs of international corporations. Recruits into this chain not only depended on body-shops for placement and maintenance between placements; they also often imagined turning knowledge of the system into creating their own body-shops, in effect capitalizing on their knowledge of the network that delivered them. In other words, body shopping, which economically functions like derivatives trading, was experienced as a chain of agents and imagined as a system of advancement or mobility up the chain or toward the ultimate goal of an IT career in the US. His other and complementary finding was that these networks reached back to Indian families, to a particular caste in Kerala that had invested in education for social mobility since the British period. What was interpreted in the body-shopping system as ethnic "Indian talent" for IT turned out, Xiang found, to be a particular dynamic of family values to invest in the education of sons who were expected in turn to remit earnings from high-wage jobs to finance dowries for their sisters, to attract husbands for them of equal status to their own. In other words, linked formations of mobility, one rooted in family values and another in just-in-time outsourcing, worked together to sustain the habitus of the system and agency within it.

If this seems peculiar, the sociologist Gina Neff described a similar system in New York City's hotbed of social media development, Silicon Alley, that she called "venture labor," by which she designated the practice of IT workers embracing the culture of risk of their entrepreneurial employers.[60] They thought of themselves as entrepreneurs, too, taking risks with only tenuous expectations of profiting if the companies employing them were successful (bought out), nonchalant about such prospects vanishing as unsecured debts in bankruptcy, and ready to change jobs like freelancers, of which New York City had a plethora of role-models in the fashion industry and the arts, closely aligned in work, leisure, and residence with Silicon Alley. Neff's addition was to trace these practices and ethos where her informants traced them, to Silicon Valley's culture of venture capital that similarly denominated the IT industry. The particular significance of this habitus may be found in another study, actually of Silicon Valley, which uncovered a pervasive sense among both tech and other workers there of "working for the Valley" over identifying with particular companies or even professions.[61] That is, they embraced a habitus of particularly volatile mobility associated with start-ups that models IT jobs on short-term projects.

Notwithstanding its various Internet "cities," or tax-free industrial zones, the Arab Middle East has no Silicon Valleys, although some returning veterans of the Valley have brought back parts of its start-up culture, partly as investment-seeking (or trading) vehicles known as incubators and accelerators that target various early stages of potential start-ups. And Silicon Valley is definitely one of the reference groups for local developers, including its practices of working for a distant pay-off (selling the company). This deferment may not be enough to account for the various aspects of working for free on the Middle Eastern Internet—from the labor of public sector technocrats, to migrations of some social practices into social media, to the extraction of value from social media elsewhere, to the developers' dilemmas of how to get paid—but it points to additional data that need to be made endogenous to modeling how the Internet that is in the Middle East actually grows there as IT work.

While comparisons to Silicon Valley, Silicon Alley, and IT body shopping may seem far-fetched, they point to kinds of data and relationships that Romer's original specification of the missing factor in economic growth identified empirically in chains of firms and supply relations which, by converting ideas into products or "human capital" (knowledge) into services, divide that labor into chains of firms that supply and draw on and draw in other firms and supporting services. This space is populated in the Arab Middle East by a whole spectrum: at one end, the meet-ups and informal networks among tech developers, such as Valeriani described;[62] at the other end, the government-sponsored media and IT "cities" or "free zones" which isolate such development from local economies. In between have emerged various so-called "incubators" and "accelerators" that provide mixes of administrative, marketing, and legal advice, as well as finance in return for ownership stakes in turning developers' ideas into IT businesses. In their jargon, they are part of an "ecosystem," and individually miniature versions of it, linking components of the tech sector (i.e. Romer's chains of firms). In proposing to link IT developers to potential investors (venture capitalists), their particular offer is training to develop a business model and how to "pitch" it to potential investors. In Amman, Jordan, incubators and accelerators have been founded by Silicon Valley returnees; others are home-grown, offering various combinations of advice, administrative, and financial support, and networking with potential customers both locally and abroad. As intermediaries that balance training, recruitment, mentoring, and investment-seeking, the form tends to morph easily, to move up or down the chain of recruitment, training, and investment-seeking, or is suspected to do so. The form itself is unstable. It includes, in addition to the Silicon Valley models, also local ones that take a looser part in training, putting on workshops and operating more like meet-ups, with a more regional view of the market for IT labor and its regional mobilities. Both take part in a rhetoric of building "ecosystems" and celebrating local potential for start-ups and entrepreneurship, which parallels that of "working for the Valley," or more precisely promotes it.[63]

This reflexivity of working for/in the "ecosystem" may be stronger in meet-ups, which come in versions modeled on precedents in high-tech hubs, channeling their glamour, and in more home-grown versions that start with IT enthusiasms channeled into the local format of voluntary associations or clubs (computer *nadiy*). In other words, the meet-up form is likewise unstable, and is liable to morph into conferences or venues for product demonstrations, which some feel betray the spirit of sharing experiences and knowledge, whereas others feel it adds a measure of professionalism and opportunity. On the whole, meet-ups give more substantial form—even if only a name—to the communities of practice that are their underlying structure. Several factors put them in the same space as incubators and start-ups, and even tech and media industrial parks further up the chain, from individual developers, to start-ups, to established firms. Some individuals circulate among these venues, or belong to networks with others who do, which transmit information about and constant comparisons between them. The rumor mill fairly twitches with gossip and speculation, which are the short-term information flow that registers the system's dynamics, and also the longer-term embodiment of the Internet habitus and experience of it, which register as "borderless" and quickly diffuse its habitus of remix and malleable forms.

By comparison to Romer's chains of firms, these arrangements display an instability or tendency to morph into different, adjacent forms: meet-ups may become conference venues, workshops may become product demonstrations, and incubators come to register as talent-scouting or financing vehicles—all like the IT body-shops described by Biao Xiang, the fragility of Silicon Alley shops, or the register of Silicon Valley firms as less permanent than "the Valley" itself. These are inherently unstable combinations of local and more global dynamics which, taken together, fit the spectrum that includes Biao Xiang's agency chains and Romer's chains of firms that unite and transform values from one sphere with another.

Conclusions and implications

Comparisons help to identify ways in which developers from the original Internet's engineers, through programmers generally, and social media developers who emerged from the phase of Web development, all form a multi-layered epistemic community, or overlapping communities of practice, and share a habitus rooted in and transmitted through the Internet that links them. Valeriani pointed to a (reflexive) "culture of the net" that is present as well in the Arab Middle East, and to its locus in the medium that spreads it, a medium at once social and technical, each conveying the experience and habitus of the other around connectivity, making connections, imagining and being (through its habitus) connected.[64] Further along this spectrum are incubators and accelerators that widen the types of relations engaged around start-ups, and begin to formalize them. Still further along this chain, tech and media "free zones" belong more to the relatively institutionalized international circulation of value through outsourcing. What may appear as a diffusion of innovations, and thus analytically accessible through parsings into the global grafted onto the local, or vice versa, is a much more complex reality of nearly instantaneous spread, accelerated through the medium of the Internet and its constant morphing, such as experimenting with social media platforms in the Middle East almost within a year of their going public in North America. In economic and political terms, this imagination may be thought of as the Internet Premium behind the various strands of the habitus that registers as "working for free."

Working for free is foundational to the Internet and its early development in the public sector, from the assiduous efforts of its creators to spread the ethos and practices of their work, to preserving those as alternatives against others that would modify the Internet. Locally, it is also reflected in common complaints in sub-communities of developers, from e-commerce Web portals in the late 1990s to social media in the first decade of the twenty-first century. One has to do with piracy (whose double-edged character is discussed by Mirgani in Chapter 6 of this volume), or the experience of early developers of Arabic-language software, who no matter how widely their work might be used, manage to "sell only one copy" in explaining why they turned to producing "middleware" components for international corporations. Some of this production involved essentially non-proprietary local cultural knowledge, such as of Arabic but also of Arab country-specific accounting, insurance, banking, and other institutional norms and procedures; others focused at the more universal technical end on the "outsourcing" economy that drives down the price of labor and makes employment more contingent, or more like a project, whatever its site.

A second way in which IT development is enmeshed in a habitus of working for free is more strictly financial than commercial. Developers, especially would-be commercial developers, from e-commerce portals to social media platforms, have consistently attributed difficulties in financing their projects to biases in Arab banking that favor trade finance, where premiums go to brokering over investment finance, which registers as speculation. That being their experience and its register in the system, some turn to personal or family sources, including spin-offs from family businesses; this is an economy of subsidizing otherwise unremunerated work partly for returns in reputation, like the engineers before them, partly for interest in the activity, partly for other pay-offs, from connection to similar others, to participation in a shared culture and extending its values and practices.

Software developers share a culture rooted in a habitus that stretches from the engineering foundations of the Internet to how that has transmitted into its structure, usage, and agencies; they combine self-administration, a work-model shaped on projects, sharing, and a vision of "pushing intelligence [knowledge built into the system] to the margins" where uses can be developed for, not just on, a general purpose technology. This vision survives and is even enhanced in the social media turn, for both ideological reasons as represented in F/OSS, and for practical ones. Social media would not exist without building on this model (of platforms), at least not in their contemporary dynamic configuration of users repurposing programs and developers incorporating that behavior, which together extend developers' programming with users' own. The unfolding of this relationship that unites developers and users could be compared to a rolling game. It would include both the engineering *amour propre* of socializing new users to Internet habits, but also socializing the Internet through additional layers that in engineering perspectives are higher-level uses, up to contemporary visions of social media focal types such as Facebook, which seeks to capture ever more of its users' social worlds, or Google's ambition to encompass "all the world's data."

At a more quotidian level, these habits of mind and work translate across a gamut, from ideologies about free and open software development, to developing free services from which can be extracted more data about user behavior that can be variously capitalized (to further automation of advertising profiles) or whose values at a higher level can be captured for buying and selling, as opposed to merely exchanged in a generalized way. This last is the economics of "working for free" that is elided in macro-perspectives, or merely deduced from them as pre-existing demands that would respond positively to exogenously increased supply. In these assumptions, both political and economic macro-perspectives analytically treat IT generally, the Internet specifically, and social media more recently as exogenous to local systems that engage them. Such conceptualization has not caught up with empirical realities identified in this volume by Zakaria (Chapter 7) for e-commerce and Radcliffe (Chapter 11) for e-government, which include important continuities not just at the level of engineering, where there is every indication in my experience that local developers in the Middle East share goals such as automation and serving uses with international-standard software with an epistemic community and often through communities of practice. It has also not caught up at the user level with fuller descriptions of what draws users to and what they do on social media, which converge on a sociological level with their counterparts more globally. Here, content may vary, but connectivity along with and for self-expression is a fundamental.

The problem is to bring such variables that register here as "working for free" into growth theory as endogenous factors in growth; that is, as part of—not as outside additions to—the phenomena, and this applies *pari parsu* to political analysis as well. In the Arab Middle East, the hypothetical contribution of IT investment to growth has been identified specifically as Solow did for growth theory generally,[65] and efforts undertaken to describe and incorporate its component factors,[66] which are summarized as "human capital." One step in this direction indicates something of the empirical gap. In a 2013 report on the IT and IT-enabled market in Jordan, the Ministry of Information and Communications Technology and its private-sector counterpart in that market for the first time adopted a standard international classification of industries in the IT and directly IT-enabled sectors,[67] which opens up identification more specifically of value flows in, within, and out of those sectors. Some of what their figures show confirms anecdotal observation and testimony from those sectors—namely, that telcos and ISPs make money, while that is still harder to identify outside established software development and service provider firms. Indeed, it is not clear how deeply data collection in those sectors goes, as percentages of firms responding to their surveys that collected their data were partial and only from firms identified, leaving out the range from start-ups to meet-ups and other formations on the margins of this economy. More telling is the report's consistent top-level breakdown into internal versus external markets, which is to say tradable value. This captures (some of) the value of trade of goods and services exchanged, but not the investment value in them, which is to say not the value developed at levels of primary production.

Among indicators of this gap in economic terms are the common developer complaints, since the first moves of the Internet into the private sector here, about a financial culture that favors loaning money against tangible values of inventory over investment finance in more virtual values; correlative emphases on building businesses to sell the business over selling its products (and reinvestment of any profit in growing the business); complaints that local markets provide no returns anyway due to piracy; and the common practice of subsidizing development from personal or family wealth. A variant of the latter includes government grants, whether in the form of subsidies or market rights such as franchises, and more recently international NGOs "investing" in social media development and developers by sponsoring conferences, workshops, training programs, and other forms of patronage.[68] Each of these represents an exogenous premium in what more nearly resembles an options market.

Economically, options are rights to buy or sell an underlying good or financial interest at a future date. Buyers of "calls" pay and sellers of "puts" receive premiums for rights ("options") to be exercised later at today's prices. In actual markets, these premiums are money that holders and non-holders receive from the other's speculation on value changes that aim to extract those values. In a virtual market, however, the premiums are something else. They range from enhancements to reputation of engineers (which may or may not translate into other values, from job advancement, to awards and prizes, to professional influence), and likewise for software developers, all the way down their chain to programmers, to enhancements of other likewise intangible or informal values, including those of informational freedom. Value in an options market is harvested up the chain from its primary producer. This nearer comparison to options markets captures the reality that Lanier analogized to derivatives being the points in the chain at which the most directly economic values are extracted from information flowing online—namely, the "reality" of investments in IT flowing as options on future values.

These realities of how developers—economically speaking, primary producers through their unification with users whose behavior they seek to capture and automate—participate in chains of value production that are hidden in analyses focusing largely on user agency or on impacts of taking up IT for all sorts of activities. Analytically, what is hidden in the study of impacts of IT generally and the Internet in particular are the agency chains that link developers' various activities in three interrelated features of social media: (1) repurposing by users and in developer efforts to incorporate new uses in their programming, (2) career patterns whereby developers emerge from users or are the first users, and (3) users in practice extending the programming of those platforms with their own data. Specifying these value and agency chains more precisely will go a long way toward resolving where and what values are extracted, and the conundrum that so much digital work of all kinds appears framed in a habitus of "working for free." Such specification analytically involves a shift from why to how this work proceeds, or what it integrates into those chains and their habitus as endogenous factors in growth, including conceptualizing those other than as additions. One practical site that makes this chain more accessible than in aggregate statistics is the spectrum that links the local emergence of "incubators" for transforming developer concepts into businesses with more informal communities of practice that feature peer-learning, and with the market represented in tech and media "cities" that, as "free zones," are separated from the local economy.

Their characteristic as options is also important, because discrepancies between abstract promises and everyday experiences in endogenous terms represent premiums attributed to the Internet and, more recently, to social media—or, for the disappointed, their discount—in "working for free." Such discounts surface in complaints that IT does not deliver what is promised, or that IT people do not, or that government or some other authority actively or passively blocks or diverts its value flows. In game-theory terms, the premium would be a bluff. More substantively, failure to generate perceptible growth in either political or economic development spells trouble from loss of faith in IT generally and the Internet in particular, to loss of faith in its promoters and apologists, to loss of faith in its purveyors' ability to congeal more supportive arrangements. Their effects may be seen in the high turnover in developers and their projects, which does not have the same registers as in Silicon Alley and Silicon Valley, where they are cast as learning experiences, but may register nevertheless in inward turns,[69] or in disappointing growth prospects where blame tends to return to local cultures of finance and governance, also of piracy and more experiences of working for free. And so for developers: "It's true," a local observer of difficulties in e-commerce development put it to me, "the customers discount promises of information technology and for good [everyday] reasons." Among those are commonly enumerated difficulties of payment, where there are few credit cards, difficulties of getting goods and services across borders and out of customs, and even, as another in the delivery business told it, apocryphal stories of e-commerce customers trying to haggle with the delivery person, who is not a party to or agent for their transaction, but is similarly drawn into working for free.

9

DIGITAL RIGHTS ACTIVISM AFTER
THE ARAB SPRING

INTERNET GOVERNANCE POLITICS
AND THE INTERNET FREEDOM PROTO-REGIME

Muzammil M. Hussain

Following the 2011–12 cascades of popular protests in the MENA states, transnational networks of technology-savvy activists, communications corporations, and foreign ministries have joined together in international policy arenas to define and enforce "Internet freedom." These stakeholders have been synthesizing policy norms to better monitor, promote, and regulate the political uses and consequences of information and communication technologies (ICTs) in non-democratic countries. In this chapter, I examine the emergence and activities of several competing technology policy arenas, debates, and stakeholders sponsored primarily by Western democratic regimes since the aftermath of the "Arab Spring."

These efforts are ongoing, and the social construction of policy norms and frameworks by multi-stakeholder communities of actors have agitated since 2011; however, recent crises, like Edward Snowden's mass surveillance revelations, have further galvanized and disrupted this process. Therefore, I ground this analysis under the rubric of examining "proto-regimes" in formation, where the involved stakeholders are engaged in introducing competing norms and goals, but are struggling to synthesize them under a coherent system.[1] So our task is to examine and critique this regime construction process and the new communities of practices that are informing contemporary communication technology governance frameworks. The involved actors have competing intersections, understandings, and practices, but have converged with the aim of influencing the political attributes and capabilities of the digital infrastructure undergirding so many recent episodes of digitally enabled social change. This discussion also identifies and traces a small Silicon Valley-based community of policy entrepreneurs—those who "from outside the formal positions of government, introduce, translate, and help implement new ideas into public practice."[2] This tech-savvy civil society network includes technologists and activists who have, since 2008, collaborated and articulated many of the new norms, vocabularies, and frameworks now referenced by officials, activists, and journalists, internationally, whenever "Internet freedom" is discussed and promoted.

This network of stakeholders and practitioners has been instrumental in driving the current ideas and discussions regarding "Internet freedom" and is increasingly important in setting the agenda for what constitutes meaningful and effective policies for securing digital infrastructures in the public's interests. Given the complexities of the transnational political setting and challenges that these diverse stakeholders (activists, corporations, and governments) are addressing, their efforts thus far have been both foundational and problematic. Their policy efforts have been foundational because the period of activities observed in this chapter (January 2012 to December 2012) contains the first major collective effort by which a large coalition of primarily Western nation states has collectively and materially supported "Internet freedom promotion." At the same time, these very states have since been found to violate the very efforts they champion, both domestically and abroad. This is why we must trace the rise of this emergent policy regime, not by assuming that it is either effective or coherent, but by noting its apparent intention to affect fundamental communicative aspects of the global system.

Bringing the state in: putting Internet freedom on the global policy agenda

The coalition of Western nation states promoting Internet freedom broadly represents advanced industrialized democracies, and is supported most substantively (both politically and materially) by the United States Department of State.[3] Although the US was the most influential sponsor, ideological and material commitment toward promoting Internet freedom has also been provided by the Netherlands Ministry of Foreign Affairs, the Swedish Ministry for Foreign Affairs, and the Foreign and Commonwealth Office of the United Kingdom, to name three key state backers. This coalition of Western democratic states advancing Internet freedom promotion was formally launched soon after major Arab Spring protests subsided, in December 2011, at The Hague by Dutch Foreign Minister Uri Rosenthal, as the Freedom Online Coalition (FOC).[4] During the December 2011 launch of the FOC in The Hague, then-Secretary of State Hillary Clinton offered the coalition its opening keynote remarks and also acknowledged Foreign Ministers Rosenthal (the Netherlands) and Carl Bildt (Sweden), corporate representative Eric Schmidt (Google), and civil society NGO leader Leon Willems (Free Press Unlimited) as "co-conspirators" of the FOC—acknowledging the intimate involvement of state, private sector, and civil society stakeholders during its early moments.[5]

Among the FOC's member states, the US has been this coalition's most prominent sponsor, and its efforts to promote Internet freedom included direct and material references to the Arab Spring protests that began in December 2010. Since 2008, the US has invested more than $US 100 million to promote Internet freedom-related research, development, and intervention projects. In addition to sponsoring dialogues and negotiations to bring together disparate digital infrastructure stakeholders, the US and the FOC provide material support to global Internet users and activists under threat for exercising their fundamental human rights through new and cutting-edge technologies, particularly censorship circumvention software and applications. According to the informational materials published and propagated by the FOC, this is primarily done with the help of funding programs from member states, exceeding 2.5 million euros. The FOC, then, is a key example illustrating the infusion of activist, state, and corporate interests in the ambiguous domain of Internet freedom promotion work involving several types of stakeholders as unlikely bedfellows.

While the FOC is a key object of examination, it is not the central case or site of study for investigating all the important norms and actors involved in Internet freedom promotion more broadly. One must be careful here not to conflate the FOC as "the" Internet freedom regime, for several reasons. First, in order to investigate Internet freedom promotion efforts, focusing solely on the activities of the FOC is not an ideal or conceptually valid strategy. This is because the diverse stakeholders working in the Internet freedom arena(s) often disagree and often misunderstand each other—consensus is not a core characteristic of Internet freedom work; consensus formation is this issue-area's core problem and challenge.

Second, the transnational context of the investigative phenomena (i.e. Internet freedom promotion) necessitates that we corroborate its multiple understandings and outcomes being championed by the competing multi-sector stakeholders. This is particularly important as proponents of Internet freedom work are situated within governmental agencies, communication corporations, transnational civil society organizations, as well as loose networks of politically-minded technologists who tinker with and manipulate digital tools and infrastructure.[6]

Finally, because Internet freedom promotion fits under the broader category of regulating or governing the global Internet infrastructure and all its surrounding and undergirding elements (i.e. what I refer to later as digital infrastructures), we must also recognize the influence of pre-existing regulatory agencies and regimes that have been operating long before the Arab Spring of 2011, and also how discussions about Internet freedom have increased both in maturity and incoherence. Indeed, a large corpus of scholarship already exists within telecommunications policy and Internet governance, and this tradition has developed a vast knowledge base about the influential bodies and policy coalitions, including the Internet Corporation for Assigned Names and Numbers (ICANN), the Internet Engineering Task Force (IETF), the Internet Governance Forum (IGF), the Internet Society (ISOC), and the UN's International Telecommunication Union (ITU), to name a few (see Figure 9.1, highlighting the FOC's positioning in the transnational ecology of Internet governance policy institutions).

Broadly, then, it would be conceptually invalid to refer to the FOC as "the" Internet freedom policy arena or treaty regime that is, or should be, worthy of singular examination. Indeed, there are many venues and arenas where the norms surrounding Internet freedom promotion are being defined and debated. However, it is the FOC's formal coalition of committed and prominent Western democratic member states, and the coalition's peculiar launch echoing strong references to the Arab Spring, that justifies the FOC as an interesting case that is conceptually distinct and empirically novel for deeper analysis. At the very least, as an international state-sponsored regime, the FOC has brought Internet freedom from the loose discussion and advocacy spaces of Internet activists and thrust it into the forefront of the global policy

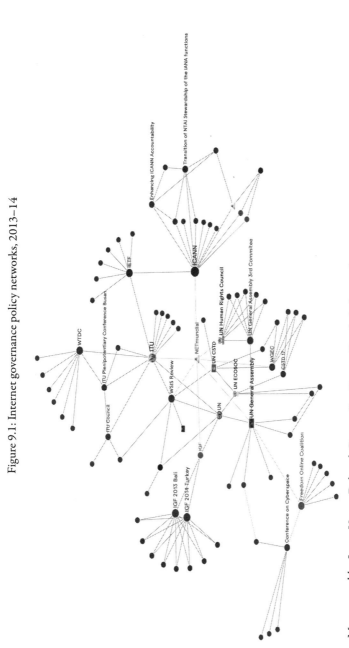

Figure 9.1: Internet governance policy networks, 2013–14

Note: Map curated by Joana Varon, Deborah Brown, Lea Kaspar, Burak Arikan at "Mapping Internet Governance," a data compiling and mapping project tracing relations between Internet governance events, processes, and organizing institutions. Replication data available at http://netgovmap.org

agenda, perhaps intentionally disrupting and expanding the Internet governance ecology beyond that which is traditionally anchored by the ITU, ICANN, and the IETF.

Furthermore, investigating the FOC and its peripheral networks of actors and their activities surrounding Internet freedom promotion after the Arab Spring not only has a unique historical importance, but is also empirically novel. Investigating the FOC and its affiliated Internet freedom stakeholders is conceptually important because no focused research has to date evaluated this particular set of stakeholders, who are vigorously justifying the establishment of an Internet regime to define and then promote "Internet freedom" globally. For these reasons, we must investigate the activities of the FOC and connected Internet freedom promotion activities, because this represents a unique case found in the empirical world, as well as a theoretically interesting case made, due to its nature of being an anomaly in the existing scholarship.[7] Thus, the following discussion progresses by establishing the FOC as a starting point for exploring the broader Internet freedom proto-regime efforts being shaped since the Arab Spring of 2011–12. Tracing the emergence of various stakeholders and their contemporary cooperating and conflicting interests makes it possible to identify connected and parallel policy arenas where substantive Internet freedom work is also being conducted, which the existing scholarship must incorporate and theorize.

The Arab Spring and the galvanizing momentum for digital rights activism

Immediately following the Arab Spring revolts, *Foreign Affairs* published an essay that reflected on the central question puzzling comparative scholars today: "Why Middle East Studies Missed the Arab Spring."[8] Other events soon to follow, like the Occupy Wall Street movement in North America and Western Europe (2011), the Greek protests against EU austerity measures (2011), collective mobilizations during Russia's elections (2011), the Spanish Indignados protests (2011–12), and Turkey's Gezi Park protests (2013), all paid symbolic homage to the Arab protests and revolutions for inspiring the organizational strategies of movement leaders and bolstering the courage of participating activists. Indeed, several waves of global protests have taken place since in sub-Saharan Africa, Europe, Asia, and the Americas, and reflect the structural connective and transnational features observed during the Arab Spring. Even far-off Oceania has been impacted: during the period when Libya was embroiled in protests that were met with a violent repression, a group of

Sydney-based Fijian democracy promoters organized to challenge the military junta in Fiji while citing the Arab Spring protests as the inspirational trigger.

These waves of unprecedented global protests have collectively provided political scientists and political sociologists with an important call to update their frameworks, theories, and assumptions about how political change is being organized today. While comparative researchers have been quick to acknowledge the novel aspects of these transnational and consecutive protests, investigating the mobilization tools necessary for organizing them is a more challenging task. There still exists considerable skepticism about drawing critical attention to the emergence of new communication technologies and digital infrastructures as serious ingredients in the causal recipes for contemporary democratization. Uncritical labels offered by enthusiastic journalists and observers, like "Facebook revolutions" and "Twitter revolutions," have also served to stall the intellectual foundation for more nuanced observations of technological interference in contemporary international politics.

Some of the skepticism about taking ICTs and digital infrastructures seriously comes from disagreement on how to define the political moment itself. Some argue that "there has been—and will be—no serial collapse of authoritarian regimes leading to a democratic future. Instead of 'revolution', the talk now is of 'uprisings', 'revolt' or simply 'crisis'."[9] This concern rests on whether the Arab Spring was "democratic" enough, or whether it is too soon to define some of the processes and attributes of the mobilizations as sufficiently democratizing. The calls to be intellectually conservative are justified, somewhat. The long-term process of political change and institutional democratization must be measured by studying the complex series of regulatory and institutional changes in the political systems and procedural practices that meaningfully engage citizens in democratic governance. In other words, some Arab societies may have ousted their ruling dictators, but the controlling interests and structural conditions embedded in the maintenance of authoritarian power have not changed much.

Despite these obvious reasons to remain critical, one cannot ignore the important and observable ways in which ICTs and digital media use have helped challenge authoritarian power and improve the prospects for democratic entrenchment. A number of recent studies examining the Arab Spring find that ICTs do have a causal influence on processes of democratization, and that recipes that account for digital infrastructure actually help explain democratic entrenchment in some of the most repressive political systems across the span of years, not just during episodic protests.[10] For example, opposition movements and civil society actors in Egypt and Tunisia may not have had much practice in organizing real elections before the Arab Spring.[11] What the gradual and exponential introduction of Internet infrastructure over the years did, though, is enable them to gain new capacities to mobilize powerfully around thematically shared grievances, again and again.

However, most comparative observers do not pay serious attention to the disruptive ways in which Arab states and societies were impacted on all levels (economic, social, and political) by the long-term introduction of new ICTs and digital infrastructures over the past two decades. These observers are agnostic to the impact of digital technologies on state-society relations and opportunities for organizing political change, often pointing to the authoritarian resilience of oil-rich monarchies in the Persian Gulf as counterfactual examples.[12] Indeed, states like Bahrain and Saudi Arabia had used those resources efficiently to better fund, secure, and co-opt new technologies in order to bolster their authoritarian capabilities and limit autonomous civic spaces, which suggests that digital media was having an anti-democratic impact on those societies. But a more discerning interpretation should note that technologies had enabled both, not either/or. They have contributed to the empowerment of pro-democracy movements and the entrenchment of civil society, on the one hand; and have helped refine the powers and practices for exercising censorship and surveillance by non-democratic regimes, on the other hand.

To emphasize the last point, interpretations of the Arab Spring that do not take into account digital technologies and new forms of organizing political change risk retelling an incomplete and inaccurate story about authoritarian exceptionalism in the twenty-first century.[13] Any analyses that ignore digital infrastructures no longer resonate as strongly with current observations. If we are to have a more nuanced understanding of why modern cascades of political change were different and unexpected, we must account for the unexpected forces and novel practices related to digitally-enabled organizing observed before and during the period of rapid mobilizations across several countries. In the years after the initial Arab uprisings, several countries, including Tunisia and Egypt, have struggled to develop long-term and sustainable democratic institutions.

In summary, a more complete understanding of contemporary political change, even in the most stalwart non-democratic regimes, requires unpacking two coexisting—even competing—dynamics: the former is the infusion of digitally-mediated political participation by democracy promoters in their organizational practices; the latter is the counter-efforts by repressive regimes to contain and repurpose the new infrastructures and tools that facilitate such practices. Activists and dictatorships have come to see digital technologies as political goods that can be used (and constructed) as both democratic scaffoldings and as authoritarian panopticons. In all these cases, the common struggle has been one pitting citizens and civil society actors against state powers and their security forces to control the political uses and affordances of digital infrastructures. But the important thread linking these opposing stakeholders (state powers vs civil society) has been the multinational technology companies (i.e. the private sector) that own and maintain key pieces of transnational digital infrastructures. So it is the case that unpacking the politics of Internet freedom promotion requires investigating at least three core categories of stakeholders: state powers, civil society, and the private sector.

With the benefit of some necessary hindsight, this different retelling of the story about the Arab Spring should acknowledge, even privilege, the real ways in which dissent was organized with the use of digital infrastructure—the very infrastructure that also put activists at grave risk of state-sanctioned retribution. Our retelling must pay close attention to the interactive relationships between the new arsenals of communication tools and strategies used by protesters to outmaneuver their dictators. Furthermore, because the infrastructure that supports these mediated political practices was located globally and transnationally to begin with, the experiences and lessons from the Arab Spring have taught us that we must begin to see digital infrastructures as an important arena for exercising state power and for shaping international politics itself. As I will demonstrate in the following discussion, the democratic activists who exploited the political capacities of digital infrastructures have, since 2011, done more than just recognize this themselves: they have gone further and begun to organize in order to protect and secure the global digital infrastructure itself. They agitated and organized transnationally to implement better support and policies to protect their digital infrastructures in the name of human rights and democratic responsibilities.

Beyond the state: civil society watchdogs for Internet freedom promotion

A digital media-focused analysis of modern political change is unique from analytical perspectives that are agnostic to the intimate and important ways in which global communications systems have come to impact on societies. Mainly, a digitally-centered analysis shows that the central puzzles surrounding contemporary political change have embedded in them the strategic uses and unexpected pitfalls of digital media and digital infrastructures. So if we were to reassess the lessons learned from the Arab Spring and acknowledge the observable ways in which contemporary communication tools and strategies were intimately tied to the process of organizing political change, how might we retell a slightly different version of events? More importantly, what might this tell us about Internet freedom politics today? Analyses sensitive to these questions may narrate as the following.

Ben Ali ruled Tunisia for over twenty years, but in early 2011, digitally-enabled protesters tossed out their dictator in less than two months. Emboldened and inspired by these events, the April 6 youth movement in Egypt mobilized to organize sustained protests to challenge the thirty-year-old Mubarak regime through surprisingly disciplined and largely peaceful demonstrations. Watching and learning from these creative strategies, discontent spread over digital media networks of family and friends to Algeria, Jordan, Yemen, and other authoritarian Arab states. These important political moments consistently drew diverse networks of people, many of whom had not been political in any traditional sense before: young entrepreneurs, government workers, women's groups, and the urban middle class. Digital media networks enabled activist networks in the Arab region to voice shared grievances and nurture transportable strategies for mobilizing against their dictators. Across the Arab Spring protests, defections from censored media and security agencies were announced on social media, mobilization tactics were shared on Facebook pages and activists' blogs, and desperate calls for global sympathy and support were spread by citizen journalists on Twitter.

But it is also myopic to tell the causal tale of digital media and political change in the Arab Spring as if it had started in 2011. In Tunisia, activists seized the opportunity when the country was hosting the high-profile UN World Summit on the Information Society in 2005 to mount an online protest movement against Ben Ali's intolerance toward civil and political freedoms.[14] In Egypt, the April 6 youth movement was cautiously testing strategies for peaceful resistance as early as 2008. In late 2009, armed with mobile phones and digital cameras, international activists from London with transnational support networks flew into Tahrir Square and demonstrated against the Egyptian-Israeli blockade of the Gaza Strip. Through innovative hybrid media campaigns relying primarily on microblogging, the conjoined networks of European and Arab activists engineered an international media event that eventually pressured Egyptian authorities temporarily to lift the blockade so that humanitarian aid could pass through to Gazans. Lebanon also experienced the first stirrings of its Cedar Revolution as early as 2005—a chain of massive demonstrations in Beirut that critically limited Syria's stronghold on Lebanese political liberalization. Because of this decisive victory, in the ongoing Syrian civil war, Beirut's Internet infrastructure, as well as Israel's neighboring Internet backbone, continues to serve as a critical node and relatively safe zone for sympathetic "hacktivists" and "fixers" who regularly use these states' more reliable communication infrastructure to transmit political information to international news agencies and human rights organizations.

Weighing multiple political, economic, demographic, and cultural conditions, then, it is components of digital infrastructures that consistently appear as key ingredients in parsimonious models helping to explain the conjoined combinations of causes behind regime fragility and social movement success in this Arab Spring. Therefore, to understand the successes and failures of contemporary political protests, we must also assess how civil society leaders and authoritarian security forces treated communication technologies as politically consequential. This perspective draws attention to the idea that it is not enough to observe the uses of digital media and ICTs—it is more important to question how these tools come into existence in the first place. Not doing so risks continuing to develop an intellectual understanding of media use and political change that is agnostic with respect to the digital infrastructures that support contemporary mediated practices of political participation, engagement, and change.

Digital tools and ICTs are not static and unchanging structures; they are constantly shaped and reshaped by both technology designers and users—a perspective well recognized by work on the social shaping of technology.[15] Digital media platforms and their forms and frequency of uses are structured and afforded by various transnationally distributed stakeholders, including engineers and regulators. Therefore, the broader Internet infrastructure that supports digital media service platforms like Facebook and Twitter exists in a complex political economy of transnational conditions governed, regulated, and contested by a highly complex set of actors, including state powers and private commerce stakeholders. To illustrate this, consider the fact that the US State Department supported the Alliance of Youth Movements network, which as early as 2009 had designed and deployed social media protest strategies to activists in Egypt; and also, during the G20 protests among others, combined digitally-enabled strategies like "smart mobbing" for political, marketing, and artistic causes. Democratic activists and political users of digital media tools and ICTs have also increasingly intervened in the construction of these tools and the underlying enabling information infrastructure. For example, Tunisian youth were attracted to the cyber activism of the online forum Takriz, a self-described citizen "cyber think tank" established in 1998, which also provided activists in the Arab Spring with technical training in counter-censorship and surveillance circumvention software.[16] So even though it was the state, in this case the Ben Ali regime, that brought Internet infrastructure to its citizens, it was the activists in Takriz that exploited the regime-sponsored infrastructure to cultivate safe spaces and digital strategies for anti-authoritarian activists to turn against the regime's interests.[17]

Obviously, democratic outcomes are not an inherent product of online technologies. Digital media can also, as has been observed across democratic and authoritarian regimes since 1995, be turned against civil societies.[18] When the Arab protests began in early 2011, authoritarian regimes did not stand idly by. In Tunisia, Egypt, Libya, Algeria, and elsewhere, regimes forcibly attempted to shut down communication networks. Some were successful, as in the case of Egypt shutting down London-based Vodafone; while others, like Algeria, did not have centralized management to coerce technology providers so easily. But surprisingly, even when unfriendly governments were successful in shutting down communication networks, transnational networks of sympathetic "information activists" skillful in technology-savvy activism also organized to redesign tools for political use and waged hacktivism campaigns to counteract the communication capacities of authoritarian regimes. This particular breed of activists was further supported by technology policy NGOs, like US-based Access, which was created by veteran activists from the "Green Revolution" in Iran, and the Bay Area-based Electronic Frontier Foundation (EFF), known informally as the "ACLU of digital rights." Both launched effective lobbying campaigns to pressure ICT companies like Vodafone to turn connectivity back on, and launched investigations to hold Western software companies accountable for selling censorship technologies to the repressive governments of Syria and Bahrain.

Considering these compelling narratives drawn directly from the experiences of the Arab Spring, it seems that we must say more than just that technologies are sometimes socially shaped and perhaps politically consequential. Based on the above events and practices, technologies are constantly being reengineered with political affordances for intentional and political outcomes, often by their designers and regulators, but also by citizen watchdogs who care about human rights and democratic norms. Unfortunately, there are limited perspectives that go beyond treating ICTs and digital infrastructures agnostically to bring critical attention to the political economic conditions which help give rise to new digital safe spaces and provide civil society actors with digital scaffolding to do their work. Most often, these perspectives are also relegated to scholarship in associated fields of telecommunications policy and mired in technical language about engineering standards that do not easily translate or explain the intimate political conditions, ideologies, and experiences shaping their uses by, and impact on, citizens[19] and activists.[20]

But since the aftermath of the Arab Spring, political activism and policy debates surrounding digital infrastructures have become highly visible and contentious at the international level, partly because NGO and citizen watchdog groups have mobilized to do this important translation work between telecommunications regulation and civic life. These efforts are novel; they are new additions to the existing exclusive forums and arenas that have traditionally existed surrounding Internet governance (including the ITU, IGF, and ICANN). Between the end of the major protests of the Tunisian, Egyptian, and Libyan revolutions (in October 2011) and when the UN's ITU organized in Dubai to revise its 25-year-old global telecommunications treaties at WCIT-12 (in December 2012), there have been at least ten major stakeholder governance summits focused explicitly on defining and promoting Internet freedom (see Table 9.1). These policy conventions and conferences have been brokered by the foreign policy offices of key Western democratic nations and others, including respected civil society organizations (e.g. Access) and influential multinational technology corporations (e.g. Google), and represent a disruptive shift in standard esoteric regulatory regimes like the ITU and ICANN.

Access was the main organization to pressure technology companies to stop selling software tools to dictators in the aftermath of Iran's Green Revolution (2009) and lobbied corporations to keep digital networks running during Egypt's national Internet shutdown (2011); it has also taken an international leadership role in organizing networks of civil society activists around issues of "Internet freedom." In October 2011, immediately following the Arab Spring protests, Access launched its first Silicon Valley Human Rights Conference. Though organized by a civil society group, this event was also sponsored and funded by Google, Facebook, Yahoo, AT&T, Mozilla, Skype, among other key multinational ICT corporations. The conference brought together corporate leaders and foreign policy officials of major Western democratic nations to design policies for corporate social responsibility with respect to international human rights.

Table 9.1: Internet freedom stakeholder meetings, 2011–12

Summit	Location	Date	Organizer
Silicon Valley Human Rights Conference I	San Francisco	Oct. 2011	Access
London Conference on Cyberspace	London	Nov. 2011	UK Foreign and Commonwealth Office
Our Internet—Our Rights—Our Freedoms	Vienna	Nov. 2011	Council of Europe
Freedom Online Conference I	The Hague	Dec. 2011	Freedom Online Coalition
Stockholm Internet Forum	Stockholm	Apr. 2012	Swedish Ministry of Foreign Affairs
Human Rights and Technology Conference II	Rio de Janeiro	May 2012	Access
Dublin Conference on Internet Freedom	Dublin	Jun. 2012	Organization for Security and Co-operation in Europe
Internet at Liberty Conference: Promoting Progress and Freedom	Washington, DC	Jul. 2012	Google
The Internet and Human Rights: Building a Free, Open and Secure Internet	Berlin	Sept. 2012	German Federal Foreign Office
Freedom Online Conference II	Nairobi	Sept. 2012	Freedom Online Coalition

Note: List prepared by author based on interview and fieldwork data collected from informant interviews and snowballing between March 2011 and December 2012. List excludes informal side-events, "hackathons," and major Internet governance summits that did not focus centrally on promoting the Internet freedom discourse or agenda. Replication data available at http://comparative-dpd.net

Similarly breaking with convention, the governments of the United States, the Netherlands, Sweden, and the European Union also publicly followed suit, creating formal funding programs of over $100 million to support digital activists working within repressive regimes under the auspices of the FOC (as discussed previously). Most of the competitive and winning responses to their requests for proposals dealt centrally with issues connected to digital infra-structures and ICTs, like helping to create secure and anonymous Internet access points for activists working within non-democratic states to communicate freely and safely on their laptops and Internet-enabled mobile devices. One of the most publicized and celebrated outcomes of these funding initiatives and state backing was a proxy Internet access protocol called "Tor," initially created by the US Naval Defense Lab, and now managed by an independent non-governmental foundation. Tor has been used across the world in places like China, Saudi Arabia, and elsewhere by activists and citizens to access content securely and anonymously. Furthermore, member states of the FOC have also organized independent, but coordinated, Internet freedom arenas to bring together global stakeholders physically in Berlin, Dublin, London, Stockholm, Vienna, and elsewhere.

The most recent efforts have also extended Internet freedom promotion work to include citizens and stakeholders in emerging powers, like Brazil, and more events have been scheduled to extend reach to the Asia-Pacific region, such as South Korea. However, since the major protests of the Arab Spring subsided, the most active supporters of Internet freedom-focused organizing have been a core collective representing technology activists and policy-makers from advanced industrialized Western democracies (reflected in the membership of the FOC). Altogether, then, in the one-year interval between the conclusion of the initial Arab Spring protests and the UN's historic quarter-century ITU treaty negotiation in Dubai, these stakeholder meetings and negotiations have worked to highlight and elucidate the complex issues surrounding digital infrastructural politics from the perspectives of activists, governments, and corporations. Because these stakeholders and their activities reflect a convergence around technology-based political activism, the remaining discussion in this essay introduces a different conceptual framework with more analytical agency than the traditional but reductive slugging between "cyber optimist" and "cyber dystopian" camps.

A "proto-regime" in formation: consolidating competing communities of practice

The discussion arc thus far has taken two broad lines of analysis. First, I argued that many elements of digital infrastructures are consequential to everyday political life and revolutionary political change, and this is particularly true in non-democratic political systems because digital infrastructures are the scaffolding upon which autonomous civic discourses and political organizing are fomenting. To that end, the Arab Spring experiences, much like other recent waves of protests like Occupy, have shown in myriad ways that both political activists and state powers are struggling to secure different kinds of digital affordances. These examples often share a common narrative, where both users and rulers increasingly target Internet service providers (who facilitate digital access) and digital media companies (who facilitate digital content). Users, particularly political activists, are increasingly pressuring these access and content providers to keep both digital networks and spaces open and safe from state powers, especially during periods of political crisis. Simultaneously, authoritarian regimes and state powers are increasingly coercing the same private-sector digital infrastructure providers to monitor and/or censor political uses of digital media for their political interests. In many repressive political systems in the Arab world, the state itself is the Internet service provider and has near total control of all aspects of its digital environment. However, the technocratic skills and necessary technologies to dominate digital infrastructure often originate from the advanced industrial economies and labor expertise of private-sector technology providers anchored in Western economies.

The second line of analysis I provided draws on several novel examples of policy initiatives that have been opened in the international policy arenas by Western state powers since the Arab Spring, related explicitly to issues and agendas promoting Internet freedom as relevant to those tensions. These policy arenas are sponsored, often independently, by several advanced industrialized Western democracies interested in supporting and regulating digital infrastructures in the global public's democratic interest,[21] or at the very least for the purpose of establishing more socially responsible standards for managing their technological exports, in compliance with established human rights norms. However, this work is made difficult because the efforts to apply human rights norms onto digital infrastructures is no simple matter, particularly due to the competing interests of the multiple stakeholders involved and the required translation of human rights and democratic norms onto a global and technical infrastructure. So what Internet freedom means and how it should be promoted within the realms of policymaking, adoption, and implementation is hitherto unclear and needs to be clarified so that an effective policy regime might emerge. The likelihood of this eventuality depends on the consolidation and establishment of a coherent system of norms that respects the various invested stakeholders' goals and needs.

How, then, can we examine the processes and outcomes of these norms-making efforts? First, the adopted approach has to have the ability to unpack the complex political economy of the involved stakeholders in the transnational arenas and their connected interests surrounding digital infrastructure.

Second, because the policy interests of these actors often conflict, the approach should view policy formation as a process that is socially constructed through debates, negotiations, and norms consolidation[22] taking place in and across various communities of practice,[23] not simply the officially sanctioned debates. For these reasons, I propose adopting the notion of a proto-regime formation from international relations theory—a concept that is particularly useful in explaining how new policy regimes are established by networks of policy entrepreneurs who transcend local contexts to solve complex transnational challenges that require knowledge exchange from different institutional backgrounds. Transnational policy regimes matter because they provide the forum or medium by which state powers cooperate to solve shared problems or allocate public goods in the transnational or global environment.[24] Regimes are necessary policy apparatuses because international activities today rely increasingly on overseas investment and trade, and the channels of global communication which make these interactions possible are "more numerous, decentralized, and diverse than ever."[25]

In order to be established, effective regimes require complex negotiations and consolidations of norms in multi-stakeholder environments to take place. Attempts to coordinate behavior among a group of countries around shared challenges, for example by setting up a global telecommunications infrastructure, are often governed by numerous semi-voluntary bilateral agreements. The number of autonomous states and stakeholder communities involved makes it extremely complex to form agreements. Examples of regulatory regimes include the International Telecommunications Union (ITU), the International Monetary Fund (IMF), the Kyoto Protocols, the Geneva Convention, and various other agreements designed to coordinate transnational cooperation between several states.[26] Furthermore, for our issue-area on freedom of expression and communication, an important history of similar initiatives, like the "World Summit on the Information Society" held in Tunis in 2005, pre-dates regime formation efforts in Arab countries that are undergoing transitions following the 2011 uprisings, and provides the basis of social networks and policy frameworks being contested today.

Regardless, all effective regimes must go through formation periods dealing with the work of aggregating and consolidating conflicting norms, disagreements, and impasses between different communities of stakeholders. This "proto-regime" period (i.e. regimes that have not yet been consolidated, and therefore lack enforceable coherence) can take many forms and directions in its advancement, but can be described as having an eclectic, rational, skeptical, or pragmatic direction. As possible causal process pathways, these dynamics deserve more than a cursory attention. The first type, eclectic regimes, tend to link issues in a tactical manner. The key actors involved do this by manipulating technical information for their strategic needs. However, because of the overt self-interests driving their functions and participation, these types of proto-regimes will likely not emerge, and instead devolve into disagreement. The second type, rational regimes, substantively link issues on the basis of agreed doctrines. However, because of the dependency on shared doctrines, the success of these regimes depends on finding simple issues with clear doctrines or clarifying issues to achieve joint doctrines. The third type, skeptical regimes, are often fragmented and only held together by the will and capability of powerful states and partners paying off their opponents. As a result, skeptical regimes tend to be weak and unstable. The fourth and final type, pragmatic regimes, attempt to narrow the scope of the regime down to a mutually beneficial range of interests acceptable to all important stakeholders. This often eventually results in a more limited but fairly stable regime that is also able to adapt and adjust to the evolving challenges and issues being addressed.

The Internet freedom proto-regime investigated in this study can be described as being in a current period of stasis best encapsulated as an eclectic regime where state actors, technology providers, and digital activists are all bringing contrasting norms and interests regarding digital infrastructure. The involved stakeholders are also engaged in the pragmatic task of nurturing a more focused (and coherent) policy framework to secure digital infrastructures. What they mean when working to promote Internet freedom and whom they intend to serve in doing so has not been defined clearly or consensually. But it is precisely this definitional period of impasse and conflict that is critical to examine, because important decisions are being made by the involved stakeholders to chisel the scope of the regime. In order to do this, we must also investigate the stakeholders, understand their norms and motivations, and identify which actors or communities of practice are producing the most viable and innovative policy ideas.

To do so, it is important to look beyond the obvious and influential actors, like governments and established policy institutions (the main focus in Internet governance and telecommunications policy scholarship). By recognizing that state powers and powerful institutions from the top down are not the only relevant actors exerting forces on periods of regime formation, we can account for newer and non-traditional stakeholders entering the mix. These include transnational advocacy networks, global civil society members, non-governmental organizations, global citizens and "international public spheres" from the bottom up that seem to be more agile and important in recent studies of international relations and regime formation.[27] In this approach, new "communities of practice" and their production of expert knowledge have become useful analytical perspectives for understanding how regimes evolve throughout their formative periods:

> Regimes are not simply static summaries of rules and norms; they may also serve as important vehicles for international learning that produce convergent state policies. This role for regimes has been seriously underestimated in the theoretical and empirical literature, which has tended to focus on two correlates of regimes—political order and economic growth—rather than on the transformative processes that regimes may imitate or foster. The literature has also paid little attention to the fact that some regimes stem from communities of shared knowledge and not simply from domestic and transnational interest groups.[28]

These growing references to "communities of shared knowledge" in international relations work refer to a concept introduced by Lave and Wenger called "communities of practice."[29] In the early formulation of communities of practice, the concept referred to the forms of learning taking place outside highly structured institutional environments. Rather, communities of practice referred to the more haphazard social contexts in which learning itself was a social activity co-created by the interactions of experts and novices—what Lave and Wenger call "Legitimate Peripheral Participation" (LPP). Applied to the case of Internet freedom promotion, it is equally important to examine the new social spaces and social practices where Internet freedom is being promoted, in addition to examining the policy ideas surrounding Internet freedom promotion itself.

Engaging the communities of practice framework also allows us to move the focus away from the narrow learning that happens in the heads of individual elite experts. Instead, we can also delve deeply into the peripheral zones of stakeholder interactions, where the new challenges and unanticipated problems of Internet freedom work are addressed in a far more observable and rich manner. Identifying important yet understudied communities of actors, then, provides an opportunity to illuminate and demystify esoteric policy-making efforts because it widens the analysis beyond the conventional focus on state powers or private interests.[30] Broadening the definition of involved stakeholders to include non-traditional actors and their interaction spaces makes it possible to examine interesting cases of civil society networks and citizen advocacy organizations that seem to be newly organizing since the Arab Spring around the critical politics of digital infrastructure management.

Thus, it is crucial to investigate the transnational politics of digital infrastructures voiced because of, and since, the Arab Spring, because the negotiations taking place between stakeholders debating Internet freedom seem distinct and disconnected from the local activists and indigenous autocrats (traditionally examined by democratization studies) or the institutional and governance stakeholders (traditionally examined in telecommunications studies). In the aftermath of the Arab Spring, the transnational stakeholders and arenas related to promoting Internet freedom are new and distinct from the Internet governance politics of the past. But it is not very clear what it means to promote Internet freedom yet because the label is, as MacKinnon eloquently states, "like a Rorschach inkblot test: different [stakeholders] look at the same ink splotch and see very different things."[31]

10

CITIZENSHIP AND CYBER POLITICS IN IRAN

Gholam Khiabany

Despite increased interest in Middle Eastern media as an area of academic inquiry, much of the existing research into mediated culture in the Middle East remains problematic, often because of an essentialism that has entrapped much of the debate about the "culture" of the region. Associated with this perceived and constructed "singular space" is the idea that the Islamic world forms a cultural unity that is based upon a common cultural core. The history of media and modernity in the region is also overshadowed by false binaries and a narrow optic of modernization dichotomies: modernity versus tradition, Islam versus the West, and secularism versus religious fundamentalism. Such binaries suppress the diversities of histories, cultures, struggles, and aspirations and obscure the real "divides" in a colorful quilt that is today's "Middle East." In the dominant narratives of the region's history, culture and media are invoked in terms of how they cause the Middle East to fit into or deviate from the narrative of the West's modernity. Iran is not an exception. This chapter examines key aspects of the contradictions and tensions in the Iranian media market and competing forms of "Islamism"/nationalism. By critically examining the role of the state in expansion of the Iranian communication system and the economic realities of the media in Iran, it challenges the essentialist reading of the Iranian state and media, and argues that the nature of Iranian media, in general, and the Internet, in particular, cannot be understood simply in terms of "Islamic ideology" or conceived in terms of the beloved dichotomy of modernization theory: modernity versus tradition.

To grasp the complex nature of cyber politics in the case of Iran calls for some historical depth. The Iranian revolution of 1979 remains problematic, both theoretically and politically, and the "trans-class" and "religious" nature of the revolution has been the main source of confusion over the precise nature of the state that replaced the monarchy. Gilbert Achcar has described the Iranian revolution as a "permanent revolution in reverse," something that started with such emancipatory potential, and could have grown into a socialist transformation, but instead produced a strange polity and state.[1] Although the revolution without a doubt had an emancipatory character, elements of counter-revolution were clearly visible from the outset. The tension between the revolution and the counter-revolution, and the existence of multiple sovereignties, aspirations, and power contentions, calls for an analytical distinction between the Iranian revolution and the Islamic Republic.[2]

The paradoxical nature of the state that came to power in 1979 is reflected in the political system that has combined elements of Islamic tradition and innovations with Iranian nationalism and a modern state structure. The Iranian constitution, as Schirazi suggests, is also a contradictory and compromised legislation that, even while it lists some democratic principles, effectively subordinates the peoples' will to the clerical establishment via the institution of *velayat-e faqih* (rule of the supreme jurist).[3] The idea of *velayat-e faqih* is presented as the intermediary between the true Islamic polity (which can be established upon resurrection of the twelfth imam, Mehdi) and the *umma* (community of faithful). This invention, however, and for the first time in Shia history, concentrated power and legitimacy of guidance (*marja'iyat*) in the hands of a single person. The "vaticanization" of Shia structure, so to speak, was against the historical pluralism of the clerical establishment, and it came as no surprise that many Grand Ayatollahs distanced themselves from the concept.[4]

The power of *vali-e faqih* (supreme leader or jurist) is unlimited. He appoints the head of judiciary, the clergy members of the powerful second chamber (Guardian Council), commanders of all armed forces, as well as the leaders of two of the most important communication channels in Iran: imams of the Friday prayers and the director general of the Islamic Republic of Iran Broadcasting (IRIB). He is also the custodian of two of the most established and powerful media organizations, *Kayhan* and *Etella't*. Azimi has argued that:

> The segmentary constitution of clerical politics and the polarity of loci of power inevitably created some scope for political debate, but civic and social liberties remained severely circumscribed. The prevailing character and configuration of governance required that the ruled be treated as subject rather than citizens; the ideal of a self-confident citizenry, imbued with civic pride and recognized as such by the rulers, remained elusive.[5]

Popular representation has always been problematic since the system as a whole revolves around an unelected central core, headed by a Supreme Leader, with truly unlimited powers. Yet, as the election of Mohammad Khatami in 1997, the "electoral coup" of 2009, and the election of Rouhani in 2013 indicate, given the faction-ridden nature of the ruling elites, the individual in charge of the executive becomes important since this appointment can affect the distribution of public resources and, to some extent, the ability of the entire state structure to function. Hence, control of elected organs, in general, and the presidency, in particular, are also hotly contested and often subject to intense bargaining among the various factions.

As far as the subject of this chapter is concerned, it is also important to remember that all developments in relation to the Internet and cyberspace in Iran have occurred in a post-revolutionary state. Furthermore, as many scholars have pointed out, the central issue is not the obvious and crude divide between a "traditional" and "religious" state and "modern," even "secular," technology, since that very state has, and many clergymen have, adopted new information technologies.[6] Nevertheless a central paradox needs to be recognized. The role of the Iranian state in facilitating, developing, and expanding the ICT capacity of the country is undeniable. At the same time, the adoption, development, and expansion of ICTs are curtailed by the centralizing state's desire to control expression in a "new technology" environment that is highly conducive to widespread and popular participation. This paradox is important to note in the case of Iran, because the contentious politics and popular protests that have marked the country's recent history are often indissociable from media dynamics.

As I discuss, the past few decades have seen the rapid emergence of the communication industry in Iran as one of the fastest growing economic sectors, and various uses of new media now constitute one of the most dynamic and vibrant politico-cultural spaces. Besides the expansion of Iranian media channels, popular desire for access to informal channels of communication and for greater cultural consumption is clearly visible in the increasing usage of mobile technology, the wide adoption of the Internet, and the astonishing rise and popularity of weblogs in the 2000s and more recently of software applications, which have become a particular site of struggle.

This chapter examines the relationship between the Internet and politics in Iran in a much broader social context. It engages with the possible lessons of digital activism, examines various organizational and media strategies by state and non-state actors, and outlines internal and external factors that help or hinder the success of rebellion against, or impede opposition to, regressive regimes and repressive state policies. It then moves on to explore the expansion of the Internet in the country, paying particular attention to the implications of the ensuing media dynamics on the wider socio-political context.

Exceptionalism, digital and otherwise

When engaging with the Iranian digital sphere, in addition to the overtly limited and narrow representation of Iran by a wide range of Western media, one is confronted with two "theoretical" perspectives that are fixated with either "culture" or "technology." On one end of the spectrum, there is a technological determinist account which tries to frame and explain the Internet in general as an "exceptional" phase in human history. The rapid expansion of technological developments in the past two decades, and in particular the innovative use of social media by various groups and movements, is indeed heralded as the clearest indication of forces of globalization, renewed faith in the role of media in social change, and prospects of democratization. The complex and evolving technologies and applications of the Internet are only the latest technology, which are supposed to shoulder the burden of realizing McLuhan's dream of "global village." Technology enthusiasts often praise the Internet not simply for the undeniable advantages it provides for big businesses and cuts in the workforce, but for its ability to transcend national boundaries, for making "space" and "distance" irrelevant, and above all for sucking away powers from political elites and economic players, and empowering individuals in the face of big businesses and encroaching governments.[7] Much of the recent literature about the role of digital technology in the recent uprisings in Iran and the Arab world is laden with optimism and the inevitability of change and progress. Technologies—the absence or limited diffusion of which in the global south was regarded as a significant index of its underdevelopment—are now praised for their revolutionary and transforming powers. The Internet and electronic media are seen as powerful weapons for mobilization of unarmed citizens against repressive states with real arms. Less emphasis has been placed on the way that imperialist forces, not to mention dictatorships and authoritarian regimes, have used and are continuing to use technologies, not for progress but for blocking it, not for civilized purposes but for barbarian ones, and not to quash fear but to inculcate the fear of God. The effective use of social media by ISIS has dented neo-liberal fascination with alternative uses of new technologies and has shown that there is nothing inevitable about the use of these tools: they are the direct outcome of broader social and economic policy and as such are subject to alteration.

In contrast to "digital exceptionalism" which overstates, exaggerates, and isolates the role of new technologies, the "Islamic exceptionalism" approach sees "culture" (which, in the case of Iran, is indissociable from Islam) as the sole variable in determining social relations.[8] With the creation of the Islamic Republic in Iran and the spread of Islamism as a dynamic mass movement in some Muslim countries, this view has apparently gained the reputation of being irrefutable. The events of the past three decades have revived the idea of Islamic "exceptionalism" and prompted local apologists of "cultural authenticity," orientalists, and "third worldists" to reject "European" models of polity. One factor that gives this view its apparent immutable quality is the breadth and variety of the persons holding it. Adopting different methodological routes and pursuing different aims, they range from racist groups in the West, to the most rabid imperialist circles, to some of the most radical political and intellectual circles in Muslim countries.[9]

In this perspective, Islam is treated as a coherent, self-sealed, and self-explanatory culture that constitutes the main obstacle in front of Islamic countries seeking full membership of the exclusive club of "modernity." Reproducing the old stories of the incompatibility of "Islam" with "modernity," Lewis argues that "the absence of a native secularism in Islam, and the widespread Muslim rejection of an imposed secularism inspired by Christian example, may be attributed to certain profound differences of belief and experiences in two religious cultures."[10] Such a reactionary account fails to acknowledge that the question of religion and religious revival is not specific or confined to Islam. The issue is not the clash of tradition with modernity, but the increased visibility of religion's involvement in the clash over global modernity. The response in the "Islamic world" to this vision of historical development has been twofold. Many share the basic assumption of Lewis and others and have begun the process of "self-examination," mapping religious and cultural traits as the key reason for failure in their engagement with modernity.[11] While challenging the Eurocentrism of "Islamic Studies" and pointing out that the contribution of "Islamic Civilization" to science and economy has been highly regulated, others do share the basic assumption of the "uniqueness" of "Islamic" culture and civilization. Such an interpretive or explanatory strategy is also evident in the call for the "Islamization" of knowledge, which is part of a much broader historical trend to Islamicize the social sciences and sociology and to effect a reconstruction of knowledge from a "Muslim" perspective.[12]

The very existence of a vibrant alternative and oppositional voices and the much fractured nature of the Iranian state and society clearly demonstrate how flawed and off target is the claim to Islamic exceptionalism. Equally, the failure of the uprising in Iran in 2009 and the setbacks to the Arab revolutions that started in 2011, which were simplistically labeled as "Twitter revolutions," clearly indicate that technology is one factor and one variable among many.

The social context of social media in Iran

Since the global financial crisis in 2008, the world has witnessed a number of protest movements. The popular uprisings in Iran in 2009, the revolutions in several Arab countries at the beginning of 2011, and the Occupy movements in the USA and elsewhere in the global north are all indicative of growing resistance to dictatorships and the past decades of neo-liberal globalization. From the streets of Tehran to Tahir Square and from Syntagma Square to Zuccotti Park, the world has witnessed a new wave of resistance to a system that has failed to generate wealth and freedom for all. The past decade has also provided some of the most evocative moments when power, whether state or corporate, confronts its opposite (people power); in some cases, in decisive and surprising ways. Technology, once again, has emerged as one of the main explanations for this new wave of revolts.

The very use of a wide range of media and communicative platforms, the innovative use of image, sound, and music to inform, organize, and mobilize dissent and demonstrations, and in particular the circulation of information via Facebook, Twitter, and other social media platforms, has prompted many commentators to suggest that it is impossible to comprehend the political nature of the existing protests in Iran, the Arab world, and elsewhere, without recognizing the centrality of new technologies.[13] For Manuel Castells, the Internet has contributed to the eruptions of such popular power, because "the more interactive and self-configurable communication is, the less hierarchical is the organisation and the more participatory is the movement.... This is why the networked social movements of the digital age represent a new species of social movement."[14] Others, however, have criticized celebratory accounts of the role of new media for neglecting or putting less emphasis on the importance of organization. For example, Gladwell has stressed that such claims fail to consider the strong organizational ties that are crucial for any social movement.[15] The question of whether and to what extent ICT can produce change has been narrowly framed, and the debate has been somewhat reduced to a false binary of "believers" and "non-believers" in power of technologies.

In addition, treating social movements' effective use of, and reliance upon, communication technologies as a sociological novelty ignores significant historical precedents and overlooks the relevance of communications and communications technology of various kinds in protests, revolts, and revolutions. What is novel, perhaps, is identifying the new waves of struggle not with the cause but the tools of these movements. There are nevertheless two important points that deserve to be highlighted. Firstly, if the impact of social media in this conjuncture has been rather overstated and exaggerated, there is little doubt that the media (social and otherwise) have been crucial in recording the events and capturing the courage and determination of thousands and millions of citizens who have managed to reclaim real public spaces and make them their own. One Egyptian demonstrator reminded us of this reality in a simple and yet powerful way: "Before, I was watching television; now it is television that's watching me."[16] Secondly, and without a doubt, social movements and significant events use media, which in turn also help make them and put them on the map. In the same way that war and turmoil made the likes of CNN and Al Jazeera into internationally recognized brands, social movements have given the likes of Facebook, Twitter, and YouTube a much needed political and social legitimacy. "Facebook generation" is no longer a negative or pejorative term used to lament the younger generation's detachment from and indifference toward politics. Political activism in Iran certainly has contributed a great deal to making technologies that were initially considered banal, benign, or irrelevant to politics into respectable and highly prized platforms. As Andy Greenberg suggested in *Forbes*: Iranian protests are good for Twitter's business.[17]

However, even if we limit our focus to the significant and visible boiling points of social movements and ignore daily, protracted, and not highly visible digital activities, we are confronted with the how and why of the outcomes of such visible and important social awakening. The failure of the Iranian uprising and the unfulfilled promise, if not collapse, of the Arab revolutions demonstrate that while such movements have shaken, at least in some instances, the foundations of the prevailing system, they have failed to form a coherent and sustainable opposition. If it is really true that we cannot begin to comprehend revolutionary movements and political activism in Iran and elsewhere without understanding the new realities of screen culture, then what does the failure of such movements reveal about the myths of new media?

The Iranian case is certainly intriguing. The phenomenon of Iranian digital activism has been recognized for over a decade by many commentators. Since the launch of the first Iranian blog in 2001, there has been an overwhelming sense of surprise over the level of computer literacy in Iran, and more insistently how and why there is such a vibrant cultural/digital scene in a country ruled by a repressive regime.[18] This very paradox is not unprecedented in Iran. Sreberny-Mohammadi and Mohammadi remind us that "the typical pattern of Iranian political life has been that when the central authority is at its weakest, a dynamic political public sphere emerges with a variety of political groupings and communicative channels. When central authority is strong, an atmosphere of repression exists, with central control over political activity and expression."[19] In addition, we also find a familiar pattern of early adoption and engagement with new forms of communication technologies and the consequent struggle between the central state and the public over use and control of communications. Such occasions, however, have been rare. Indeed, we can only recall six occasions or significant examples of flourishing media engagements and political participations: the constitutional revolution (1906), the collapse of Reza Khan Pahlavi in 1941, the premiership of Mosaddeq (late 1940s, early 1950s), the Spring of Freedom (1979–80), the emergence of a reform movement inside the Islamic Republic (1998–2000), and the Iranian popular uprising (2009). In all these periods, not only have the media played a crucial role in "spreading the word"—to use Nabavai's description of the role of the press during the constitutional revolution—but they were also important in the struggle for democracy.[20] Throughout Iranian history, and contrary to ahistorical assumptions about the religious establishment in Iran, the clergy have also been quick in adapting, adopting, and using new communication technologies.[21] The recent fascination with the "present" and the "wow" reaction to digital activism in Iran is only possible with a large degree of historical amnesia. A technological determinist perspective is both apolitical and ahistorical insofar as it fails to consider the wealth of activities by various players in various locations, over the course of decades, which paved the ground for the eruptions and uprising. As Rashid Khalidi reminds us with particular reference to the Arab revolutions of 2011:

> It is a mistake to focus excessively on the specifics of the technology, whether Facebook, Twitter, cell phones or satellite TV. Such a common public sphere existed in the past, relying on earlier forms of technology, whether the printing press or radio. As with all revolutions, this one is the result not of technology but of a ceaseless struggle over many years, in this case by workers' unions, women's groups, human rights activists, Islamists, intellectuals, campaigners for democracy, and many others who have paid dearly for their efforts.[22]

The other paradox that is worth remembering, despite ruling with an iron fist and wary of the emergence of any independent source of social power, is the fact that the central Iranian state has been a developmentalist state and, certainly since the end of war with Iraq, a liberalizing state. The state, therefore, has been not only the repressor but also and at the same time the principal agent for the expansion and development of media, as well as the key player in the media market. Indeed, the Iranian state has been and remains the main media conglomerate.[23]

Discussion of the media environment in Iran also inevitably follows the pattern of the political upheavals in the country and somehow fits closely with changes at elected organs, most notably the presidency. For example, there was a renewed hope for prospects of democracy when Khatami unexpectedly and against the odds, and against wishes of the supreme leader, won a landslide victory in 1997. That period was followed by two controversial terms of Ahmadinejad. Hopes for change and reform were then renewed with the victory of Rouhani in 2013. As I have already pointed out, the executive is important, but the focus on changes at the executive level always risks missing the broader picture, which encompasses the reality of the Iranian state as a whole. A cursory look at the production and expansion of certain media in Iran illustrates this point. For example, during Khamenei's presidency (1981–9) just over 40,000 books were published. During Rafsanjani's two terms (1989–97) this number increased to over 79,000. In the heyday of the reform period and under Khatami (1997–2005), it more than tripled to reach over 250,000 books. Under Ahmadinejad (2005–13) the trend continued (rather than faltered) and more than 450,000 books were published, of which 19 per cent were titles by women.[24] The same pattern can be observed across the field. The number of TV channels since 1979 has increased from two to eight national channels and thirty regional channels. In addition, the Islamic Republic of Iran Broadcasting (IRIB) operates four international news television channels, six satellite television channels for international viewers, and a number of regional, national, and international radio channels. The development of basic communications infrastructure, including telecommunication, has also been emphasized, and the sector developed rather rapidly. By 2013, 38 per cent of Iranians had access to fixed-line telephones, over 80 per cent had mobile phones, 44 per cent of households had access to a computer, and nearly 7 per cent had broadband. The number of Internet users had increased from a quarter of a million in 2000 to over 41 million in 2013, over half of the country's population.

In examining the Iranian case we have to recognize the reality of global digital divides and the fact that Iran is lagging behind some of its richer regional neighbors; in particular, the Gulf states. However, the disparity of access and usage only tells part of a more complex story of communicative experiences in Iran and elsewhere. After all, despite claims around the role of new technologies in democratization and social change, social movements for democracy and against dictatorship were stronger in countries with less access to the Internet (Egypt and Iran compared with Gulf monarchies). However, the more significant challenge in Iran lies in the use of the Internet as a channel of political and cultural communication. Considering the absence of genuinely free political parties, regular clampdowns on the semi-independent press, and the total control of broadcasting, it is no accident that the Internet has come to the fore as a space for various alternative political and cultural voices and has created a strong link between activists inside and outside Iran. With the closure of many semi-independent publications in 2000 and later in 2009, the Internet became the main battleground between various factions and between the state and independent voices. The vibrant and dynamic blogging culture was the most vivid expression of this reality.

However, the rapid transformation or, to be precise, the decline of blogging activities in Iran clearly indicates that not only is the digital environment not static, but it can furnish no "fountain of eternal youth" to oppositional politics and culture in Iran. Without a doubt, the framing of the digital as anti-hierarchical by Castells and others is not entirely inaccurate. Nevertheless, there are a number of issues that arise out of such a broad characterization. In the first place, it is important to ask if this "anti-hierarchical" feature is inherent in the "digital" itself, or a reflection of key features in recent social movements. Significant social movements are always spontaneous movements at the beginning, and the logic of "horizontal" organization allows the movements to gain momentum. The rapid expansion of the Occupy movements is obvious. Use of social media by social actors in these movements reflects this reality and not the other way around. In addition, we have to remember that by far the most significant examples of challenges to the existing order have come not in the most advanced capitalist economy (with far more digital resources and access), but in the southern and marginal countries of the Eurozone (Greece, Spain, Italy, and Portugal) or in Latin America and the Middle East.

The digital, however, is praised not only for its anti-hierarchical feature but, as a result, also for empowering the public. This framing, as Kuntsman and Stein have argued, fails "to account for the ways that hegemonic institutions and oppressive regimes marshal new media for their end—but also because it stills the hermeneutic operation within the digital sphere and assumes rather than interrogates the nature of the digital itself."[25] Similarly, Srinivasan and Fish point out how "dictatorial and monarchic regimes have found ways to disrupt, shut down, or monitor dissident activities, and these practices discourage any euphoric celebration of "liberation technologies."[26] Iran is no exception. The digital environment in Iran has been subject to the friction and competition between government factions of the state, the institutional interests of various state agencies, as well as the tension between the state and the public. Even though the Islamic Republic has officially encouraged the use of the Internet, the issues of access and control over content remain controversial.[27] Fearful of the formation of any alternative source of social power, the state has taken a leading role in providing Internet access and services. The "selling" of the majority of shares of the Telecommunication Company of Iran to the Revolutionary Guards for $5 billion in 2009 clearly demonstrates the significance of the Internet to the state. This military takeover, which was done under the banner of "privatization," points to the security dimension of the Internet in Iran. In addition, the Iranian state has devised a range of controls which are implemented with a greater or lesser degree of efficiency. These controls include ISP licensing, Internet filtering, censorship of sites, control of the speed of the Internet, attempts to inundate the net with favorable content, the criminalization of digital activities, and the arrest of activists.[28] In short, the Iranian state, rather unsurprisingly, relies on the use of coercion and violence (physical as well as symbolic) as its ultimate sanction.

If the lack of independent media, the closure of many reformist newspapers, and erosion of state legitimacy, on the one hand, and the growing popular dissatisfaction in Iran, on the other hand, helped to increase activism in the blogosphere and to develop a vigorous cyber culture (a Blogistan, so to speak), the collapse of the Iranian uprising in 2009 and the massive state crackdown on activism (digital and otherwise) put an end to the phenomenon of Blogistan. One recent study confirmed that there was a "high rate of blog abandonment with only around 20 per cent of the prominent blogs from 2008–2009" continuing to be active in September 2013. The same study also "shows a general decrease in the frequency of posting: 70 per cent of bloggers surveyed publish one post per month or less—in contrast to earlier years."[29] The same report insists that the decline of Blogistan is partly due to the growth of social media and the migration of many Iranian bloggers to new platforms: "Our audience survey shows that although social networking sites are perceived as both catalyst and impediment for blog usage, these platforms have significantly altered the way readers interact with blogs." The study further notes that Social Networking Sites (SNSs) "facilitate publication and instant promotion of any content, including short, often less analytical, and re-used content. They also provide a consistent, seamless and cross platform experience for readers."[30] It is important to note that many analysts highlight the technical advantages of SNSs in terms of their seamless, consistent, and cross-platform elements. But SNSs are also operating in the same historical society and, as such, have all the marks of existing realities, constraints, and limits.

Significantly, the popularity of and controversy over SNSs are consistent with previous phases of new media in Iran. In 2014, Al Jazeera reported that of those who have access to the Internet, 58 per cent use Facebook regularly and 37 per cent use Google+. Facebook and Twitter are still officially banned in Iran, although that has not deterred key Iranian officials, including the supreme leader, or institutions, from using such platforms. The most interesting success stories, however, relate to the use of Viber, WhatsApp, and, more recently, Telegram. In contrast to the country's 4.5 million Facebook users, around 10 million people (12 per cent of the Iranian population) were using Viber. In fact, in 2015, Iranians were the leading group of Viber users internationally, a trend that is not dissimilar to their adoption of blogs. According to Alexa.com, Viber was ranked 6,644 globally, but it is ranked in Iran at 776. Nearly 18 per cent of Viber users in 2015 were in Iran, ahead of Russia (8.8 per cent of Viber users), USA (8.4 per cent), India (7 per cent), and Brazil (4.9 per cent).

Viber itself emerged as a top news item after the Iranian police announced the arrest of eleven people in September 2014 for circulating jokes about Ayatollah Khomeini on Viber. In the same week, in a letter to Mahmood

Vaezi, Communication Minister, Gholam-Hossein Mohseni-Ejei, first deputy of the judiciary branch, threatened that if he did not take action, the judiciary would "take the appropriate measures." In his letter, Mohseni-Ejei described applications such as Viber, WhatsApp, and Tango as networks "with immoral and criminal content," and gave the government a month to block them. The Communication Minister replied that blocking such networks would not solve any problem.[31] Iranian officials and institutions were also among Viber users, and the fact that it was developed by Israel has not stopped for example Press TV or Rafsanjani's website from using the app. Even the security officials are divided over how to tackle these networks. Ahmadi-Moghadam, the chief of Iranian police, has admitted that using such apps is inevitable, but added that the state needs to find ways of monitoring and controlling inappropriate use of these services.[32] He did urge the Supreme Council on Cyberspace (SCC) to come up with appropriate guidelines regulating the use of networks such as Facebook and Viber. Prior to the Viber controversy and confusion, there was more unhappy news for users of SNSs in Iran when an Iranian court charged seven young men and women in May 2014 for posting their version of Pharrell Williams' music video on YouTube.

The Viber controversy, however, has more than a political dimension; it is not simply over jokes about statesmen or irreverence toward the clergy, even though, according to a report by BBC Persian, 29 per cent of all SMSs in Iran are jokes.[33] Tools such as Viber and WhatsApp are also denting the profit of the Telecommunication Company of Iran. Viber and WhatsApp are providing Iranians with what Voice over the Internet Protocol (VoIP) had done in the early 2000s: low-cost telephone communication. TCI had reported $20 million profit in 1998, but in 2002, despite a threefold increase in the number of people with access to telephone lines in that period, TCI had reported a loss of $23 million. Unsurprisingly, private Internet and telephone providers were blamed for this loss in profit and the reversal of TCI fortune, and in reaction the government began to close many cyber cafés. The Revolutionary Guards, owner of TCI, are reacting yet again with the same "moral" crusade and waging their own war against what certain factions of the Iranian state are labelling a "soft war."

The controversy over SNSs in Iran continued as Telegram started to replace Viber and WhatsApp as Iranians' favorite method of communication. In October 2015, Mahmood Vaezi suggested that approximately 14 million Iranians use Telegram, although the social networking company claims that the number of users is around 20 million.[34] In October 2015, Pavel Durov, the co-founder of Telegram, revealed that Iran's Ministry of Information and Communications Technology requested "spying and censorship tools" from the service. When Telegram refused to give in to the minister's request, the ministry moved to block the service—a claim that was vehemently denied by officials. Because of their ease of use and accessibility via mobile devices, SNSs have started to replace blogs and emails. Their popularity is such that many state officials, including the supreme leader, news organizations, political parties, musicians, and various social groups have opened their own channels on Telegram to share and disseminate their works, ideas, and analysis. As an emerging company, Telegram cannot ignore such a big market in Iran and many organizations have expressed concerns over the nature of its negotiations and possible cooperation with the Iranian state. For example, on 18 November 2015 a British human rights organization urged Telegram to "clarify the nature of its negotiations with Iranian officials, including the nature of any data, technology, and censorship being requested, as well as the date on which discussions began, and which elements of the Iranian regime have been involved."[35] Such expressions of concern about privacy and Iranian government interference with popular communication tools and applications are not without precedent. In 2009, Nokia Siemens Network was forced to confirm that it had provided the Telecommunication Company of Iran with equipment that allowed it to spy on its customers. This led to a campaign against the Finnish information technology company and "Nokia: Disconnecting People" became one of the slogans of Iranian activists in 2009.

Mobile phones equipped with SNS capability are also politically relevant for other reasons:

> [they] not only permit the exchange of information between the individuals but also enable each person to act as an amateur photojournalist during demonstrations and their repression, sending photos and short videos to channels (in Tunisia, Al Jazeera did not have an authorized official journalist, and it broadcast the images and short sequences it received from the young 'amateur journalists').[36]

During the 2009 Iranian uprising, Yahoo Messenger and Bluetooth technologies allowed individuals to maintain connectivity and exchange information; this made it possible either to bypass the government censorship wall or to remain connected when the Internet was either down or too slow.

New media as new political tools: reformist and women's movements

Throughout modern history, the democratic potential of communication technologies—variously "new" in different historical epochs—for the expansion of the public sphere has been trumpeted.[37] The printing press revolutionized European intellectuals within a few decades of its development, and remains an epoch-defining technology.[38] Walter Benjamin clearly saw the revolutionary potential of film and the mechanical reproduction of works of art.[39] Brecht argued for the possibility of making radio into something really democratic, arguing that radio was more than an "acoustical department store" and that it could be turned into a two-way communication that was "capable not only of transmitting but of receiving, of making the listeners not only hear but also speak, not of isolating him but connecting him."[40] As such, the debate over new technologies—namely, whether new communication technologies or forms of media (press, TV, and the Internet) are catalysts for the emergence and formation of a new public sphere—is not all that new. Lest we forget that prior to the uprising in Iran, the Arab world reformist press and Al Jazeera were hailed as crucial in debating and promoting political and social change. While any discussion about democracy is incomplete without reference to the media, it is also clear that the process of democratization is always much more complex. Democracy and democratization are impossible without media; and yet, in all dictatorships media figure prominently.

To be sure, even in recent years, those that are using media technologies to record and write about events (bloggers, citizen journalists, etc.) have been heralded as new types of activists.[41] However, such categorization tends to ignore the complex, nuanced, and dialectical relationship between media, technology, and politics. For example, citizen journalism is a broad term, which is used to refer to often untrained, unpaid, non-unionized, and highly politicized forms of journalism. One can argue that the boundaries and practices of journalism (professional or otherwise) are being blurred, and in some respects (unionized and paid) fine lines are harder to draw. Nevertheless, citizen journalism can, and indeed does, contain different interests, focus, forms, and levels of politics. In a chaotic cyberspace there are many diverse voices; not all these are critical, not all about matters of public life, and not all about challenging the authority of the state or opposing the capitalistic ethos. If the issue of tools and access to the means of communication is significant, so is the issue of content and concerns. Furthermore, as I have stressed, identifying the new waves of struggle with the tools of movements carries the danger of neglecting the fact that digital technologies do not instigate the movements on their own, but rather provide new channels for the expression and amplification of oppositional and alternative voices. As Rahimi and Gheytanchi have argued, "online activism has served as an extension of Iranian dissident groups' channels of expression, allowing them to circumvent the established propaganda mechanisms and more directly exchange information and mobilize protests with other social movements."[42]

Rahimi and Gheytanchi rightly identify reformists and dissident voices inside the state apparatus as "Internet exploiters." Internal dispute and factionalism within the Iranian state are not just the product of the contradictions between the "Islamic" and republican elements of its constitutions. Caught between imperatives of the market and its ideology and the straitjacket of *velayat-e faqih*, the Iranian state has produced many dissidents from its own rank and supporters. Since the Supreme Leader controls state television, a president or officials with views different from the *rahbar* (leader) have to resort to other media. Publishing (newspapers, magazines, pamphlets, and books) was the medium of choice, particularly in the 1990s, which witnessed a boom in publishing. It was during this period that the works and writings of some reformists, such as Soroush, Kadivar, Eshkevari, and Ebadi, generated significant debates about the very nature of the Islamic Republic. Arjomand has argued that this new political space was "disorderly but also pluralistic and boisterously public, and is inextricably linked with government. It is the arena of competition among various social, economic and regional interests."[43] Despite the closure of many reformist and semi-independent press initiatives, however, the debate continued. The Internet became the new tool for many dissident voices on a much broader scale, which allowed them to reach a much larger audience inside and outside Iran. Almost all major figures within the Shia establishment developed their own websites as fora to disseminate their views. Lacking access to state-controlled broadcasting, many reformist officials and members of the parliament launched their own blogs. By 2004, blogging in Iran had attracted so much attention that Persianblog, the biggest blog service provider, organized a three-day festival of blogging, possibly the first in the world. The festival was opened by Mohammad Ali Abtahi, then vice president, who was an active blogger himself. Weblogs also played a key role in the 2005 elections, with all candidates having their own dedicated sites and blogs.[44]

The Iranian state, rather unexceptionally, has been the primary actor in engineering political legitimacy and the definer of the "national" character and culture. Yet, the factionalism and internal disputes are also a clear indication of the failure of the Islamic state to impose its monopoly over the legitimate use of symbolic violence and its continuing struggle to manufacture consent to its rule. The 2009 uprising highlighted this reality more than ever before.

Indeed, the 2009 presidential elections triggered unprecedented and impassioned involvement inside Iran and brought to the surface many simmering dissatisfactions about the lack of rights, the limits of freedoms, rising inflation, and growing inequality. A historic campaign grew in support of Mir-Hussein Mousavi, who put forward a modest, reformist program, with his "green" campaign quickly mobilizing to contest the proclaimed re-election of Ahmadinejad that had rendered political participation simply a charade in a predetermined outcome. The importance of factionalism inside the Iranian state cannot be overlooked for many reasons. Two issues in particular are highly relevant here. First, in contrast to the 2011 events in Egypt and Tunisia, which were sparked by anger against rising unemployment and growing social inequality, the 2009 revolt in Iran grew out of divisions and disagreements within the state apparatus when the Iranian state tried to entice people to the polls and give the electoral game a democratic gloss. With the deepening of the crisis and the increased mobilization of the people, the revolt against the "electoral coup" went further and acquired an added dimension. The initial motto of "where is my vote" soon gave way to "down with Khamenei" and "down with the dictator."[45] Second, the Iranian experience demonstrates the significance of resources and networks in staging and maintaining coherent and organized resistance against the state. It is undeniable that without the reformist networks and resources in Iran, no other social group could maintain an organized and sustained resistance. What this suggests is that the Internet on its own is no substitute for strong organizational ties such as political parties, associations, and unions.

How strongly and vigorously different groups could, want, or are willing to fight is also more than about social media dynamics. The struggle of the women's movement against gender discrimination in Iran provides us with additional insights into the strength, weakness, and contradictory nature of online activism. Before delving into these dynamics, it is fitting to point out yet another relevant difference between the Iranian uprising of 2009 and the 2011 uprisings in Egypt and Tunisia. Without a doubt, all three were revolts against dictatorship. However, the Islamic Republic is a religious dictatorship with totalitarian ambitions, a regime that combines political repression with widespread civil and cultural repression. The dictatorships of Tunisia and Egypt, as repressive as they were, were not based primarily on aggressive civil oppression. In both countries, sexual segregation and the imposition of the hijab were not official state policy, nor was "morality" a state priority; likewise, regular attacks and crackdowns to confiscate satellite dishes, interrupt weddings and parties, and humiliate citizens for their choice of clothing and hairstyles were not a regular feature of social life. Unlike the political establishment in the Islamic Republic of Iran, Ben Ali and Mubarak tolerated trade unions, allowed relative freedom in the media, and were apt at managing—rather than merely suppressing—dissent.[46] As such, and in the Iranian context, the "political" is always contentious and contingent, not least in an environment where even simple "private" acts in people's everyday lives (such as holding hands with a member of the opposite sex, or choosing not to wear the hijab) can become a "public" affair and a matter of national concern. Yet, from the beginning, violent measures taken by the Iranian state have provoked the persistent opposition of Iranian women, who have refused to conform to the moral conceptions of conservative Islamists in the country. For thirty-six years Iranian women have used every opportunity to challenge those very "moral" conceptions, including the compulsory hijab.

The struggle for equality, evident in various campaigns, meetings, and demonstrations, is supported and supplemented by a powerful presence in the online environment. Among the notable sites supporting and promoting various campaigns were Meydaan Zanan (Women's Field), Iranian Feminists' Tribune, Women in Iran, Focus of Iranian Women, Zanestan, and Feminist School, along with thousands of individual and collective blogs by Iranian women activists. A distinguishing feature of many of these sites, building on previous offline media experiences, was their conscious attempt at bridging activism and intellectual debate, as well as combining practice and theory. Some of the activities and campaigns, Rahimi and Gheytanchi suggest, generated new campaigns and spurred further activism. For example, in response to the arrest of many of the participants in the One Million Signatures campaign, the mothers of arrested activists and other Iranians concerned about government repression and the prospects of war against Iran formed Mothers for Peace, a non-profit and politically diverse forum which campaigns against violence, poverty, and oppression.[47] Another notable campaign is Mothers of Park Laleh. Inspired by the Madres de Plaza de Mayo, many Iranian women whose children, spouses, or close relatives were victims of the Islamic Republic have been campaigning against the death penalty, while advocating freedom for all political prisoners and the need to bring to justice those responsible for the death of their loved ones.

The most successful campaign is probably the Stealthy Freedom (*Azadiye Yawaschaki*) Facebook page. Set up in May 2014 by Iranian journalist and activist Massih Alinejad, the page is dedicated to posting hundreds of images of women with the hijab removed. Within a few days of its launch the page had received over 100,000 likes, and by the end of 2015 it had over 900,000 followers—a much bigger following than the Facebook page of the presidential candidate Mir-Hossein Musavi at the peak of the 2009 Iranian uprising. The Stealthy Freedom campaign can be seen as a continuation of the challenges, concerns, and anxieties over the hijab in Iran. Although the campaign is not free from contradictions and limits, it reveals the great potential for civil disobedience against "moral" concerns in the Iranian state.

In contrast to the virtual and real attacks and threats against the Stealthy Freedom campaign by Iranian state officials, the overwhelming feeling outside Iran has been one of support, solidarity, and encouragement. However, the problem with such expressions of solidarity is not that the information provided about the lack of freedom in Iran is inaccurate; but rather, as Haleh Anvari suggested in the *New York Times*, the Western fetish and obsession with gazing at Iranian women has turned them into "Iran's Eiffel Tower or Big Ben."[48] Since the 9/11 terrorist attacks, these "cultural icons" in particular have come to represent the dividing line between "us" and "them," modern and traditional, civilized and barbaric. The Stealthy Freedom Facebook campaign is not immune from such prejudices and stereotypes. No new technology, and no matter how global, can override assumptions, prejudices, and stereotypes about real spaces and concerns. In addition, and as Azadeh Davachi has suggested,[49] the campaign effectively reduces the concerns over gender equality in Iran to a compulsory hijab, when in fact for many Iranian women the core issue is simply not about the hijab; rather, it concerns a whole set of policies of control, monitoring, and in many cases traditions (including the hijab) which act as instruments for denying—and violently suppressing—women's rights. The campaign's focus on publishing pictures of veil-less Iranian women also effectively divides them into two distinct groups defined exclusively in terms of their attitudes toward the hijab. As suggested above, this false dichotomy might appeal to international media, but fails to provide any concrete and comprehensive model for achieving women's liberation in Iran.

The Stealthy Freedom campaign has also reinforced the myth of the role of social media in the Iranian context, thus confusing, or perhaps even substituting, media for the movement. "You are the media" was one of the claims of the so-called Green Movement. Masih Alinejad is still promoting the same idea in her campaign. Yet, it is worth remembering that at the time when activists were being confined to the realm of small media, many of the well-known figures of the Green Movement appeared on mainstream media as the voice of the movement. Effectively, such trends have tended to privilege select individual voices and their political philosophies. Who actually gets to speak inside the Islamic Republic of Iran, who gets noticed, and how individuals are recognized as "representing" the public is by definition a public process. In addition, it is rather interesting that in the current campaign, which has been hailed as a step toward "reclaiming individuality," the only recognized individual is Masih Alinejad herself.[50] Similar concerns have been raised by Gilda Seddighi, whose study of the Iranian group Mothers of Park Laleh and the organization of privileges in online spaces demonstrates how the networks of Iranian mothers who were inspired by the Madres de Plaza de Mayo were excluded from the online activism launched in their names.[51]

Finally, it is worth remembering that many such campaigns, irrespective of whether they take up a single issue or are animated by a range of issues, have come and gone without leaving much trace, or establishing a sustained, influential, long-term activist base. As I have already highlighted in my discussion of the power of real networks of reformists' circles in Iran, it is hard to effect social change without a sustained and well-established form of organization. Campaigns of this kind cannot possibly mount a significant challenge to repression and injustice if they are not transformed into real networks of activists. The experiences of Iran, Tunisia, and Egypt in the aftermath of the uprisings in these countries are powerful reminders of what can happen in the absence of real networks and political organizations.

Conclusion

The fairly rapid Internet development in Iran has been enacted amid political, economic, and cultural contestation at both national and international levels. The central paradox remains, that despite a top-heavy and controlling state, Iran enjoys a vibrant Persian-language cyberspace that is far more eclectic and disputed than might be imagined. This combines competition between the burgeoning cultural and communication industries of the private sector; and significant public demands for greater political and cultural openness, expressed most vehemently by various groups and their creative uses of these new technologies. In Iran, the combination of market forces and state policies is suppressing the democratic and participatory potential of the Internet. While demonstrating the real "potential" of new information technologies for the empowerment of citizens, the case of Iran also shows that the realization of this dream—in fact the potential of the Internet—depends on access and (political/cultural) entitlements for all. The digital environment in Iran also demonstrates how the very factionalism of the Iranian state inevitably makes for an intriguing and contradictory political and digital environment, and how the potential of new media is constrained by such factors as confusion in government policies, varied institutional interests, the dialectical tension between the imperative of the market and the "revolutionary" claims of the Iranian state, as well as external forces. New technologies have to be studied within specific and complex skeins of political, economic, and social issues, as the case of Iran vividly demonstrates.

· 11

E-GOVERNMENT IN THE GCC COUNTRIES

PROMISES AND IMPEDIMENTS

Damian Radcliffe

E-government is the process of using electronic tools to engage citizens, businesses, and residents with government-related information and services. Although there is no standard definition of e-government, there is a consistency to the key benefits that different actors attribute to it. These often focus on enablement and facilitation.[1] More specifically, e-government can contribute to increased government transparency, greater convenience for citizens and businesses, revenue growth, and/or cost reductions,[2] as well as enhance efforts to encourage civic participation in decision-making processes. Such moves can, in turn, help to make government bodies more accountable, transparent, and effective.[3]

These impacts are consistently present in definitions of e-government offered by major international institutions. For the World Bank, "e-Government refers to the use by government agencies of information technologies (such as Wide Area Networks, the Internet, and mobile computing) that have the ability to transform relations with citizens, businesses, and other arms of government."[4] UNESCO builds on these themes by also noting that e-government can support different actors "with the aim to improve their access to information and to build their capacities."[5] Meanwhile, the United Nations, a body which produces regular large-scale reports on the global progress of e-government, highlights the role that e-government can play in streamlining public administration workflows and processes, enhanced public service delivery, and the creation—and expansion—of communication channels for the engagement and empowerment of people.[6]

The management consultancy firm Strategy& (formerly Booz & Co.) adds another dimension to the potential socio-economic impacts created by e-government by arguing that "structured correctly, e-government initiatives can even generate economic value for governments, in addition to social and civic value, by helping create new jobs."[7] Because of these wide-ranging potential benefits, governments around the world have embraced the concept of e-government—although the emphasis and success of these efforts vary substantially from country to country.

The aim of this chapter is to explore the extent to which e-government has become embedded in policy and practice across the countries of the Gulf Cooperation Council (GCC), and to identify the challenges which need to be overcome and the opportunities that need to be embraced if the region is to realize the potential that e-government affords. Given the pace of change in this environment, the chapter encompasses academic literature, industry perspectives, and news reports to tell this emerging story.

Birthing pains: the initial adoption of e-government

In the first decade of the twenty-first century, the implementation of e-government across the six countries in the Gulf Cooperation Council (Bahrain, Kuwait, Oman, Qatar, Saudi Arabia, and the UAE) was often slow and protracted. Although the volume of academic literature in this arena is quite shallow, it consistently describes the paucity of these early efforts.

Much of the literature focused on e-government in Kuwait, for example, is notably critical of efforts by the Kuwaiti government to establish different e-government programs; especially when benchmarked against the efforts of their Gulf neighbors. Kuwait's services are typically identified as being less advanced and sophisticated than its GCC counterparts. Kraetzschmar and Lahlali are in line with many of their peers when they comment on "the limited availability of full e-services across government agencies, the absence of any integrated e-services involving multiple agencies, and the questionable value to users of some of the e-services provided."[8]

Disappointment among scholars in the progress of e-government is not confined to Kuwait. Examining the case of Saudi Arabia, the Gulf's largest and most populous country, Basamh, Qudaih, and Suhaimi observe that "despite the improvement in online presence in Saudi Arabia for the past five years, many citizens are still not able to access e-government services, and that the quality of e-government services are not as per expectations of citizens since most of the information the Saudis expect to be available is not available."[9]

Al-Shafi and Weerakkody express similar sentiments when studying e-government in Qatar—a country that has "superior ICT infrastructure" and which is "one of the regional broadband leaders in the Arab World."[10] Despite this, "the initial period of [e-government] strategy formulation and implementation" was "laggard compared to e-government efforts during the same period in developed countries," they state; but the authors do note that the establishment of a single body (ictQATAR) with responsibility for national e-government had "accelerated progress."[11]

Similarly, in nearby Oman, despite the establishment of a single government organization (Oman Digital) in 2003 to take the lead on these issues, little was achieved for some time, with the new agency spending half a decade identifying the information and technological needs for different government agencies in the country to participate in e-government.[12]

These efforts, or lack thereof, are in marked contrast with UAE and Bahrain, where earlier e-government initiatives appear to be more energized, with a more aggressive implementation of services and infrastructure, led by both government and the leading telecoms companies. Bahrain's e-government strategy goes back to 2007. As Karolak and Razzaque note, "the innovative approach to e-government has made Bahrain a leader in e-government and a model for other countries. The approach, which combines needs of a multicultural society and future economic development considerations, reflects a commitment to quality and growth."[13] Bahrain's small population and geographic land mass have also aided this implementation, although the lower levels of smartphone access in the country—compared to several of its neighbors—may hamper the next stage of this e-government evolution.

Meanwhile, "the UAE is considered to have one of the most advanced and world-class information and communication technology infrastructures."[14] This has created a strong foundation for e-government with efforts in this space mirroring the wider modernization agenda seen across the country and most clearly manifest in the cities of Dubai and Abu Dhabi. Despite this, however, the country dropped four places to 32nd in the 2014 UN e-governance rankings. One factor affecting the country's standing is the variance behind Dubai's enthusiasm for e-government and the attitudes and progress manifest in the other Emirates. A further consideration is the federal structure of the UAE, which may bring with it unique challenges in terms of developing e-government. Either way, the UAE's recent fall in the global e-government ranking is a reminder of how quickly early efforts can be overshadowed by energized neighbors eager to catch up and potentially leapfrog their Arab peers.

Gaining impetus: more recent progress

After a slow start, e-government in the region has begun to gain some momentum. The reasons for this are multiple and include a gradual acceptance of the e-government concept by stakeholders and concerted efforts to address key considerations such as usefulness, ease of use, reforming bureaucracy, cultural and social influences, technology issues, and lack of awareness.[15] Although countries in the GCC are still a long way behind leading e-government economies like Singapore, they have nonetheless made progress in recent years.

Measurement of e-government advancement, both in terms of deployment and wider socio-economic impacts, is formally performed and reported by a range of national and international bodies. Of these, the most notable is the United Nations e-Government Survey, which is produced every two years by the Department of Economic and Social Affairs. The publication features an assessment of the online presence of all 193 United Nations member states, including how member states harness ICTs for the "delivery of essential services."

Other prominent studies in this space include the World Economic Forum's annual Global Information Technology Report—which features their "Networked Readiness Index"[16]—and the analysis "Measuring the Information Society," which is published each year by the International Telecommunication Union (ITU).[17] Although each report deploys its own methodology, these studies blend a range of technical indices, stakeholder interviews, attitudinal analysis, and usage data to determine the progress of e-government implementation at a national, regional, and international level.

GCC countries place considerable emphasis on improving their ranking in these different reports; and this desire can be a key driver in shaping particular e-government initiatives. The publication of a higher rank in these studies is a source of pride for countries in the region, with the results frequently trumpeted in the national press and by different government bodies. Media coverage also reflects the frequently competitive nature of this activity, by often highlighting where progress is more favorable to that of their neighbors. However, with e-government scores potentially boosted by the presence of online portals, strategies, and services (rather than a more nuanced assessment of their quality and impact), cosmetic changes can sometimes produce a disproportional boost in rankings which are not necessarily underpinned by changes in behavior and practice.

Nonetheless, despite the small field of academic literature in this space—particularly in terms of cross-country analysis—the development of e-government in the Gulf states during the past decade and a half is discernible. As a result, the governments of the GCC countries have consistently seen a rise in their global e-government rankings. A review of materials published by the United Nations in 2012 finds that "The Networked Readiness Index of the 2012 Global Information Technology Report ranked three Arab countries in the top 30." In the United Nations' e-Government Survey 2012, the UAE was "among the top third of 190 countries in telecommunications infrastructure index value, along with Qatar, Saudi Arabia, and Bahrain."[18] Two years later, with 2014 the most recent year for which this ranking is available, all GCC countries were to be found in the top third of UN-ranked countries for e-government (see Figure 11.1). Within this, all countries—with the exception of the UAE—had seen a rise in their ranking, and all six GCC countries scored considerably above the world average.

E-government maturity

There are a number of different frameworks to determine the progress of e-government. Of these, Forrester's e-Government Maturity Continuum is perhaps the best known and most cited. It outlines how the form of e-government typically evolves as the concept of e-government becomes more deeply rooted in a country. The three distinct phases of e-government are: 1) "the era of access," whereby citizens can access government information online; 2) "the era of interaction and transaction," which has a transactional focus with some activities (such as the payment of bills or applications for driving licenses) being undertaken by electronic means; and lastly 3) "the era of engagement," which involves an active two-way relationship between government bodies and the public aimed at shaping decisions, policies and practices.[19]

Figure 11.1: E-government development in the GCC

Country Name	Organization	E-Government Development Index 2014	2014 Rank	2012 Rank	Change in Rank
Very High EGDI					
Bahrain	GCC Member	0.8089	18	36	18
High EGDI					
United Arab Emirates	GCC Member	0.7136	32	28	4
Saudi Arabia	GCC Member	0.6900	36	41	5
Qatar	GCC Member	0.6362	44	48	4
Oman	GCC Member	0.6273	48	64	16
Kuwait	GCC Member	0.6268	49	63	14
Regional Average		0.6838			
World Average		0.4712			

Source: Ismael Peña-López, "UN e-Government Survey 2014"

GCC governments find themselves at different stages of maturity across this continuum, although most countries in the region have made particularly good progress in the first two of these areas, most notably providing online information and access to e-services. Early successes found in a number of GCC countries include the creation of government networks, digital identity programs, growth and choice in broadband and mobile markets, as well as investment in next generation ICT networks.

As the United Nations noted in 2012, "over the past five to seven years, no other part of the world has advanced as rapidly. Through investments in telecommunications infrastructure, digital readiness initiatives, and competitive arrangements for network providers, the region has closed the digital gap with North America, Europe, and Asia."[20] Alongside these infrastructure investments and wider market developments, earlier e-government efforts in the region have also included the creation of national e-government portals. Although these served a domestic purpose—and their presence is part of the assessment process in gauging the e-readiness of a country—they also played a vital international role in terms of projecting the image of countries that are modern, open, and forward looking. As Kostopoulos noted, these "worldwide showcases" acted as "permanent promoters" of the countries' transition to a knowledge-based society and their efforts to offer a pro-business environment.[21]

There is, however, a big difference between these externally focused portals and the more sophisticated internal channels needed to support residents and businesses. Although external portals can help project a modern pro-business and technology environment, this external image does not always reflect the reality on the ground, where change can be much slower to effect. In terms of e-government across the region, the breadth of services used by both citizens and businesses typically remains limited, with many transactions continuing to be processed face-to-face. These issues need to be addressed if GCC countries are to create genuine e-societies.

Challenges to e-government progress

Although studies show that Gulf countries have consistently become more e-government-friendly, there remain a number of areas where further progress can be made. Without this, maintaining and enhancing their e-government rankings—as the UAE has recently found—will become increasingly difficult.

As the foregoing analysis suggests, early gains can—and have—been made through investment in ICT infrastructure, a change that is easier to implement than changes in consumer and business behavior. Potential barriers to address in order to drive greater consumer and business engagement include performance expectancy, effort expectancy, and peer influence.[22] It is these more advanced behavioral elements—along with lack of awareness, bureaucratic business practices, sociocultural issues, and citizens' satisfaction levels of current service provision—that GCC governments will need to focus on if they are to continue their rise in the global e-government rankings.[23] The following section explores key areas that merit particular attention if momentum in e-government maturity is to be maintained across the region.

Defining success

Governments across the region have developed and implemented e-government action plans. However, there are considerable variances in their proposals, including any proposed success measures. This can make it difficult to undertake cross-country analysis, as well as determine success within any given country. For example, the roll-out of services is meaningless if these services are not used. Yet, governments often highlight the number of services they have launched rather than focus on the number of users, or more complex indices such as time saved, or other potential cost-benefit analysis.

This diversity of approach—and the granularity of proposed goals and performance indicators—is particularly apparent when exploring the experiences of e-government in Oman, Qatar, and Bahrain. Oman, ranked 48th in the UN's 2014 e-government rankings, just above Kuwait, explicitly identifies links between e-government and efforts to achieve Millennium Development Goals.[24] Often cited as a benefit of e-government in other literature,[25] these wider developmental links are seldom made by other GCC nations. Moreover, most GCC countries typically publish broad indicators of e-government success, rather than very specific measurements. Bahrain, which is the leading county for e-government—ranked 18th globally on the UN's e-government index and second (to Singapore) in the UN's index of Small Island Developing States[26]—is one of the exceptions. Alongside broader e-government ambitions, it has committed to a number of very specific goals, including producing forty new e-services and the creation of ten new mobile applications every year. Bahrain's 2016 e-government strategy also undertook that "by 2014, 50% of government entities will interact with constituents through social networks" and that awareness of e-government programs would be at 90 per cent, with consumer satisfaction levels maintained over 80 per cent.[27]

The Qatari government published a new strategy for e-government in 2014, featuring a series of ambitious targets, including the commitment to have "100% of government services available online by 2020, 80% adoption of government shared services and 20% increase per annum in users participating on forums moderated by government."[28] This was Qatar's second e-government strategy document, following a master plan for integrated e-government in 2006.[29]

The types of measurable goals that we see in the cases of Bahrain and Qatar make it much easier for governments to define success, as well as to identify where remedial action might be needed. For external audiences, these tangible outcomes also make it easier to determine progress and assess the scope of ambition from these government agencies.

Who is e-government for?

Alongside these types of specific measurable pledges, many national e-government strategies in the region also include wider philosophical statements, which outline their intentions. The UAE government, for example, has expressed a commitment whereby "Emiratis will benefit from customer-focused government services whose quality is rigorously monitored and constantly improved. Interactive e-government will provide citizens with an especially responsive and efficient channel of service from public authorities."[30]

This last example hints at one of the unique challenges for e-government development in the region, namely defining who it is for. The unique demographics of many Gulf countries constitute an additional layer of complexity to e-government strategies. High levels of skilled and unskilled migration mean that national citizens in Gulf states such as the UAE and Qatar are a minority in their own countries. E-government strategies often prioritize the national population first, followed by skilled Arab, Asian, and Western expats.

The lack of e-government service provision for low-skilled workers, many of whom may have low literacy levels or are unable to use services that are often only provided in Arabic (or English, which is often the only other available language for e-government services in the region), is a barrier for widespread e-government adoption. Addressing this consideration and supporting this cohort will, in all likelihood, help countries in the region to boost their e-government standing. Similarly, specific efforts to support other groups less likely to use these services—such as women, who often have lower levels of both digital access and ICT skills—could also have an impact on international standing.

Understanding and accommodating interdependencies

Alongside these key strategic considerations, governments also need to understand and reflect the complexity of overlapping relationships upon which successful, integrated e-government relies. As identified by the e-Government for Development Information Exchange Project (coordinated by the University of Manchester's Institute for Development Policy and Management), the wider economic and social benefits of e-government are typically delivered through three main pillars of activity: e-administration (improving government processes), e-citizens and e-services (connecting citizens with government), and e-society (building external interactions by connecting stakeholders with each other).[31]

Although these different elements can operate independently, they have more impact when part of a holistic approach that recognizes potential interdependencies and the benefits of closer ties between different focal domains. Effective e-government strategies should reflect this framework and ensure that different elements do not operate in isolation.

Willingness to change

Rogers W'O Okot-Uma, of the Commonwealth Secretariat, has argued that "electronic Governance involves new styles of leadership, new ways of debating and deciding strategies, new ways of accessing services, new ways of transacting business, new ways of accessing education, new ways of listening to citizens and communities of practice and new ways of organizing and delivering information."[32] As manifest in Forrester's "era of engagement," this final phase of e-government maturity witnesses the embodiment of a very different relationship between governments and their stakeholders (citizens and businesses). However, many government workers are either unwilling or unable to work in this way. Many of them do not have the skills required to succeed in this new environment.[33] As Boujarwah notes in his study of e-government in Kuwait, "the majority of Kuwaiti citizens are employed by the government in service delivery tasks. Many of these people would have to be re-trained if services were automated and delivered online."[34] Government workers may also be bound by bureaucratic processes that hamper their ability to embrace new behaviors and ways of working. The World Economic Forum, for example, has highlighted red tape as a major barrier to Saudi Arabia's progress, ranking KSA the 107th worst country globally in this domain.[35] By contrast, the World Economic Forum typically ranks the country quite highly on many other important business indices. These obstacles are not unique to the GCC. Nonetheless, a culture that is willing to do things differently is essential for any government that wishes to enhance its e-government presence and global ranking.[36]

Ownership

Allied to the importance of government agencies being willing to change—in terms of both their approach and their attitude toward e-government—other important strategic questions which need to be addressed include issues of ownership, advocacy, and responsibility for e-government. Countries in the region have taken different approaches to the implementation of e-government, and these may have an impact on the success, or otherwise, of e-government implementation.

In Saudi Arabia, unlike most GCC countries, *Yesser*—the government's e-government program, meaning to "make easy"—is not owned by a single ministry, but rather by a "higher supervisory committee composed of the Minister of Finance, the Minister of MCIT and the Governor of CIT Commission. A steering committee has emerged from the higher committee with members representing the Ministry of Finance, MCIT and CIT Commission in addition to the Program's Director General."[37] This complexity of ownership may be one reason why the pace of e-government take-up in Saudi Arabia has been slower than anticipated. These shortcomings have also been noted in the case of Qatar and Oman, two Gulf countries that entrusted e-government transformation to the hands of a lead organization. Although Saudi Arabia's original aspiration had been that everyone should benefit from e-government by 2010,[38] only basic services had been implemented at that point.[39] A study revealed that by 2011 the transition to e-government was far from satisfactory: "10 ministries (45.4%) were completely or partially in the first stage (web presence); 3 ministries (13.6%) were in the second stage (one-way interaction); and 6 ministries had no online service at all."[40]

Engaging citizens and business

In their 2009 study of risks associated with e-government development, Al-Shehab et al. noted that "e-Government readiness is determined not just by government initiatives aimed at making comprehensive government services available online to citizens, but also the level of acceptance and participation of the society in e-services."[41] This willingness, or lack thereof, to engage in e-government can be driven by a number of factors. Take-up in Qatar has arguably been hindered by the perception that initial e-government efforts were aimed more at the business community than the average citizens, and this is reflected in the continued low usage—and awareness—of the service by residents.[42] In Kuwait, *wasta* (or nepotism) in government services constitutes a hindrance to e-government adoption. A large number of participants (86 per cent) in a survey by Al Awadhi and Morris stated that they might be more encouraged to use e-government services if they thought it would help to reduce *wasta* so "that all people would be given an equal chance to carry out their governmental transactions."[43] A quarter of the participants in the survey (24 per cent) indicated that they believed *wasta* was so engrained in their culture that it would be impossible to overcome. "*Wasta* in our society will be used in everything, even if it is electronic," one respondent noted.[44]

Lack of awareness

Although the emphasis in most e-government literature is on governments to modernize and adopt e-government, both businesses and end-users are also key to the success of e-government adoption. Boujarwah argues that e-government services will become obsolete if they are not widely used by the general public, and so "a public education and training campaign must be part of the whole formula for success."[45] Boujarwah's observations are especially pertinent given the prevalent perception that there is a lack of awareness amongst citizens and residents across the Gulf region regarding the range of e-government services that are available, and the potential benefits that such services can bring to end-users. In 2014, *Gulf News* reported that "residents in the emirate of Abu Dhabi appear to be unaware of the availability of most customer service apps from government departments, despite their easy availability and the number of transactions they claim to enable."[46] Many services are either available only in Arabic or simply do not work, they noted in their news story. Addressing these technical issues—as well as raising awareness about the provision of e-government services—is fundamental to delivering a step-change in e-government usage.

Security

Security and privacy issues,[47] alongside a lack of awareness of e-government services and their benefits, are key considerations for citizens across the region and globally. Some of these concerns are justified: according to Boujarwah's 2006 review of e-government services in Kuwait, "all e-government sites lack proper provisions for privacy and security of personal information. Anyone having the Civil ID number of a person can access all of his or her personal information."[48] Considering these risks, it is perhaps not surprising that one third of participants (30 per cent) in a subsequent study of 249 Kuwait University students identified security and privacy as factors that might prevent them from trusting, and therefore using, e-government services.[49] As Al Awadhi and Morris note, "many participants thought that if e-government services were not secure enough, their personal data would be under threat and could be altered or misused by hackers."[50] Clearly, this is a major concern for potential e-government users and one which needs to be addressed through improved robust technical standards, as well as effective communications to provide the reassurance that users obviously need.

Opportunities

The digital world does not stand still and technological change is "disruptive" across all aspects of our lives, including e-government. According to Kostpoulos, "more and more government agencies are moving employees from the front office to the back office of government service. Ultimately, the front office of government will be the Web, kiosks strategically located in areas of high foot traffic, as well as the SMS capabilities of the omnipresent mobile phones."[51] This statement from 2004 demonstrates just how quickly consumer and business behaviors change, and the speed with which governments need to pivot and modify their plans in order to stay relevant. As a result, e-government services and communication are in a perpetual state of evolution.

For GCC governments, this amplifies the ongoing challenges they are already contending with around engaging citizens and business with e-government: whether it is security concerns, lack of awareness, or resistance to change. Although mainstream penetration of ICT devices is high, breadth of usage by individuals in GCC countries is typically shallow.[52] For example, few small- and medium-size enterprises (SMEs) have a web presence,[53] or are familiar with everyday business technologies such as the Cloud.[54]

These findings point to the extent of the technological and cultural challenges that governments in the region need to address if they are to increase participation in e-government initiatives, and if this is to have an impact across the demographic spectrum. At the same time, there is cause for optimism. After a slow start, the building blocks for a more advanced e-society are in place across all nations in the GCC. The following section explores how these foundations can be built upon.

Promoting the benefits

Across the region, lack of awareness of the key constituents of e-government services—and their ancillary benefits—prevents the full potential of this sector being realized. This lack of awareness remains present amongst both businesses and consumers, despite the plethora of services already offered by different countries in the region. To remedy this, government agencies will need to work with digital marketing agencies, employers, telecoms providers, and civil society organizations to ensure that the workforce and general population are aware of e-government services and the potential benefits (such as financial and time savings, ease of use, and efficiency) that they can provide.

The regional e-government forerunner, Bahrain, like many of its counterparts, offers a number of standard e-government services, such as utilities payments or traffic services. The Bahraini government is also very active in highlighting the role that e-government can play in making many important government-related tasks easier to do—a trait not necessarily seen in other GCC countries. Among the many uses of e-government in Bahrain is the issuing of birth and death certificates and generating notifications for medical check-ups, to name a few.

Not every country in the region has such an advanced e-government program. If anything, evidence suggests that awareness of even the simplest applications can often be surprisingly low. A 2012 study on the Arab digital generation (ADG) reported that

> online payment of government services or fines is widely available in GCC countries. Despite this, 42 percent of the ADG in GCC countries are seemingly unaware that such services are available. This is more so for the older ADG age group in the GCC. About 49 percent of those between the ages of 25 and 35 were not aware of the provision of such services.[55]

At the same time, the report also noted that "the ADG has high expectations for transparency and e-government services."[56] This suggests that they would be willing to use these services, if only they knew about them. Marketing and awareness campaigns therefore will need to target all groups, as lack of awareness about e-government can be found across the demographic spectrum.

Acknowledging and addressing security concerns

Alongside lack of awareness, the other leading barrier to e-government adoption in the GCC countries relates to privacy and security concerns. This concern about online transactions is not just restricted to the e-government arena; e-commerce in the region has similarly been held back by security fears. Insights into e-commerce in the Middle East, published in September 2013 by PayPal, noted that "security is a concern for all online shoppers, whether it comes in the form of payment fraud, non-delivery or counterfeiting. MENA shoppers listed security as their number one concern for shopping online in 40% of cases."[57] More broadly, growing concerns about the ability to protect privacy and secrecy in a post-Snowden age mean that governments must provide citizens with reassurance about the security of their personal data more urgently than ever.

Digital inclusion

Some of these security concerns can be addressed by ensuring that citizens and residents are equipped with the skills they need to be active netizens. Equipping potential users with digital literacy skills will help to create a potential user base that is more confident about their ability to use e-government. Prerequisite skills include being able to determine the legitimacy and security levels of websites and transactions, as well as mitigating risks associated with phishing and spam.

Investment in this space can have a palpable impact. In Oman, large-scale capacity-building efforts provided IT training to 160,000 individuals, including government employees and people with disabilities. Alongside this, nineteen Community Knowledge Centers have been established to provide access to equipment and support. As a result of these and other interventions (such as a Central 24/7 Call Center offering free advice to users of the central government e-portal), Oman has seen a dramatic growth in IT and e-government take-up. In 2005, their Internet penetration rate was less than 17 per cent; by the end of 2013, it had grown to 67 per cent, whilst the PC penetration rate hit 80 per cent.[58]

Of course, there also needs to be a recognition that some citizens will be unable or unwilling to go digital-only. This realization is not unique to the Gulf. It is a reality that has been acknowledged in more mature e-government nations such as Britain,[59] which has outlined plans to provide "digital assistance" for those people who have rarely or never been online.[60] This assistance will include the provision of offline services, although the overall percentage of transactions conducted in this manner is expected to decline substantially. The British government is also aware of the potential afforded by proxy use, whereby users work with friends and family or other trusted parties who can help them to enter details online or undertake transactions on their behalf. In Britain, many Internet non-users have a link to the Internet via a proxy user.[61] Given the prevalence of extended families in the Middle East region, proxy use would seem to be a sensible way to help grow e-government engagement. Citizens and residents may be aware of e-government services, but unable or unwilling to use them online. Being able to work with friends and family to do so is a potentially viable way forward.

Finally, in the digital inclusion field, the other issue for GCC governments to address is the provision of services and support for low-skilled migrant workers. With many e-government services only available in Arabic or English, this group risks being excluded on linguistic grounds. Moreover, e-government content is typically designed for use on a desktop or smartphone, technologies to which this demographic often has very limited access (and may not have the ICT skills to use). Understanding, and catering for, the linguistic and technological realities of this sizeable population are important steps if e-government in the region is to be a truly inclusive service. This will mean provision of e-government services in other languages such as Tamil, Hindi, and Bengali, as well as ensuring that e-government materials can be accessed via 2G networks and non-smartphones. The work being led by Internet.org and Facebook offers one potential approach for data-friendly mobile services, which can help to promote digital inclusion. Meanwhile, innovations using SMS and m-payment systems in Africa offer replicable models for GCC governments, which can be used to create valuable e-government services for the Gulf's low-skilled labor force. Undertaking such efforts will help meet real socio-economic needs amongst this substantial cohort, and would no doubt also be well received internationally.

User-centric design

Across the GCC, governments may face some resistance from communities who prefer to undertake activity in traditional ways, such as face-to-face, or who distrust the security and privacy of online services. Understanding user preferences and barriers can go a long way toward improving service delivery and enhancing digital inclusion efforts. As the UK government has recognized with their digital strategy, "these services must be designed to meet user needs... The approach includes a range of possible ways to provide services ... depending on what the user needs are and how complex the service is."[62]

This approach has seen support in the region. The authors of a 2013 report titled "Generations A: Differences and Similarities across the Arab Generations" argue that "to successfully implement e-government models, Arab region states must take a customer-centric approach to their government services, understanding each service from their constituents' perspective to determine how best to provide them."[63] A similar recommendation was made by the Economist Intelligence Unit, which suggested "a focus on local adaptability—to target what it is the population needs and provide this via a variety of channels, including both stationary and mobile devices—will buttress e-government development further."[64] The report further noted that "the leading e-government countries of the future are likely to be those that tailor their online offerings to local norms and to their level of development. They are also likely to be those that listen to constituents before launching or refining services."[65]

Bahrain's success in this field is due, in part, to their adoption of such principles. Their e-government authority holds focus groups to develop services, undertakes regular field studies, and conducts customer satisfaction surveys, so that initiatives can be based on the feedback and interaction of citizens. This approach also means offering services that users want, rather than simply those which are technically feasible or which allow e-government targets to be hit. Saudi Arabia offers e-services that include registering for unemployment benefits online or by SMS, whilst Oman has launched tools such as Mobile ID—the equivalent of a physical e-ID card on the user's mobile phone—and e-Passport.[66]

In the UAE, "Tawajody" (meaning "My Presence") is a service provided to UAE citizens staying abroad that facilitates communication between them and diplomatic missions in cases of emergencies—an example of a service that looks to meet a clearly defined need. Other useful UAE services include a smart app from Dubai Police, which allows users to view and pay traffic fines, as well as allowing access to electronic copies of their national ID, driver's license, and car ownership documents; and an interactive electronic system for case management released in 2014 by the Dubai Courts, where defendants can receive notification by email and Short Message Service (SMS) when a plaintiff registers a case.[67]

As consumers and businesses increasingly use social media, apps, data, and cloud computing services, government agencies will need to adopt these tools if they are to ensure that their e-government services remain relevant to the needs, expectations, and behavior of their citizens. User-centric design will therefore need to be at the heart of the e-government future.

M-government

Given the high take-up of mobile devices in the region, user-centric design will often mean that it will be essential for services to be mobile-friendly. The proliferation of smartphones, apps, and tablets has resulted in a shift to interaction through mobile—instead of desktop—devices, whilst social networks have also played a role in changing communication dynamics, making them less formal and more immediate.

Across the wider MENA region, there are 404 million mobile connections and 195 million subscribers, with 3G and 4G connections growing from nearly 9 million connections in 2008 to 106 million by 2013.[68] Harnessing this potential entails, among other initiatives, dedicated apps as well as mobile responsive design.[69] Whatever happens, the future of e-government will continue to evolve, and e-government providers will need to acknowledge the multi-channel reality of today's e-citizen.

In June 2013, the UAE government changed the name of their e-government initiative to m-government, a symbolic indication of their shift to service delivery aimed at mobile phone users.[70] The move is not too surprising, perhaps, given that the UAE—alongside affluent Qatar—has the highest levels of smartphone penetration in the world.[71] Gulf countries are also releasing dedicated apps for citizens, residents, and businesses to use, whilst also embracing third-party services like Instagram as tools for m-government. Although the myriad of available apps can be daunting—with many apps often offering one function or services from one government body instead of multiple services from different government entities—they are starting to gain popularity. In Bahrain, use of their dedicated e-government app store (bahrain.bh/apps) increased by 27 per cent in September 2014, with applications downloaded 146,991 times.[72] The initial success of the Dubai government's single sign-on service, where one log-in enables users to access over 250 e-services from eleven government entities, gives an indication of how these services might evolve. Thus far 40,000 users are harnessing this service,[73] although the number is likely to grow in the coming years.

E-engagement and open government

As measured by numerous international indices and definitions of e-government, for e-government to deliver on its full potential, it should be used as a tool that promotes genuine two-way dialogue between governments and other stakeholders, with feedback used to shape services. Tools like mobile phones and apps make the technological process for two-way dialogue infinitely easier and more immediate. This is not easy, although it is an important characteristic for the success of more sophisticated e-government efforts. As the OECD notes:

> The challenge is not to introduce digital technologies into public administrations; it is to integrate their use into public sector modernisation efforts.... Failures of governments to make the transition to the new digital environment can have important consequences including poor service delivery, underperformance of

spending, privacy and security breaches, and loss of citizen trust. For this reason, strategies for effective digital government need to reflect public expectations in terms of economic and social value, openness, innovation, personalised service delivery and dialogue with citizens and businesses.[74]

While the potential of e-government is not developed to its fullest in the region, there are encouraging trends. Bahrain's 2016 e-Government National Strategy has had some results, and their approach benefits from pan-agency partnerships and engagement. In particular, it is notable that they have sought to develop relationships with NGOs such as the Bahrain Internet Society, Social Media Club, and the Bahrain Society of Engineers. This type of multi-stakeholder approach is seldom seen in the region, although it can be essential to promoting engagement, buy-in, and positive perceptions of open government.

Qatar's 2020 e-government plan includes targets for citizen-based e-engagement and a commitment to open data, whilst also recognizing that no single body can make an integrated e-government a reality; "each affected entity will need to develop and implement e-Government services," and "the effort to achieve this will be significant, and requires energy and stamina. The rewards will be substantial, for people and government alike."[75] This approach also recognizes the value of a multi-stakeholder approach to engender an e-government culture, although civil society organizations in Qatar generally lack the profile and impact of their counterparts in Bahrain. Furthermore, although the Qatar government has set targets for year-on-year growth for e-engagement, these are percentages, and thus quite easy to attain if the starting sample is quite small. Nonetheless, this represents a step in the right direction and the Qatari government will hope to see the benefit of this approach.

In this regard, Saudi Arabia is seen in some quarters as a pioneer. In 2013, an Economist Intelligence Unit report noted that "the kingdom has developed numerous surveys, public consultations and further engagement initiatives using social media, such as Facebook and Twitter."[76] The report went on to say that, like Saudi Arabia, "some of the countries in the UN survey which perform best on this measure—creating online tools for citizen participation—are not Western-style democracies. Among the UN's top ten performers in e-government participation are Singapore (tied for second), Kazakhstan (tied for second) and the UAE (tied for sixth)."[77] The finding that active e-government participation can be found in non-democratic nations may be unexpected, and the point that these "are not Western-style democracies" is well made, reflecting the cultural challenge of identifying global best practice. However, considering that the online impact of these tools is not clearly addressed, it is difficult to see how impactful they are.

Although not a tool for consultation per se, Oman has identified a clear way to promote transparency, after Oman's State Financial and Administrative Audit Institution (SFAAI) implemented an automated e-form on their portal. This allows confidential feedback related to any wrongdoings in any public services, government-owned organizations, and private companies. Based on these inputs, the SFAAI carries out specific audits and investigations designed to remove corrupt practices. The initiative—which won first place in the 2013 United Nations Public Service Award (UNPSA) in the category "preventing and combating corruption in the public service"—offers an interesting case study for their Gulf peers.[78]

Promotion and engagement through social media

Finally, it is worth noting the potential afforded by social media as a platform for addressing many of the issues and opportunities outlined in this paper. Engaging with citizens in the digital spaces that they already inhabit may be one way to address concerns such as security, as well as to raise awareness and promote e-engagement. Across the wider Middle East and North Africa region, Facebook penetration is over 74 million,[79] whilst services like WhatsApp, Twitter, and Instagram also have growing audiences. By providing opportunities for engagement within a digital environment in which users are already proficient and comfortable may be part of the solution. To some extent, the UAE government acknowledged this in 2014 when it introduced a unified Instagram brand for government news.[80] The Emirate of Dubai in particular is proactive in promoting its services through a variety of channels, including social media. The Twitter account of the Ruler of Dubai (@ HHShkMohd) is followed by 31.1 per cent of the population, with each tweet typically being retweeted 557 times.[81]

As the World Bank has stated, "social networking tools have the potential to enhance citizen engagement in the region, promote social inclusion, and create opportunities for employment, entrepreneurial activities, and social development."[82] In the social media savvy Gulf region, it may well be the most effective route to enhanced e-government promotion and engagement.

Conclusion and research recommendations

Governments in the GCC countries are all focused on developing new knowledge-based economies and ensuring that their products and services are competitive on a regional and global scale. As a result, "there are serious efforts in these countries to develop electronic operating environments, with advanced capabilities to build the right conditions for the e-Citizens concept to evolve."[83] Making this happen, however, is not without its challenges. Alongside challenging and changing the status quo, barriers to progress identified in a number of studies include: IT infrastructural weakness of government public sectors, lack of knowledge, limited ability to use ICT, and low awareness of government services.[84] Looking within the government entities, the behavior and competence of government employees in the public sectors can be seen as an added internal challenge to the implementation of e-government systems in many organizations. Therefore, it is necessary to develop the public sector and train its employees to have a clear vision about the new nature of their public service, including their job descriptions, tasks, and application to customer service.

Without this, the transformative potential of e-government cannot be fully harnessed. However, governments across the Gulf region are aware of these challenges and have put many of the instruments in place needed to address these considerations. These plans, when coupled with earlier investments in the e-government space, have the potential to see a step-change in e-government activity across the region in the next decade. Meanwhile, Dubai's proposal to use drones to deliver government documents provides an example of how innovations in this space may evolve. It will be fascinating to see this future unfold.[85]

In the future, capitalizing on the potential of such developments will require more research on e-government. Academic analysis of this field in the region remains relatively small. This is particularly true at the regional level, as most academic studies tend to focus on the development of e-government within a specific GCC country, with the result that there is little in the way of comparative analyses, either across GCC countries, or with other regions. This should be remedied in the near future.

Alongside the need for greater cross-country analysis, the literature in this field would also benefit from further exploration of some culturally specific issues, which may in turn hinder adoption of e-government services. Of these, the role of *wasta* emerged in only one study,[86] and whilst this suggested that in an electronic environment this influence may be reduced, there were those who felt that the concept was too culturally engrained to be overcome by technology alone. This is an area that would merit further study.

Other aspects of e-government that may benefit from more detailed analysis include a focus on specific demographics. Typically studies cover an entire population, or a particular cohort such as students or government workers. In the Gulf, the use of services by women, and by the sizeable non-English and non-Arabic speaking populations, may also need to be addressed separately by both researchers and governments. Progress in supporting the unique needs of these cohorts could prove to be essential if respective governments are to continue their rise in the relevant international e-government rankings.

EPILOGUE

ON THE DIGITAL MIDDLE EAST
AND COMPUTATIONAL SOCIAL SCIENCE

Ingmar Weber

Changes in the global digital landscape over the past decade or so have transformed many aspects of society, including how people communicate, socialize, and organize. These transformations have also reconfigured how companies conduct their businesses and altered how states think about security and interact with their citizens. Glancing into the future, there is good reason to believe that nascent technologies such as augmented reality will continue to change how people connect, blurring the lines between our online and offline worlds. Recent breakthroughs in the field of artificial intelligence will also have a profound impact on many aspects of our lives, ranging from the mundane—chat bots as convenient, always available customer support—to the disruptive—replacing medical doctors with automated diagnosis tools.

The ubiquity and ever-increasing use of ICTs are not merely changing society, they are also changing the way we study society. With nearly every digital activity, whether it is a simple search on Google, a short message on Twitter, or a casual posting of a selfie to Instagram, users leave behind digital breadcrumbs. Digital traces of what we do, what we write, what we share, and what we consume are a by-product of Internet use and provide a record of human behavior at an unimaginable scale. Notwithstanding the concerns that data permanence raises in relation to the issue of privacy,[1] these generated digital footprints open up exciting research possibilities. As such, they constitute a new opportunity for understanding the individual, the state, and society in an unfolding digital era.

The emergent field of computational social science is tapping into such data sources, using them as a kind of telescope, or rather socioscope,[2] to fuel research that would have been unthinkable only a few years ago. This new type of research is truly interdisciplinary, applying computational and "big data" approaches to address research questions that are posed by sociologists, political scientists, demographic researchers, and experts from other fields. The effect of this new field on our ability to generate knowledge in the digital era is profound.

The digital Middle East is particularly interesting to study from the perspective of computational social science. The rapid diffusion of digital media infrastructure and the wide adoption of digital technologies in the region have put new methodological avenues for scientifically observing these ongoing changes at the disposal of Middle East scholars, Internet researchers, and data scientists. Social media in particular provide a valuable source of data to make sense of evolving Middle Eastern societies. Digital networks can serve as "observatories" of transformation in the region that are due to, and go beyond, the adopted digital technologies themselves.[3]

A few examples can help elucidate the potential that computational social science holds for the study of emergent trends and subtle changes in the region. It is common for social networking sites like Facebook to provide its advertisers with aggregate anonymized data about its users. Out of this, computational social scientists can gain useful insights about health, for instance, including how many young women in the individual countries of the Middle East have expressed interest in diabetes-related information on Facebook. Researchers equipped with computational tools can use such data sources to study levels of awareness of different health concerns among Facebook users in the region.[4] To take another example, the longitudinal nature of Twitter, with many users having tweeted for several years, enables an investigation of what eventual supporters of ISIS had been discussing long before the terrorist group even existed, thus shedding light on potential antecedents for ISIS support.[5] Big social data also have potential value in predicting offline events.

More generally, what the study of digital traces enables researchers to do is not only enlarge the scope of inquiry, but also increase the ability to measure trends. What this means is that theories previously argued about qualitatively or demonstrated quantitatively using a limited sample can now be tested empirically using big social data. Among the advantages that computational social science offers over traditional survey-based methods is access to longitudinal data, often spanning several years; access to social network data; and access to rich, multifaceted data not limited to answering small sets of questions.

At the same time, there are considerable methodological challenges that need to be addressed, in particular concerning selection bias and non-representativeness issues. Whereas these challenges are fairly universal to most studies in computational social science, there are a number of challenges that do not apply to the same degree to data from the Middle East and data from, say, the United States. To start with, most available natural language processing (NLP) tools, such as sentiment analysis tools, are well-tuned for English but typically less reliable or non-existent for Arabic. Naturally, this limits the insights that computational social scientists can obtain without first advancing the state-of-art in foundational methods. Additionally, cultural norms around publicly sharing details about one's private life are different in the MENA region, particularly among Muslim-majority nations.[6]

Furthermore, and especially in the case of Gulf nations that are considerably more heterogeneous in terms of the nationalities represented, different parts of society use different online services, making it particularly challenging to obtain a truly global picture of such societies. For example, Twitter usage is comparatively higher among Western expats than among blue-collar workers from the Indian subcontinent. Furthermore, the usage of online services by the lowest income bracket is influenced by tariff particulars, more so than in other regions of the world. In the instance of Qatar, the Facebook usage of blue-collar workers is surprisingly high, partly due to special tariffs from Vodafone Qatar with (partly) free Facebook data traffic.

Apart from challenges related to the availability of tools and data in the Middle East, there are concerns about ethics and human subject research when harvesting digital traces, which are amplified due to the sensitivities of the region's geo-cultural politics. In spite of these challenges and limitations, computational social science comes with enormous opportunities for interdisciplinary research, particularly in instances where social scientists and computer scientists work together to tackle difficult research questions of societal research. Computational social science tools and methods can help acquire valuable knowledge from digital communication. The ensuing measurements and comparisons can provide valuable insights into society's complex realities, which traditional social science methods like interviews and surveys may not be as adept in obtaining from within developing regions. Yet, the scientific appeal of data science like computational social science is most revealing when its quantitative insights are complemented with insights from traditional social sciences inquiries that provide interpretative depth and take heed of the specificity of the region.

At the same time, just as unidirectional broadcast media are losing ground to multidirectional interactive media, researchers have to make more of an effort to have knowledge flow back to the wider public. In particular, more efforts are needed to develop a digital literacy that goes beyond acquiring the knowledge and ability to use an ever-expanding array of tools—one that can instill wider awareness of the privacy risks associated with digital communication and feed a deeper curiosity in learning how to create such tools. Without these ingredients, societies in the Middle East and elsewhere risk becoming passive users of technology, rather than active agents involved in shaping the technologies and, in doing so, their future.

NOTES

1. MAPPING THE DIGITAL MIDDLE EAST: TRENDS AND DISJUNCTIONS

1. Manuel Castells, "The Internet and the Network Society," in *The Internet in Everyday Life*, ed. Barry Wellman and Caroline Haythornthwaite (Oxford: Blackwell, 2002), xxvii-xxx.

2. Manuel Castells, *The Rise of the Network Society* (Oxford: Blackwell, 2000).

3. Annabelle Sreberny, "Television, Gender and Democratization in the Middle East," in *De-Westernizing Media Studies*, ed. James Curran and Myung-Jin Park (London: Routledge, 2000), 66.

4. Arjun Appadurai, "Disjunction and Difference in the Global Cultural Economy," *Theory Culture and Society* 7 (1990): 296.

5. Henry Jenkins, *Convergence Media: Where Old and New Media Collide* (New York: New York University Press, 2006), 5–6.

6. Andrew Chadwick, *The Hybrid Media System: Politics and Power* (Oxford: Oxford University Press, 2013), 4.

7. For recent book-length studies on how the adoption of ICTs in the region has impacted various aspects of the political sphere, broadly defined, see Niki Akhavan, *Electronic Iran: The Cultural Politics of an Online Evolution* (New Brunswick, NJ: Rutgers University Press, 2013); David Faris, *Dissent and Revolution in a Digital Age: Social Media, Blogging and Activism in Egypt* (London: I. B. Tauris, 2012); Linda Herrera, *Revolution in the Age of Social Media: The Egyptian Popular Insurrection and the Internet* (London: Verso: 2014); Philip Howard, *The Digital Origins of Dictatorship and Democracy: Information Technology and Political Islam* (Oxford: Oxford University Press, 2010); Philip Howard and Muzammil M. Hussain, *Democracy's Fourth Wave? Digital Media and the Arab Spring* (Oxford: Oxford University Press, 2013); Marwan Kraidy, *The Naked Blogger of Cairo: Creative Insurgency in the Arab World* (Cambridge, MA: Harvard University Press, 2016); Negar Mottahedeh, *#iranelection: Hashtag Solidarity and the Transformation of Online Life* (Stanford, CA: Stanford University Press, 2015); Courtney Radsch,

Cyberactivism and Citizen Journalism in Egypt: Digital Dissidence and Political Change (New York: Palgrave Macmillan, 2016); Annabelle Sreberny and Gholam Khiabany, *Blogistan: The Internet and Politics in Iran* (London: I. B. Tauris, 2010); Deborah Wheeler, *Digital Resistance in the Middle East: New Media Activism in Everyday Life* (Edinburgh: Edinburgh University Press, 2017); Mohamed Zayani, *Networked Publics and Digital Contention: The Politics of Everyday Life in Tunisia* (Oxford: Oxford University Press, 2015); Mohamed Zayani and Suzi Mirgani, eds, *Bullets and Bulletins: Media and Politics in the Wake of the Arab Uprisings* (New York: Oxford University Press, 2016).

8. Taylor Owen, *Disruptive Power: The Crisis of the State in the Digital Age* (Oxford: Oxford University Press, 2015).

9. Matt Duffy, "Despite Arab Uprisings, Press Freedom Still Elusive," *Jadaliyya*, 5 June 2013, http://www.jadaliyya.com/pages/index/12035/despite-arab-uprisings-press-freedom-still-elusive

10. "YouTube and the Middle East: The Story of 6 Arab Web Superstars," Digital in the Round, 5 February 2014, http://www.digitalintheround.com/youtube-arab-web-stars

11. Nahlah Ayed, "Why Saudi Arabia is the World's Top YouTube Nation," CBC News, 1 April 2013, http://www.cbc.ca/news/world/nahlah-ayed-why-saudi-arabia-is-the-world-s-top-youtube-nation-1.1359187

12. Joe Khalil, "Youth-Generated Media," in *The Handbook of Development Communication and Social Change*, ed. Karin Gwinn Wilkins, Thomas Tuft, and Rafael Obregon (Oxford: Wiley-Blackwell, 2014), 439–45.

13. "Media Use in the Middle East: A Six Nation Survey," 2016, http://www.qatar.northwestern.edu/docs/publications/research-media-use/2016-middle-east-media-use-report.pdf

14. "Twitter in the Arab Region," Arab Social Media Report, Dubai School of Government, 2014, http://www.arabsocialmediareport.com/Twitter/LineChart.aspx

15. Raja Abdallah Al Sania, *Girls of Riyadh* (New York: Penguin, 2007).

16. Touria Khannous, "Virtual Gender: Moroccan and Saudi Women's Cyberspace," *Hawwa: Journal of Women in the Middle East and the Islamic World* 8 (2011): 358–87.

17. Sultan Sooud Al-Qassemi, "Gulf Governments Take to Social Media," *Huffington Post*, 31 May 2011, http://www.huffingtonpost.com/sultan-sooud-alqassemi/gulf-governments-take-to-_b_868815.html

18. Ifran Chaudhry, "#Hashtags for Change: Can Twitter Promote Social Progress in Saudi Arabia," *International Journal of Communication* 8 (2014): 943–61.

19. Courtney C. Radsch, "Treating the Internet as the Enemy in the Middle East," Committee to Protect Journalists, 27 April 2015, https://cpj.org/2015/04/attacks-on-the-press-treating-internet-as-enemy-in-middle-east.php

20. Abdel Bari Atwan, *Islamic State: The Digital Caliphate* (London: Saqi Books, 2015), 15–31. On digital media and terrorism, see also Suzi Mirgani, *Target Markets: International Terrorism Meets Global Capitalism* (Bielefeld: Transcript, 2017), 98–102.

21. Ronald J. Deibert, *Black Code: Surveillance, Privacy and the Dark Side of the Internet* (Toronto: Signal, 2013), 4–5.

22. Mehran Kamrava, "Contemporary Port Cities in the Persian Gulf: Local Gateways and Global Networks," in *Gateways to the World: Port Cities in the Persian Gulf*, ed. Mehran Kamrava (Oxford: Oxford University Press, 2016), 44.

23. Mark Andrejevic, "The Big Data Divide," *International Journal of Communication* 8 (2014): 1673–89; Jennifer Sunrise Winter, "Big Data Analytics and the Right to Privacy," *Media Development* 1 (2016): 10–13; Danah Byd and Kate Crawford, "Critical Questions for Big Data," *Information, Communication and Society* 15, no. 5 (2012): 662–79.

24. Javier Borge-Holthoefer, Muzammil M. Hussain, and Ingmar Weber, "Studying Networked Communication in the Middle East: Social Disrupter and Social Observatory," in *Communication in the Networked Age*, ed. S. Gonzalez-Bailon and B. Foucault Wells (forthcoming, Oxford University Press).

25. Rasha S. Abdul Wahab, "Data Mining's Capabilities for Knowledge Creation in the GCC Countries," *International Journal of Innovation and Knowledge Management in Middle East and North Africa* 1, no. 1 (2011): 129–42.

26. Jens-Erik Mai, "Big Data Privacy: The Datafication of Personal Information," *Information Society* 32, no. 3 (2016): 192–9.

27. "Transforming Education in the Arab World: Breaking Barriers in the Age of Social Learning," Arab Social Media Report, June 2013, http://www.arabsocial-mediareport.com/UserManagement/PDF/ASMR_5_Report_Final.pdf

28. Btihaj Ajana, *Governing Through Biometrics: The Biopolitics of Identity* (Basingstoke: Palgrave Macmillan, 2013), 5.

29. Alanoud Alsharekh, "Social Media and the Struggle for Authority in the GCC," *Canadian Journal for Middle East Studies* 1, no. 2 (2016): 8–33.

30. Jon Gambrell, "Amazon Buys Souq.com," *US News and World Report*, 28 March 2017, https://www.usnews.com/news/business/articles/2017–03–28/souqcom-says-amazon-has-bought-it-after-800m-counteroffer; Robert Cyran, "Amazon Takes a Gamble on Middle Eastern E-Commerce," *New York Times*, 24 March 2017, https://www.nytimes.com/2017/03/23/business/dealbook/amazon-takes-a-gamble-on-middle-eastern-e-commerce.html?_r=0

31. Chris Vein, "Why Increasing Digital Arabic Content is Key for Global Development," *Guardian*, 28 April 2014, http://www.theguardian.com/media-network/media-network-blog/2014/apr/28/global-development-digital-arabic-content

32. Remah Gharib, Evren Tok, and Mohammad Zebian, "Neoliberal Urbanization

and Smart Cities in the Gulf Region: The Case of Abu Dhabi's Masdar City," in *Gateways to the World: Port Cities in the Persian Gulf*, ed. Mehran Kamrava (New York: Oxford University Press, 2016), 183–202; Evren Tok, Jason James McSparren, Maha Al Merekhi, Hanaa Elghaish, and Fatema Al Mohammad, "Crafting Smart Cities in the Gulf Region: A Comparison of Masdar and Lusail," in *Handbook of Research on Digital Media and Creative Technologies*, ed. Dew Harrison (Hershey, PA: Information Science Reference/IGI Global, 2015), 448–60.

33. Becky P. Y. Loo, *The E-Society* (New York: Nova Science Publishers, 2012), 187.

34. Pippa Norris, *The Digital Divide: Civic Engagement, Information Poverty, and the Internet Worldwide* (Cambridge: Cambridge University Press, 2009), 6.

35. "Middle East Internet Users, Population and Facebook Statistics 2016," Internet World Stats, http://www.internetworldstats.com/stats4.htm

36. Emma C. Murphy, "ICT and the Gulf Arab States: A Force for Democracy," in *Reform in the Middle East Oil Monarchies*, ed. Anoushiravan Ehteshami and Steven Wright (Reading, Berks: Ithaca Press, 2008), 189.

37. Fadi Salem, Racha Mourtada, and Sara Alshaer, "The Arab World Online 2014: Trends in Internet and Mobile Usage in the Arab Region," Mohammed Bin Rashid School of Government, 2014, http://www.mbrsg.ae/getattachment/ff70c2c5–0fce-405d-b23f-93c198d4ca44/The-Arab-World-Online-2014-Trends-in-Internet-and.aspx

38. Amr Al Roubai and Abdul Wahab Rasha Shakr, "Building a Knowledge Society in the Arab World," in *The Islamic World and the West: Managing Religious and Cultural Identities*, ed. Christoph Marcinkowski (Zurich: LIT Verlag, 2009), 231–42.

39. Natalija Gelvanovska, Michel Rogy, and Carlo Maria Rossotto, "Broadband Networks in the Middle East and North Africa: Accelerating High-Speed Internet Access," in *Directions in Development: Communication and Information Technologies* (World Bank, 2014), xi, https://openknowledge.worldbank.org/handle/10986/16680

40. David Sholle, "What is Information? The Flow of Bits and the Control of Chaos," in *Democracy and New Media*, ed. Henry Jenkins and David Thornburn (Cambridge, MA: MIT Press, 2003), 343–63.

41. Luis Suarez-Villa, *Technocapitalism: A Critical Perspective on Technological Innovation and Corporatism* (Philadelphia, PA: Temple University Press, 2009), 9–10.

42. John Carroll, "Intellectual Property Rights in the Middle East: A Cultural Perspective," *Fordham Intellectual Property, Media and Entertainment Law Journal* 11, no. 3 (2001): 555–600, particularly 556.

43. According to World Bank estimates, Arabic digital content is an abysmal 0.16 per cent of global digital content, and the number of websites hosted in the

region is barely 0.2 per cent of the global total. See Chris Vein, "Why Increasing Digital Arabic Content is Key for Global Development," *Guardian*, 28 April 2014, https://www.theguardian.com/media-network/media-network-blog/2014/apr/28/global-development-digital-arabic-content

44. Salem, Mourtada, and Alshaer, "The Arab World Online 2014: Trends in Internet and Mobile Usage," 6, http://www.mbrsg.ae/getattachment/ff70c2c5–0fce-405d-b23f-93c198d4ca44/The-Arab-World-Online-2014-Trends-in-Internet-and.aspx

45. Ulises Ali Mejias, *Off the Network: Disrupting the Digital World* (Minneapolis, MN: University of Minnesota Press, 2013), 25.

46. Norma Claire Moruzzi, "Gender and Revolutions," *Middle East Report* 268 (2013), http://www.merip.org/mer/mer268/gender-revolutions

47. Annabelle Sreberny, "Women's Digital Activism in a Changing Middle East," *International Journal of Middle East Studies* 47, no. 2 (2015): 357.

48. Sami Ben Gharbia, "The Internet Freedom Fallacy and the Arab Digital Activism," Nawaat.org, 17 September 2010, https://nawaat.org/portail/2010/09/17/the-internet-freedom-fallacy-and-the-arab-digital-activism/

2. THE CHANGING NATURE OF SOCIALIZATION AMONG ARAB YOUTH: INSIGHTS FROM ONLINE PRACTICES

1. "Social Media Adds Excitement to the Arab World," WPP Report, 2015, http://www.wpp.com/govtpractice/~/media/wppgov/files/wpp-lky-cpp-2016.pdf

2. When it comes to defining the youth bracket, research studies use different age groups for the purpose of their statistics. For example, Booz & Co. consider youth to be 15–35 years; Brookings 15–29; NU-Q 18–24; and UNESCO 15–24.

3. Everette Dennis, Justin Martin, and Robb Wood, "Arab Media Use Survey," 2016, http://menamediasurvey.northwestern.edu/#section=media_usage&q=1

4. Ilhem Allagui and Harris Breslow, "The Internet and the Evolving UAE," 2013, http://www.aus.edu/download/downloads/id/1332/emirates_internet_project_year_4

5. Dennis, Martin, and Wood, "Arab Media Use Survey."

6. "The Arab World Online 2014: Trends in Internet and Mobile Usage in the Arab Region," Mohammed Bin Rashid School of Government, www.ArabSocialMediaReport.com

7. Zizi Papacharissi and Alan M Rubin, "Predictors of Internet Use," *Journal of Broadcasting and Electronic Media* 44, no. 2 (2000): 175–96.

8. Norman H. Nie, Sunshine D. Hillygus, and Lutz Erbring, "The Impact of Internet Use on Sociability: A Time Diary Study," in *The Internet in Everyday Life*, ed. Barry Wellman and Caroline Haythornthwaite (Oxford: Blackwell Publishing, 2002), 215–43.

9. See Andrew Ledbetter, "Media Use and Relational Closeness in Long-term Friendships: Interpreting Patterns of Multimodality," *New Media and Society* 10,

no. 4 (2008): 547–64; Nancy K. Baym, Yan Bing Zhang, and Mei-Chen Lin, "Social Interactions Across Media: Interpersonal Communication on the Internet, Telephone and Face-to-Face," *New Media and Society* 6, no. 3 (2004): 299–318; Caroline Haythornthwaite, "Social Networks and Internet Connectivity Effects," *Information, Communication and Society* 8, no. 2 (2005): 125–47; Barry Wellman, Anabel Quan-Haase, Jeffrey Boase, and Wenhong Chen, "The Social Affordances of the Internet for Networked Individualism," *Journal of Computer-Mediated Communication* 8, no. 3 (2003), http://onlinelibrary.wiley.com/doi/10.1111/ j.1083–6101.2003.tb00216.x/full.

10. Sonia Livingstone, *Children and the Internet* (Cambridge: Polity Press, 2009); Danah Boyd, "Why Youth (Heart) Social Network Sites: The Role of Networked Publics in Teenage Social Life," in *Youth, Identity, and Digital Media*, ed. David Buckingham (Cambridge, MA: MIT Press, 2008), 119–42.

11. Denise E. Agosto and June Abbas, "Youth and Online Social Networking: What do we Know so Far?" in *The Information Behavior of a New Generation: Children and Teens in the 21st Century*, ed. Jamshid Beheshti and Andrew Large (Plymouth, UK: Scarecrow Press, 2013), 123–4.

12. Gustavo Mesch, "The Internet and Youth Culture," *Hedgehog Review* (Spring 2009): 55, http://www.iasc-culture.org/THR/archives/YouthCulture/Mesch. pdf

13. For example, the Department of Telecommunications at Indiana University reports: 92 per cent said they use it to keep in touch with friends, 88 per cent to make plans with friends, 61.5 per cent to play games with IM software, 60 per cent to play a trick on someone, 44 per cent to ask someone out, 42 per cent to write something you would not say in person, 38.5 per cent to send non-text information, and 24 per cent to break up with someone. See Christine Greenhow and Beth Robelia, "Old Communications, New Literacies: Social Network Sites as Social Learning Resources," *Journal of Computer-Mediated Communication* 14, no. 4 (2009): 1130–61.

14. Candice M. Kelsey, *Generation MySpace: Helping Your Teen Survive Online Adolescence* (New York: Marlowe & Co., 2007).

15. Agosto and Abbas, *Teens and Social Networking*; Danah Boyd, *It's Complicated: The Social Lives of Networked Teens* (New Haven, CT: Yale University Press, 2014).

16. Paul Adams, *Grouped: How Small Groups of Friends are the Key to Influence on the Social Web* (Berkeley, CA: New Riders, 2012).

17. Ibid.

18. Barbie H. Clarke, "Early Adolescents' Use of Social Networking Sites to Maintain Friendship and Explore Identity: Implications for Policy," *Policy and Internet* 1, no. 1 (2009): 55–89.

19. Michele Fleming and Debra Rickwood, "Teens in Cyberspace: Do They Encounter Friend or Foe?" *Youth Studies Australia* 23, no. 3 (2004): 46–52.

20. Chia-Chen Yang and B. Bradford Brown, "Motives for Using Facebook, Patterns of Facebook Activities, and Late Adolescents' Social Adjustment to College," *Journal of Youth and Adolescence* 42 (2013): 403–16; Pinar L. Tosun, "Motives for Facebook Use and Expressing 'True Self' on the Internet," *Computers in Human Behavior* 28 (2012): 1510–17.

21. Agosto and Abbas, *Teens and Social Networking*, 126.

22. Adams, *Grouped*, 17.

23. Ibid., 20.

24. Samuel D. Gosling et al., "Manifestations of Personality in Online Social Networks: Self-Reported Facebook-Related Behaviors and Observable Profile Information," *Cyberpsychology, Behavior and Social Networking* 14, no. 9 (2011): 483–8, http://online.liebertpub.com/doi/pdf/10.1089/cyber.2010.0087

25. Khaled S. Al Omoush, Saad G. Yaseen, and Mohammed A. Alma'aitah, "The Impact of Arab Cultural Values on Online Social Networking: The Case of Facebook," *Computers in Human Behavior* 28 (2012): 2397.

26. "ASDA'A Burson-Marsteller Arab Youth Survey 2014," http://www.arabyouth-survey.com/en/whitepaper

27. "Social Media in the Arab World 2015 Report," *Arabian Gazette*, 18 March 2015, http://www.arabiangazette.com/social-media-in-the-arab-world-2015-report/

28. See for instance Yeslam Al-Saggaf, "The Effect of Online Community on Offline Community in Saudi Arabia," *Electronic Journal on Information Systems in Developing Countries* 16, no. 2 (2004): 1–16. The study shows that Saudi online communities tend to be open-minded, more confident, and more appreciative of the other gender.

29. Al Omoush, Yaseen, and Alma'aitah, "The Impact of Arab Cultural Values," 2397. See also Karen D. Loch, Detmar W. Straub, and Sherif Kamel, "Diffusing the Internet in the Arab World: The Role of Social Norms and Technological Culturation," *IEEE Transactions on Engineering Management* 50, no. 1 (2003): 45–63.

30. Kathy N. Shen and Mohamad Khalifa, "Facebook Usage among Arab College Students: Preliminary Findings on Gender Differences," *International Journal of e-Business Management* 4, no. 1 (2010): 53–65.

31. Insofar as it exists, research has focused on Arab youth education (UNESCO, OECD), media and culture among the youth, youth, TV and reality TV, in addition to opinion polls covering identity or concerns about the future (such as public opinion research by the Zogby Institute, Arab Barometer and Strategy). See Marwan Kraidi and Joe Khalil, "Youth, Media, and Culture in the Arab World," in *International Handbook of Children, Media and Culture*, ed. Kirsten Drotner and Sonia Livingstone (London: Sage, 2008), 330–44; Imad Karam, "Satellite Television: A Breathing Space for Arab Youth," in *Arab Media and Political*

Renewal: Community, Legitimacy, and Public Life, ed. Naomi Sakr (London: I. B. Tauris, 2007).

32. Deborah L. Wheeler, *The Internet in the Middle East: Global Expectations and Local Imaginations in Kuwait* (Albany, NY: State University of New York Press, 2006).

33. Samia Mihoub-Dramé, "Particularités de l'Appropriation du Réseau Internet en Tunisie," *Archive Ouverte en Sciences de l'Information et de la Communication* (17 November 2003), http://archivesic.ccsd.cnrs.fr/sic_00000804

34. Miriyam Aouragh, *Palestine Online: Transnationalism, the Internet and the Construction of Identity* (London: I. B. Tauris, 2011).

35. Harry T. Reis and Charles M. Judd, *Handbook of Research Methods in Social and Personality Psychology* (Cambridge: Cambridge University Press, 2000), 331.

36. Keith Punch, *Introduction to Social Research: Quantitative and Qualitative Approaches*, 3rd edn (London: Sage, 2014), 187–8.

37. Joann Keyton, *Communication Research: Asking Questions, Finding Answers*, 3rd edn (New York: McGraw Hill, 2011).

38. John W. Creswell, *Research Design: Qualitative, Quantitative and Mixed Methods Approaches*, 4th edn (Thousand Oaks, CA: Sage, 2013).

39. Maria Pramaggiore and Tom Wallis, *Film: A Critical Introduction*, 3rd edn (London: Laurence King, 2011), 27.

40. Michel de Certeau, *The Practice of Everyday Life* (Berkeley, CA: University of California Press, 1984).

41. Marie Gillespie and Jason Toynbee, *Analyzing Media Texts* (Maidenhead, Berks: Open University Press, 2006), 83.

42. To protect the informants' privacy, all names have been anonymized.

43. On the evolution of media in Saudi Arabia, see Naomi Sakr, *Satellite Realms: Transnational Television, Globalization and the Middle East* (London: I. B. Tauris, 2001); Marwan M. Kraidy, "Saudi Arabia, Lebanon and the Changing Arab Information Order," *International Journal of Communication* 1 (2007): 139–56; Mohamed Zayani, "Transnational Media, Regional Politics and State Security: Saudi Arabia Between Tradition and Modernity," *British Journal of Middle East Studies* 39, no. 3 (2012): 307–27.

44. "Media Use in the Middle East, 2015 Report," http://www.mideastmedia.org/survey/2015/

45. Interview with Mohammed Makki, Doha, Qatar, 2015.

46. Laura Bashraheel, "'Takki': Drama for Change," *Arab News*, 7 March 2012, http://www.arabnews.com/node/408037

47. "No Country for Movie Buffs," *Economist*, 18 October 2013, http://www.economist.com/blogs/pomegranate/2013/10/film-making-saudi-arabia

48. Maria Bakardjieva, "Social Media and the McDonaldization of Friendship," *Communications* 39, no. 4 (2014): 371.

49. Margaret K. Nydell, *Understanding Arabs. A Guide for Modern Times*, 4th edn (Boston, MA: Intercultural Press, 2006).

50. Nydell, *Understanding Arabs*, 17.

51. Tarik Sabry, *Cultural Encounters in the Arab World: On Media, the Modern and the Everyday* (London: I. B. Tauris, 2010).

52. Ibid.

53. Adams, *Grouped*, 17.

54. Rassed Research Team at ictQATAR, "The Attitudes of Online Users in the MENA Region: Cybersafety, Security and Data Privacy," 2014, http://www.ictqatar.qa/en/rassed/major-studies?v12

55. Adams, *Grouped*, 97.

56. Samir Khalaf and Roseanne Saad Khalaf, eds, *Arab Society and Culture: An Essential Reader* (Beirut: Saqi Books, 2009).

57. Wendy Hollway, "Gender Difference and the Production of Subjectivity," in *Changing the Subject: Psychology, Social Regulation and Subjectivity*, ed. Julian Henriques et al. (London: Methuen, 1984), 227–63.

58. Francisco Tirado and Ana Gálvez, "Positioning Theory and Discourse Analysis: Some Tools for Social Interaction Analysis," *Qualitative Social Research* 8, no. 2 (2007).

59. Steven Sabat and Rom Harré, "Positioning and the Recovery of Social Identity," in *Positioning Theory: Moral Contexts of Intentional Action*, ed. Rom Harré and Van Langenhove (Oxford: Blackwell Publishing, 1999), 87–101.

60. This refers to Maslow's hierarchy of needs, which is based on the theory of human motivation. A. H. Maslow, "A Theory of Human Motivation," *Psychological Review* 50, no. 4 (1943): 370–96.

61. Boyd, *It's Complicated*, 148.

62. Khaled Saleh Al Omoush, Saad Ghaleb Yaseen, and Mohammad Atwah Alma'aitah, "The Impact of Arab Cultural Values on Online Social Networking: The Case of Facebook," *Computers in Human Behavior* 28, no. 6 (2012): 2397.

63. Stephan Winter et al., "The Digital Quest for Love—The Role of Relationship Status in Self-Presentation on Social Networking Sites," *Cyberpsychology: Journal of Psychosocial Research on Cyberspace* 5, no. 2 (2011).

64. Ilhem Allagui, "Arab Youth on the Internet: A Journey between Websites and Blogs," paper presented at the German Arab Media Dialogue Conference on Youth and Media, Amman, Jordan, 26–27 June 2007.

65. Sherry Turkle, *Life on the Screen: Identity in the Age of the Internet* (New York: Simon & Schuster, 1995).

66. Boyd, *It's Complicated*.

67. Josephine D. Korchmaros, Michele L. Ybarra, and Kimberley L. Mitchell, "Adolescent Online Romantic Initiation: Differences by Sexual and Gender Identification," *Journal of Adolescence* 40 (2015): 54–64.

3. VIRTUAL WORLDS, DIGITAL DREAMS: IMAGINARY SPACES OF MIDDLE EASTERN VIDEO GAMES

1. This study was supported by Charles University's Progres Q15, Primus/Hum/03 and European Regional Development Fund-Project No. CZ.02.1.01/0.0/0.0/16 _019/0000734.
2. Ibid.
3. Ibid.
4. Jane McGonigal, *Reality is Broken: Why Games Make Us Better and How They Can Change the World* (New York: Penguin Press, 2011).
5. Entertainment Software Association, "The 2015 Essential Facts about the Computer and Video Game Industry," http://www.theesa.com/wp-content/uploads/2015/04/ESA-Essential-Facts-2015.pdf
6. "Worldwide Video Game Market to Total $93 Billion in 2013," Gartner, http://www.gartner.com/newsroom/id/2614915
7. Entertainment Software Association, "The 2015 Essential Facts about the Computer and Video Game Industry."
8. "Worldwide Video Game Market to Total $93 Billion in 2013," Gartner.
9. Arjun Appadurai, *Modernity at Large: Cultural Dimensions of Globalization* (Minneapolis, MN: University of Minnesota Press, 2005), 33.
10. Ibid., 35.
11. Ibid., 35.
12. Ben Aslinger and Nina B. Huntemann, "Introduction," in *Gaming Globally: Production, Play and Place*, ed. Nina B. Huntemann and Ben Aslinger (New York: Palgrave Macmillan, 2013), 4.
13. Ibid.
14. See, for instance, Larissa Hjorth and Dean Chan, eds, *Gaming Cultures and Place in Asia-Pacific* (New York: Routledge, 2009); Nina B. Huntemann and Ben Aslinger, *Gaming Globally: Production, Play and Place* (New York: Palgrave Macmillan, 2013).
15. "Media Use in the Middle East 2015," Northwestern University in Qatar, 2015, http://mideastmedia.org/2015
16. Ibid.
17. Ibid.
18. Vít Šisler, "Videogame Development in the Middle East: Iran, the Arab World and Beyond," in *Gaming Globally: Production, Play and Place*, ed. Nina B. Huntemann and Ben Aslinger (New York: Palgrave Macmillan, 2013), 251–72.
19. Šisler, "Videogame Development in the Middle East."
20. "Middle East, North African (MENA), and Turkish Game Markets," LAI Global Game Services, http://www.lai.com/en/middle-east-north-african-mena-turkish-game-markets

21. Ibid.
22. Karin E. Skoog, "Insights Learned from Indie Game Developers in Latin America and the Middle East," LAI Blog, http://www.lai.com/blog/?p=123
23. Vít Šisler, "Video Games, Video Clips, and Islam: New Media and the Communication of Values," in *Muslim Societies in the Age of Mass Consumption*, ed. Johanna Pink (Newcastle, UK: Cambridge Scholars Publishing, 2009), 231–58.
24. Šisler, "Videogame Development in the Middle East."
25. Mohammed Taher, "Game Gulf," *The Magazine*, http://the-magazine.org/11/game-gulf#.Vo-aZU_Xliw
26. Ibid.
27. Muhammad Hamza, *The Stone Throwers* (Damascus, 2000).
28. Šisler, "Videogame Development in the Middle East."
29. Ibid.
30. Ibrahim Marashi, "The Depiction of Arabs in Combat Video Games," paper presented at the Beirut Institute of Media Arts, Lebanese American University, 5–9 November 2001; Philipp Reichmuth and Stefan Werning, "Pixel Pashas, Digital Djinns," *ISIM Review* 18 (2006): 46–7; Johan Höglund, "Electronic Empire: Orientalism Revisited in the Military Shooter," *Game Studies* 8 (2008); Anandam Kavoori, "Gaming, Terrorism and the Right to Communicate," *Global Media Journal* 7 (2008), http://www.globalmediajournal.com/open-access/gaming-terrorism-and-the-right-to-communicate.pdf
31. Alexander Galloway, "Social Realism in Gaming," *Game Studies* 4, no. 1 (2004), http://www.gamestudies.org/0401/galloway/; David Machin and Usama Suleiman, "Arab and American Computer War Games: The Influence of a Global Technology on Discourse," *Critical Discourse Studies* 3, no. 1 (2006): 1–22; Helga Tawil-Souri, "The Political Battlefield of Pro-Arab Video Games on Palestinian Screens," *Comparative Studies of South Asia, Africa and the Middle East* 27 (2007): 536–51.
32. Vít Šisler, "Digital Arabs: Representation in Video Games," *European Journal of Cultural Studies* 2, no. 11 (2008): 203–20.
33. Vít Šisler, "Digital Heroes: Identity Construction in Iranian Video Games," in *Cultural Revolution in Iran: Contemporary Popular Culture in the Islamic Republic*, ed. Annabelle Sreberny and Massoumeh Torfeh (New York: I. B. Tauris, 2013), 171–91; Vít Šisler, "From Kuma\War to Quraish: Representation of Islam in Arab and American Video Games," in *Playing with Religion in Digital Games*, ed. Heidi A. Campbell and Gregory Price Grieve (Bloomington, IN: Indiana University Press, 2014), 109–33.
34. Šisler, "Video Games, Video Clips, and Islam."
35. Šisler, "Videogame Development in the Middle East."

36. Kerstin Radde-Antweiler, Michael Waltemathe, and Xenia Zeiler, "Video Gaming, Let's Plays, and Religion: The Relevance of Researching Gamevironments," *Gamevironments* 1 (2014): 1–36.

37. Ibid., 14.

38. Abbas Amanat, "Introduction: Is There a Middle East? Problematizing a Virtual Space," in *Is There a Middle East? The Evolution of a Geopolitical Concept*, ed. Michael E. Bonine, Abbas Amanat, and Michael Ezekiel Gasper (Stanford, CA: Stanford University Press, 2011), 2.

39. Johannes Fromme and Alexander Unger, "Computer Games and Digital Game Cultures: An Introduction," in *Computer Games and New Media Cultures: A Handbook of Digital Games Studies*, ed. Johannes Fromme and Alexander Unger (London: Springer, 2012), 4.

40. Ibid.

41. Ibid.

42. Campbell and Grieve, *Playing with Religion in Digital Games*, 4.

43. Ibid.

44. Reichmuth and Werning, "Pixel Pashas, Digital Djinns," 47.

45. Ian Bogost, *How to Do Things with Videogames* (Minneapolis, MN: University of Minnesota Press, 2011), 4.

46. Ibid.

47. Gonzalo Frasca, "Videogames of the Oppressed: Critical Thinking, Education, Tolerance, and Other Trivial Issues," in *First Person: New Media as Story, Performance, and Game*, ed. Noah Wardrip-Fruin and Pat Harrigan (Cambridge, MA: MIT Press, 2004), 21.

48. Bogost, *How to Do Things with Videogames*, 4.

49. Ian Bogost, *Persuasive Games: The Expressive Power of Videogames* (Cambridge, MA: MIT Press, 2007).

50. Bogost, *Persuasive Games*, 287.

51. Jesper Juul, "The Game, the Player, the World: Looking for a Heart of Gameness," in *Level Up: Digital Games Research Conference Proceedings*, ed. Marinka Copier and Joost Raessens (Utrecht: Utrecht University, 2003), 30–45.

52. Brøderbund Software, *Prince of Persia* (Novato, CA: Brøderbund Software, 1989).

53. Vít Šisler, "Revolution Reloaded: Spaces of Encounter and Resistance in Iranian Video Games," paper presented at the conference Context Collapse: Reassembling the Spatial organized by the Annenberg School for Communication at the University of Pennsylvania, Philadelphia, 6 December 2013.

54. Tarik Sabry, *Cultural Encounters in the Arab World: On Media, the Modern and the Everyday* (London: I. B.Tauris, 2010), 11.

55. Šisler, "Videogame Development in the Middle East."

56. Šisler, "Videogame Development in the Middle East."

57. Mark Allen Peterson, *Connected in Cairo: Growing Up Cosmopolitan in the Modern Middle East* (Bloomington, IN: Indiana University Press, 2011), 3.
58. Peterson, *Connected in Cairo*, 3.
59. Šisler, "From Kuma\War to Quraish."
60. Ibid.
61. Šisler, "Digital Arabs."
62. Machin and Suleiman, "Arab and American Computer War Games."
63. Šisler, "Digital Arabs."
64. Höglund, "Electronic Empire."
65. Ibid.
66. Šisler, "Digital Arabs."
67. Edward Said, *Orientalism* (New York: Pantheon Books, 1978).
68. Šisler, "Digital Arabs."
69. Reichmuth and Werning, "Pixel Pashas, Digital Djinns."
70. Ibid., 46.
71. Šisler, "Videogame Development in the Middle East."
72. Šisler, "Digital Arabs."
73. Henri Lefebvre, *The Production of Space* (Oxford: Blackwell, 1991).
74. Šisler, "Videogame Development in the Middle East."
75. Šisler, "Digital Heroes."
76. Solution, *Special Force* (Beirut: Solution, 2003); W3DTEK, *Special Force 2* (Beirut: W3DTEK, 2007).
77. Šisler, "Digital Heroes."
78. Espris, *Mir Mahna* (Tehran: Espris, 2011).
79. Iran Computer and Video Games Foundation, "Mir Mahna," Iran Computer and Video Games Foundation, http://irvgame.com/GamesInfo.aspx?Game_id=4
80. Machin and Suleiman, "Arab and American Computer War Games."
81. Šisler, "Digital Heroes."
82. "The Liberation of Palestine," www.freepal.ps/
83. "New Palestinian Computer Game," YouTube, www.youtube.com/watch?v=mPTcvbne2gc
84. Ibid.
85. Ibid.
86. "Black Years," Iran Computer and Video Games Foundation, http://irvgame.com/GamesInfo.aspx?Game_id=46
87. Ibid.
88. Taher, "Game Gulf."
89. Šisler, "Video Games, Video Clips, and Islam."
90. Vít Šisler, "Preaching Islam to the Video Game Generation: New Media Literacies and Religious Edutainment in the Arab World," in *Media Evolution on the Eve of the Arab Spring*, ed. Leila Hudson, Adel Iskandar, and Mimi Kirk (New York: Palgrave Macmillan, 2014), 103–25.

91. Sebastian Weiss and Wolfgang Müller, "The Potential of Interactive Digital Storytelling for the Creation of Educational Computer Games," *Lecture Notes in Computer Science* 5093 (2008): 475–86.

92. FutureSoft, *The Prophet's Wars* (FutureSoft, 2007).

93. Šisler, "Preaching Islam to the Video Game Generation."

94. Iran Computer and Video Games Foundation, "About Us," Iran Computer and Video Games Foundation, http://irvgame.com/aboutus.aspx.

95. Tebyan, "The Honor," Tebyan, http://www.tebyangame.com/Rahe-Eftekhar

96. "Black Gold," Iran Computer and Video Games Foundation, http://irvgame.com/GamesInfo.aspx?Game_id=7

97. Tebyan, "Earth 2124," Tebyan, http://www.tebyangame.com/Earth2124

98. Šisler, "Preaching Islam to the Video Game Generation."

99. Šisler, "Digital Heroes."

100. Šisler, "Digital Arabs."

101. Puya Arts Software, *Quest of Persia* (Tehran: Puya Arts Software, 2005).

102. Šisler, "Digital Heroes," 179.

103. Ibid., 180.

104. Connor Sears, "Making Games in Qatar," Polygon, http://www.polygon.com/features/2014/5/13/5542406/qatar-girnaas-giddam

105. Sears, "Making Games in Qatar."

106. Personal interview with Fatima Al-Kuwari (Doha, 2014).

107. Diana Farid, "Giddam: From 'Karak' to 'Eshrij,' A Game that's Quintessentially Qatar," *Just Here*, http://www.justhere.qa/2014/02/giddam-karak-eshrij-quintessentially-qatar/

108. Omar Chatriwala, "Colorful Characters, Karak to Feature in New Qatar-produced Video Game," *Doha News*, http://dohanews.co/colorful-characters-karak-to-feature-in-new-qatar-produced-video-game/

109. Sabry, *Cultural Encounters in the Arab World*, 11.

110. Šisler, "Videogame Development in the Middle East."

111. Šisler, "Digital Heroes."

112. Šisler, "Video Games, Video Clips, and Islam."

113. Farid, "Giddam."

114. Peterson, *Connected in Cairo*, 134.

115. Ibid., 25.

116. Christa Salamandra, *A New Old Damascus: Authenticity and Distinction in Urban Syria* (Bloomington, IN: Indiana University Press, 2004).

117. Šisler, "Videogame Development in the Middle East."

118. Ibid.

119. Peterson, *Connected in Cairo*, 25.

120. Šisler, "Digital Heroes."

121. Marwan Kraidy and Joe F. Khalil, *Arab Television Industries* (London: British Film Institute, 2009), 123.

122. Sahar Khamis and Vít Šisler, "The New Arab Cyberscape: Redefining Boundaries and Reconstructing Public Spheres," in *Communication Yearbook 34*, ed. Charles T. Salmon (New York: Routledge, 2010), 277–315.

123. Šisler, "Videogame Development in the Middle East."

124. Sears, "Making Games in Qatar."

125. Ibid.

126. "About the Gaming Lab," Gaming Lab, http://gaminglab.jo/jo/about-2/

127. Chris Boots-Faubert, "Islamic Video Game Rating System Announced," Gaming Update, http://www.gamingupdate.com/articles/5/Islamic-Video-Game-Rating-System-Announced

128. Ibid.

129. Šisler, "Videogame Development in the Middle East."

130. Adam Ostrow, "Happy Oasis Wants to be FarmVille of the Middle East," *Mashable*, http://mashable.com/2011/07/18/happy-oasis/

131. Zynga Game Network, *FarmVille* (Zynga Game Network, 2009).

132. Ostrow, "Happy Oasis wants to be FarmVille of the Middle East."

133. "Media Use in the Middle East 2015."

134. Ibid.

135. Ibid.

136. Constance Steinkuehler and Dmitri Williams, "Where Everybody Knows Your (Screen) Name: Online Games as 'Third Places,'" *Journal of Computer-Mediated Communication* 11 (2006): 885–909.

137. Henry Jenkins, *Convergence Culture: Where Old and New Media Collide* (New York: New York University Press, 2006), 20.

138. Kurt Squire and Constance Steinkuehler, "Meet the Gamers," *Library Journal*, 15 April 2005, https://www.academia.edu/1317092/Meet_the_gamers

139. Jane Brown, Carol Dykers, Jeanne Steele, and Anne White, "Teenage Room Culture: Where Media and Identities Intersect," *Communication Research* 21 (1994): 813–27.

140. MENA Games Conference, www.menagames.com

141. Dubai World Game Expo, www.gameexpo.ae

142. Arabic Game Developer Network, http://agdn-online.com

143. GameTako, www.gametako.com

144. GameZanga, www.gamezanga.com

145. Iran Game Development Institute, http://irangdi.com/.; SAE Institute, "Bachelor of Game Development," SAE Institute, http://dubai.sae.edu/en-gb/course/8692/BSc_(Honours)_in_Games_Programming

146. Šisler, "From Kuma\War to Quraish."

147. Šisler, "Videogame Development in the Middle East."

148. Stéphane Natkin and Liliana Vega, "Petri Net Modelling for the Analysis of the Ordering of Actions in Computer Games," in *GAME-ON*, 4th International

Conference on Intelligent Games and Simulation (London: EUROSIS, 2003), 82–92.

149. Ibid., 82.

150. Šisler, "From Kuma\War to Quraish."

151. Ibid.

152. Peterson, *Connected in Cairo*, 3.

4. MEDIATED EXPERIENCE IN THE EGYPTIAN REVOLUTION

1. Stacey Philbrick Yadav, "Bodies in Motion: Adjudicating and Materializing Normality in Cairo," *International Feminist Journal of Politics* 17, no. 2 (2015): 5.

2. Bjørn Thomassen, "Notes toward an Anthropology of Political Revolution," *Comparative Studies in Society and History* 54, no. 3 (2012): 684.

3. Periodicizing events in Egypt is a challenge, as many see the Egyptian revolution as having ceased with the election of Abdel Fattah El-Sisi in 2014. Others insist that the revolution is ongoing. For the purpose of providing a coherent account, I will limit the period to the "eighteen days" of protests centered in public spaces, especially Tahrir Square.

4. See, for example, Bjørn Thomassen, *Liminality and the Modern: Living through the In-Between* (Farnham: Ashgate, 2014); Agnes Horvath, Bjørn Thomassen, and Harald Wydra, eds, *Breaking Boundaries: Varieties of Liminality* (Oxford: Berghahn Books, 2015); John Postill, "Fields as Dynamic Clusters of Practices, Games and Socialities," in *Sociality: An Anthropological Interrogation*, ed. Vered Amit (Oxford and New York: Berghahn, 2015), 47–68.

5. Diane Singerman and Paul Amar, eds, *Cairo Cosmopolitan: Politics, Culture, and Urban Space in the New Global Middle East* (Cairo: American University in Cairo Press, 2006); Paul Amar, *The Security Archipelago: Human-Security States, Sexuality Politics, and the End of Neoliberalism* (Durham, NC: Duke University Press, 2013).

6. Salwa Ismail, "Authoritarian Government, Neoliberalism and Everyday Civilities in Egypt," *Third World Quarterly* 32, no. 5 (2011): 845–62.

7. Mark Allen Peterson, "Egypt's Media Ecology in a Time of Revolution," in *Three Years Since the Spring: A Collection of Essays on the State of Arab Media*, ed. Sarah El-Shaarawi (Cairo: American University in Cairo, Kamal Adham Center for Television and Digital Journalism, 2014), 81–95.

8. Joel Beinin, "Egyptian Workers and January 25th: A Social Movement in Historical Context," *Social Research* 79, no. 2 (2012): 323–48; Michaelle Browers, "The Egyptian Movement for Change: Intellectual Antecedents and Generational Conflicts," *Contemporary Islam* 1, no. 1 (2007): 69–88.

9. Brecht De Smet, "Egyptian Workers and 'Their' Intellectuals: The Dialectical Pedagogy of the Mahalla Strike Movement," *Mind, Culture and Activity* 19, no. 2 (2012): 139–55.

10. Bassem Nabil Hafez, "New Social Movements and the Egyptian Spring: A Comparative Analysis between the April 6 Movement and the Revolutionary Socialists," *Perspectives on Global Development and Technology* 12 (2013): 98–113.

11. Peter Dahlgren, *Media and Political Engagement: Citizens, Communication and Democracy* (Cambridge: Cambridge University Press, 2009), 5.

12. Peterson, "Egypt's Media Ecology in a Time of Revolution," 81–95.

13. Courtney Radsch, "Core to Commonplace: The Evolution of Egypt's Blogosphere," *Arab Media and Society* 6 (2008), http://www.arabmediasociety.com/UserFiles/AMS6%20Courtney%20Radsch.pdf

14. Jon W. Anderson and Dale F. Eickelman, "Media Convergence and its Consequences," *Middle East Insight* 14, no. 2 (1999): 59–61.

15. Mark Allen Peterson and Ivan Panovic, "Accessing Egypt: Making Myths and Producing Web Sites in Cyber-Cairo," *New Reviews in Hypermedia and Multimedia* 10, no. 2 (2004): 199–219.

16. See Naila Hamdy, "Arab Citizen Journalism in Action: Challenging Mainstream Media, Authorities and Media Laws," *Westminster Papers in Communication and Culture* 6, no. 1 (2009): 92–112; Ali Sayed Mohamed, "On the Road to Democracy: Egyptian Bloggers and the Internet 2010," *Journal of Arab and Muslim Media Research* 4 (2011): 253–72.

17. For example, the arrests of bloggers like al-Sharkawi and Abd El Fattah received more international criticism than punitive measures against crusading newspaper journalists like Ibrahim Issa, editor of the independent newspaper *Al-Dustour*, because influential bloggers in the West wrote in solidarity with their Egyptian co-practitioners. See Negar Azimi, "Bloggers against Torture," *The Nation* 284 (2007): 11–16; Nora Boustany, "Crackdowns on Bloggers Increasing, Survey Finds," *Washington Post*, 17 October 2007, http://www.washingtonpost.com/wp-dyn/content/article/2007/10/16/AR2007101601843.html; Amr Gharbeia, "Lost in Process," *Index on Censorship* 36 (2007): 51–5.

18. Farhad Khosrokhavar, *The New Arab Revolutions that Shook the World* (Boulder, CO: Paradigm Publishers, 2012).

19. Kurt Squire and Matthew Gaydos, "From Egypt to Wisconsin: Tactical Innovation with Digital Media," *Critical Studies in Education* 54, no. 1 (2013): 57–71.

20. Eli Pariser, *The Filter Bubble: What the Internet is Hiding from You* (London: Penguin Press, 2011).

21. Peterson, "Egypt's Media Ecology in a Time of Revolution," 88.

22. Melissa Wall and Sahar El-Zahed, "'I'll Be Waiting for You Guys': A YouTube Call to Action in the Egyptian Revolution," *International Journal of Communication* 5 (2011): 1333–43.

23. Emad El-Din Aysha, "January 25: The Day of Egypt's Revolutionary Historical Makeover," *Studies in Political Economy: A Socialist Review* 87, no. 1 (2011): 29–47.

24. Alexandra Dunn, "Unplugging a Nation: State Media Strategy during Egypt's January 25 Uprising," *Fletcher Forum of World Affairs* 35, no. 2 (2011): 15–24.

25. Nezar Alsayyad, "The Virtual Square: Urban Space, Media, and the Egyptian Uprising," *Harvard International Review* 34 (2012): 58.

26. Elliott Colla, "The Poetry of the Arab Revolt," in *The Dawn of the Arab Uprisings: End of an Old Order?* ed. Bassam Haddad, Rosie Basher, and Ziad Abu-Rish (London: Pluto Press, 2012), 77–82.

27. For a comparable summative account of the roles that new media played in the Tunisian uprising, see Mohamed Zayani, *Networked Publics and Digital Contention: The Politics of Everyday Life in Tunisia* (New York: Oxford University Press, 2015); Anita Breuer, "The Role of Social Media in Mobilizing Political Protest: Evidence from the Tunisian Revolution," German Development Institute Discussion Paper 10 (2012), https://www.die-gdi.de/uploads/media/DP_10.2012.pdf

28. Wael Ghonim, *Revolution 2.0: The Power of the People is Greater than the People in Power: A Memoir* (New York: Houghton Mifflin Harcourt, 2012).

29. Ilana Gershon, "Media Ideologies: An Introduction," *Journal of Linguistic Anthropology* 20, no. 2 (2010): 283–93.

30. See J. C. Mitchell, "Case and Situation Analysis," *Sociological Review* 31 (1983): 187–211; J. Van Velson, "The Extended-case Method and Situational Analysis," in *The Craft of Anthropology*, ed. A. L. Epstein (London: Tavistock, 1967), 129–53.

31. Michel Foucault, "Of Other Spaces," *Diacritics* 16 (1986): 22–7.

32. Summer Harlow, "It was a 'Facebook Revolution': Exploring the Meme-like Spread of Narratives during the Egyptian Protests," *Revista de Comunicación* 12, no. 1 (2013): 59–82.

33. Abeer Bassiouny Radwan, "Egypt's Facebook Revolution," *American Diplomacy* 21 (2011): 1–3.

34. Ghonim, *Revolution 2.0*.

35. On mediation, see Richard Parmentier, "Signs' Place *In Medias Res*: Peirce's Concept of Semiotic Mediation," in *Semiotic Mediation: Sociocultural and Psychological Perspectives*, ed. Elizabeth Mertz and Richard Parmentier (Orlando, FL: Academic Press, 1985), 23–48; William Mazzarella, "Culture, Globalization, Mediation," *Annual Review of Anthropology* 33 (2004): 345–67; Jesus Martín-Barbero, "A Latin American Perspective on Communication/Cultural mediation," *Global Media and Communication* 2 (2006): 279–97; Nick Couldry, "Mediatization or Mediation? Alternative Understandings of the Emergent Space of Digital Storytelling," *New Media and Society* 10 (2008): 373–91; Sonia Livingstone, "On the Mediation of Everything: ICA Presidential Address 2008," *Journal of Communication* 59 (2009): 1–18; Birgit Meyer, "Mediation and Immediacy: Sensational Forms, Semiotic Ideologies and the Question of the Medium," *Social Anthropology/Anthropologie Sociale* 19 (2011): 23–39; Birgit Meyer, "Material Mediations and Religious Practices of World-Making," in *Religion Across Media* (New York: Peter Lang, 2013): 1–19; Birgit Meyer, "Mediation and the Genesis of Presence," *Religion and Society: Advances in Research* 5 (2014): 205–54.

36. See Mark Allen Peterson, "In Search of Antistructure: The Meaning of Tahrir Square in Egypt's Ongoing Social Drama," in *Breaking Boundaries: Varieties of Liminality*, ed. Agnes Horvath, Bjørn Thomassen, and Harald Wydra (Oxford: Berghahn Books, 2015); Mark Allen Peterson, "Re-Envisioning Tahrir: The Changing Meanings of Tahrir Square in Egypt's Ongoing Revolution," in *Revolutionary Egypt: Connecting Domestic and International Struggles*, ed. Reem Abou-El-Fadl (London: Routledge, 2015).

37. Jessica Winegar, "The Privilege of Revolution: Gender, Class, Space, and Affect in Egypt," *American Ethnologist* 39, no. 1 (2012): 67–70.

38. Lila Abu-Lughod, "Living the 'Revolution' in an Egyptian Village: Moral Action in a National Space," *American Ethnologist* 39, no. 1 (2012): 21–5.

39. Margaret Mead and Rhoda Métraux, eds, *The Study of Culture at a Distance* (New York: Berghahn, [1953] 2000).

40. Antonius C. G. M. Robben, *Iraq at a Distance: What Anthropologists Can Teach Us about the War* (Philadelphia, PA: University of Pennsylvania Press, 2009); Irene Kucera, "Follow the Afghan War: Methods, Interpretations, Imagination," *Anthropology of the Middle East* 7, no. 1 (2012): 38–50; Charles Lindholm, "Culture, Charisma, and Consciousness: The Case of the Rajneeshee," *Ethos* 30, no. 4 (2002): 357–75.

41. George E. Marcus and Fernando Mascarenhas, *Ocasião: The Marquis and the Anthropologist, A Collaboration* (Walnut Creek, CA: Rowman Altamira, 2005).

42. Livingstone, "On the Mediation of Everything."

43. On assemblages, see Manuel DeLanda, *A New Philosophy of Society: Assemblage Theory and Social Complexity* (New York: Continuum, 2006); Gilles Deleuze and Félix Guattari, *A Thousand Plateaus: Capitalism and Schizophrenia* (Minneapolis, MN: University of Minnesota Press, [1987] 2007); and George E. Marcus and Erkan Saka, "Assemblage," *Theory, Culture and Society* 23 (2006): 101–6.

44. Bruno Latour, *Reassembling the Social: An Introduction to Actor-Network-Theory* (New York: Oxford University Press, 2005).

45. On mediatization, see Knut Lundby, "Mediatization as Key Concept," in *Mediatization: Concept, Changes, Consequences* (New York: Peter Lang, 2009): 1–20; Knut Lundby, "Media Logic: Looking for Social Interaction," in *Mediatization: Concept, Changes, Consequences* (New York: Peter Lang, 2009): 101–19; Knut Lundby, "Mediatization of Communication," in *The Mediatization of Communication* (Berlin: De Gruyter/Mouton, 2014): 3–38; Nick Couldry and Andreas Hepp, "A Conceptualizing Mediatization: Contexts, Traditions, Arguments," *Communication Theory* 23 (2013): 191–202.

46. Mobile telephony is a crucial part of the digital revolution in Egypt that has been under-emphasized. See Kira C. Allmann, "Mobile Revolution: Toward a History of Technology, Telephony and Political Activism in Egypt," *CyberOrient* 8 (2014), http://www.cyberorient.net/article.do?articleId=9145. While fewer than

15 per cent of people in Egypt had landlines, mobile phone use reached 113 per cent by July 2012, with the number of landlines dropping to little more than 10 per cent. See Mona F. Badran, "Young People and the Digital Divide in Egypt: An Empirical Study," *Eurasian Economic Review* 4 (2014): 223–50.

47. John Postill, "Freedom Technologists and the New Protest Movements: A Theory of Protest Formulas," *Convergence* 20, no. 4 (2014): 402–18.

48. Asef Bayat, *Life as Politics: How Ordinary People Change the Middle East* (Stanford, CA: Stanford University Press, 2013); Asef Bayat, *Making Islam Democratic: Social Movements and the Post-Islamist Turn* (Stanford, CA: Stanford University Press, 2007); Alice Mattoni and Emiliano Treré, "Media Practices, Mediation Processes, and Mediatization in the Study of Social Movements," *Communication Theory* 24, no. 3 (2014): 252–71.

49. David Faris, *Dissent and Revolution in a Digital Age: Social Media, Blogging and Activism in Egypt* (London: I. B. Tauris, 2013), 22.

50. Ibid.

51. Victor W. Turner, *The Ritual Process: Structure and Anti-Structure* (Chicago, IL: Aldine, 1969); Pierre Bourdieu, *The Field of Cultural Production: Essays on Art and Literature* (Cambridge, MA: Polity Press, 1993); John L. Martin, "What is Field Theory?" *American Journal of Sociology* 109 (2003): 1–49; Postill, "Fields as Dynamic Clusters of Practices, Games and Socialities."

52. Max Gluckman, *Politics, Law and Ritual in Tribal Society* (Chicago, IL: Aldine, 1965).

53. John Gledhill, *Power and its Disguises: Anthropological Perspectives on Politics* (London: Pluto, 2000).

54. Pierre Bourdieu, *Language and Symbolic Power* (Cambridge, MA: Harvard University Press, 1999).

55. Thomassen, "Notes Toward an Anthropology of Political Revolution," 683.

56. Turner, *The Ritual Process*, 128.

57. Turner, *The Ritual Process*, 128.

58. Emily Crane, Personal Communication, 6 January 2016.

59. Mark Allen Peterson, "From Microblogging to Microperformance in Egypt," *Anthropology News* 53, no. 4 (2012): 35–6; Ramesh Srinivasan, "Bridges Between Cultural and Digital Worlds in Revolutionary Egypt," *Information Society* 29 (2013): 49–60.

60. John Sutter, "When the Internet Actually Helps Dictators," CNN, 22 February 2011, http://www.cnn.com/2011/TECH/web/02/22/authoritarian.internet. morozov/

61. President El-Sisi, for example, from the time he announced his candidacy for office, maintained not only a website but also Facebook, Twitter, Instagram, YouTube, and Google+ accounts.

62. Ramzy Baroud, "The Age of TV Jokers: Arab Media on the Brink," *Arab Media and Society* 20 (2015), http://www.arabmediasociety.com/?article=858

63. Sheila Peuchaud, "Social Media Activism and Egyptians' Use of Social Media to Combat Sexual Violence: An HiAP Case Study," *Health Promotion International* 29, no. 1 (2014): 113–20.

64. Postill, "Freedom Technologists and the New Protest Movements."

65. Randa Aboubakr, "New Directions of Internet Activism in Egypt," *Communications: The European Journal of Communication Research* 38, no. 3 (2013): 251–65.

5. WOMEN'S DIGITAL ACTIVISM: MAKING CHANGE IN THE MIDDLE EAST

1. See Clay Shirky, *Here Comes Everybody: The Power of Organizing without Organizations* (New York: Penguin, 2008); Evgeny Morozov, *The Net Delusion: The Dark Side of Internet Freedom* (New York: Public Affairs, 2011).

2. Annabelle Sreberny-Mohammadi and Ali Mohammadi, *Small Media, Big Revolution: Communication, Culture, and the Iranian Revolution* (Minneapolis, MN: University of Minnesota, 1985), 36.

3. Kimberle Crenshaw, "Mapping the Margins: Intersectionality, Identity Politics, and Violence against Women of Color," *Stanford Law Review* 43, no. 6 (1991): 1241–99; Nira Yuval-Davis, "Intersectionality and Feminist Politics," *European Journal of Women's Studies* 13, no. 3 (2006): 193–209.

4. Cynthia Enloe, "Masculinities, Policing, Women and International Politics of Sexual Harassment," *International Feminist Journal of Politics* 1 (2013): 77–81, specifically 80.

5. Yakin Erturk, "The Missing Link in Women's Rights," *Open Democracy*, 6 March 2015, https://www.opendemocracy.net/5050/yakin-erturk/missing-link-in-women's-human-rights

6. Joshua Meyrowitz, *No Sense of Place: The Impact of Electronic Media on Social Behavior* (New York: Oxford University Press, 1985).

7. John B. Thompson, *The Media and Modernity: A Social Theory of the Media* (Stanford, CA: Stanford University Press, 1995).

8. See the range of contributions about gender equality on 50/50 Open Democracy, http://bit.ly/2lF21p0

9. Soumitra Dutta, Thierry Geiger, and Bruno Lanvin, "The Global Information Technology Report 2015: ICTs for Inclusive Growth," http://www3.weforum.org/docs/WEF_Global_IT_Report_2015.pdf. See also Thierry Geiger, "The Top 10 Nations for Bridging the Digital Divide," World Economic Forum, 15 April 2015, http://www.weforum.org/agenda/2015/04/which-nations-are-top-for-digital/

10. World Economic Forum, "The Global Gender Gap Report 2014," http://www3.weforum.org/docs/GGGR14/GGGR_CompleteReport_2014.pdf

11. Arab Social Media Report, "Citizen Engagement and Public Services in the Arab

World: The Potential of Social Media," 2014, http://www.mbrsg.ae/getattachment/5e2c447f-c02b-438f-a42a-f41ea16206ec/6

12. We Are Social, "Social, Digital and Mobile in the Middle East, North Africa and Turkey," 2014, http://www.slideshare.net/wearesocialsg/social-digital-mobile-in-the-middle-east-north-africa-turkey

13. See, for example, Emirati Media Forum, "2014 UAE Social Media Outlook: Increasing Connectivity between Government and Citizen," http://www.mbrsg.ae/getattachment/3122bce8-b0e3-48e7-872e-2644fceb71ff/2014-UAE-Social-Media-Outlook-Increasing-coneectiv.aspx

14. Everette Dennis, Justin Martin, and Robb Woods, "Media Use in the Middle East: An Eight-Nation Survey," Northwestern University in Qatar/Harris Interactive, 2013, https://www.sribd.com/fullscreen/148423818?access_key=key-hhrn kzjb5s6ns9vu3md&allow_share=true&view_mode=scroll

15. See also Mohammed Bin Rashid School of Government (MBRSG), "The Arab World Online 2014: Trends in Internet and Mobile Usage in the Arab Region," http://www.mbrsg.ae/getattachment/ff70c2c5-0fce-405d-b23f-93c198d4ca44/The-Arab-World-Online-2014-Trends-in-Internet-and.aspx

16. World Economic Forum, "Global Gender Gap Report," http://www3.weforum.org/docs/GGGR14/GGGR_CompleteReport_2014.pdf

17. Dennis et al., "Media Use in the Middle East."

18. Ulrich Beck, *Power in the Global Age: A New Global Political Economy* (Malden, MA: Polity, 2005).

19. Annabelle Sreberny and Gholam Khiabany, *Blogistan: The Internet and Politics in Iran* (London: I. B. Tauris, 2010).

20. Paul Amar, "Turning the Gendered Politics of the Security State Inside Out? Charging the Police with Sexual Harassment in Egypt," *International Feminist Journal of Politics* 13, no. 3 (2011): 299–328, specifically 309.

21. Chantal Mouffe, *On the Political* (London: Routledge, 2005), 18.

22. Issandr El Amrani, "The Girl," *The Arabist*, 17 December 2011, http://arabist.net/blog/2011/12/17/the-girl.html; Isobel Coleman, "'Blue Bra Girl' Rallies Egypt's Women vs. Oppression," CNN, 22 December 2011, http://edition.cnn.com/2011/12/22/opinion/coleman-women-egypt-protest/

23. "Egypt's 'Girl in the Blue Bra,'" *On the Media*, 23 December 2011, http://www.onthemedia.org/story/177561-egypts-girl-blue-bra/

24. Coleman, "'Blue Bra Girl' Rallies Egypt's Women vs. Oppression."

25. HarassMap, http://harassmap.org/en/

26. See "Women under Siege: Documenting Sexualized Violence in Syria," Women's Media Center, https://womenundersiegesyria.crowdmap.com/. The site also includes considerable documentation of the specific difficulties that women and mothers experience in the refugee flight to Europe. See http://www.womenunder-siegeproject.org/

27. "My Stealthy Freedom" Facebook Page, www.facebook.com/StealthyFreedom

28. Masih Alinejad, "My Stealthy Freedom," 24 February 2015, http://bit.ly/1RKfHYh

29. Babak Dehghanpisheh, "Acid Attacks in Iran Sharpen Row over Islamic Dress and Vigilantism," Reuters, 5 November 2015, http://www.reuters.com/article/2014/11/05/us-iran-politics-women-attacks-idUSKBN0IP15K20141105

30. Maya Gebeily, "Meet Estayqazat, Syria's Online Feminist Movement," *Al-Monitor*, 16 March 2015, http://www.al-monitor.com/pulse/ru/contents/articles/originals/2015/03/syria-women-estayqazat-movement-sexuality.html#

31. Ibid.

32. Ahwaa, ahwaa.org.

33. Ikhtyar, www.ikhtyar.org.

34. Bintelnas, www.bintelnas.org.

35. Helem, www.helem.net, and Bedayaa, http://bedayaa.webs.com

36. Annabelle Sreberny, "Violence against Women Journalists," in *Media and Gender: A Scholarly Agenda for the Global Alliance on Media and Gender*, ed. Aimée Vega Montiel (Paris: UNESCO/IAMCR, 2014), 35–9.

37. Rose Troup Buchanan, "Turkish Men Take to Istanbul's Streets in Skirts to Protest Death of Young Woman," *Independent*, 23 February 2015, http://www.independent.co.uk/news/world/asia/turkish-men-take-to-istanbuls-streets-in-skirts-to-protest-death-of-young-woman-10065020.html

38. Sherine Hafez, *An Islam of Her Own: Reconsidering Religion and Secularism in Women's Islamic Movements* (New York: New York University Press, 2011); Valentine Moghadam, "Islamic Feminism and its Discontents: Toward a Resolution of the Debate," *Signs* 27, no. 4 (2002): 1135–71.

39. Deborah Amos, "A Tweet on Women's Veils, Followed by Raging Debate in Saudi Arabia," NPR, 17 December 2014, http://n.pr/13p1fhC

40. Belinda Robinson, "Saudi Cleric, Who Once Headed Mecca's Religious Police, Receives Death Threats After His Wife Appears with Him on TV Wearing Make-up and Without a Veil," *Daily Mail*, 19 December 2014, http://www.dailymail.co.uk/news/article-2880791/Saudi-cleric-headed-Mecca-s-religious-police-receives-death-threats-wife-appears-TV-wearing-make-without-veil.html

41. Daniel Regalado, Nart Villeneuve, and John Scott Railton, "Behind the Syrian Conflict's Digital Front Lines," FireEye, February 2015, https://www.fireeye.com/content/dam/fireeye-www/global/en/current-threats/pdfs/rpt-behind-the-syria-conflict.pdf

42. "Egypt Warns Women against Marrying ISIS Fighters Online," *Al Arabiya*, 5 March 2015, http://english.alarabiya.net/en/News/middle-east/2015/03/05/Egypt-warns-women-against-marrying-ISIS-fighters-online.html

43. Valentine Moghadam, "Explaining Divergent Outcomes of the Arab Spring: The Significance of Gender Relations and Women's Mobilizations," Upholding

Gendered Peace at a Time of War International Conference, Beirut, 9 June 2015, http://womeninwar.org/wordpress/beirut-conference-publications-and-videos

6. DOMESTICATING FOREIGN INTELLECTUAL PROPERTY LAWS IN THE DIGITAL AGE: OF PIRATES AND *QARSANA* IN THE GCC STATES

1. David Price, *The Development of Intellectual Property Regimes in the Arabian Gulf States: Infidels at the Gates* (London: Routledge, 2009), 32; Neil Partrick, "Nationalism in the Gulf States," Research Paper, Kuwait Programme on Development, Governance and Globalisation in the Gulf States, 2009, http://www.lse.ac.uk/middleEastCentre/kuwait/documents/NeilPartrick.pdf

2. Price, *The Development of Intellectual Property Regimes in the Arabian Gulf States*, 3.

3. The Organization of the Petroleum Exporting Countries (OPEC), "Brief History," http://www.opec.org/opec_web/en/about_us/24.htm

4. Price, *The Development of Intellectual Property Regimes in the Arabian Gulf States*, 3.

5. John Duke Anthony, "U.S.-GCC Trade and Investment Relations," U.S.-GCC Occasional Paper Series Number Six (Washington, DC: U.S.-GCC Corporate Cooperation Committee, 1999).

6. Organisation for Economic Co-operation and Development, "The Knowledge-Based Economy," 1996, http://www.oecd.org/sti/sci-tech/1913021.pdf

7. World Trade Organization, "Intellectual Property: Protection and Enforcement," http://www.wto.org/english/thewto_e/whatis_e/tif_e/agrm7_e.htm

8. Beñat Bilbao-Osorio, Soumitra Dutta, and Bruno Lanvin, eds, "The Global Information Technology Report 2014 Rewards and Risks of Big Data," 2014, http://global-indices.insead.edu/documents/GITR2014.pdf

9. Adrian Johns, *Piracy: The Intellectual Property Wars from Gutenberg to Gates* (Chicago, IL: University of Chicago Press, 2010).

10. Price, *The Development of Intellectual Property Regimes in the Arabian Gulf States*, 6.

11. Ibid., 5.

12. Cooperation Council for the Arab States of the Gulf Secretariat General, "The Charter," http://www.gcc-sg.org/eng/index.html; Cooperation Council for the Arab States of the Gulf Secretariat General, "The Economic Agreement between the GCC States," file:///C:/Users/sm623/Desktop/Copyright%20GCC/1274258747.pdf

13. Wang Hui, "Postcolonial Approaches," in *Routledge Encyclopedia of Translation Studies*, ed. Mona Baker and Gabriela Saldanha (London: Routledge, 2009), 201.

14. David Price, "The GCC Intellectual Property Regimes," in *The GCC Economies: Stepping Up to Future Challenges*, ed. Mohamed A. Ramady (London: Springer, 2012), 143.

15. Ibid.

16. ICT Qatar, Ministry of Information and Communications Technology, "Media, Culture and Heritage (MCH) National Digitization Plan," 10 July 2104, file:///C:/Users/sm623/Desktop/Copyright%20GCC/media_culture_and_heritage_national_digitization_plan_-_english_0.pdf.

17. Ibid.

18. World Intellectual Property Organization (WIPO), International Conference on Intellectual Property, the Internet, Electronic Commerce and Traditional Knowledge, Sofia, Bulgaria, 29–31 May 2001.

19. World Trade Organization, "The WTO: In Brief," http://www.wto.org/english/thewto_e/whatis_e/inbrief_e/inbr00_e.htm

20. World Trade Organization, "Agreement on Trade-Related Aspects of Intellectual Property Rights," http://www.wto.org/english/docs_e/legal_e/27-trips.pdf

21. Howard L. Stovall, "Arab Commercial Laws—Into the Future," *International Lawyer* 34, no. 3 (2000): 842.

22. Peter Drahos, "Expanding Intellectual Property's Empire: the Role of FTAs," 2003, http://www.grain.org/system/old/rights_files/drahos-fta-2003-en.pdf

23. Just when GCC governments were attempting to align their newly codified laws with TRIPS stipulations, developed nations, especially the US and EU, began insisting on even more stringent regulations, known as "TRIPS-plus," that go beyond the minimum requirements enshrined in TRIPS. In accordance with TRIPS-plus, the US and EU have entered into bilateral Free Trade Agreements (FTAs) with individual Gulf states in order to enforce more aggressive intellectual property protections in an era of increased digitalization of information. "Many WTO members tried to negotiate higher standards than were eventually agreed and they now have higher levels of protection in their laws than those set out in the TRIPS Agreement and consequently, for those Members, the TRIPS Agreement is a floor rather than a ceiling," Susy Frankel, "Challenging Trips-Plus Agreements: The Potential Utility of Non-Violation Disputes," *Journal of International Economic Law* 12, no. 4 (2009): 1024, http://jiel.oxfordjournals.org/content/12/4/1023.full.pdf

24. Price, *The Development of Intellectual Property Regimes in the Arabian Gulf States*, 7.

25. John Carroll, "Intellectual Property Rights in the Middle East: A Cultural Perspective," *Fordham Intellectual Property, Media and Entertainment Law Journal* 11 (2001): 555.

26. Matthew Dames, "Framing the Copyright Debate," *Information Today* 23, no. 8 (2006); Ben Willis, "The Arguments For and Against the TRIPS Agreement," E-International Relations, 23 December 2003, http://www.e-ir.info/2013/12/23/the-arguments-for-and-against-the-trips-agreement/

27. Willis, "The Arguments For and Against the TRIPS Agreement."

28. Peter Drahos and John Braithwaite, *Information Feudalism* (London: Earthscan Publications, 2002).

29. Peter Drahos, "Developing Countries and International Intellectual Property Standard-Setting," *Journal of World Intellectual Property* 5, no. 5 (2002): 766.

30. John Barkley Rosser, Jr and Marina V. Rosser, *Comparative Economics in a Transforming World Economy*, 2nd edn (Cambridge, MA: MIT Press, 2004), 99.

31. Carroll, "Intellectual Property Rights in the Middle East," 566.

32. Ibid., 596.

33. Susan Sell, *Private Power, Public Law: The Globalization of Intellectual Property Rights* (Cambridge: Cambridge University Press, 2003).

34. International Intellectual Property Alliance, "Description of the IIPA," 2014, http://www.iipawebsite.com/aboutiipa.html

35. Ibid.

36. Carroll, "Intellectual Property Rights in the Middle East," 556.

37. International Intellectual Property Alliance (IIPA), "United Arab Emirates: 2014 Special 301 Report on Copyright Protection and Enforcement," 2014, http://www.iipa.com/rbc/2014/2014SPEC301UAE.PDF

38. Carroll, "Intellectual Property Rights in the Middle East," 566–7.

39. IIPA, "United Arab Emirates."

40. Ibid.

41. Ibid.

42. Price, *The Development of Intellectual Property Regimes in the Arabian Gulf States*, 4.

43. Commission on Intellectual Property Rights, "Integrating Intellectual Property Rights and Development Policy," Report of the Commission on Intellectual Property Rights, 2002, http://www.cipr.org.uk/papers/text/final_report/report-webfinal.htm

44. Ibid.

45. IIPA, "United Arab Emirates."

46. Carroll, "Intellectual Property Rights in the Middle East," 556.

47. Yale Law School, "The Statute of Anne; 10 April 1710," 2008, http://avalon.law.yale.edu/18th_century/anne_1710.asp

48. Johns, *Piracy*, 33.

49. Ben Willis, "The Arguments For and Against the TRIPS Agreement," E-International Relations, 23 December 2003, http://www.e-ir.info/2013/12/23/the-arguments-for-and-against-the-trips-agreement/

50. Ibid.

51. World Intellectual Property Organization (WIPO), *Intellectual Property Handbook*, 2008, http://www.wipo.int/edocs/pubdocs/en/intproperty/489/wipo_pub_489.pdf

52. Amir H. Khoury, "Ancient and Islamic Sources of Intellectual Property Protection in the Middle East: A Focus on Trademarks," *IDEA The Journal of Law and Technology* 43, no. 2 (2003): 153.

53. Jonathan Lethem, "The Ecstasy of Influence: A Plagiarism," *Harper's Magazine*, February 2007, http://www.harpers.org/archive/2007/02/0081387

54. Price, *The Development of Intellectual Property Regimes in the Arabian Gulf States*, 27.

55. Ibid., 16.

56. Cooperation Council for the Arab States of the Gulf Secretariat General, "Common Customs Law of the GCC States Rules of Implementation and Explanatory Notes Thereof" (Riyadh: Secretariat General, 2008), file:///C:/Users/sm623/Desktop/1282120184.pdf

57. Johns, *Piracy*, 320.

58. Peter W. Hansen, *Intellectual Property Law and Practice of the United Arab Emirates* (Oxford: Oxford University Press, 2009), xxi.

59. James Onley, "The Politics of Protection in the Gulf: The Arab Rulers and the British Resident in the Nineteenth Century," *New Arabian Studies* 6 (2014), 30–92; James Onley, "Britain and the Gulf Shaikhdoms, 1820–1971: The Politics of Protection," CIRS Occasional Paper no. 4 (Doha: Center for International and Regional Studies, 2009), 4. For more on piracy in Gulf history, see Louise Sweet, "Pirates or Polities? Arab Societies of the Persian or Arabian Gulf, 18th Century," *Ethnohistory* 11, no. 3 (1964): 262–80; Charles Belgrave, *The Pirate Coast* (London: G. Bell & Sons, 1966); Hubert Moyse-Bartlett, *The Pirates of Trucial Oman* (London: Macdonald, 1966); Patricia Risso Dubuisson, "Qasimi Piracy and the General Treaty of Peace (1820)," *Arabian Studies* 4 (1978): 47–57; Sulṭan Muḥammad Al-Qasimi, *The Myth of Arab Piracy in the Gulf* (London: Routledge, 1986); Charles Davies, *The Blood-Red Arab Flag: An Investigation into Qasimi Piracy, 1797–1820* (Exeter: University of Exeter Press, 1997); Patricia Risso, "Cross-Cultural Perceptions of Piracy: Maritime Violence in the Western Indian Ocean and Persian Gulf Region during a Long Eighteenth Century," *Journal of World History* 12 (2001): 293–319; Sulṭan Bin Muḥammad Al-Qasimi, *Power Struggles and Trade in the Gulf: 1620–1820* (Exeter: Forest Row, 1999).

60. See, for example, how the word "qarsana" is used in the title of the Arabian Anti-Piracy Alliance, which is translated into Arabic literally as: "*alitihad al'araby limukafhat alqarsana*." See also an example of public discourse on the issue of copyright and the "normalizing"everyday use of the term "qarsana" in a newspaper article: "*Wazir al'adl: 'itifāqiyyat 'TRIPs' tatawafaq m'a anzimat almamlaka liḥimayat almlkia alfikria*." Al-Jazirah, December 19, 2013, http://www.al-jazirah.com/2013/20131219/fe23.htm.

61. Rights Direct, "International Copyright Basics," 2015, http://www.rightsdirect.com/content/rd/en/toolbar/copyright_education/International_Copyright_Basics.html

62. Price, *The Development of Intellectual Property Regimes in the Arabian Gulf States*, 54–5.

63. Broadband Commission for Digital Development, "The State of Broadband 2014: Broadband for All," September 2014, http://www.broadbandcommission.org/

Documents/reports/bb-annualreport2014.pdf. The Broadband Commission for Digital Development was launched by the International Telecommunication Union (ITU) and the United Nations Educational, Scientific and Cultural Organization (UNESCO).

64. IIPA, "United Arab Emirates."

65. Sulaiman Al-Rafee and Kamel Rouibah, "The Fight against Digital Piracy: An Experiment," *Telematics and Informatics* 27 (2010): 283–92.

66. Joanne Bladd quotes Kevin Ridgely, managing director of Sony Music Entertainment Middle East, saying that the "biggest challenge is in Saudi Arabia. Piracy is an issue there, much more so than it is in the UAE." See Joanne Bladd, "Saudi Arabia Worst for Music Piracy in Gulf," *Arabian Business*, 5 June 2009, http://www.arabianbusiness.com/saudi-arabia-worst-for-music-piracy-in-gulf-17545.html

67. United Nations, "E-Government Survey," 2014, http://unpan3.un.org/egovkb/Portals/egovkb/Documents/un/2014-Survey/E-Gov_Complete_Survey-2014.pdf; "21ˢᵗ Century GCC Smart Government and Smart Services Conference, 2015," http://www.gccsmartgovernment.com/

68. Alhanoof Al Debasi and David Price, "Intellectual Property in the New Era in the GCC States: Enforcement and Opportunity," Gulf Research Meeting, Cambridge, 24–27 August 2015, http://gulfresearchmeeting.net/index.php?pgid=Njk=&wid=MTA0&yr=2015

69. IIPA, "United Arab Emirates."

70. Carroll, "Intellectual Property Rights in the Middle East," 558.

71. Ibid.

72. Ibid.

73. IIPA, "United Arab Emirates."

74. ICT Qatar, Ministry of Information and Communications Technology, "ICT Legal Landscape," http://www.ictqatar.qa/en/smetoolkit/about-us/qatar-legal-infrastructure-and-landscape

75. Government of the State of Qatar, Ministry of Interior, "Thousands of Fake Products Seized in 'Shaheen' Operation," 17 March 2014, http://www.moi.gov.qa/site/english/news/2014/03/17/31724.html?highlightQuery=Intellectual%20property

76. Price, *The Development of Intellectual Property Regimes in the Arabian Gulf States*, 8.

77. Ibid.

78. In partnership with Qatar Foundation and Qatar Museums, University College London (UCL) instituted UCL Qatar, which specializes in the study of cultural heritage, offering an MSc in Conservation Studies, an MA in Museum and Gallery Practice, and an MA in the Archaeology of the Arab and Islamic World. UCL Qatar's "objectives is to work to support the development of Qatar's cultural heritage sector, as outlined in the National Vision 2030," http://www.ucl.ac.uk/qatar/

discover. Each Gulf state has its own national museum and heritage centers, and throughout the year there are government-funded conferences and oral history projects all designed in the digital age to keep alive a notion of a past identity that continues unbroken to the present, despite decades of colonial rule and exploitation. Other heritage activities include regular government- and university-funded annual forums and conferences hosting experts, academics, researchers, and historians all dedicated to the production of heritage knowledge.

79. ICT Qatar, Ministry of Information and Communications Technology, "Media, Culture and Heritage (MCH) National Digitization Plan."

80. World Trade Organization, "The Doha Round," 2015, http://www.wto.org/english/tratop_e/dda_e/dda_e.htm

7. FROM SOUK TO CYBER SOUK: ACCULTURATING TO E-COMMERCE IN THE MENA REGION

1. Bernard Dubois and Gilles Laurent, "Attitudes Towards the Concept of Luxury: An Exploratory Analysis," *Asia Pacific Advances in Consumer Research* 1 (1994): 273–8; Kuisma Taavi, "Conspicuous Consumption: An Analysis of Finnish and Malaysian Luxury Good Consumers," Masters dissertation, University of Science, Malaysia, 2008.

2. K. Prakash Vel, Alia Captain, Rabab Al-Abbas, and Balqees Al Hashemi, "Luxury Buying in the United Arab Emirates," *Journal of Business and Behavioural Sciences* 23, no. 1 (2011): 145–60.

3. Doreen Massey, "Power-Geometry and a Progressive Sense of Place," in *Mapping The Futures: Local Cultures, Global Change*, ed. John Bird, Barry Curtis, Tim Putnam, and Lisa Tickner (London: Routledge, 1993).

4. Pasi Falk, "The Scopic Regimes of Shopping," in *The Shopping Experience*, ed. Pasi Falk and Colin B. Campbell (New York: Sage, 1997).

5. Oana Şeitan, Cristina Gherman, and Cătălin Nicolae Bulgărea, "E-Commerce with Online Payment through Bank Card," Annals of the University of Petrosani, *Economics* 10, no. 4 (2010): 309–16.

6. Zhenhui Jiang and Izak Benbasat, "Virtual Product Experience: Effects of Visual and Functional Control of Products on Perceived Diagnosticity and Flow in Electronic Shopping," *Journal of Management Information Systems* 21, no. 3 (2004): 111–47.

7. Ellen Feghali, "Arab Cultural Communication Patterns," *International Journal of Intercultural Relations* 21, no. 2 (1997): 345–78; Gillian Rice, "Doing Business in Saudi Arabia," *Thunderbird International Business Review* 46, no. 1 (2004): 59–84.

8. Raphael Patai, *The Arab Mind* (Tucson, AZ: Red Brick Press, 1997); Margaret K. Nydell, *Understanding Arabs: A Guide for Westerners* (Yarmouth, ME: Intercultural Press, 2007); A. J. lmaney and A. J. Alwan, *Communicating with the Arabs: A Handbook for the Business Executive* (Prospect Heights, IL: Waveland Press,

1982); Rhonda Zaharna, "Bridging Cultural Differences: American Public Relations Practices and Arab Communication Patterns," *Public Relations Review* 21 (1995): 241–55.

9. Bob Lauterborn, "New Marketing Litany: Four Ps Passe; C-Words Take Over," *Advertising Age* 61 (1990): 26.

10. Karim Sabbagh, Mohamad Mourad, Wassim Kabbara, Ramez T. Shehadi, and Hatem Samman, "Understanding the Arab Digital Generation," Booz & Co., 9 October 2012, http://www.strategyand.pwc.com/reports/understanding-arab-digital-generation

11. Naushad K. Cherrayil, "PayPal Launches Middle East Operations with Aramex Deal," *Gulf News*, 14 November 2012, http://gulfnews.com/business/sectors/technology/paypal-launches-mideast-operations-with-aramex-deal-1.1104963

12. Giovanni Fantasia, "Who are the Global Consumers?" Nielsen, July 2013, http://www.nielsen.com/content/dam/nielsenglobal/eu/docs/pdf/Who%20are%20the%20Global%20Consumers.pdf

13. "B2C E-Commerce Volume Exceeded US$ 4.87 Billion in Kuwait, Lebanon, Saudi Arabia and UAE in 2007," Arab Advisors Group, 4 February 2008, http://www.arabadvisors.com/Pressers/presser-040208.htm-0

14. "E-Commerce in the Middle East, Statistics and Trends," Go-Gulf, 29 May 2013, http://www.go-gulf.ae/blog/ecommerce-middle-east/

15. R. Chadha, J. Enberg, R. Kats, and D. Marcec, "Digital and the Middle East: A Spotlight on the Gulf Cooperation Council Countries," *E-Marketer*, 4 December 2013, http://www.emarketer.com/articles/results.aspx?q=Digital%20and%20the%20Middle%20East

16. Everette E. Dennis, Justin, D. Martin, Robb Wood, and Marium Saeed, "Media Use in the Middle East 2016: A Six-Nation Survey," 27 March 2017, http://www.qatar.northwestern.edu/docs/...use/2016-middle-east-media-use-report.pdf

17. Patrick D. Lynch and John C. Beck, "Profiles of Internet Buyers in 20 Countries: Evidence for Region-Specific Strategies," *Journal of International Business Studies* 32, no. 4 (2001): 725–48; Patricia M. Doney, Joseph P. Cannon, and Michael R. Mullen, "Understanding the Influence of National Culture on the Development of Trust," *Academy of Management Review* 23, no. 3 (1998): 601–20.

18. Abdel Nasser H. Zaied, "Barriers to E-Commerce Adoption in Egyptian SMEs," *International Journal of Information Engineering and Electronic Business* 4, no. 3 (2012): 9–18.

19. Laura Shovlowsky, "Major Barrier to E-Commerce in Middle East and North Africa is Fear about Data Security," Proskauer, 4 September 2014, http://privacylaw.proskauer.com/2014/09/articles/articles/major-barrier-to-e-commerce-in-middle-east-and-north-africa-is-fear-about-data-security/

20. N. Anubhav Reddy and Brig Rajiv Divekar, "A Study of Challenges Faced by

e-Commerce Companies in India and Methods Employed to Overcome Them," *Procedia Economics and Finance* 11 (2014): 553–60.

21. Zhijie Lin, "An Empirical Investigation of User and System Recommendations in e-Commerce," *Decision Support Systems* 68, no. 3 (2014): 111–24.

22. Steven S. Aanen, Damir Vandic, and Flavius Frasincar, "Automated Product Taxonomy Mapping in an e-Commerce Environment," *Expert Systems with Applications* 42, no. 3 (2015): 1298–1313.

23. Tom R. Tyler, "Is the Internet Changing Social Life? It Seems the More Things Change, the More they Stay the Same," *Journal of Social Issues* 58, no. 1 (2002): 195–205.

24. Ibid., 200.

25. Jintao Wu, Junsong Chen, and Wenyu Dou, "The Internet of Things and Interaction Style: The Effect of Smart Interaction on Brand Attachment," *Journal of Marketing Management* 33, nos. 1–2 (2017): 61–75.

26. Yun J. Lee and Alan J. Dubinsky, "Consumers' Desire to Interact with a Salesperson During e-Shopping: Development of a Scale," *International Journal of Retail and Distribution Management* 45, no. 1 (2017): 20–39.

27. Jeffrey Inman and Hristina Nikolova, "Shopper-Facing Retail Technology: A Retailer Adoption Decision Framework Incorporating Shopper Attitudes and Privacy Concerns," *Journal of Retailing* 93, no. 1 (2017): 7–28.

28. Harry C. Triandis, "Cultural Aspects of Globalization," *Journal of International Management* 12, no. 2 (2006): 208–17.

29. Robert Jeyakumar Nathan, "Electronic Commerce Adoption in the Arab Countries: An Empirical Study," *International Arab Journal of e-Technology* 1 (2009): 29–37.

30. Paul A. Pavlou and Lin Chai, "What Drives Electronic Commerce across Cultures? A Cross-cultural Empirical Investigation of the Theory of Planned Behavior," *Journal of Electronic Commerce Research* 3, no. 4 (2002): 240–53; Qi-Ying Su and Carl Adams, "Will B2C E-Commerce Developed in One Cultural Environment Be Suitable for Another Culture?" in ICEC, 2005 Proceedings of the 7th International Conference on Electronic Commerce, 236–43; Nitish Singh, Vikas Kumar, and Daniel Baack, "Adaptation of Cultural Content: Evidence from B2C E-Commerce Firms," *European Journal of Marketing* 39, nos. 1–2 (2005): 71–86.

31. Geert Hofstede, *Culture's Consequences: International Differences in Work-Related Values* (Newbury Park, CA: Sage, 1984).

32. Pavlou and Chai, "What Drives Electronic Commerce across Cultures?" 240.

33. Singh, Kumar, and Baack, "Adaptation of Cultural Content."

34. Bhuvan Unhelkar, "Understanding the Impact of Cultural Issues in Global E-Business Alliances," in Proceedings of We-B Conference, Edith Cowan University, Australia, 2003.

35. Shaheen Al Hosni, "The Utilization of the World Wide Web for Decision-Making

in the United Arab Emirates (UAE) Business Settings: The Case of Dubai," PhD dissertation, Florida State University, 2000.

36. Morris Kalliny, Anshu Saran, Salma Ghanem, and Caroline Fisher, "Cultural Differences and Similarities in Television Commercials in the Arab World and the United States," *Journal of Global Marketing* 24, no. 1 (2011): 41–57.

37. S. Tamer Cavusgil, Gary A Knight, and John R Riesenberger, *International Business: The New Realities*, 2nd edn (Upper Saddle River, NJ: Pearson Education, 2012).

38. Victor Danciu, "The Impact of Culture on International Negotiations: An Analysis Based on Contextual Comparisons," *Theoretical and Applied Economics* 17, no. 8 (2010): 87–102.

39. Charles W. L. Hill, *International Business: Competing in the Global Marketplace* (New York: McGraw Hill, 2010), 112.

40. Christopher Bartlett and Paul Beamish, *Transnational Management: Text-Cases and Readings in Cross Border Management*, 6th edn (Burr Ridge, IL: McGraw Hill/ Irwin, 2011); Michael Czinkota and Masaaki Kotabe, *Trends in International Business: Critical Perspectives* (Cambridge, MA: Blackwell, 1998); David A. Griffith, "Cultural Meaning of Retail Institutions," *Journal of Global Marketing* 12 (1998): 47–59.

41. Geert Hofstede, *Culture's Consequences: International Differences in Work-Related Values* (Newbury Park, CA: Sage, 1984); Edward T. Hall, *Beyond Culture* (New York: Doubleday, 1976); Alfons Trompenaars and Charles Hampden-Turner, *Riding the Waves of Culture: Understanding Cultural Diversity in Business* (New York: McGraw-Hill, 1997).

42. Hofstede, *Culture's Consequences*.

43. Harry Triandis, *Individualism and Collectivism* (San Francisco, CA: Westview Press, 1995).

44. Charles W. L. Hill, Krishna Udayasankar, and Chow Hou Wee, *Global Business Today*, 8th edn (New York: McGraw-Hill, 2013).

45. Triandis. *Individualism and Collectivism*.

46. Hills, Udayansankar, and Wee, *Global Business Today*.

47. Shadi Ahmed Khattab, Amer Al-Manasra, Mohammed Khair Saleem Abu Zaid, and Fadi Taher Qutaishat, "Individualist, Collectivist and Gender-moderated Differences toward Online Purchase Intentions in Jordan," *International Business Research* 5 (2012): 85–93.

48. Lisa M. Hunter, Chickery J. Kasouf, Kevin G. Celuch, and Kathryn A. Curry, "A Classification of Business-to-Business Buying Decisions: Risk Importance and Probability as a Framework for e-Business Benefits," *Industrial Marketing Management* 33 (2004): 145–54.

49. Hofstede, *Culture's Consequences*.

50. Sandra M. Forsythe and Bo Shi, "Consumer Patronage and Risk Perceptions in

Internet Shopping," *Journal of Business Research* 56 (2003): 867–75; David W. Salisbury, Rodney A. Pearson, Allison W. Pearson, and David W. Miller, "Perceived Security and World Wide Web Purchase Intention." *Industrial Management and Data Systems* 101 (2001): 165–77; Yehoshua Liebermann and Shmuel Stashevsky, "Perceived Risks as Barriers to Internet and E-Commerce Usage," *Qualitative Market Research* 5 (2002): 291–300.

51. Ali Al-Kandari and T. Kenn Gaither, "Arabs, the West and Public Relations: A Critical/Cultural Study of Arab Cultural Values," *Public Relations Review* 37 (2011): 266–73; Margaret K. Nydell, *Understanding Arabs: A Guide for Modern Times* (Boston, MA: Intercultural Press, 2005).

52. Zaharna, "Bridging Cultural Differences."

53. Robert J. Nathan, Paul H. P. Yeow, and San Murugesan, "Key Usability Factors of Service-Oriented Web Sites for Students: An Empirical Study," *Online Information Review* 32 (2008): 302–24; Hyoung Yong Lee, Hyunchul Ahn, and Ingoo Han, "Analysis of Trust in the E-Commerce Adoption," paper presented at the 39th Annual Hawaii International Conference on System Sciences, Hawaii, 4–7 January 2006.

54. Lisa Anderson, "Policy-Making and Theory Building: American Political Science and the Islamic Middle East," in *Theory, Politics and the Arab World: Critical Responses*, ed. Hisham Sharabi (New York: Routledge, 1990).

55. William K. Darley, Denise J. Luethge, and Charles Blankson, "Culture and International Marketing: A Sub-Saharan African Context," *Journal of Global Marketing* 26 (2013): 188–202.

56. Hall, *Beyond Culture*.

57. Cavusgil, Knight, and Riesenberger, *International Business*.

58. William K. Darley and Charles Blankson, "African Culture and Business Markets: Implications for Marketing Practices," *Journal of Business and Industrial Marketing* 23 (2008): 374–83; Rice, "Doing Business in Saudi Arabia."

59. Morris Kalliny, Salma Ghanem, and Mary Kalliny, "The Influence of Cultural Orientation and Communication Style on Consumer Behavior: A Comparative Study of the Arab World and the United States," *Journal of Global Marketing* 27 (2014): 145–60.

60. Carolina Gómez, Bradley L. Kirkman, and Debra L. Shapiro, "The Impact of Collectivism and In-Group/Out-Group Membership on the Evaluation Generosity of Team Members," *Academy of Management Journal* 43 (2000): 1097–1106; Harry C. Triandis, "The Many Dimensions of Culture," *Academy of Management Perspectives* 18 (2004): 88–93.

61. Norhayati Zakaria and Derrick L. Cogburn, "Context-Dependent vs. Content-Dependent: An Exploration of the Cultural Behavioural Patterns of Online Intercultural Communication Using E-Mail," *International Journal of Business and Systems Research* 4 (2010): 330.

62. Trompenaars and Hampden-Turner, *Riding the Waves of Culture*.

63. Ibid.

64. William B. Gudykunst, Ge Gao, Karen L. Schmidt, Tsukasa Nishida, Michael H. Bond, Kwok Leung, Georgette Wang, and Robert A. Barraclough, "The Influence of Individualism-Collectivism, Self-Monitoring, and Predicted-Outcome Value on Communication in Ingroup and Outgroup Relationships," *Journal of Cross-Cultural Psychology* 23 (1992): 196–213.

8. WORKING FOR FREE: HIDDEN SOCIAL AND POLITICAL ECONOMIES OF THE INTERNET IN THE MIDDLE EAST

1. This chapter draws on research conducted between 1995 and 2014 principally in Jordan and also in Egypt, Syria, and Saudi Arabia, which unless otherwise specified constitute the "Middle East" referred to here. This research has been supported by an NMERTA Fulbright Fellowship at the American Center for Oriental Research (Amman), USIS travel-lecturing grants, a grant (with Michael C. Hudson) from the United States Institute of Peace, a research professorship at the Centre for Middle Eastern Studies of Lund University, and small grants from the Faculty Research Fund of the Catholic University of America. Ithiel de Sola Pool, *Technologies without Boundaries: On Telecommunications in a Global Age*, ed. Eli M. Noam (Cambridge, MA: Harvard University Press, 1990).

2. Pierre Bourdieu, *Outline of a Theory of Practice*, trans. Richard Nice (Cambridge: Cambridge University Press, 1977). His formal definition emphasizing this linkage was "systems of durable, transposable dispositions, structured structures predisposed to function as structuring structures, that is, as principles which generate and organize practices and representations that can be objectively adapted to their outcomes without presupposing a conscious aiming at ends or an express mastery of the operations necessary in order to attain them" (p. 4).

3. The same extended practice perspective is applied by Peterson in this volume to media studies, where it was introduced as an advance over values-in-action formulations by Nick Couldry, "Theorizing Media as Practice," in *Theorizing Media and Practice*, ed. Birgit Bräuchler and John Postill (New York: Berghahn Books, 2010).

4. Jodi Dean, *Democracy and Other Neoliberal Fantasies: Communicative Capitalism and Left Politics* (Durham, NC: Duke University Press, 2009).

5. Manuel Castells, *The Information Age: Economy, Society and Culture, Vol. 1: The Rise of the Network Society* (Malden, MA: Blackwell, 1996), 496.

6. Ibid., 21.

7. Fundamentally, they lead to "magic bullet" thinking, whether as soft technological determinism or in social constructionist treatments of both political and economic development as "reprogramming."

8. Robert Solow, "We'd Better Watch Out," *New York Times Book Review*, 12 July 1987, 36.

9. Paul M. Romer, "Endogenous Technological Change," *Journal of Political Economy* 98, no. 5 (1990).

10. *The Arab Human Development Report 2002: Creating Opportunities for Future Generations* (New York: United Nations Development Programme (UNDP), Regional Bureau for Arab states, 2002).

11. Erik Brynjolfsson, "The Productivity Paradox of Information Technology," *Communications of the ACM* 36, no. 12 (1993).

12. Nicholas Negroponte, *Being Digital* (New York: Simon & Schuster, 1995); Chris Anderson, *Free: The Future of a Radical Price* (London: Random House Business, 2009).

13. A. Burson-Marsteller, "After the Spring: Arab Youth Survey 2012" (Dubai Media City: Asda'a Burson-Marsteller, 2012); Emma C. Murphy, "Problematizing Arab Youth: Generational Narratives of Systemic Failure," *Mediterranean Politics* 17, no. 1 (2012); ESCWA, "Impact of ICT on Arab Youth: Employment, Education and Social Change" (New York: United Nations, 2013); Tobias Olsson and Peter Dahlgren, *Young People, ICTs and Democracy: Theories, Policies, Identities and Websites* (Göteborg, Sweden: Nordicom, 2010).

14. Deborah L. Wheeler, "The Internet and Youth Subculture in Kuwait," *Journal of Computer-Mediated Communication* 8, no. 2 (2003); Linda Herrera, "Youth and Citizenship in the Digital Age: A View from Egypt," *Harvard Educational Review* 82, no. 3 (2012); Michael Hoffman and Amaney Jamal, "The Youth and the Arab Spring: Cohort Differences and Similarities," *Middle Eastern Law and Governance* 4, no. 1 (2012); Pamela Ann Smith, "ICT: The Arab World's Bright Hope?" *Middle East* 422 (2011); Olsson and Dahlgren, *Young People, ICTs and Democracy*; Peter Dahlgren, *Young Citizens and New Media: Learning for Democratic Participation*, Routledge Studies in Social and Political Thought (New York: Routledge, 2007).

15. Danah Boyd, "Why Youth (Heart) Social Network Sites," in *Youth, Identity, and Digital Media*, ed. David Buckingham (Cambridge, MA: MIT Press, 2008); George Weyman, "Speaking the Unspeakable: Personal Blogs in Egypt," http://www.arabmediasociety.com/topics/index.php?t_article=164&printarticle; Khaled Saleh Al Omoush, Saad Ghaleb Yaseen, and Mohammad Atwah Alma'aitah, "The Impact of Arab Cultural Values on Online Social Networking: The Case of Facebook," *Computers in Human Behavior* 28, no. 6 (2012); Dominika Sokol and Vít Šisler, "Socializing on the Internet: Case Study of Internet Use among University Students in the United Arab Emirates," *Global Media Journal: American Edition* 9, no. 16 (2010); Paul Leslie, "Post-Secondary Students' Purposes for Blogging" (MR42033, Memorial University of Newfoundland, 2008); Yeslam Al-Saggaf, "Saudi Females on Facebook: An Ethnographic Study," *International Journal of Emerging Technologies and Society* 9, no. 1 (2011).

16. Courtney C. Radsch, "Core to Commonplace: The Evolution of Egypt's Blogosphere," *Arab Media and Society* 6 (Fall 2008), http://www.arabmediasociety.com/?article=692

17. Augusto Valeriani, "Bridges of the Revolution: Linking People, Sharing Information, and Remixing Practices," *Sociologica* 3 (2011); Donatella Della Ratta and Augusto Valeriani, "Remixing the Spring! Connective Leadership and Read-Write Practices in the 2011 Arab Uprisings," www.cyberorient.net/article. do?articleid=7763

18. Valeriani, "Bridges of the Revolution."

19. Abdelmajid Bouazza and Hamyar Al-Mahrooqi, "Use of the Internet by Arts and Social Science Students as a Source of Information: The Case of the Sultanate of Oman," *DOMES: Digest of Middle East Studies* 18, no. 2 (2009); Salim Said Ali Al kindi and Saadat M. Alhashmi, "Use of Social Networking Sites among Shinas College of Technology Students in Oman," *Journal of Information and Knowledge Management* 11, no. 1 (2012).

20. This layering is built into the very concept of the Internet, the TCP/IP protocol, for "delivering" lower level services (e.g. telecommunications) to higher level operations that packet and address information to destinations, and thence to the programs that use them. As such, it is taken for granted or "naturalized" in Bourdieu's (1977) terms within the developer realm.

21. Janet Abbate, *Inventing the Internet* (Cambridge, MA: MIT Press, 1999).

22. Barry M. Leiner et al., "A Brief History of the Internet," *SIGCOMM Computer Communication Review* 39, no. 5 (2009).

23. Jeffrey A. Hart, Robert R. Reed, and François Bar, "The Building of the Internet: Implications for the Future of Broadband Networks," *Telecommunications Policy* 16, no. 8 (1992).

24. Harold Rheingold, *The Virtual Community: Homesteading on the Electronic Frontier* (New York: HarperCollins, 1993).

25. Tim Berners-Lee and Mark Fischetti, *Weaving the Web: The Past, Present and Future of the World Wide Web* (London: Orion Business, 1999).

26. Tim O'Reilly, "What Is Web 2.0: Design Patterns and Business Models for the Next Generation of Software," http://oreilly.com/web2/archive/what-is-web-20. html

27. Jon W. Anderson and Michael C. Hudson, "Internet Pioneering in Four Arab Countries: The Internet as a Force for Democracy in the Middle East," http:// aipnew.wordpress.com/2008/09/15/ internet-pioneering-in-four-arab-countries-the-internet-as-a-force-for-democracy-in-the-middle-east/

28. Heba El Sayed and Chris Westrup, "Egypt and ICTs: How ICTs Bring National Initiatives, Global Organizations and Local Companies Together," *Information Technology and People* 16, no. 1 (2003): 76; Jon W. Anderson, "Producers and Middle East Internet Technology: Getting Beyond 'Impacts,'" *Middle East Journal* 54, no. 3 (2000).

29. Jon B. Alterman, *New Media, New Politics? From Satellite Television to the Internet*

in the Arab World, Policy Paper No. 48 (Washington, DC: Washington Institute for Near East Policy, 1998).

30. Jon W. Anderson, "Between Freedom and Coercion: Inside Internet Implantation in the Middle East," in *The New Arab Media: Technology, Image and Perception*, ed. Majhoob Zweiri and Emma C. Murphy (Reading, UK: Ithaca Press, 2011).

31. International Telecommunications Union Annual Reports for 2001, 2006.

32. International Telecommunications Union Annual Reports for 2006, 2011.

33. The second phase of the UN's World Summit on the Information Society (WSIS) was hosted in Tunis in 2005 by the Tunisian government, which attracted criticism for its restrictive Internet policies, particularly by civil society activists which the Summit was intended to incorporate into its stakeholder broadening. For an account of the aftermath up to the Arab Spring, see Mike Elkin, "Tunisia Internet Chief Gives Inside Look at Cyber Uprising," wired.com, http://www.wired.com/dangerroom/2011/01/as-egypt-tightens-its-internet-grip-tunisia-seeks-to-open-up/

34. Marc Lynch, *Voices of the New Arab Public: Iraq, Al-Jazeera and Middle East Politics Today* (New York: Columbia University Press, 2006); Marc Lynch, "Blogging the New Arab Public,"http://www.arabmediasociety.com/topics/index.php?t_article=32

35. Ethan Zuckerman, "Meet the Bridgebloggers," *Public Choice* 1/2 (2008); Kevin Wallsten, "Political Blogs: Transmission Belts, Soapboxes, Mobilizers, or Conversation Starters?" *Journal of Information Technology and Politics* 4, no. 3 (2008).

36. Weyman, "Speaking the Unspeakable: Personal Blogs in Egypt."

37. Valeriani, "Bridges of the Revolution." See also David D. Kirkpatrick and David E. Sanger, "A Tunisian-Egyptian Link That Shook Arab History," http://www.nytimes.com/2011/02/14/world/middleeast/14egypt-tunisia-protests.html?pagewanted=all; John Pollock, "Streetbook: How Egyptian and Tunisian Youth Hacked the Arab Spring," http://www.technologyreview.com/featuredstory/425137/streetbook/

38. Lawrence Lessig, *Remix: Making Art and Commerce Thrive in the Hybrid Economy* (New York: Penguin Press, 2008).

39. Christopher Kelty, "Geeks, Social Imaginaries, and Recursive Publics," *Cultural Anthropology* 20, no. 4 (2005); Christopher Kelty, *Two Bits: The Cultural Significance of Free Software* (Durham, NC: Duke University Press, 2008).

40. Jean Lave and Etienne Wenger, *Situated Learning: Legitimate Peripheral Participation* (Cambridge: Cambridge University Press, 1991). They generated this concept for the site of "informal" learning, which they specified as including peer-to-peer information sharing, mentoring, and apprenticeships, apart from formal learning marked by hierarchical relationships.

41. Castells, *The Information Age: Economy, Society and Culture, Vol. 1: The Rise of the Network Society*, 500.

42. Chris Anderson, *The Long Tail: How Endless Choice Is Creating Unlimited Demand* (London: Random House Business, 2006); *Free: The Future of a Radical Price*.

43. Boyd, "Why Youth (Heart) Social Network Sites"; "Social Network Sites as Networked Publics: Affordances, Dynamics, and Implications," in *Networked Self: Identity, Community, and Culture on Social Network Sites*, ed. Zizi Papacharissi (New York: Routledge, 2010); Mizuko Ito, ed., *Hanging out, Messing around, and Geeking Out: Kids Living and Learning with New Media*, John D. and Catherine T. Macarthur Foundation Series on Digital Media and Learning (Cambridge, MA: MIT Press, 2010).

44. Al Kindi and Alhashmi, "Use of Social Networking Sites among Shinas College of Technology Students in Oman; Matthew Clarke, "The Discursive Construction of Interpersonal Relations in an Online Community of Practice," *Journal of Pragmatics* 41 (2009); Sokol and Šisler, "Socializing on the Internet: Case Study of Internet Use among University Students in the United Arab Emirates."

45. Meriem Dhaouadi, "Tunisian Bloggers Meet During 45th International Sahara Festival in Douz," 27 December 2012, Nawaat.org, http://nawaat.org/portail/2012/12/27/tunisian-bloggers-meet-during-45th-international-sahara-festival-in-douz/; Hisham Almiraat, "Arab Bloggers: A Blessed Generation?" http://advocacy.globalvoicesonline.org/2014/02/25/arab-bloggers-a-blessed-generation/print/; Amaar Abdulhamid, "Blogging and the Future of Democracy in the Arab World," http://amarji.blogspot.se/2006/07/blogging-and-future-of-democracy-in.html; Tarek Amr, "Three Years Blogging," 19 February 2008, http://notgr33ndata.blogspot.se/2008/02/three-years-blogging.html; Ahmed Jadoo and Thalia Rahme, "Made in Libya: Blogger Ahmed Ben Wafaa," http://globalvoicesonline.org/2012/11/24/made-in-libya-blogger-ahmed-ben-wafaa/; Amy Aisen Kallander, "From Tunezine to Nhar 3la 3mmar: A Reconsideration of the Role of Bloggers in Tunisia's Revolution," http://www.arabmediasociety.com/?article=818

46. Teresa Pepe, "Improper Narratives: Egyptian Personal Blogs and the Arabic Notion of Adab," *LEA—Lingue e letterature d'Oriente e d'Occidente* 1, no. 1 (2012); Weyman, "Speaking the Unspeakable: Personal Blogs in Egypt"; Chiara Bernardi, "Saudi Bloggers, Women's Issues and Ngos," http://www.arabmediasociety.com/topics/index.php?t_article=309

47. "Social Media in the Arab World: Influencing Societal and Cultural Change?" in *Arab Social Media Report* (Dubai: Dubai School of Government, 2012).

48. Sara Alshaer and Fadi Salem, "The Arab World Online: Trends in Internet Usage in the Arab Region," http://www.dsg.ae/en/Publication/Pdf_En/424201311017185100000.pdf

49. "Transforming Education in the Arab World: Breaking Barriers in the Age of Social Learning," in *Arab Social Media Report 5* (Dubai: Dubai School of Government, 2013).

50. Gilad Lotan et al., "The Revolutions Were Tweeted: Information Flows During the 2011 Tunisian and Egyptian Revolutions," *International Journal of Communication* 5 (2011): 1390.

51. Nojin Kwak et al., "To Broadband or Not to Broadband: The Relationship between High-Speed Internet and Knowledge and Participation," *Journal of Broadcasting and Electronic Media* 48, no. 3 (2004).

52. "Citizen Engagement and Public Services in the Arab World: The Potential of Social Media," in *Arab Social Media Report 6* (Dubai: Mohammed bin Rashid School of Government, 2014).

53. Eisa Al Nashmi et al., "Internet Political Discussions in the Arab World: A Look at Online Forums from Kuwait, Saudi Arabia, Egypt and Jordan," *International Communication Gazette* 72, no. 8 (2010); Yeslam Al-Saggaf and Mohamed M. Begg, "Online Communities Versus Offline Communities in the Arab/Muslim World," *Journal of Information, Communication and Ethics in Society* 2, no. 1 (2004); Yeslam Al-Saggaf and Kirsty Williamson, "Online Communities in Saudi Arabia: Evaluating the Impact on Culture through Online Semi-Structured Interviews," *Forum: Qualitative Social Research* 5, no. 3 (2004); Stephanie Ryan Cate and Annemarie Profanter, "Frontier Triptych: Saudi Arabia in Motion. Liminal Digital Frontier Spaces," *Journal of New Media Studies in MENA* 1 (2012); Nadav Samin, "Dynamics of Internet Use: Saudi Youth, Religious Minorities and Tribal Communities," *Middle East Journal of Culture and Communication* 1, no. 2 (2008).

54. Tamer Samedi, "Jordanian Youth Inaugurate 'Facebook Parliament,'" 4 March 2013, http://www.al-monitor.com/pulse/politics/2013/03/jordan-facebook-parliament.html; Murphy, "Problematizing Arab Youth: Generational Narratives of Systemic Failure."

55. Jaron Lanier, *Who Owns the Future?* (New York: Simon & Schuster, 2013).

56. Steven Levy, *In the Plex: How Google Thinks, Works, and Shapes Our Lives* (New York: Simon & Schuster, 2011).

57. Emma C. Murphy, "Theorizing ICTs in the Arab World: Informational Capitalism and the Public Sphere," *International Studies Quarterly* 4 (2009).

58. Ibid., 1147.

59. Biao Xiang, *Global "Body Shopping": An Indian Labor System in the Information Technology Industry* (Princeton, NJ: Princeton University Press, 2007).

60. Gina Neff, *Venture Labor: Work and the Burden of Risk in Innovative Industries* (Cambridge, MA: MIT Press, 2012).

61. Jan A. English-Lueck, *Cultures@Siliconvalley* (Stanford, CA: Stanford University Press, 2002).

62. Valeriani, "Bridges of the Revolution."

63. Christopher M. Schroeder, *Startup Rising: The Entrepreneurial Revolution Remaking the Middle East* (New York: Palgrave Macmillan, 2013).

64. Valeriani, "Bridges of the Revolution."

65. Khaled Abdel-Kader, "The Impact of Information and Communication Technology on Economic Growth in MENA Countries," in *EUI Working Papers RSCAA No. 2006/31* (Florence: European University Institute, 2006).

66. Krishna B. Kumar and Desiree van Welsum, "Knowledge-Based Economies and Basing Economies on Knowledge," (Santa Monica, CA: RAND Corporation, 2013).

67. "ICT & ITES Industry Statistics and Industry Yearbook 2013" (Amman: INT@J & Ministry of Information and Communications Technology, 2013).

68. Examples range from but are not limited to a series of Arab blogger conferences sponsored by Germany's Heinrich-Böll-Stiftung starting in 2008, to the Global Voices online aggregator sponsored by the Berkman Center for Internet and Society of the Harvard University Law School, the Hivos foundation in the Netherlands, and the Open Society Institute—just in the media space.

69. Radsch identified digital participants in the April 6 Youth Movement turning from activism in the events to documenting the records of their participation in its aftermath. For a similar turn in the Green Movement following Iran's 2009 elections, see Babak Rahimi, "Affinities of Dissent: Cyberspace, Performative Networks and the Iranian Green Movement," www.cyberorient.net/article.do?articleId=7357

9. DIGITAL RIGHTS ACTIVISM AFTER THE ARAB SPRING: INTERNET GOVERNANCE POLITICS AND THE INTERNET FREEDOM PROTO-REGIME

1. Oran R. Young, "The Politics of International Regime Formation: Managing Natural Resources and the Environment," *International Organization* 43, no. 3 (1989): 349–75.

2. Nancy C. Roberts and Paula J. King, "Policy Entrepreneurs: Their Activity Structure and Function in the Policy Process," *Journal of Public Administration Research and Theory* 1, no. 2 (1991): 147.

3. State-based coalitions are often referred to as international treaty or policy regimes; but such a coalition is not a formal "international regime"; rather, a core component of this investigation is to unpack the political economy of this coalition, help make explicit its implicit norms, and evaluate its operational utility in achieving its normative goals.

4. The "Freedom Online Coalition" (FOC) was initially endorsed by the following governments: Austria, Canada, Costa Rica, Czech Republic, Estonia, Finland, France, Georgia, Germany, Ghana, Ireland, Kenya, Latvia, Republic of Maldives, Mexico, Mongolia, Netherlands, Sweden, Tunisia, United Kingdom, and United States. Since then, it has expanded to include other nations.

5. See "Secretary Clinton's Remarks on Internet Freedom," 21 January 2010, http://www.humanrights.gov/2011/12/09/secretary-clinton-on-Internet-freedom-transcript/

6. For an activist's perspective, see Rebecca MacKinnon, *Consent of the Networked: The Worldwide Struggle for Internet Freedom* (New York: Basic Books, 2012).

7. Charles C. Ragin and Howard S. Becker, *What is a Case? Exploring the Foundations of Social Inquiry* (Cambridge: Cambridge University Press, 1992).

8. Gregory F. Gause, III, "Why Middle East Studies Missed the Arab Spring: The Myth of Authoritarian Stability," *Foreign Affairs* 90 (2011): 81.

9. Katerina Dalacoura, "The 2011 Uprisings in the Arab Middle East: Political Change and Geopolitical Implications," *International Affairs* 88, no. 1 (2012): 63.

10. Muzammil M. Hussain and Philip N. Howard, "What Best Explains Successful Protest Cascades? ICTs and the Fuzzy Causes of the Arab Spring," *International Studies Review* 15, no. 1 (2013): 48–66.

11. Vickie Langohr, "Too Much Civil Society, Too Little Politics: Egypt and Liberalizing Arab Regimes," *Comparative Politics* 36, no. 2 (2004): 181–204.

12. See also Anoushiravan Ehteshami, "Reform from Above: The Politics of Participation in the Oil Monarchies," *International Affairs* 79, no. 1 (2003): 53–75; Anoushiravan Ehteshami and Steven Wright, "Political Change in the Arab Oil Monarchies: From Liberalization to Enfranchisement," *International Affairs* 83, no. 5 (2007): 913–32.

13. Eva Bellin, "Reconsidering the Robustness of Authoritarianism in the Middle East: Lessons from the Arab Spring," *Comparative Politics* 44, no. 2 (2012): 127–49; Marsha P. Posusney, "Enduring Authoritarianism: Middle East Lessons for Comparative Theory," *Comparative Politics* 36, no. 2 (2004): 127–38.

14. Mohamed Zayani, *Networked Publics and Digital Contention: The Politics of Everyday Life in Tunisia* (New York: Oxford University Press, 2015), 100–103.

15. Gina Neff, *Venture Labor: Work and the Burden of Risk in Innovative Industries* (Cambridge, MA: MIT Press, 2012).

16. John Pollock, "Streetbook: How Egyptian and Tunisian Youth Hacked the Arab Spring," *MIT Technology Review* 14, no. 5 (2011): 70–89.

17. Habibul H. Khondker, "Role of the New Media in the Arab Spring," *Globalizations* 8, no. 5 (2011): 675–9.

18. Philip N. Howard, Sheetal D. Agarwal, and Muzammil M. Hussain, "When do States Disconnect their Digital Networks? Regime Responses to the Political Uses of Social Media," *Communication Review* 14, no. 3 (2011): 216–32.

19. Laura DeNardis, *Protocol Politics: The Globalization of Internet Governance* (Cambridge, MA: MIT Press, 2009).

20. Milton L. Mueller, *Networks and States: The Global Politics of Internet Governance* (Cambridge, MA: MIT Press, 2010).

21. Again, the Freedom Online Coalition (FOC) is the most public and cohesive expression of this state-supported policy phenomenon, but is not the sole proprietor of Internet freedom concerns. See Table 9.1 for a complete list.

22. Emanuel Adler, "The Spread of Security Communities: Communities of Practice,

Self-Restraint, and NATO's Post-Cold War Transformation," *European Journal of International Relations* 14, no. 2 (2008): 195–230.

23. Jean Lave and Etienne Wenger, *Situated Learning: Legitimate Peripheral Participation* (Cambridge: Cambridge University Press, 1991).

24. Stephan Haggard and Beth A. Simmons, "Theories of International Regimes," *International Organization* 41, no. 3 (1987): 491–517.

25. Ernst B. Haas, "Why Collaborate: Issue-Linkage and International Regimes," *World Politics* 32, no. 3 (1980): 357.

26. Eric Neumayer, "Do International Human Rights Treaties Improve Respect for Human Rights?" *Journal of Conflict Resolution* 49, no. 6 (2005): 925–53.

27. Molly Cochran, "Deweyan Pragmatism and Post-Positivist Social Science in IR," *Millennium: Journal of International Studies* 31, no. 3 (2002): 525–48.

28. Haas, "Why Collaborate: Issue-Linkage and International Regimes," 377.

29. Lave and Wenger, *Situated Learning*, 98.

30. Andrew Moravcsik, "The Origins of Human Rights Regimes: Democratic Delegation in Postwar Europe," *International Organization* 54, no. 2 (2000): 217–52.

31. MacKinnon, *Consent of the Networked*, 188.

10. CITIZENSHIP AND CYBER POLITICS IN IRAN

1. Gilbert Achcar, *Eastern Cauldron: Islam, Afghanistan, Palestine and Iraq in a Marxist Mirror* (London: Pluto, 2004).

2. Val Moghadam, "One Revolution or Two? The Iranian Revolution and the Islamic Republic," in *Socialist Register: Revolution Today, Aspirations and Realities*, ed. Ralph Miliband, Leo Panitch, and John Saville (London: Merlin, 1989), 74–101.

3. Asghar Schirazi, *The Constitution of Iran: Politics and the State in the Islamic Republic* (London: I. B. Tauris, 1998).

4. Maziar Behrooz, "The Islamic State and the Crisis of *Marja'iyat* in Iran," *Comparative Studies of South Asia, Africa and the Middle East* 16, no. 2 (1996): 93–100.

5. Fakhreddin Azimi, *The Quest for Democracy in Iran* (Cambridge, MA: Harvard University Press, 2009), 413–14.

6. Elizabeth Shakman Hurd, "Iran, in Search of a Nonsecular and Nontheocratic Politics," *Public Culture* 22, no. 1 (2010): 25–32; Annabelle Sreberny and Gholam Khiabany, *Blogistan: The Internet and Politics in Iran* (London: I. B. Tauris, 2010); Niki Akhavan, *Electronic Iran: The Cultural Politics of an Online Evolution* (New Brunswick, NJ: Rutgers University Press, 2013).

7. Gholam Khiabany, "Globalization and the Internet: Myths and realities," *Trends in Communication* 11, no. 2 (2003): 137–53.

8. Gholam Khiabany, *Iranian Media: The Paradox of Modernity* (New York: Routledge, 2010).

9. Aziz Al-Azmeh, *Islams and Modernities* (London: Verso, 1993); Sami Zubaida, *Islam, the People and the State: essays on political ideas and movements in the Middle East* (London: I. B. Tauris, 1993).

10. Bernard Lewis, *What Went Wrong? Western Impact and Middle Eastern Response* (New York: Oxford University Press, 2002), 10.

11. Afshin Matin-Asgari, "Islamic Studies and the Spirit of Max Weber: A Critique of Cultural Essentialism," *Critique: Critical Middle Eastern Studies* 13, no. 3 (2004): 293–312.

12. Nilüfer Göle, "Snapshots of Islamic Modernities," *Daedalus* (2000): 91–117; Ali Hassan Zaidi, "Muslim Reconstructions of Knowledge and the Re-enchantment of Modernity," *Theory, Culture and Society* 23, no. 5 (2006): 69–91

13. Henry Giroux, "The Iranian Uprisings and the Challenge of the New Media: Rethinking the Politics of Representation," *Fast Capitalism* 5, no. 2 (2009), http://www.uta.edu/huma/agger/fastcapitalism/5_2/Giroux5_2.html

14. Manuel Castells, *Networks of Outrage and Hope: Social Movements in the Internet Age* (Cambridge: Polity, 2012), 15.

15. Malcolm Gladwell, "Twitter, Facebook, and Social Activism," *New Yorker*, 4 October 2010, 1–6.

16. Alain Badiou, *The Rebirth of History: Times of Riots and Uprisings* (London: Verso, 2012), 110.

17. Andy Greenberg, "Twitter's Activist Initiation," *Forbes*, 16 June 2009, http://www.forbes.com/2009/06/16/twitter-iran-election-markets-equity-dissent.html

18. Sreberny and Khiabany, *Blogistan*.

19. Annabelle Sreberny-Mohammadi and Ali Mohammadi, *Small Media, Big Revolution: Communication, Culture, and the Iranian Revolution* (Minneapolis, MI: University of Minnesota Press, 1994), 54.

20. Negin Nabavi, "Spreading the Word: Iran's First Constitutional Press and the Shaping of a 'New Era,'" *Critique: Critical Middle Eastern Studies* 14, no. 3 (2005): 307–21.

21. Asghar Fathi, "The Role of the Islamic Pulpit," *Journal of Communication* 29, no. 3 (1979): 102–6; Sreberny-Mohammadi and Mohammadi, *Small Media, Big Revolution*.

22. Rashid Khalidi, "Preliminary Historical Observations on the Arab Revolutions of 2011," *Jadaliyya, 21 March 2011*, http://www.jadaliyya.com/pages/index/970/preliminary-historical-observations

23. Khiabany, *Iranian Media*.

24. "Writer's Block: The Story of Censorship in Iran," *Small Media*, 6 May 2015, http://www.smallmedia.org.uk/writersblock/file/Writer'sBlock.pdf

25. Adi Kuntsman and Rebecca L. Stein, "Digital Suspicion, Politics, and the Middle East," *Critical Inquiry* (2011): 1–10, http://criticalinquiry.uchicago.edu/digital_suspicion_politics_and_the_middle_east/

26. Ramesh Srinivasan and Adam Fish, "Revolutionary Tactics, Media Ecologies, and Repressive States," *Public Culture* 23, no. 3 (2011): 509.

27. Babak Rahimi, "Cyberdissent: The Internet in Revolutionary Iran," *Middle East Review of International Affairs* 7, no. 3 (2003): 101–15.

28. Sreberny and Khiabany, *Blogistan.*

29. Laurent Giacobino, Arash Abadpour, Collin Anderson, Fred Petrossian, and Caroline Nellemann, "Whither Blogestan [*sic*]: Evaluating Shifts in Persian Cyberspace," Iran Media Program, Annenberg School for Communications, University of Pennsylvania (2014), 3.

30. Ibid., 4.

31. "Iran Communication Minister: The problem will not be Solved by Closure of SNSs," BBC Persian, 1 October 2014, http://www.bbc.co.uk/persian/iran/2014/10/141001_filter_communication_vaezi

32. "Iran's Police Chief: Inevitability of use of Viber and Facebook," BBC Persian, 24 September 2014, http://www.bbc. co.uk/persian/iran/2014/09/140924_l45_police_filtering_ahmadimoghaddam

33. "Nearly One Third of all SMSs [Short Message Services] are Jokes," BBC Persian, 3 March 2015, http://www.bbc.co.uk/persian/iran/2015/03/150301_me_sms_iran

34. "Communication Minister: 13 to 14 Million use Telegram in Iran," BBC Persian, 25 October 2015, http://www.bbc.com/persian/iran/2015/10/151025_l26_iran_ict_minister_telegram

35. "Iran: Privacy and Censorship Fears around Telegram Messaging App," Article 19, 18 November 2015, https://www.article19.org/resources.php/resource/38196/en/iran:-privacy-and-censorship-fears-around-telegram-messaging-app

36. Farhad Khosrokhavar, *The New Arab Revolutions that Shook the World* (Boulder, CO: Paradigm Publishers, 2012), 152.

37. Douglas Kellner, "Intellectuals and New Technologies," *Media, Culture and Society* 17, no. 3 (1995): 427–48.

38. Elizabeth Eisenstein, *The Printing Press as an Agent of Change* (Cambridge: Cambridge University Press, 1980).

39. Walter Benjamin, *Illuminations* (New York: Schocken Books Inc., 1968).

40. Bertolt Brecht, "Radio as a Means of Communication: A Talk on the Function of Radio," *Screen* 20, nos. 3–4 (1979): 25.

41. Khosrokhavar, *The New Arab Revolutions.*

42. Babak Rahimi and Elham Gheytanchi, "Iran's Reformists and Activists: Internet Exploiters," *Middle East Policy* 15, no. 1 (2008): 46.

43. Said Amir Arjomand, "Civil Society and the Rule of Law in the Constitutional Politics of Iran under Khatami," *Social Research* (2000): 296–7.

44. Sreberny and Khiabany, *Blogistan.*

45. For more detailed comparative discussion, see Khosrokhavar, *The New Arab*

Revolutions; and Arshin Adib-Moghaddam, *On the Arab Revolts and the Iranian Revolution: Power and Resistance Today* (London: Bloomsbury Academic, 2013).

46. Mona El-Ghobashy, "The Praxis of the Egyptian Revolution," *Middle East Report* 258 (2011): 2–13, http://www.merip.org/mer/mer258/praxis-egyptian-revolution?ip_login_no_cache=e09109d1aa0cffd76b991472093d087b

47. Rahimi and Gheytanchi, "Iran's Reformists and Activists," 57.

48. Haleh Anvari, "The Fetish of Staring at Iran's Women," *New York Times*, 16 June 2014, http://www.nytimes.com/2014/06/17/opinion/the-fetish-of-staring-at-irans-women.html?_r=0

49. Azadeh Davachi, "Stealthy Freedom: The Hidden and Visible Voice of Iranian Women?" *Jahan Zan*, 20 May 2014, https://jahanezan.wordpress.com/2014/05/20/12345–2006/

50. Naureen Zaina Azizee, "My Stealthy Freedom: The Reclaiming of Individuality," *Alochonaa*, 23 June 2014, http://alochonaa.com/2014/06/23/my-stealthy-freedom-the-reclaiming-of-individuality/

51. Gilda Seddighi, "Mothers' Affective Networking and Privileges in Online Space: The Case of Iranian Mothers of Park Laleh," *Feminist Media Studies* 14, no. 3 (2014): 523–7.

11. E-GOVERNMENT IN THE GCC COUNTRIES: PROMISES AND IMPEDIMENTS

1. Ali M. Al-Khouri, "e-Government in Arab Countries: A 6-Staged Roadmap to Develop the Public Sector," *Journal of Management and Strategy* 4, no. 1 (2013): 80–107.

2. World Bank, "E-Government," 19 May 2015, http://www.worldbank.org/en/topic/ict/brief/e-government

3. UNESCO, "E-Governance," n.d., http://portal.unesco.org/ci/en/ev.php-URL_ID=3038&URL_DO=DO_TOPIC&URL_SECTION=201.htmln.d

4. World Bank, "E-Government."

5. UNESCO, "E-Governance."

6. Department of Economic and Social Affairs, Division for Public Administration and Development Management (UNPAN), "UN e-Government Survey 2014: E-Government for the Future We Want," 2014, https://publicadministration.un.org/egovkb/Portals/egovkb/Documents/un/2014-Survey/E-Gov_Complete_Survey-2014.pdf

7. Ramez T. Shehadi, Raymond Khoury, Fady Kassatly, and Abdulkader Lamaa, "Self-Sustainable e-Government: A Road Map to Financial Independence and Value Creation," Booz & Co., 2013, quoted in Richard Shediac, Ramez T. Shehadi, Jayant Bhargava, and Hatem Samman, "Generations A: Differences and Similarities across the Arab Generations," Booz & Co., 2013, http://www.strategyand.pwc.com/global/home/what-we-think/reports-white-papers/article-display/arab-generations

8. Hendrik Kraetzschmar and El Mustapha Lahlali, "The State of e-Services Delivery in Kuwait: Opportunities and Challenges," London School of Economics and Political Science, the Kuwait Programme on Development, Governance and Globalisation in the Gulf States Research Paper no. 20 (January 2012), http://eprints.lse.ac.uk/55253/1/Kraetzschmar_2012.pdf

9. Saeed Saleem Basamh, Hani A. Qudaih, and Mohd Adam Suhaimi, "e-Government Implementation in the Kingdom of Saudi Arabia: An Exploratory Study on Current Practices, Obstacles and Challenges," *International Journal of Humanities and Social Science* 4, no. 2 (2014): 296–300.

10. Shafi Al-Shafi and Vishanth Weerakkody, "Factors Affecting e-Government Adoption in the State of Qatar," European and Mediterranean Conference on Information Systems, 12–13 April 2009 (Abu Dhabi, 2010).

11. Al-Shafi and Weerakkody, "Qatar."

12. Moaman Al-Busaidy and Vishanth Weerakkody, "The e-Government Implementation Directions in Oman: A Preliminary Investigation," European and Mediterranean Conference on Information Systems 2010 (EMCIS2010), https://core.ac.uk/download/pdf/336834.pdf

13. Magdalena Karolak and Anjum Razzaque, "Bahraini Government and the e-Government Initiative: An Assessment," paper presented at the Proceedings of the Asian Group for Public Administration (AGPA) Annual Conference, Maldives, 8–12 May 2012, https://www.academia.edu/16083147/Bahraini_Government_and_the_e-Government_Initiative_an_Assessment

14. Ali M. Al-Khouri, "e-Government Strategies: The Case of the United Arab Emirates," *European Journal of ePractice* 17 (2012): 126–50.

15. Suha Al Awadhi and Anne Morris, "Factors Influencing the Adoption of e-Government Services," *Journal of Software* 4, no. 6 (2009): 584–90.

16. Beñat Bilbao-Osorio, Soumitra Dutta, and Bruno Lanvin, "The Global Information Technology Report 2014," World Economic Forum, 2014, http://www3.weforum.org/docs/WEF_GlobalInformationTechnology_Report_2014.pdf

17. International Telecommunication Union, "Measuring the Information Society Report, 2014," http://www.itu.int/en/ITU-D/Statistics/Documents/publications/mis2014/MIS2014_without_Annex_4.pdf

18. United Nations, Department of Economic and Social Affairs, "E-Government Survey 2012: E-Government for the People" (New York: UN DESA, 2012), https://publicadministration.un.org/egovkb/Portals/egovkb/Documents/un/2012-Survey/unpan048065.pdf

19. Cited in Al-Khouri, "e-Government in Arab Countries," 80.

20. United Nations, "E-Government Survey."

21. George K. Kostopoulos, "E-government in the Arabian Gulf: A Vision toward Reality," Proceedings of the 2003 Annual National Conference on Digital Government Research, Digital Government Society of North America, Boston, 18–21 May 2003.

22. Suha Al Awadhi and Anne Morris, "The Use of the UTAUT Model in the Adoption of e-Government Services in Kuwait," Proceedings of the 41st Annual Hawaii International Conference on System Sciences, IEEE, 2008, https://www.computer.org/csdl/proceedings/hicss/2008/3075/00/30750219.pdf

23. Al-Shafi Shafi and Vishanth Weerakkody, "Understanding Citizens' Behavioural Intention in the Adoption of e-Government Services in the State of Qatar," 17th European Conference on Information Systems, 2009, http://unpan1.un.org/intra-doc/groups/public/documents/un-dpadm/unpan035996.pdf

24. Information Technology Authority, Sultanate of Oman, "Sultanate of Oman Progress Report on the Information Society 2003–2013," n.d., http://www.itu.int/wsis/review/inc/docs/rcreports/WSIS10_Country_Reporting-OMA.pdf

25. United Nations 2014 Survey.

26. Ibid.

27. Kingdom of Bahrain, "e-Government Strategy 2016," http://www.ega.gov.bh/wps/wcm/connect/1f75f0004af9c3b2b84cb978e38c6a11/eGov%2BStrategy_Brochure_Eng.pdf?MOD=AJPERES

28. ictQATAR, "Qatar e-Government 2020 Strategy," www.ictqatar.qa/en/file/10921/download?token=3fekKLvM

29. ictQATAR. "The Qatari i-Gov Program: Government Wide, Customer Centric," November 2008, http://unpan1.un.org/intradoc/groups/public/documents/unpan/unpan032975.pdf

30. UAE Government, "UAE National Charter 2021," dubai.ae/SiteCollection Documents/UAE_Vision_2021_English.pdf

31. eGovernment for Development, "What is eGovernment?" 2008, http://www.egov4dev.org/success/definitions.shtml

32. Rogers W'O Okot-Uma, "Electronic Governance: Re-Inventing Good Governance" (London: Commonwealth Secretariat, 2000).

33. OECD, "Recommendation of the Council on Digital Government Strategies," Public Governance and Territorial Development Directorate, 2014, http://www.oecd.org/gov/public-innovation/Recommendation-digital-government-strategies.pdf

34. Abdulazeez S. Boujarwah, "e-Government in Kuwait: From Vision to Reality," Proceedings of the 8th International Conference on Information Integration and Web-based Applications & Services (iiWAS2006).

35. Damian Radcliffe, "The Middle East's Tech Hotspots to Watch: Where are the Region's IT Leaders?" ZDNet, 3 June 2014, http://www.zdnet.com/article/the-middle-easts-tech-hotspots-to-watch-where-are-the-regions-it-leaders/

36. Mohammed Alshehri and Steve Drew, "Challenges of e-Government Services Adoption in Saudi Arabia from an e-Ready Citizen Perspective," Education 29, no. 5.1 (2010).

37. Government of the Kingdom of Saudi Arabia, "Saudi Arabia e-Government Program," http://www.yesser.gov.sa/en/ProgramDefinition/Pages/Overview.aspx

38. These targets can be found in Omar S. Al-Mushayt, Yusuf Perwej, and Kashiful Haq, "Electronic-Government in Saudi Arabia: A Positive Revolution in the Peninsula," 2012.

39. Mohammed Alshehri, Steve Drew, and Osama Alfarraj, "A Comprehensive Analysis of e-Government Services Adoption in Saudi Arabia: Obstacles and Challenges," *Higher Education* 6 (2012): 8–2.

40. Cited in ibid.

41. Abdullah Al-Shehab, Thalaya Al-Fozan, Gilberto Montibeller, Robert T. Hughes, and Graham Winstanley, "Structuring Risk in e-Government Development Projects Using a Causal Model," 8th European Conference on Information Warfare and Security, ECIW2009, 2009.

42. Ministry of Information and Communications Technology (ictQATAR), "Qatar's ICT Landscape 2014: Households and Individuals," http://www.ictqatar.qa/en/documents/document/qatars-ict-landscape-2014-households-and-individuals

43. Al Awadhi and Morris, "Factors Influencing the Adoption of e-Government Services."

44. Al Awadhi and Morris. "Factors Influencing the Adoption of e-Government Services."

45. Boujarwah, "e-Government in Kuwait."

46. Samihah Zaman, Nada Al Taher, and Binsal Abdul Kader, "Abu Dhabi Residents still not Convinced about Government Apps," *Gulf News*, 2 August 2014, http://gulfnews.com/news/gulf/uae/general/abu-dhabi-residents-still-not-convinced-about-government-apps-1.1347823

47. Faris Al-Sobhi, Vishanth Weerakkody, and Muhammad Mustafa Kamal, "An Exploratory Study on the Role of Intermediaries in Delivering Public Services in Madinah City: The Case of Saudi Arabia," *Transforming Government: People, Process and Policy* 4, no. 1 (2010): 14–36.

48. Boujarwah, "E-Government in Kuwait."

49. Al Awadhi and Morris, "Factors Influencing the Adoption of e-Government Services."

50. Ibid.

51. Kostopoulos, "E-government in the Arabian Gulf."

52. ictQATAR, "Qatar's Smartphone Market Q4 2011 Consumers' Perspective: A Nielsen syndicated study," 3 February 2012, http://www.ictqatar.qa/sites/default/files/documents/Qatar%20Smartphone%20Market%20-%20Q4%202011.pdf

53. "The UAE has nearly 300,000 SMEs who, according to recent statistics from Dun and Bradstreet, are providing over 86% of employment opportunities in the private sector alone. With an Internet penetration rate of 88% in the UAE, the highest in the Middle East, it is vital that businesses have a robust online presence. However, as revealed by a Google survey last year, only 18% of businesses in the UAE are online, which highlights significant room for growth." *Zawya*, Press

Release, "Google and in5 welcome smes to learn about the online tools available to grow a business," 24 February 2015, https://www.zawya.com/story/Google_and_in5_welcome_smes_to_learn_about_the_online_tools_available_to_grow_a_business-ZAWYA20150224104719/

54. ictQATAR, "Start-ups in Qatar Benefit From ICT and Built Strong Foundations," 3 June 2013, http://www.ictqatar.qa/en/news-events/news/start-ups-qatar-benefit-ict-and-built-strong-foundations

55. The Arab digital generation refers to a cohort born between 1977 and 1997, which is a demographic group constituting 40 per cent of the MENA population. Sabbagh et al., "Understanding the Arab Digital Generation."

56. Ibid.

57. PayPal, "PayPal Insights: E-commerce in the Middle East, 2012–2015," September 2013, http://www.slideshare.net/meaoist/paypal-insights-ecommerce-in-the-middle-east

58. Sultanate of Oman, Oman Information Technology Authority, "E.Oman," http://www.ita.gov.om/ITAPortal/ITA/

59. See, for example, UK Cabinet Office, "Government Digital Strategy: December 2013," 10 December 2013, https://www.gov.uk/government/publications/government-digital-strategy/government-digital-strategy

60. UK Cabinet Office and Government Digital Service, "Government Approach to Assisted Digital," 4 December 2013, https://www.gov.uk/government/publications/government-approach-to-assisted-digital

61. Grant Black, "Most Internet Non-users have a Link to the Internet via a Proxy User," Oxford Internet Institute Blog, 3 September 2013, http://oxis.oii.ox.ac.uk/blog/most-internet-non-users-have-link-internet-proxy-user/

62. UK Cabinet Office, "Digital Strategy."

63. Shediac et al., "Differences and Similarities across the Arab Generations."

64. Economist Intelligence Unit, "E-government in Europe, the Middle East and Africa, Expert Views on the UN e-Government Survey," 2013, http://workspace.unpan.org/sites/Internet/Documents/Expert_views_egov_surveyEMEA_EIU.pdf

65. Ibid.

66. "Oman: The Middle East's eGov Pioneer," *Gemalto*, 17 March 2015, http://review.gemalto.com/post/oman-the-middle-easts-egov-pioneer

67. World Economic Forum, "The Competitiveness of Cities," 2014, http://www3.weforum.org/docs/GAC/2014/WEF_GAC_CompetitivenessOfCities_Report_2014.pdf

68. Damian Radcliffe, "10 New Insights into Mobile in the Middle East," *ZDNet*, 30 October 2014, http://www.zdnet.com/article/10-new-insights-into-mobile-in-the-middle-east/

69. Bahrain's eGov app store (bahrain.bh/apps) contains twenty-five different apps:

Fix2Go, Bahrain Elections 2014, Civil Service Bureau, Health Locator, Electricity and Water Bill Payment, Gasoline Octane Inquiry, Student Exam Results, Profile Manager, Postal Services, eGuide Bahrain, Traffic Services, Bahrain Today, NGO Directory, Members Guide, Bahrain Shura Council Guide, eGov SMS Services, Foreign Affairs Ministry, eKiosk eService Centre Locator, Islamiyat, and Bahrain International eGovernment Forum. Priya Viswanathan notes that "responsive Web Design, or RWD as it is commonly referred to, implies the formatting of Website design in a way that is most optimal for viewing and navigation across a wide range of devices, including traditional PCs, smartphones and tablet devices." "Responsive Web Design: Definition," 19 October 2016, http://mobiledevices.about.com/od/glossary/g/Responsive-Web-Design-Definition.htm

70. "Mohammed Renames Dubai e-Government Department," Emirates 24/7, 20 June 2013, http://www.emirates247.com/news/government/mohammed-renames-dubai-e-government-department-2013–06–20–1.511278

71. GSMA, "The Mobile Economy: Arab States 2014," http://arabstates.gsmamobileeconomy.com/

72. "eGov App Store Boost as Downloads Hit 147,000," *Gulf Digital News*, 25 November 2014, http://archives.gdnonline.com/NewsDetails.aspx?date=04/07/2015&storyid=390675

73. Government of Dubai, *Dubai Smart Gov Magazine* no. 135, January 2015, http://www.dsg.gov.ae/SiteCollectionImages/Content/DeG%20Documents/January–2015-en.pdf

74. OECD, "Recommendation of the Council on Digital Government Strategies."

75. ictQATAR, "Qatar e-Government 2020 Strategy," http://www.ictqatar.qa/sites/default/files/documents/Qatar%20e-Government%202020%20Strategy%20Executive%20Summary%20English.pdf

76. Economist Intelligence Unit, "e-Government."

77. Ibid.

78. Ibid.

79. Mary Sophia, "Facebook Cashing in on Video Ads as MENA Users Reach 74m," *Gulf Business*, 4 November 2014, http://www.gulfbusiness.com/articles/industry/facebook-cashing-in-on-video-ads-as-mena-users-reach-74m/#.VH1ZAhaUfhA

80. "UAE Government Launches Instagram Account," *The National*, November 2014, http://www.thenational.ae/uae/government/uae-government-launches-instagram-account

81. Arthur Mickoleit, "Social Media Use by Governments: A Policy Primer to Discuss Trends, Identify Policy Opportunities and Guide Decision Makers," OECD Working Papers on Public Governance, no. 26, 2014, http://dx.doi.org/10.1787/5jxrcmghmk0s-en

82. GSMA, "The Mobile Economy."

83. Al-Khouri, "e-Government in Arab Countries."

84. Ibid.

85. Dara Kerr, "Drone Deliveries Get off the Ground in Dubai," CNet, 11 February 2014, http://www.cnet.com/uk/news/drone-deliveries-get-off-the-ground-in-dubai

86. Kate Hutchings and David Weir, "Understanding Networking in China and the Arab World: Lessons for international managers," *Journal of European Industrial Training* 30, no. 4 (2006): 272–90. Al Awadhi and Morris, "Factors Influencing the Adoption of e-Government Services."

EPILOGUE: ON THE DIGITAL MIDDLE EAST AND COMPUTATIONAL SOCIAL SCIENCE

1. Meg Leta Jones, *Cont + Z: The Right to be Forgotten* (New York: New York University Press, 2016).

2. Yelena Mejova, Ingmar Weber, and Michael W. Macy, eds, *Twitter: A Digital Socioscope* (Cambridge: Cambridge University Press, 2015).

3. Javier Borge-Holthoefer, Muzammil M. Hussain, and Ingmar Weber, "Studying Networked Communication in the Middle East: Social Disrupter and Social Observatory," in *Communication in the Networked Age*, ed. S. Gonzalez-Bailon and B. Foucault Wells (forthcoming, Oxford University Press).

4. Matheus Lima Diniz Araujo, Yelena Mejova, Michael Aupetit, and Ingmar Weber, "Visualizing Health Awareness in the Middle East," *Proceedings of the Eleventh International AAAI Conference on Web and Social Media* (ICWSM 2017), 725–726, https://aaai.org/ocs/index.php/ICWSM/ICWSM17/paper/view/15576

5. Walid Magdy, Kareem Darwish, and Ingmar Weber, "#FailedRevolutions: Using Twitter to Study the Antecedents of ISIS Support," *First Monday* 21, no. 2 (2016), http://firstmonday.org/ojs/index.php/fm/article/view/6372

6. Norah Abokhodair and Sarah Vieweg, "Privacy and Social Media in the Context of the Arab Gulf," Proceedings of the ACM Conference on Design Interactive Systems (2016): 672–83.

INDEX